CITY OF QUARTERS

City of Quarters

Urban Villages in the Contemporary City

Edited by
DAVID BELL and MARK JAYNE
Cultural Trends Unit
Staffordshire University

ASHGATE

Published by
Ashgate Publishing Limited
Gower House
Croft Road
Aldershot
Hants GU11 3HR
England

Ashgate Publishing Company
Suite 420
101 Cherry Street
Burlington, VT 05401-4405
USA

Ashgate website: http://www.ashgate.com

British Library Cataloguing in Publication Data
City of quarters : urban villages in the contemporary city
   1. Sociology, Urban 2. Cities and towns 3. Neighborhood
   I. Bell, David, 1965- II. Jayne, Mark
   307. 3'36216

Library of Congress Cataloging-in-Publication Data
City of quarters : urban villages in the contemporary city / edited by David Bell and Mark Jayne.
   p. cm.
   Includes bibliographical references and index.
   ISBN 0-7546-3414-0
   1. Cities and towns. 2. Neighborhood. 3. Community life. I. Bell, David, 1965 Feb. 12-
II. Jayne, Mark, 1970-

HT119.C594 2004
307.76--dc22

2003064702

ISBN 0 7546 34140

Printed and bound in Great Britain by MPG Books Ltd, Bodmin, Cornwall

Contents

Part 3: Identities, Lifestyles and Forms of Sociability

Part 4: Rethinking Neighbourhoods/Rethinking Quarters

Acknowledgements

The Editors would like to thank all of the contributors for ensuring that the compilation of this book was a straightforward and enjoyable process. We would also like to thank colleagues and students from the Cultural Studies Department at Staffordshire University, and friends and family who have been understanding and supportive as ever. We would especially like to thank Valerie Rose and Carolyn Court at Ashgate for their patience, encouragement and help and the Ordnance Survey and Government of Ireland for allowing the 'Ulysses Map of Dublin' to be reproduced. Special thanks to Ruth and Daisy.

List of Figures and Tables

Figures

Tables

List of Contributors

Nasreen Akhtar has lived her whole life in Walsall. She works as a community development worker for the Primary Care Trust and is involved in a wide range of health issues from drugs to prostitution. She says that the most important thing for her is to 'empower the community she works with'.

David Bell is Professor of Cultural Studies and Director of the Cultural Trends Unit at Staffordshire University. He is author of *Introduction to Cybercultures* (Routledge, 2001), and co-author of *Consuming Geographies* (Routledge, 1997), *The Sexual Citizen* (Polity, 2000), and *Pleasure Zones* (Syracuse University Press, 2000). He is co-editor of *Mapping Desire* (Routledge, 1995), *The Cybercultures Reader* (Routledge, 2000), and *City Visions* (Prentice Hall, 2000). David is currently working on two further books, *Key Concepts in Cyberculture* (co-authored with B. Loader, N. Pleace and D. Schuler, Routledge, 2004), and *Science, Technology and Culture* (Open University Press, 2004).

Franco Bianchini is Reader in Cultural Planning and Policy, Director of the International Cultural Planning and Policy Unit, and Programme Leader for the MA in European Cultural Planning at De Montfort University, Leicester. His books include *Culture and Neighbourhoods: A Comparative Report* (with L. Ghilardi, Santacatterina, Strasbourg, Council of Europe, 1997), *The Creative City* (with C. Landry, Demos, 1995), *Cultural Policy and Urban Regeneration: the West European Experience* (with M. Parkinson, Manchester University Press, 1993) and *City Centres, City Cultures* (with M. Fisher *et al.*, CLES, 1988). He has acted as adviser and researcher on cultural planning strategies and projects in various European countries, on behalf of organizations including the Arts Council of England, the Council of Europe, the European Commission and the European Task force on Culture and Development. Franco has lectured on urban cultural policy and planning issues in countries including Ireland, the UK, Sweden, Finland, Denmark, Russia, Poland, Spain, Greece and Italy.

Jon Binnie lectures in human geography at Manchester Metropolitan University. His work has appeared in *Society and Space, Gender, Place and Culture, Environment and Planning A,* and *Progress in Human Geography*. His books include *The Sexual Citizen* (with D. Bell, Polity, 2000), *Pleasure Zones* (with D. Bell, R. Holliday, R. Longhurst and R. Peace, Syracuse University Press, 2001) and *Queer Globalization* (Sage, 2004).

Rosie Campbell is a freelance consultant with 14 years experience of applied social research. She has also provided policy advice to a range of multi-agency community safety bodies in the UK developing strategic responses to prostitution.

She is now an independent research consultant, having been based in the Applied Research Centre of Liverpool Hope until March 2002. As Chair of the UK Network of Sex Worker Projects and Chair of the network's Safety, Violence and Policing Group, she works with sex work projects throughout the UK.

Wun Chan is Lecturer in Geography at the University of Strathclyde. He teaches and writes in the areas of urban studies and cultural geography, with a particular interest in the relationship between immigration, multiculturalism and city building.

James DeFilippis is an Assistant Professor in the Department of Black and Hispanic Studies at Baruch College, City University of New York. He has written about issues of public space, gentrification and neighbourhood change, community development and local economic development policy. He is the author of *Unmaking Goliath: Community Control in the Face of Global Capital* (Routledge, 2003).

Phil Denning is Chief Executive of PAULO, the National Training Organization for community-based learning and development. Previous to this he worked for Community Learning Scotland. For the last eight years he has served on the Executive of the Coalfield Learning Initiatives Partnership (CLIP), a multi-organization UK-wide partnership dedicated to emphasizing the role of learning in regeneration for coalfield and other former industrial communities.

Graeme Evans is Professor of Cultural Studies and Head of Research at Central Saint Martin's College of Art & Design, The London Institute. He has undertaken numerous studies of the arts and cultural industries for local and regional authorities, including a longitudinal study of the crafts quarter of Clerkenwell and Islington in north London, where he recently undertook the mapping exercise for the Local Cultural Strategy. Ken Worpole considered the results of his research as: 'to date ... the best detailed and quantified analyses we have of just how important the cultural industries are to the successful urban economies'. His book *Cultural Planning: An Urban Renaissance?* (Routledge, 2001) is the first to link town planning and city design with the arts and cultural facilities.

Tom Fleming is an independent consultant specializing in research and development work for the creative industries sector. His work includes developing strategies for the support of the sector, ranging from the very local to the regional. Key 'intervention areas' include the development of cultural quarters and clusters, intermediary support agencies, and individual policy instruments (such as creative industries finance). Recent clients range from the London Development Agency to the Council of Europe, where Tom is supporting a 'cultural entrepreneurialism' programme in Russia. Tom worked previously as Programme Manager at the Cultural Industries Development Agency in East London, and as Research Associate at Manchester Institute for Popular Culture, Manchester Metropolitan University – where he developed 'best practice' support models for the creative industries sector. Tom has a Doctorate from Sheffield University, where he specialized in issues of cultural identity, diaspora and senses of place through a focus on Carnival in the UK.

Lia Ghilardi is the founder and director of Noema Research and Planning Ltd, a UK-based cultural planning consultancy. As well as assisting public institutions in the implementation of cultural planning strategies across Europe, since 1994 she has worked as a member of the special committee of advisers for the selection of projects concerning the regeneration of cities through cultural initiatives for DG XVI of the European Commission. During the past ten years she has lectured regularly on cultural planning and policies in the UK, Sweden and Italy. Her recent publications include *Culture and Neighbourhoods: A Comparative Report* with Franco Bianchini (Strasbourg, Council of Europe, 1997), 'Why Cities Need To Be Creative' in S. Dingli (ed.), *Creative Thinking: Towards Broader Horizons* (Malta University Press, 1998); and 'Cultural Planning and Cultural Diversity' in T. Bennett (ed.), *Differing Diversities* (Strasbourg, Council of Europe, 2000).

Abigail Gilmore works at Staffordshire University, in the Cultural Studies team and as part of the Cultural Trends Unit. Her research has primarily been on urban cultural policy and planning, with particular interest in the cross-over (or otherwise) between academic research and cultural policy, and on the relationship between popular music and place. She is currently fanatical about Nordic music scenes, having abandoned Irish traditional music for closer harmonies.

Kate Green has worked as a freelance photographer and digital artist for fourteen years, specializing in community arts work. Most of her work is issue-based and she encourages those with whom she works to create images that express experiences, and feelings about issues relevant to them. She strives to be adventurous with her digital outputs and creates large-scale artworks including giant banners, enormous light transparencies and architectural projections.

Anne James has just retired from the Health Service where she worked as a health visitor and a nurse manager. Her interest in women's issues led her to become a director of The Haven Wolverhampton, so for the past 10 years she has been involved in the provision of services for homeless women and their children. Locally, she is vice-chair of Caldmore Local Committee, a Director of Walsall Youth Arts and sits on the South HAZ Steering Group and Walsall Prostitution Forum.

Mark Jayne has taught Cultural Studies and Sociology at the University of Birmingham and Staffordshire University, where he is currently a Research Fellow in the Cultural Trends Unit (CTU). His research interests include consumption, city cultures, urban regeneration, creative industries and cultural policy. Mark is currently writing a book entitled *Cities and Consumption* (Routledge, 2004).

Malcolm Miles is Reader in Cultural Theory at the University of Plymouth. He is author of *Art, Space and the City* (Routledge, 1997) and *The Uses of Decoration: Essays in the Architectural Everyday* (Wiley, 2000), and co-editor of *The City Cultures Reader* (Routledge, 2000, 2nd edition revised 2003) and *Urban Futures* (Routledge, 2003).

Chris Murray is Director of Learning and Development with CABE (the Commission for Architecture and the Built Environment), the Government's watchdog for better quality buildings and the spaces around them. Chris joined CABE from Milton Keynes Council where he led the UK's first Local Authority Cultural Planning Division, bringing together services concerned with cultural, economic and urban development, creating a powerful tool for urban innovation and renewal. Trained originally in art and design, as a sculptor, Chris is also professionally qualified in business and marketing, education and cultural planning. He has worked in community arts, art therapy, as a teacher, lecturer and art centre manager, before moving into public and cultural policy. Author of *Making Sense of Place: New Approaches to Place Marketing* (Comedia and De Montfort University, 2001), Chris is concerned that the way we design, inhabit and promote the places we live should be more closely connected.

Maggie O'Neill is a Reader in Sociology at Staffordshire University. She specializes in Participatory Action Research. The majority of her empirical research is conducted with sex workers, refugees and asylum seekers, and is community-based. Her concept of ethno-mimesis involves a combination of ethnography and artistic re-presentation (PAR and Participatory Arts) to re-present lived experience in challenging, thought-provoking, and change-causing ways. Her recent publications include *Prostitution and Feminism: Towards a Politics of Feeling* (Polity Press, 2001); *Prostitution: a Reader*, co-edited with R. Matthews (Ashgate, 2002); and *Dilemmas in Managing Professionalism and Gender in the Public Sector*, co-edited with J. Barry and M. Dent (Routledge, 2002)

Jay Patel is a member of the Caldmore Local Committee (Walsall). With experience in pharmacy, Jay became Chair of the Health and Environmental Sub-Group and took a keen interest in the health issues of particular concern, namely drugs and prostitution. As a member of PAF (Prostitution Action Forum) Jay helped to pick the researchers for Walsall Prostitution Consultation Research and played an active part in the research, including helping to run focus groups, liaising with local businesses about the effects of prostitution and helping to create one of the art images to go with the research.

Stephanie Rains studied at Dublin City University and University College Dublin and has taught Communications at Dundalk Institute of Technology. Stephanie is currently completing a PhD at Dublin City University on Irish-American representations of Irishness within popular culture and has published articles on cultural policy and cultural tourism.

Waheed Saleem gained his first degree from the London School of Economics and is currently a Labour councillor in Walsall, committed to serving and empowering the local community.

Jim Shorthose has been project co-ordinator at the Cultural Policy and Planning Research Unit at Nottingham Trent University since 1999. His current academic work focuses upon an analysis of D-I-Y approaches to social, economic and cultural life, and the 'micro-experiments' that people refer to in their everyday lives in an attempt to meet the material and existential needs that formal systems do not, or will not respond to. He is currently planning a self-built house using the Walter Segal method and tries to find time for some artwork, which is not easy, as his partner and he have just had a baby called George.

Gordon Waitt teaches Human Geography in the School of Geosciences at the University of Wollongong, Australia. He is co-author of *Introducing Human Geography* (Pearson, 2000). His research centres on tourism geographies, particularly the relationship between tourism activities and place-making processes.

Mark Webster is a community arts worker and lover of cities. He has worked in Walsall on and off for the last 14 years and despite attempts to escape he keeps coming back for more. He is the editor of *Finding Voices Making Choices: Creativity for Social Change* (Educational Heretics Press, Nottingham, 1997), which focuses on creative work to empower local people in Walsall.

Chapter 1

Conceptualizing the City of Quarters

David Bell and Mark Jayne

This book examines the increasingly ubiquitous presence of distinct social and spatial areas – urban villages – in our cities. Created either through the enhancement of historically distinctive areas, or by developing and generating signatures for previously economically, culturally or spatially ambiguous areas, urban villages or quarters seek to appeal to the consumption practices of the emerging nouveau riche of the professional, managerial and service classes. Promotion of conspicuous consumption – art, food, music, fashion, housing and entertainment – is at the fore in these urban 'shop windows' (Hall and Hubbard, 1998: 199). Moreover, in recognition of the complex plurality of the contemporary urban villages, more prosaic 'low' street culture, working-class traditions, ethnicity, sex and sexuality are also increasingly commodified in narratives of place. In urban villages, the symbolic framing of culture becomes a powerful tool as capital and cultural symbolism intertwine; the symbolic and cultural assets of the city are vigorously promoted – but also contested – as cities are branded as attractive places to live, work and play in.

In contrast to these planned or institutionally-developed urban villages, however, there are a host of other areas, districts or neighbourhoods that must be added to the kind of spaces and places that what we think about when we think of the city of quarters. Ghettos, red-light zones, neighbourhoods and areas where there are concentrations of marginalized groups and activities, often divided along the lines of class and ethnicity, are bound up in the political, economic, social, spatial and cultural forces which have led to the proliferation of the kind of urban villages outlined above.

Over the past 15 years, there have been a growing number of essays theorizing urban villages as part of broader structural transformations associated with urban change. A major aim of this book is to synthesize the concepts and arguments associated with this literature into one volume for the first time. However, while urban villages are present in cities across the world, no one story or example tells all (Thrift, 2000). While the same kind of gentrified residential city enclaves, gay villages, ethnic quarters, ghettos, red-light zones and creative and cultural quarters, can be a commonplace feature of the urban landscape, there are significant differences between them. The theoretical and case-study material presented in *City of Quarters* examines the role of urban quarters in terms of structural, political, economic, social, cultural and spatial change, and also investigates how specific urban villages are discursively and differentially constructed. This introductory chapter initially outlines the theoretical terrain that has informed understanding of urban villages and finishes with a brief overview of each chapter.

Conceptualizing Quarters

The past twenty years have witnessed the global reconstruction of economic, political, social, cultural and spatial practices and processes, which have had a profound impact upon the nature of urban life. This has been theorized as a movement to late or advanced capitalism, underpinned by a shift from Fordism to post-Fordist flexible accumulation. Related to these profound changes has been the decline of manufacturing industries and an increase in the importance of the service sector. This has been coupled with social and demographic forces that saw the simultaneous increase in mass unemployment, and the rise of a 'new petite bourgeoisie' (Giddens, 1973). These processes have been reproduced in space by conditioning the social production of the built environment (Knox, 1987).

In 1989 Peter Marcuse outlined how political and economic change was leading to American cities becoming increasingly quartered. Identifying five types of residential quarters – the dominating city, the gentrified city, the suburban city, the tenement city and the abandoned city – Marcuse showed that these city quarters were not separate isolated units, but that each was intimately and intricately linked to each other, forming a mutually dependent whole. Although he described a city becoming increasingly fragmented, Marcuse argued that this was not a random spatialization, but quartered through new urban social and spatial patterns that reflected economic, cultural and symbolic hierarchies.

These new socio-spatial urban configurations – variously labelled as post-industrial, post-Fordist, or post-modern – have been described by theorists such as Davis (1990), Harvey (1989a), Knox (1987), Soja (1989) and Zukin (1982), as being very different from their predecessors. Underpinning such urban change was economic recession that led to a dramatically declining manufacturing base, unemployment and physical decline in North American and European cities. City authorities (previously focused on local welfare and service provision) met this 'urban crisis' with 'a new urban politics', designed to foster economic development and local growth (Harvey, 1989b). Competition between cities engendered an entrepreneurial risk-taking by local government agencies in an attempt to respond to economic, social and cultural change. This 'new' city is not only characterized by programmes of place promotion or new public-private partnerships, but is visibly more spectacular. Economically and symbolically rejuvenated city centres with agglomerated business and financial districts feature gleaming high-rise office blocks, waterfront developments, and 'urban villages' surrounded by high-technology business clusters, a veritable archipelago of elite enclaves, out of town mega-malls, fragmented neighbourhoods and 'edge cities' (Knox, 1987; Soja, 1989; Zukin, 1982).

These physical and symbolic attempts to improve the urban environment are what Landry (1995) considers as initiatives to promote a 'creative city'.

Designed to make the city more liveable, these encompass aesthetic improvements of soft infrastructure, ranging from the building of squares, the provision of benches and fountains, to the greening of streets and improved public spaces, the establishment of late-night shopping and 'happy hours', and cultural events and festivals. Augmenting this has been the support and promotion of creative and cultural industries such as advertising, architecture, visual and performing art, crafts, design, film, music, performing art, publishing, media and new media. With buildings and facilities such as museums, art galleries and art centres, theatres, convention and exhibition centres, as well a supporting cast of restaurants, café bars, delicatessens, fashion boutiques, and other cultural facilities – the buzz of 'creativity, innovation and entrepreneurialism' brought about by the clustering of these activities in certain areas of the city centre is seen as crucial to contributing to the competitiveness of cities (Florida, 2002).

Such strategies of urban redevelopment seek to cultivate a symbolic economy based upon activities and products such as finance, investment, information and culture (art, food, fashion, music and tourism). Following the language of urban decline pre-1970s, and the dominance of residential, retail and business growth in suburban areas, it is clear that these economic and cultural discourses have now become overwhelmingly focused on city centre regeneration. Whether as a pro-growth economic strategy in more successful cites or an attempt to stabilize a declining economy in cities further down the urban hierarchy, the city centre is now seen as having great potential for a new cycle of economic, social and cultural post-industrial investment (Castells, 1977; Harvey, 1989a; Knox, 1987; Sassen, 1991, 1994; Soja, 1989, 1996).

This is graphically shown by Sharon Zukin (1982) in her famous study of the development of *Loft Living* in SoHo, New York. This exemplar of the growth of an urban village unpacked the political and cultural economy of consumption-led gentrification of a run-down and abandoned area of the city. Zukin describes the colonization of old industrial buildings that enabled and sustained an infrastructure of musicians, artists, craftworkers, entrepreneurs and cultural producers. These 'urban pioneers' created a vibrant scene that was youthful, dynamic and attractive to particular market segments of consumers and producers that in turn attracted other creative and entrepreneurial people as well as middle-class professional and managerial gentrifiers (see also O'Connor, 1998; O'Connor and Wynne, 1996). This final group, however, brought higher house prices, concerns with visual standardization, clean streetscapes and expensive shops, thus displacing the initial wave of gentrifiers to other parts of the city.

Central to the vitality of new city spaces are the social identities, lifestyles and consumption practices of managerial, professional and service classes. Similarly, the presence and promotion of, among others, lesbian and gay, youth and ethnic social groups, help to create a vibrant atmosphere in the city centre. This is an urban renaissance based on wealth creation associated with consumption (and the production of consumption), the cultural and service industries, with a focus on visual attractions which encourage people to spend money – including an array of consumption spaces from restaurants, museums, casinos, sports stadia and specialist and designer stores (and not traditional industry and manufacturing).

This is a post-industrial economy based on the interrelated production of such economic and cultural symbols and the spaces in which they are created and consumed. As such, 'sociability, urban lifestyles and social identities are not only the result, but also the raw materials of the growth of the symbolic economy' (Zukin, 1998: 830).

Such urban spaces are dominated by consumption, urban lifestyles and cultural events that Mafessoli (1996) describes as epitomizing post-industrial/post-modern urbanity. The new 'carnivalesque' spaces (such as urban villages), while being centred on private consumption, are argued to create a collective sense of *belonging* (to those with the symbolic and economic capital to join in). In these areas, membership is expressed by paraphernalia (clothes, lifestyle, taste). Post-industrial identities and lifestyles, while being distinctively grounded in local social relations, are expressed in terms of a fluidity of social relations no longer limited to the physical spaces of the city but expanded into virtual spaces – in, for example, advertising and media images – of the consumer society (Mort, 1998; Wynne and O'Connor, 1998). Thus, as Zukin (1998) shows, while there has been a global proliferation of the same kinds of malls, office complexes and urban villages, it must be remembered that it is the very specific localized social relations that makes each of these spaces and places unique.

Increasingly, then, the economic and cultural vitality of cities is founded on provision of consumption spaces that include the broadest variety of restaurants, theatres, shops and nightclubs and so on (Crewe and Lowe, 1995). The presence of such consumption spaces is vital precisely because they represent cultural and economic success. In general, the most successful cities contain the most culturally and socially diverse and innovative spaces of consumption. Hence, more successful cities attract a broader range of capital and investment, tourists and visitors, and in turn attract other innovative and entrepreneurial people: the symbolic success of cities is central to creating a sustainable broad economic base.

However, it has been shown that the kind of cosmopolitan, entertaining, vibrant, and 'happening' post-industrial spaces such as urban villages are underpinned by strong regional economies with professional post-industrial business cores (Castells, 1977; Sassen, 1991, 1994; Soja, 1989, 1996; Wynne and O'Connor, 1998). The stimulus for these conditions often appears to be the existence of an innovative political and institutional vision, and/or the activities of entrepreneurs and cultural intermediaries – urban 'movers and shakers' who are mediators and representatives of 'good taste' (whether as part of a structured media and advertising strategy or as fashionable individuals about town) – and cultural producers and artists who stimulate a snowballing of economic and cultural innovation. These instigators create a critical infrastructure of sites, citizens, social relations and forms of sociability relevant to the urban post-industrial symbolic economy.

Central to the vitality of such redevelopment strategies is the attraction of mobile capital, culture and people that could potentially go elsewhere. Cities must attempt to offer something unique in terms of generalized 'aesthetic' features and attractions (such as public art, theatres and historic buildings), plus chic places to live and work, if they are to add symbolic weight to their competitiveness (Zukin,

1998). For example, each city strives to identify/promote itself with reference to unique activities, places, events or people associated with its city/region/country. In order to compete, the ability of cities to innovate and attract the widest variety of symbolic and economic activities, new spectacular experiences, events and spaces of consumption, is paramount.

It is clear, then, that in this vision of the restructuring of cities (particularly those that have most successfully moved to a service- and consumption-based economy from a historic focus on manufacturing production), that particular social and spatial forms of urban life have been produced. However, while some urban spaces are developed around the consumption practices of the 'new petite bourgeoisie', as Marcuse (1989) showed, in other parts of the city (such as inner-city or suburban residential areas) there is an ever-widening gulf between the 'haves' and 'have-nots'. For example, the declining industrial city with unemployment, fiscal problems from the erosion of the tax base, and poor households in poor areas, is characterized as being plagued with violence, vandalism, housing, abandonment and urban unrest. Moreover, new kinds of flexible deregulation of the labour market ensure that it is only insecure, low status and low paid jobs that are generated by the demands of gentrifiers, tourists, conference delegates and other affluent consumers. It is this regime of flexible accumulation that creates these new spatial and social relations; landscapes of consumption and devastation co-exist in intimate relationship to one another (Davis, 1990; Harvey, 1985; Zukin, 1982). Moreover, uneven development is not only manifest within but also between cities in a new urban order (Harvey, 1989a; Savage and Warde, 1993).

Reading *City of Quarters*

In *Revitalizing Historic Urban Quarters* (1996), Tiesdell *et al.* outline interesting and useful case studies, ranging from downtown USA and historic *quartiers* of Europe, in order to discuss a number of issues concerning the economic potential of quarter gentrification, architectural design, heritage, tourism and housing associated with structural urban change as outlined by Zukin (1982), Soja (1989), and Harvey (1989). *City of Quarters* seeks to build on that progress, but advocates a more critical stance in order to unpack the political, economic, social, cultural and spatial construction (and contestation) of the conceptualization not only of planned or institutionally-developed urban quarters, but also of a range of other associated urban spaces and places. In doing so the collection of essays brings together thinking and case studies relating to Marcuse's mutually dependant city quarters, not only within, but between cities in different parts of the world and at different positions in the urban hierarchy.

City of Quarters is divided into four parts that reflect the urban practices and processes noted above – urban regeneration; production and consumption; identities, lifestyles and forms of sociability; and excluded and marginalized neighbourhoods. While individual chapters to some degree touch on each of these interrelated topics, each has a specific weighting.

Part 1 is a series of theoretical and empirical contributions that address how cultural quarters have been utilized as motors of economic and physical regeneration. Chapters discuss the development, branding and 'marking out' of quarters within particular urban and regional contexts and point to the accompanying social and spatial polarization of cities. Part 2 looks at the interface of production and consumption in urban quarters as cities try to compete in a post-industrial urban hierarchy characterized by intense competition. Chapters are focused on the creative industries, tourism and the cultural economy of villages and quarters. Part 3 presents case-study material and theoretical discussion relating to the importance of identities, lifestyles and forms of sociability in urban villages as cities seek to attract flows of global capital, culture and people by generating ambiences of cosmopolitan urbanity. Topics covered include conviviality, multiculturalism and sexuality. Part 4 opens up debate on how urban quarters and neighbourhoods are conceptualized by policy-makers, and identifies the need for a more integrated approach to planning for urban living. Chapters discuss the concept of the urban village as a socio-spatial model; community responses to prostitution in red-light districts; the mis-match between 'top-down' urban regeneration initiatives and community agendas in former industrial urban areas. The final substantive chapter outlines a blueprint for progressive planning for localities in urban areas. This is followed by a concluding chapter that draws together the themes discussed in this volume, and identifies key issues relating to the *City of Quarters*.

Part 1 opens with Gordon Waitt's examination of Pyrmont-Ultimo, which he describes as the newest 'chic quarter' of Sydney (Australia). Waitt's chapter tells an archetypal tale of the social and spatial transformations of a post-industrial city. Practices and processes are identified relating to economic and cultural globalization; neo-liberal urban politics; place marketing, civic boosterism; and the gentrification of historic manufacturing and industrial areas by property developers (on behalf of white-collar professionals). Waitt describes the development of the urban village in parallel with the 'corralling' of excluded and marginalized social groups into decaying neighbourhoods, thus highlighting a cityscape dominated by social divisions – an exemplar of uneven post-industrial urban life.

Pyrmont-Ultimo is thus a shining example; a symbol of successful inner-city revitalization, one element of a re-imagining of the city by an urban elite seeking to establish Sydney as a world city. This urban village is the location of financial institutions and knowledge-rich global companies, and offers a haven of cosmopolitan consumption cultures for middle-class residents and tourists. However, as Waitt notes, Pyrmont-Ultimo is also a symbol of the growing divisions between the 'haves' and 'have-nots' in our cities. Nevertheless, while café-bars, delicatessens, loft apartments and harbour views make up a landscape of cosmopolitan consumption, this particular urban village lacks an essential facility of city centre living: Pyrmont-Ultimo does not have a supermarket to service its residents.

Following on from Waitt's Australian tale of social and spatial polarisation, Malcolm Miles takes us to Spain and, with a similar tale of gentrification, outlines an historic precedent for the contemporary urban change that has unfolded in el

Raval, Barcelona. In line with the city's desire to further raise its profile as a locus of cultural tourism, Miles argues that the redevelopment of el Raval as a cultural quarter (with its flagship building the Museu d'Art Contemporani, MACBA) is centred on provision of tourist attractions rather than locally-embedded production and consumption cultures. Miles shows that the development of this residential area represents a new colonialism where the needs of the city's diverse publics have been disregarded under pressure from the demands of the global tourism market.

Miles goes on to contextualize the development of el Raval with reference to two contrasting and famous urban planning traditions: firstly, Idelfons Cerdà's plan for the city of Barcelona in 1854 and secondly, Baron Haussmann's infamous redevelopment of Paris around the same time. Miles concludes that the contemporary redevelopment of el Raval is more akin to Haussmann's oppressive planning regime than to Cerdà's liberalism. Urban planning in contemporary Barcelona is underpinned by a 'Haussmannization' of the city – urban change oriented towards gentrifiers and tourists rather than for egalitarian or socially beneficial regulation; an argument that is easily applicable to the previous case study as it is to the following iconic urban space in New York, USA.

In Chapter 4, James DeFilippis discusses the plans for the redevelopment of what is arguably *the* most high-profile urban space on this planet – lower Manhattan. Following terrorist attacks that led to the collapse of the World Trade Center (WTC), in New York on September 11th 2001, DeFilippis addresses two main issues that have arisen around the redevelopment of the 16-acre site where the 'Twin Towers' used to stand as a symbol of America's economic superpower status. First is the broad issue of the prominence of economic growth-oriented urban authorities in the USA, and second is the production and proliferation of 'public' spaces that are inherently exclusionary.

DeFilippis argues that plans for the reconstruction of the WTC site represent a further intensification of the privatization of public space in the USA, and that this is bound up in the increasingly oppressive nature of the socio-spatial production of American cities. He shows that plans for the redevelopment of 'Ground Zero' thus represent a cruel irony, that following the events of 9/11 (which he argues effectively reinvigorated *public* life in the city of New York and offered a glimpse of the city's diversity), should essentially lead to the deepening of already-entrenched class and race-based exclusions and segregations. Such an assertion ultimately summarizes the debate on urban regeneration in this part of the book. Waitt, Miles and DeFilippis all offer beguilingly simple structural accounts of urban change, that can be relevantly applied to cities throughout the urban hierarchy as much as they can to New York, Sydney or Barcelona or the city where you are from; or the city where you are reading this; the city you might soon visit, or have seen at the movies. Contemporary urban redevelopment is overwhelmingly based on a globalized capitalist ideology of economic growth – rather than social justice. This is ultimately leading to increasingly socially and spatially polarized cities.

Part 2 argues that production and consumption cultures are now central to the ability of cities to maintain their position in an urban hierarchy based on intense competition. If cities are to maintain or develop competitive advantage they must attract global flows of capital and culture; footloose investment and professional, managerial and business employers as well as tourists and people to sustain a creative post-industrial economy. The focus in this part of the book is not on the landing place of global capital, the home of financial institutions as with the examples of New York and Sydney above, but rather other activities associated with post-industrial competitiveness, such as creative and cultural industries development and tourism.

Graeme Evans discusses the contemporary form of the post-industrial cultural quarter while acknowledging its pre-industrial precedents. With examples from all around the world, Evans unpacks the importance of the clustering of creative and cultural industries, from those based on a craft ethos to multi-media and post-Fordist flexible design-led businesses. Evans writes that over the past twenty years cultural industries quarters have emerged as part of urban regeneration regimes. However such spaces tend to be given only limited institutional support, and a limited time to flourish; Evans questions whether these are indeed quarters in the sense of clustering and networking necessary to develop a critical mass of buildings, institutions, businesses and people that make up a creative milieu. With a detailed focus on Clerkenwell, London (UK), Evans charts the morphology of creative businesses, as well as flagging the intimate relationship between the creative industries cluster in Clerkenwell and its proximity to the financial centre of the City of London and renowned cultural institutions such as the Tate Modern. Above all, Evans argues that the proliferation of such organic creative urban spaces, as well as the prominence of (often less convincing) planned cultural and creative quarters, ultimately stands and falls on their relationship to broader economic and cultural flows that operate in and between cities – and further that state intervention with creative clustering must ensure the retention of the cultural values and distinctiveness of local contexts and activities.

Tom Fleming's chapter follows on neatly from the previous chapter to address Evans's contention about the role of the state in supporting or developing creative and cultural quarters. Fleming looks at the role of creative intermediaries who support the development of cultural and creative quarters and whose job it is to attract or generate creative industries activity in order to augment the physical gentrification of quarters. Fleming thus focuses on publicly-funded creative intermediaries rather than those from the new petit bourgeois professional class, as identified by Bourdieu (1984) and Featherstone (1991). The chapter addresses three central questions: firstly, what are the dynamics of the local creative industries sector? Secondly, what is the best way to support the retention and growth of the sector? And finally, what is the position and role of the creative intermediary? In addressing these questions, Fleming argues that a successful creative/cultural industries quarter can be characterized as being networked, knowledge-reliant, founded on risk and trust, shy, and as an 'evanescent' economy. Fleming praises certain creative intermediary services in the UK for undertaking progressive and effective work. However, he questions the efficacy of intervention, while acknowledging the necessity of state-led involvement in creative industries development initiatives and the value the sector to urban regeneration. Fleming ultimately advocates a locally sensitive and tailored creative intermediary service, plus embedded development teams and individuals who retain a sense of the explorative, flexible, resourceful and entrepreneurial in order to make quarters work.

Abigail Gilmore addresses a particular creative industries quarter, focused on popular music. The Rope Walks, Liverpool (UK) has been developed to capture music-related tourism as well as to enhance local music production and consumption cultures. The quarter has been constructed around the city's historical association with The Beatles and more contemporarily the high-profile clubbing attraction Cream. The quarter has been central to the branding of Liverpool as 'Music City', and Gilmore traces the conflicts and connections between music, local economic development and city image. She explores the interconnection between the production and consumption of music and sense of place. Rope Walks is, however, a property-led initiative largely funded through national and European funding projects that focus on public realm and infrastructural improvement. While there is an acknowledgement of the need for an integrated approach, including creative industries support and development, the level of actual support for cultural production and its relationship to consumption is unconvincing. Gilmore concludes that local music spaces are still present in the area, defiant or oblivious to the gentrification that might ultimately pose a threat to their existence.

The final chapter in this part of the book turns more explicitly to the relationship between tourism, heritage and the production and consumption of urban space. Stephanie Rains' (1999) previous work on the Temple Bar cultural quarter in Dublin (Eire), identified that Dublin's heritage industry is a delicate and only recently negotiated method of rehabilitating Dublin's colonial and Anglo-Irish identity in a way that appeals to both tourists and the city's inhabitants. Rains shows how the re-imagining of the city has been based around the 'safe' area of Dublin's Literary Heritage, aligning the city to its creative rather than political past.

Rains extends this understanding of a specific urban village in her chapter here, to a process that she describes as the 'quarterization' of the city. She unpacks the most emblematic feature of Dublin's tourist industry, the *Ulysses* Walks – which are based on walking routes through the city taken from Joyce's novel. Rains suggests that *Ulysses* Walks represent a particular image of city living, and a way of emphasizing national pride in its culture and history, by marking the city as a 'site' that is representative of the 'common man'. Rains argues that *Ulysses* Walks represents a 'painful' symbolic re-configuring of the city's material form. She shows that the quartering of the city via urban regeneration initiatives such as Temple Bar cultural quarter, or the quarterization of the city by the *Ulysses* Walks, exhibits a post-colonial negotiation of a city seeking to capture flows of global tourism and economic advantage.

Part 3 follows on from Rains' examination of the conflict that surrounds the production and consumption of urban space with a critical focus on the relationship between identity, lifestyle and forms of sociability and the construction and experience of urban villages. Jim Shorthose focuses on the Lace Market, Nottingham (UK) which he describes as a *de facto* cultural quarter, grown organically from its industrial textile past into a thriving creative industries district. Shorthose describes the Lace Market as an ecology of inter-dependent relationships founded on flows of work and information between independent producers and other cultural organizations and businesses. He describes this as a convivial ecology with a high value placed on everyday living/working ambience – of cultural, rather than culture-for-money, individuals and businesses. Utilizing quantitative research, Shorthose identifies that location, sense of belonging and sustainability are central concerns of the Lace Market's populace. The chapter concludes that the success of the Lace Market is in danger of being undermined by large-scale redevelopments attracted to the quarter by its entrepreneurial potency and innovative economy.

Jon Binnie is more critical about the ways in which urban villages are constructed around particular identities, activities and ways of behaving. His chapter examines the development of 'gay villages' and unpacks the conflicts that surround these urban spaces. Binnie offers a specific focus on sexual citizenship, and the role the state plays in the production of gay space. His argument centres on Manchester (UK), where the local state is actively promoting the city's gay village as a cosmopolitan symbol of Manchester's aspiration to be seen as a European city. Binnie questions the models of citizenship that are being promoted as part of this process, arguing that there is a disciplining and normalizing agenda that ultimately reinforces exclusionary discourses that surround 'boundaries' in cities. While he argues that homophobia is associated with anti-cosmopolitanism, Binnie suggests that quartering in essence fixes queers in place. The chapter suggests that quarters produce a weak, less dynamic lesbian and gay culture and that in gay quarters difference is annihilated.

Wun Chan's chapter on the proliferation of Chinatowns provides a similar critical review of the kind of processes of control and regulation outlined by Binnie. Chan notes that British planning regards Chinese culture as both a source of inspiration and as contemptuous. The chapter outlines a relationship of appropriation and ethnocentrism reiterated through UK planning discourses. Chan shows how the development of the Chinese Quarter in Birmingham (UK) was central to attempts to market the city as a model of multi-cultural integration in order to generate an international trading advantage. Chan shows that there was also the very specific aim to attracting flows of capital, people and businesses wishing to leave Hong Kong in anticipation of the island returning to Chinese rule. He concludes that despite allusions to multicultural difference, and rather than being a genuine engagement with planning for a diverse and inclusive city, the central aim of developing a Chinese Quarter in Birmingham was limited to adding an aesthetic 'Chinese flavour' to the city in order to aid physical regeneration and to attract financial investment and support business tourism.

Part 4 provides an exploration of marginalized neighbourhoods and offers an alternative approach to planning for urban living. The authors attempt to challenge the orthodox and market-led responses to urban change – to think differently about the contemporary city, and to outline an agenda that seeks to overcome many of the problems associated with the social and spatial polarizations outlined in preceding chapters. In doing so the authors contribute to increasing academic interest in the concept of the neighbourhood (see for example, Atkinson and Kinetra, 2001; Forrest and Kearns, 2001; Meegan and Mitchell, 2001; Whithead, 2003). Chris Murray's chapter begins with an introduction to the work of the Urban Villages Forum in the UK, and outlines a definition of what constitutes a successful urban village. He then shows how the urban village model is ingrained in English culture, underpinned by historical precedents such as the model village movement and suburbian utopias. Murray then investigates what he considers a best-practice case study – Christiania, Denmark. Outlining an agenda for action, Murray includes eight key objectives, advocating that neighbourhoods should not be seen as isolated spatial phenomena, but that planning for each neighbourhood must be embedded within a broader context of city-wide or even regional planning. The chapter commends the concept of the urban village and quarter in recognizing the importance of localized policy and planning and the acknowledgment that specialized cultural centres need planning and provision. However, Murray concludes that the proliferation of urban villages has to date been problematic because of the failure to develop villages and neighbourhoods in a way which seeks to overcome or tackle in a convincing way the seemingly inevitable impacts on those who are marginalized by practices and processes of global urban change.

The following two chapters present case studies of empirical research and policy intervention within peripheral urban areas. The final chapter in this part of the book draws on substantial research from across Europe and outlines an agenda for an integrated planning approach to neighbourhoods and cities. O'Neill *et al.* discuss a particular (but nonetheless worldwide) phenomenon, that of urban red-light districts. The chapter highlights community responses to prostitution in Walsall (UK), and draws on research undertaken with prostitutes and local residents. Utilizing creative consultation methods such as participatory action research and participatory arts, all local voices are valued and the research is community driven; it led to actionable and sustainable recommendations and outcomes. The chapter advocates the development of tolerance zones, where sex workers can work in strategic locations; the intention of these is not to ghettoize sex workers, but to ensure safer working conditions and attempt to reduce nuisance to residents. The chapter highlights how resistance emerges around forms of subjectivity (class, race, sexuality, etc.) that are usually marginalized in and through space.

Phil Denning investigates regeneration initiatives relating to former industrial neighbourhoods, particularly those associated with coal mining and steel. His chapter discusses examples of these 'Coketowns' in Scotland, Germany and Hungary. Denning laments the prevalence of top-down regeneration schemes that fail to address the needs of the local community and fail to engage with local agendas. The chapter then focuses on the Scottish case study, Craigmillar. Denning identifies a number of community groups, institutions and events that define the spirit of the place, but that are being undermined or silenced by local authority urban regeneration initiatives. He argues that the wealth of tradition, identity and memory is not being supported at the level of public policy, and that urban regeneration is being led by bulldozers and demolition that leads to the proliferation of ghost towns.

The final substantive chapter in the book, by Bianchini and Ghilardi, focuses on European cities and offers a review of a major research project commissioned by the Council of Europe into the 'Culture of Neighbourhoods'. The project was undertaken between 1993 and 1996 and included neighbourhoods from eleven European cities. Its objectives include identifying ways in which local communities can shape and evaluate their own cultural policies; and exploring and maximizing the potential contribution of neighbourhood culture to the cultural, economic and social dynamics and development of cities and regions. The chapter outlines the concept of neighbourhood culture – neighbourhoods rooted in buildings and memory and the complex activity and networks of residents, where individuals obtain ontological security. Bianchini and Ghilardi point to the ways in which culture can be used to aid physical regeneration, and highlight organic approaches to regeneration mobilizing responses to local aspirations. This is contrasted to flagship cultural projects and city centre redevelopment. The chapter identifies particular policy implications based around a cultural planning approach that accounts for many facets of neighbourhood life.

The authors show a need for the retraining of policy-makers so that they better understand how neighbourhoods and cities develop. This stresses the importance of cross-cutting issues and problems, but most importantly, the imperative of overcoming problems of social exclusion marked by economic and lifestyle differences. Bianchini and Ghilardi argue for an egalitarian notion of public space at city and neighbourhood level, with procedures and institutional arrangements to co-ordinate cultural policies at city-wide and neighbourhood level; an assertion which has been propagated by many of the writers in this volume. In doing so, this chapter offers an alternative agenda for the development of urban neighbourhoods, one that is relevant to the development of urban villages and quarters as well as city-regions throughout the urban hierarchy.

City of Quarters offers insights into the relationship between structural transformations associated with urban change and everyday life. By addressing political, economic, social, spatial and cultural practices and processes, each chapter offers a focused critique of urban living and the development of our cities. We hope that these essays together constitute an experiential review of case studies complemented with conceptual debate that contributes to the crucial task of unpacking both broad trends and local specificities in urban spaces and places in different kinds of cities throughout the world.

Part 1
Urban Regeneration

Chapter 2

Pyrmont-Ultimo: the Newest Chic Quarter of Sydney

Gordon Waitt

Pyrmont-Ultimo, on the western edge of Sydney's Central Business District (CBD), has become the Australian city's newest 'chic quarter' (Figure 2.1). Abandoned industrial buildings born of maritime and industrial capitalism are being refurbished and converted into either boutique office space for the burgeoning creative industries sector or loft apartments for urban professionals. Empty shops are being converted into cafés and boutique retail outlets. New high-rise luxury apartment blocks are being built on derelict waterfront industrial sites. The harbour foreshore is being reopened to the public, as walkways and parklands. Pyrmont-Ultimo is one of the latest locations of Sydney's inner-city urban renaissance following policies that embrace the 'New Right' political ideology emphasizing urban consolidation and 'village lifestyles' and an economic climate encouraging rapid expansion of the creative industries sector. However, the emergence of Sydney's chic inner-city urban quarter has also brought its own physical and symbolic barriers that effectively wall-out Sydney's least affluent residents from all but a passing curiosity.

Pyrmont-Ultimo provides an example through which to examine the processes of social exclusion that accompany the social transformation of an inner-city precinct from urban dereliction to urban chic. Three questions guide this chapter. It begins by addressing what is new about the emergence of Pyrmont-Ultimo as Sydney's urban chic quarter, given that social divisions have always characterized the city. To an extent this question is examined by reference to geographical analyses of economic restructuring. Next, the chapter examines questions regarding the residential pattern or social mosaic arising from economic restructuring in Sydney. These questions require a more detailed consideration of the arguments examining the processes of residential segregation, particularly socio-economic polarization. Finally, the chapter turns to a detailed examination of how the process of social polarization is exemplified in Pyrmont-Ultimo. First, a description is given of the transformation of Pyrmont-Ultimo from the centre of Sydney's nineteenth- and early twentieth-century manufacturing and port activities, to one of Sydney's latest most fashionable postcodes. This is followed by a discussion

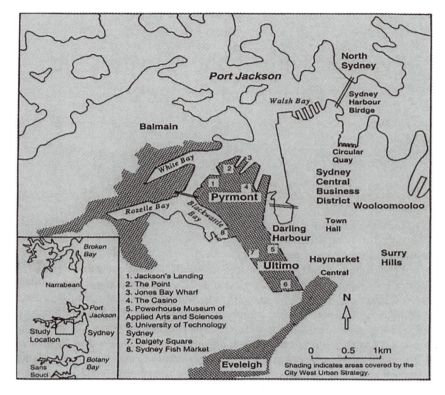

Figure 2.1 Map of Central Sydney

of how Pyrmont-Ultimo was refashioned as a residential location for the almost exclusive occupancy of urban professionals. Readings of the architecture and development corporation's advertisements are offered to illustrate the repackaging of Pyrmont-Ultimo.

Sydney's Urban and Political Economies

Social divisions have always characterized Sydney's residential structures. Gender, class and ethnic inequalities have been manifested in the spaces its residents have occupied since its establishment as a convict settlement in early 1788 (Aplin, 1982). The undemocratic pattern of urban life has remained apparent throughout the several phases of Sydney's integration into the global economy, beginning with its role as a commercial trade centre in the 1820s and, most recently, with its emergence as Australia's only 'world city' (Connell, 2000).

Whilst social divisions within Sydney are certainly old, much is new. An acute over-supply of commercial CBD property in the early 1990s caused many developers to look towards residential development. Changing demographics have seen a growth in the number of single parents, singles, childless couples, women executives and dual income families. The ageing of the population and increasing numbers of retirees has resulted in the process of downsizing, involving the movement from large suburban properties to high-rise apartments. Higher density housing has been strongly encouraged by all levels of government through urban consolidation policies and legislation permitting pre-construction sales (New South Wales Department of Environment and Planning, 1984).

The broader process of economic globalization has also resulted in the progressive restructuring of Sydney's urban economy, particularly since the political-economic crisis of the 1970s and 1980s (Bounds and Morris, 2001; Lepani *et al.*, 1995; Murphy and Watson, 1990; O'Connor and Stimson, 1995). A new spatial 'fix' was required for a Sydney profoundly affected and reshaped by massive deindustrialization and the new demands of global capitalism. In this context, property developers seized the opportunity to restructure Sydney's CBD into the orbit of global capitalism through international banking (Daly, 1982), and its former central industrial area by constructing purpose-built facilities catering for emerging 'high-tech' industries (Watson, 1990).

In addition, this new economic context, in which cities increasingly compete with one another for new forms of investment, encouraged Australia's state and commonwealth governments to embrace entrepreneurial rather than welfare goals in response to the problems following from deindustrialization (McGuirk *et al.,* 1996; Pusey, 1991). Since the mid-1980s, urban policies have been increasingly informed by the 'New Right' agenda, including the virtues of individualism, self-help, and private property. Entrepreneurial private-public partnerships of the urban development corporations were heralded as the solution to urban blight, such as in Pyrmont-Ultimo. Urban development corporations embrace business goals and objectives. A blurring has thus occurred of the distinction between public provision for social goals and private production for economic opportunity and individual profit. Therefore, urban development corporations and the spaces they have created have generally favoured the interests of those with access to capital. Furthermore, in this policy climate obstacles to attaining economic growth included planning regulations, public participation and social equity considerations. Consequently, the urban social movements apparent in Sydney's inner-city precincts in the 1970s were effectively curtailed. In the 1970s resident action groups, forming informal alliances with building unionists, and utilizing green bans, halted inner-city redevelopment (Nittim, 1980). The gentrification that did occur in precincts such as Balmain, Glebe and Paddington was predominantly through private redevelopment (Hovarth and Engels, 1985).

The prominence amongst entrepreneurial public-private partnerships of a decision-making environment in which business tactics of the profit-making sector take precedence over policies of welfare provision has enabled urban development corporations to refashion cityscapes to facilitate forms of capital accumulation emphasizing consumption rather than production (Roche, 1994). Such refashioning emphasizes the broader transformation of cities' economies away from manufacturing to production of commodities satisfying the growing demands of business, entertainment, education and culture. In this process Sydney's cityscapes have been reconstituted as products which generate cultural capital. Sydney's cityscapes and social environments have thus been transformed by various public and private authorities into a variety of aesthetic products aiming to sell inner-city locations not only to potential homebuyers but also to overseas tourists, investors and businesses (Waitt, 1999). In this competitive promotional environment, two new sets of city attributes have become prominent locational determinants: amenity and services (Ashworth and Voogd, 1990).

In rendering Sydney's social and physical attributes as attractive commodities to be consumed, images have gained greater importance over substance in the so-called 'promotional culture' of marketing places (Urry, 1995). Marketing processes, operating across all geographical scales, have been strongly criticized as destroying a place's integrity by a repackaging process that dismissively rearranges social, environmental and historical resources into new patterns that might earn money and acceptance (Harvey, 1989a; Zukin, 1992). The repackaging of Sydney's inner city to white-collar professionals by property developers, either independently or in partnership with the state, exemplifies this process of decontextualization. This process removes anything controversial, offering a contemporary lifestyle that promises an exclusive neighbourhood combining security with convenience to places of work, services and leisure. The promotional language employs a universal vocabulary that describes inner-city lifestyles as 'New York Style' or 'village living'. The act of promoting to urban professionals the glossy image of the symbolic capital offered by inner-city living silences and denies alternative lifestyles, particularly those marginalized by the process of de-industrialization – including the homeless, and the discarded unskilled, blue-collar workers. Repackaging casts many 'realities' of inner-city lifestyles as irrelevant and/or 'unchic': local maritime histories and lifestyles that include prostitution, squatting, begging, crime and drug and alcohol addiction. In place of variety, contrast and historic attachment, the commodification of inner-city lifestyles generates de-contextualization, sameness and blandness through apathy to the difference of place.

Sydney's Residential Spaces

The globalization/polarization thesis suggests those processes of globalization, economic restructuring and employment shift are combining to restructure city spaces by the demands of mobile global capital. City residential spaces are argued to be increasingly polarized, differentiated between the educated who can participate in the 'new economy', and those skilled in the 'old economy' and vulnerable groups who are increasingly marginalized (Sassen, 1991; Savage and Warde, 1993; Smith and Williams, 1986). The dichotomy between the 'inner city' and the 'outer suburb' is receiving increased media attention, which employs discourses of a divided society that implies a group of people are separated off spatially, socially and economically (Murphy and Watson, 1997). But this is a simplistic and often misleading binary division.

Socio-economic polarization within Australian cities is a highly contested issue, engendering debates over such matters as appropriate measures (Walmsely and Weinand, 1997), attention to geographical scale (Baum, 1997), boundaries (Withers *et al.,* 1995), models (Badcock, 1997) and representations (Mee, 1994; Hodge, 1996). Nevertheless, there is general agreement among many researchers that in terms of real income the greatest divergence has occurred in Sydney between the outer (western) and inner suburbs, both from analysis conducted with data collected at the neighbourhood (census collectors district) (Gregory and Hunter, 1995, 1997) and the more aggregated spatial scale of the postcode (Gregory and Sheehan, 1998). A spatial disparity in income and employment is readily apparent in Sydney. The locational disadvantage hypothesis suggests that in Sydney's case, the outer western suburbs were negatively effected by the transition to global capitalism because their growth was associated with processes of chain migration from Europe, refugee hostels, higher concentrations of public housing and manufacturing activity, dependence upon the motor car and the suburban dream (NHS, 1991). In contrast, Sydney's inner city revitalization has become associated with creative industries, which tend to cluster at a relatively few locations that offer ease of access to both their international and national markets and workforce (Stimson, 2001). Transformation of the inner city is in part an outcome of an iterative process between the agglomerative requirements of creative industries and symbolic analysts choosing 24/7 city lifestyles and ease of access to work.

Housing markets, through a process of social tenure polarization, represent a key mechanism that operates to divide the city between the increasingly affluent inner city and socially marginalized outer suburb. In Australia, Fincher and Wulff (1998) claim a 'new geography of property' is emerging with heightened socio-economic disparities in large cities. In Sydney, poorer families are increasingly compressed into the outer municipalities that have concentrations of lower priced private rental housing and higher concentrations of public housing (such as Campbelltown, Green Valley and Mount Druitt) (Flood, 2000). Lower-income households still able to contemplate home purchasing are also increasingly being forced into the low-density outer southwestern suburbs and beyond. In the year to July 2002, median house and unit prices in the outer southwestern suburbs were AU$251,00 and AU$150,000; in inner suburbs the medians were AU$523,000 and AU$322,000 respectively (Australian Property Monitor www.apm.com.au). For the year to July 2002, in Pyrmont the median house and unit price was more than double Sydney's outer southwestern suburbs, at AU$644,000 and AU$391,000, respectively (Australian Property Monitor, www.apm.com.au). Fifteen years earlier, in 1987, when gentrification began, the median property prices in Pyrmont-Ultimo and Sydney were almost equal; AU$86,000 and AU$89,000, respectively. A decade earlier in 1977, during the height of Pyrmont-Ultimo's urban blight, property was sold for almost half the Sydney median price. The median Pyrmont-Ultimo property sale price was AU$18,800, whereas that of Sydney was AU$38,000 (BIS Schrapnel, 1987). Inner-city living is thus being restricted to the higher income and professional upwardly mobile households.

Whilst mapping and statistical analysis of social differences may highlight diverging inequalities, such quantitative exercises mask residents' lived experience. When analysis turns to how residents experience and contribute to a particular city locality, a far more complex, even chaotic pattern of cityspaces emerges. Marcuse (1995) argues that behind the chaos there is order. When conceptualizing the socio-spatial structure along qualitative lines, a city of fragments is revealed that is not random but hierarchical in power, walled in and walled out by boundaries sometimes physical, but more often symbolic and dependent on outside social forces. Although Marcuse (1989) identified five types of residential quarters for larger cities in the United States – the dominating city, the gentrified city, the suburban city, the tenement city and the abandoned city – these are not conceptualized as separate, isolated units, given that each distinct entity or division is intimately and intricately linked to all other parts of the metropolitan area, forming a mutually dependent city.

Mapping Marcuse's residential quarters onto Sydney suggests that the classification has some limited relevance here, particularly the 'dominating city' and 'gentrified city'. However, Marcuse's categories do not wholly match Sydney's social divisions (Murphy and Watson, 1997). In Sydney there is no significant inner 'tenement city' with high-density state-owned housing, though there is, in Surry Hills, a limited high-rise development from the 1950s, constructed to replace cleared 'slum housing'. Equally, the 'abandoned city' is almost inappropriate. Whilst a significant degree of homelessness exists and is particularly visible on inner-city streets of Haymarket, Surry Hills and Wooloomooloo, charity organizations and the Australian government welfare provisions have prevented the emergence of this problem on a scale comparable with that in comparably sized American cities. Sydney's 'suburban city' is also differentiated by the specificities of Australian suburbanization; the 1960s 'Great Australian Dream' as involving 3-4 children, the detached house and garden (the quarter acre block); successive waves of overseas migrants from the 1950s; and substantial public housing construction in the 1970s (Dowling and Mee, 2000).

However, following Marcuse's argument, Sydney's metropolitan spaces are intricately linked to social diversity and power differences. Sydney has become a place of wide-ranging social and cultural diversity. Social divisions are increasingly apparent along a number of axes of difference including education, employment, sexuality, ethnicity, religion, age, gender and other variables. Some groups have economic and social power, ensuring that their needs are met in the urban system, others do not. Individuals constituting themselves as groups because they have little economic, social or political power are not the same as the spatial separation of the affluent.

Those who conform to the cultural norm and have economic or political power have the choice of luxury homes set in suburbs with high environmental amenity value, for example the dominating city with its luxury housing in the elite suburbia of the North Shore and Eastern Suburbs. Their spatial segregation is commonly marked by the walls of mansions, with gates and security devices to protect from physical intrusion. Equally the gentrification and displacement of the earlier working-class populations has occurred in a swathe of inner-city suburbs ranging from Balmain, through Glebe, Eveleigh, Surry Hills and Newtown. In Sydney, the process of gentrification within Surry Hills and Darlinghurst cannot be separated from the assertion of gay identities since the late 1970s and more recently in Newtown and Erskinville through the queering of space. Here the walls are symbolic rather than physical: the rainbow flag, the pink triangle, the dress codes and other performances of identity. Spatial segregation offers not merely an opportunity to enjoy services and community facilities offered by a critical mass of like-minded people but also acts as a form of resistance and solidarity against an often hostile world (McInnes, 2001).

In contrast, where difference from the cultural norm is combined with a lack of economic or political power, the spatial concentration of marginalized individuals in the suburb may arise through lack of choice, including many single parents and indigenous Australians. Watson (1988) argues that residents may perceive the physical walls of housing estates as a form of confinement to poor services and peripheral locations. Another manifestation of individuals constituting themselves as groups because of their cultural difference and powerlessness is the spatial segregation of overseas migrants, encapsulated in colloquial references to Campsie as 'Korea Town' and Cabramatta as 'Vietnammatta'. For international migrants, bounded spaces offer protection where minorities can establish themselves. Common interest arises from a shared culture, from intra-community business opportunities and from shared financial and family concerns. The protective walls of migrants' spatial concentration are symbolic, including the language of shop signs and the prevalence of languages other than English on the street as well as in the home (Dunn, 1993).

The emergence of Pyrmont-Ultimo as one of Sydney's 'urban chic quarters' can be explored through this lens. What processes have operated to delimit Pyrmont-Ultimo as a space bounded by exclusionary walls? The entrepreneurial planning policies that have revitalized Pyrmont-Ultimo have fostered symbolic and physical walls that favour those who conform to the cultural norm, have political and economic power, desire a salubrious environment and fear incursions by the poor. The outcome exemplifies the emergence of high-rise apartment living in inner Sydney as an alternative to the suburb and the increasing spatial segregation and concentration of white-collar professionals within the inner city. In Pyrmont-Ultimo, once the centre of Sydney's manufacturing and port activities, private developers combine city lifestyle with suburban living to market the precinct's local distinctiveness.

Pyrmont-Ultimo

Pyrmont-Ultimo is located on a peninsula on the western edge of Sydney's central business district, which physically separates it from the rest of the city. To the west, physical boundaries are the foreshore of Blackwattle Bay, Wentworth Park and a main northwestern arterial road, Wattle Street. To the east the foreshore of Darling Harbour (Sydney's entertainment and conference precinct) and a University of Technology Sydney campus physically designate the precinct, while to the south the boundary is Sydney's major western arterial highway, Broadway (see Figure 2.1).

Until the late 1940s, waterfront location and proximity to the urban core resulted in the emergence of an urban infrastructure born of nineteenth-century maritime servicing and manufacturing activities including shipping, storage, cartage, shipbuilding, foundries, breweries, sugar refining and flour milling (Matthews, 1982). From the late 1880s, the construction of large-scale warehouses and wool stores on the flat harbour foreshore effectively created an 'urban wall' along both the western and eastern boundaries (DUAP, 1995a). At the beginning of the twentieth century, Pyrmont was an industrial suburb housing over 30,000 people, the majority of whom lived in terrace housing confined to the central spine of the peninsula (Keilhacker, 1998). Homes along the foreshore were demolished when the Sydney Harbour Trust (established 1901) resumed all the harbour foreshores to clear them of rats, the alleged culprit of Sydney's worst bubonic plague outbreak. Profitable waterfront industries were encouraged through the state's provision of modernized and expanded wharves at Pyrmont Bay (Gibbons, 1980). During the early decades of the twentieth century, industrial expansion continued and many homes were destroyed, including those to make room for the expansion of the Colonial Sugar Refining Ltd's plant (CWDC and Park, 1997). As one of Sydney's key industrial locations, Pyrmont was also the obvious location for a power station (1904) and incinerator (1937) (Matthews, 1982).

After World War II, many of the manufacturing industries closed or progressively relocated to Sydney's suburbs from the central industrial area. By 1954 the population had decline to 5,000 (Fitzgerald and Golder, 1994). Homes were progressively demolished for a second Pyrmont power station in 1955, the Government Printing Office in 1959 and Fairfax Press newsprint store in the 1960s (Ashton, 1993). In that decade, too, Pyrmont's maritime activities were curtailed by the rapid growth of freight containerization serviced by new container facilities in Port Botany and by the relocation of wool brokering to Yennora, in southwestern Sydney (Sant and Jackson, 1991). The sixteen wool stores that lined the peninsula were vacated, signalling the end of industrial expansion and the beginning of two decades of instability and uncertainty (Fitzgerald and Golder, 1994).

By the 1970s the majority of the obsolete industrial sites had been abandoned (see Figure 2.2). In land use terms, Pyrmont-Ultimo was regarded by planners as little more than an expressway route to the city. Much of the deteriorating housing stock was either occupied by squatters or was derelict. Government bodies resumed properties as they fell into disrepair. The residential population fell below 1,800 and local amenities vanished. Indeed, throughout the 1970s residential regeneration was prohibited under the provisions of the Sydney City Council's 'light industrial' zoning (Hillier and Searle, 1995). However, the remaining long-term residents formed a small, stable and tightly-knit community, a place where everyone knew one another. Moreover, this sense of community was heightened by physical isolation from the rest of Sydney, the density of housing and, for most residents, walking distances that defined the boundaries of their lived experiences (Fitzgerald and Golder, 1994).

Figure 2.2 Abandoned Nineteenth-Century Industrial Sites (Photo: G. Waitt)
Top – One of the last redundant manufacturing sites in Pyrmont-Ultimo. Bottom – Wattle Street Depot was closed in 1989, having operated for sixty years as a store for Council vehicles, horses and equipment. The depot was central to road construction operation of the city. Previously this site had been the location of a tar distillation plant and a sandstone quarry (Fitzgerald and Golder, 1994).

The 1980s signalled the beginning of a new era of entrepreneurial urban development. In September 1984, an Act of Parliament established the Darling Harbour Authority, whose objective was to transform the obsolete goods yards in the adjoining suburb into an international exhibition and convention centre (Webber, 1988). Earmarked for special Commonwealth funding from the Bicentennial Project financing the celebration of two hundred years of European 'settlement' in Australia and with a completion date of 1988, the Authority was exempt from the normal development controls, in complete disregard of the concerns of UPROAR (Ultimo-Pyrmont Residents Opposed to Arbitrary Re-development) (Fitzgerald and Golder, 1994). Consequently, and without any residential consultation, Pyrmont's eastern boundary was redefined by a new physical barrier, the rear faces of the multi-storied Novotel and Ibis Hotels. Additionally, Pyrmont-Ultimo was bisected by the construction of the Darling Harbour freeway, part of the Western Distributor connecting the city with the western suburbs.

The City of Sydney Strategic Plan of 1980 envisaged the residential restructuring that was to occur by rezoning to allow a mix of residential, commercial and industrial uses (Sydney City Council, 1980). In 1981 the process of gentrification began and property prices began to rise in Pyrmont-Ultimo (Sant and Jackson, 1991). New residents sought not only the 'charm' of terrace housing but were also aware of the benefits of inner-city living as well as the appreciation of land and dwelling prices that would occur.

By 1991 the population had begun to increase slowly, reaching some 3,200 residents. However, the 1990s saw a major turnaround in the fortunes of the area, making the social and urban transformations of the initial private gentrification now appear almost insignificant. With over 50 per cent of the land owned by a multiplicity of government instrumentalities, including the Maritime Service Board and State Housing Commission, the state, in partnership with private enterprise, took a proactive role in planning Pyrmont-Ultimo's urban future. In 1992 the future of the peninsula changed with the announcement of the Pyrmont-Ultimo Regional Environmental Plan, establishing a public-private partnership governed by the City West Development Corporation (CWDC) (Griffiths, 1996). So began what City West marketed as a 'partnership in progress' (CWDC, n.d.: 1) and what Reid (1992: 22) proclaimed was Australia's largest ever 'urban experiment' in redevelopment.

The City West Development Corporation 1992-1999

The CWDC, staffed from the New South Wales Department of Urban Affairs Planning (DUAP), was responsible for determining the re-use or sale of four precincts of government land, including Pyrmont-Ultimo. In 1990 the envisaged outcomes had been documented in the City West Urban Strategy: to maximize the value of government land, to enact urban consolidation policies, to provide open space and foreshore access, to conserve the area's industrial heritage and to promote developments that complemented the area's existing character (Hillier and Searle, 1995). In 1999 the CWDW was incorporated into a new statutory authority, the Sydney Harbour Foreshore Authority, managing some 400 hectares of prime foreshore land.

Initial funding was secured from several sources. In 1992, one-off funding was provided from the Commonwealth's Building Better Cities Program, aimed at reforming urban management processes through partnerships between government, the private sector and the community (Keilhacker, 1998). The Building Better Cities Program embraced the idea of the urban village initially voiced by Newman and Kenworthy (1991). This initiative aimed to improve the economic efficiency, social equity and environmental sustainability of Australia's cities by reducing car dependency. To this end they envisaged light rail services linking areas of urban consolidation with the city. As a result of Pyrmont-Ultimo embracing Newman and Kenworthy's urban village concept, the CWDC was allocated AU$117 million of the Building Better Cities Program funds, matched by AU$124 million of State government funds. The Commonwealth funding was staggered, its continuation being conditional on the CWDC demonstrating its commitment to the provision of open space, harbour foreshore access, light rail transport and affordable housing. One-off funding also came from the sale of public land, in what was dubbed by the local media as the biggest concentrated land sell-off in Australian history. Estimates suggest that the New South Wales government sold off at least AU$97 million worth of property (Russell, 1996). Private developer contribution schemes were also an essential source of funding. The initial City West Urban Strategy statement was written as if it were a 'prospectus' designed to attract domestic as well as overseas capital (Sant and Jackson, 1991). The essence of this approach is captured in the CWDC slogan 'Pyrmont a place of opportunity' (CWDC, n.d.). To attract developers the CWDC initially portrayed Pyrmont-Ultimo as an area of predominantly public-owned land, where redevelopment could occur almost effortlessly, and offering a prime location with proximity to the city, Darling Harbour as well as offering harbour views (Hillier and Searle, 1995). Locating the Sydney Harbour Casino on the former site of the Pyrmont power station was also a key incentive to secure private funding. Similarly, the construction of the Sydney Light Rail, connecting the peninsula with Central Railway Station, acted as a marketing tool that drew on the theme of clean modern technology. Private developers responded. Estimates place total construction consortium investment in excess of AU$2 billion. In 1995, Meriton Apartments allegedly paid nearly AU$10 million for the Farmer and Graziers wool store (O'Brien, 1995). Lend Lease alone is alleged to have invested over AU$800 million in the transformation of the CSR sugar refinery site into Jackson's Landing, touted as a high-tech city waterfront village (Totaro, 1997).

The strategy envisaged a residential population of over 16,000, mostly living in medium to high-density accommodations. The rhetoric of the plan implied the maintenance of the socio-economic diversity of the area through the inclusion of a further 600 (6-7 per cent) rental units of affordable housing (public rental housing) (DUAP, 1995b). Funding for a third of these units came from the Building Better Cities Program; the remainder was to be secured by either development proposals to include affordable housing dwellings or by means of a monetary contribution towards their construction (Williams, 1997). City West Housing Pty Ltd, a non-profit housing company, was established in 1994 to manage the program and 'protect' the local residents.

By 1997, nearly 5,000 dwellings had been approved and the population had increased by over 3,200 in 1991 to nearly 7,000. The demographic profile of Pyrmont-Ultimo suggests that, despite plans for socio-economic diversity, the suburb is now home to predominantly young (20-39 years old), single, tertiary-educated persons with household annual salaries in excess of AU$78,000, with the exception of a minority accessing the affordable housing. In 2001, the largest proportion of households contained 'dinkies' – dual income couples with no children (31 per cent). Between 1996 and 2001, the sharp increase in the number of people over fifty (from 7 per cent to 18 per cent) suggests Pyrmont-Ultimo is also attracting retirees. The most recent *Ultimo Pyrmont Post Occupancy Survey* suggests that this age group is comprised of particularly 'empty nesters', those professional couples who are selling their suburban homes once their children have left home and buying waterfront units and a city lifestyle (Sydney Harbour Foreshore Authority, 2000).

The occupation of residents in the precinct is predominantly in white-collar jobs of the tertiary and quaternary sectors. Employment figures from the 1976 and 1991 census show that the number of those employed in professional and para-professional occupations increased from 5 to 29 per cent. In contrast, those in blue-collar occupations fell from 42 per cent to 24 per cent (ABS, 1976, 1991). In 2000, of the new residents, 27 per cent were employed in finance, property and business services, 26 per cent worked in the recreation and personal service industries, whilst 13 per cent worked in the communication industry (Sydney Harbour Foreshore Authority, 2000).

The strategy also envisaged the creation of 40,000 new jobs in 1991 (New South Wales Department of Planning, 1991). The precinct was to have a twin role, providing a 'traditional' service support centre for the CBD as well as a site for new 'creative' industries. In other words, Pyrmont-Ultimo's new economic base was to be derived from the cultural economy, 'producing and marketing goods and services that are infused in one way or another with broadly aesthetic or semiotic attributes' (Scott, 1997: 323). The cultural economy is often referred to as having two components, the 'core' arts or creative industries component, including music, film, television and design, and 'related activities'. These have a significant 'symbolic' element that underpins production and the appeal of particular goods and services (such as fashion, advertising or architectural services) or where intellectual property constitutes a unifying element and commodity in itself (such as music, software and web design) (Connell and Gibson, 2002).

Pyrmont-Ultimo's businesses are now characterized by both 'traditional' services and core and related activities of the cultural economy. The area is also attracting back-office operations of banks, legal and accounting firms. In 2002, a major city legal firm moved to Jackson's Landing. Similarly, in 2000 a large Finnish mobile telephone company moved its headquarters to Jackson's Landing with other telecommunications companies moving to Pyrmont-Ultimo (see Figure 2.3). Core cultural economy activities include the headquarters of several media companies; publishing companies are also present. Related activities of the cultural economy are illustrated by the presence of high-profile internet corporations; market research companies; advertising agencies; as well as numerous internet service providers and computer software firms. Estimates by commercial real estate agents suggest that of the 220,000 square metres of office space now available in Pyrmont, 80,000 has been let to IT companies; 40,000 to media companies; and 15,000 to entertainment-related outfits (Morris, 2000).

Another expression of the social transformation of Pyrmont-Ultimo is illustrated in its places of consumption, such as boutique retail outlets and cafés. No consumption space in the precinct makes reference to modernist themes of order, standardization and convenience (Pritchard, 2000). Instead, boutique retail outlets and cafés play an important symbolic role for white-collar inner-urban residents through their references to individuality, quality, localness, specialization, smallness and variety. Consumption spaces are designed explicitly to provide a contrast with the 1960s suburban supermarket. Indeed, there is no supermarket, a fact often lamented by some residents (Sydney Harbour Foreshore Authority, 2000).

Pyrmont-Ultimo's café culture also plays a role in the process of social exclusion. Pyrmont-Ultimo's new 'quality' cafés are designed to not only facilitate economic value being attached to and extracted from commodities, but also because acts of consumption establish locations that help construct subjectivities and power relations (Cook and Crang, 1996). In the words of Bell and Valentine (1997), 'we are where we eat'. The setting, the foods and drinks consumed and the cultural performances of both the customer and waiter, are markers that help distinguish a particular personal taste, style and identity (see Figure 2.4).

The café's role in redefining Pyrmont-Ultimo is acknowledged by residents. In the view of one new resident, drinking coffee is an important part of the lifestyle. 'We enjoy living here. It is a café society. Very villagey, very friendly population. There is a nice mix. ... There has always been a sense of community here but I think it is growing even more' (quoted in Bounds *et al.,* 2000: 14). In contrast, a Housing Commission resident, in reference to drinking coffee at a café, scornfully said, 'I don't have time for that'. Long-established and less-affluent residents lament the lack of a common sense of community that previously existed. In the view of one long-established resident, 'It was a nice suburb .... That sense of it being a village – that's gone' (quoted in Bounds *et al.,* 2000: 13). Hence, Pyrmont-Ultimo's café culture serves not only a practical role of networking and information gathering that has always been important in the IT industry, but is also an urban experience with specific signifiers of identity, social inclusion and exclusion. Linda Morris (2000: 37), a local media business reporter, described the café culture's ambience as having a 'trendy, casual feel [which] is a magnet for a niche market that thrives on an image of unruffled cool'. In other words, those who choose to sit in a Pyrmont-Ultimo café and sip their decaffeinated lattes declare their elite urban identity as white-collar professionals, whilst simultaneously displaying their sophisticated yet chic taste. In a mutually constitutive process, these practices help construct knowledges or representations of Pyrmont-Ultimo as spatially segregated, having urban experiences appealing to white-collar, inner-urban residents.

Figure 2.3 Creative Industries, Waterfront 'Village' and 'Breathtaking' Views
(Photo: G.Waitt)
Top left – Nokia telecommunication headquarters, Jackson's Landing, and a façade from one of the former sugar refinery buildings. Top right – IBM e-business, Pyrmont Street. Bottom left – Jackson's Landing, medium-density apartments for 3,000 people. Jackson's Landing is marketed as offering a 'subtle mix of the new and old ... [P]ositioned on the premier waterfront ... an unrivalled harbourside location just 2km from the CBD. Waterfront boardwalks and tree lined paths link apartments to cafés, restaurants and leisure facilities, provide a unique community environment', (Lend Lease). Bottom right – Penthouse apartments, harbour and city views, The Point, Pyrmont Point.

Figure 2.4 Café Cultures (Photo: G.Waitt)

Top left – Hennessy's cultural capital is derived from its nineteenth-century 'charm'. Top right – Union Street cafés increasingly rely upon performances of waiting staff to provide the cultural capital being sold to its clients. Bottom left – Jackson's Landing's café, No. 1 Harris, derives its cultural capital from *haute cuisine* and as a specialty delicatessen, supplying luxury and exotic food items. Bottom right – Concrete Café's cultural capital is dependent upon an appreciation of minimalist design (polished concrete floors, halogen lighting and stainless steel tables and chairs).

Repackaging Pyrmont-Ultimo

Infrastructure improvements alone do not explain the social and economic transformations of Pyrmont-Ultimo. As elsewhere, the imagery of the former industrial precinct remains part of a well-documented process of refashioning into post-industrial space (Dunn *et al.,* 1995; Goodwin, 1993; Goss, 1997; Keith and Pile, 1996; Mein, 1997; Short *et al.,* 1993). Place marketing has been essential in displacing the nineteenth-century industrial legacy and its associated pollution, obsolescence, decay and dereliction. This repackaging is here examined within the general context of Pyrmont-Ultimo's redevelopment authority, then more specifically for both commercial and residential properties.

The CWDC portrayal of Pyrmont-Ultimo was always as a return to 'human' scale design and use that characterized pre-industrial waterfronts, where homes, retail establishments and workshops, and the public and private, were combined in the same location. However, this is a contemporary urban village offering sophisticated living, leisure and working environments which are clean and modern. The social exclusiveness of this urban village is implied in the CWDW slogan 'Pyrmont – *the* address for business, living and leisure' (*Australian Financial Review,* 26th September 1997). The accompanying images are of small boutique-style shopping facilities and leisure pursuits of walking or jogging along the harbour foreshore or passively gazing at harbour or city views whilst picnicking. The CWDW particularly promoted public and especially visual access to Sydney Harbour. The centrepiece of the public's access to the water is Pyrmont Point Park and a foreshore walkway linking Darling Harbour to the Sydney Fish Market. The walkway and seating is organized to maximize visual access to water views, offering a recreational pursuit traditionally more appealing to Sydney's upper and middle social stratum (see Figure 2.5). Interestingly, there are no portrayals of more traditional waterfront leisure activities among Pyrmont-Ultimo's former blue-collar workers (collective socializing, ocean swimming and fishing). Indeed, there are regulations controlling leisure activities in Pyrmont Park that prohibit amplified sound, consumption of alcoholic beverages and fishing, since they are viewed as noisy, disorderly or ecologically unsustainable. CWDC's imagery of a sophisticated waterfront village has undoubtedly sought to create a sense of authentic belonging and a connection with place and the environment among urban professionals, most of whom will have no personal connections in living generations with Pyrmont-Ultimo through family, friends or work. Equally, the actions of the CWDC that promoted the cultural ascendancy of white-collar professionals have increasingly alienated those working-class residents who do remain (Bounds *et al.,* 2000).

New business tenants in the precinct are attracted not only by the relative scarcity of office rental space in the CBD, but also by competitive rents (approximately only half those of the CBD), easy parking and proximity to the CBD. Property developers have remodeled Pyrmont-Ultimo as 'Dot Com Bay'. Sydney's 'inner-city information technology quarter' has become the northerly point of an information technology corridor extending north from Sydney Airport through the Australian Technology Park at Eveleigh. In other words, Sydney's commercial property marketers successfully employed creative industry activities as new sources of promotional material for strategies aimed at attracting mobile investment capital.

Integral to this promotion strategy has been the specific use of selected elements of Pyrmont-Ultimo's industrial heritage to enhance its appeal, for example by the refurbishment of wharves and warehouses. The architecture of refurbishment, and how it recycles imagery of Pyrmont-Ultimo's industrial past, is integral to the ideological apparatus of place marketing. Industrial heritage is employed both to mediate perceptions of the redevelopment and to enhance the location's appeal for the creative economy. Industrial wharf and warehouse architecture of the nineteenth century is used, like other dimensions of the heritage industry, to proclaim a retention of tradition in a society often disillusioned by the urban prophecies of modernism (Hewison, 1987; Crilley, 1993). Revitalization of buildings and wharves within the guidelines of historical preservation orders often defuses local resident protests through maintaining continuity with the past. Designing urban futures to look like the past has been one means of ensuring higher levels of popular consensus and less controversy than if more glitzy alternatives had been followed. Heritage preservation, however, masks the inequities of social polarization. Whilst at first appearance the structure suggests nothing has changed, behind the carefully manicured façade nothing remains of lived working experience of maritime and/or industrial labourers in the luxury appointed apartments where executives now live and work (see Figure 2.5).

A marketable aesthetic is also provided by refurbished wharf and warehouse architecture through imbuing the neighbourhood with a ready-made aura of tradition and familiarity that presently appeals to upmarket tastes. The architectural codes of an aestheticized industrial history are culturally encoded with popular meanings that have certain uniformity. Themes of this code centre upon authenticity of design and building materials and reiterate those being expressed in the process of gentrification elsewhere in Sydney at Walsh Bay and Wooloomooloo. For example the designer Cameron Algie, referring to the refurbishment of the Engineers Workshop in Pyrmont-Ultimo, is reported to have said, 'refurbishment ensured the original character and charm of the building had been enhanced, incorporating original timber columns, combined with stainless steel and iron inter-floor staircases' (Cummins, 2001: 70). In the language of commercial property agents, the aesthetics of warehouse and wharf refurbishment translate into stylish, boutique office space offering a unique character, generous proportions and natural light that resonate with the buildings' industrial past (Loneragan, 2001). Hence, architectural codes drawing upon industrial heritage themes help sustain an ambience appropriate for a work environment for executives and employees within the creative industries.

Corporate prestige is also offered to owners or tenants of refurbished building through the symbolic capital derived from association with the name of an 'internationally recognized' architect. For this reason City West Development Corporation ran competitions for designs or appointed award-winning architects (such as for the redevelopment of Jones Bay Wharf). High-profile architects provide redevelopment projects with a 'designer label', providing patrons with

Figure 2.5 City Lifestyles (Photo: G. Waitt)
Top left – Point Street apartments, offering 'panoramic' city, harbour and water views. Top right –
Jones Bay Wharf, constructed from 1913-20, as part of massive investment by the state through the
Sydney Harbour Trust in the 'modernization' and standardization of shipping facilities to support the
expansion of trade in livestock, grain and frozen meats. In 2002, a AU$150 million revitalization is
being undertaken in a joint venture between the Toga Group and Multiplex to transform the wharf into
a complex containing apartments, hotel, function centre, offices and restaurants. Bottom left – Pyrmont
Bay Park, opened in 1995, and pitched by City West as returning 2.2 hectares of waterfront parkland to
the public. Recreational activities in this manicured, palm fringed park, however, are restricted through
design and regulation to picnicking and waterfront promenades. Bottom right – Union Street, Pyrmont-
Ultimo's 'village centre', derives its cultural capital from the 'charm' of heritage, rather than hardships
of the past. A sense of belonging is created amongst white-collar professionals through the up-market
ambience that refashions nineteenth-century terraces as cafés and restaurants. References to being in
'another time' are subtly incorporated into the built environment through preventing car access, the use
of sandstone and cobblestones, and prioritizing a memorial to local residents killed in World War I.

integrity and distinction in good taste.

Pyrmont-Ultimo has not been immune to the emergence of the conversion of warehouses into luxury loft apartments that has been discussed elsewhere (Zukin, 1982; Podmore, 1998). Indeed, the advertisements for loft apartments appear to imitate those of SoHo in New York City by offering new urban lifestyles through an alternative form of built environment. Meriton used explicit New York referencing for its conversion of the Farmers and Graziers building into 'Dalgety Square: New York Style!' and 'New York Style Living in Sydney's thriving heart'. New York references are also employed to portray a sophisticated urban lifestyle (Shaw, 2000). Pyrmont-Ultimo, along with other New York styled inner-city Sydney precincts, has become a site of influence, power, style and fashion. A New York lifestyle of elegant loft living becomes a component of the cultural capital of Pyrmont-Ultimo, with its accompanying pool, gymnasium, and security of fortress technologies (intercoms, security cameras, alarms). New York imaginaries also promise minimum engagement with inner-city residents, the socially dysfunctional or those who have been marginalized by the process of social polarization – the homeless, the unemployed and the unskilled. Loft residents are effectively protected from the difficulties of everyday streetlife and, if they desire, from localized politics and struggles. The loft apartment is an appeal to quality, sophistication, power and safety, focused upon the real and imagined needs of urban professionals. Purchasing or leasing a loft apartment is therefore buying into the spatial narrative and cultural capital associated with this particular urban lifestyle (Zukin, 1990) and thereby acquiring its specific signifiers of taste and distinction (Bourdieu, 1984).

However, as Podmore (1998: 284) has argued, the 'SoHo Syndrome is a spatial and cultural process that involves more than simply copying the aesthetic of SoHo [New York] as a redevelopment strategy ... cities are "locales"... [and the SoHo Syndrome is] more than a universal valorization strategy'. In Sydney, Shaw (forthcoming) explores the complexities of the socio-cultural processes surrounding loft apartments by examining the 'Manhattanization' of Sydney's warehouse accommodation. She concludes that promotional strategies alone cannot explain the attractiveness of loft apartments at the turn of the century. In addition, over a century of successive Commonwealth government promotional films have embedded an affinity with New York in Sydney's collective imagery of Manhattan as a marker of modernism and progress. Equally, although largely unrecorded and unofficial, Sydney's warehouses have a local history connected with alternative/bohemian lifestyles, made notorious through one-off events such as demolition protests, evictions, dance parties, music venues and art galleries. These lifestyles, and their remaining traces, form an essential component of the cultural capital that was traded on in legitimizing the commercial version that is now available.

Property developers use a number of marketing strategies to portray Pyrmont-Ultimo's new apartments as offering a prestigious lifestyle. In part this is defined through the presence of leisure facilities like pools, gyms, spas and saunas. Such pastimes are commonly associated with affluence and personal indulgence. Design is also called upon to symbolically differentiate the precinct as elite. The language of private developers describing the newly-constructed high-rise apartments is rich with superlatives that suggest a differentiation from other inner-city locations on the basis of quality alone, for example 'unique', 'best', 'sophisticated', 'benchmark' (Austland, Lend Lease). Indeed the Walker Development Corporation marketed luxury apartments of The Point using the slogan 'city-linked living ... a style apart' (*Sydney Morning Herald,* 24th April 1997). Apparently, in this suburb residents are distinguished by their 'good' taste, as defined by an appreciation of architecture, interior design and European kitchen appliances.

Residential prestige also underpins Lend Lease's slogan 'Reflecting the best of harbourside living', designed to market 'Reflections' apartments of Jackson's Landing as 'a new waterfront village' (*Sydney Morning Herald,* 8th June 2002). In this case status is derived from a waterside frontage and views of Sydney Harbour. Harbour views in Sydney have been variously coded by residential property developers as 'uninterrupted', 'commanding', 'panoramic', 'spectacular', 'stunning', 'breathtaking' or 'exciting'. Advertisements for most of Pyrmont Point's apartments are coded with the 'uninterrupted and commanding' views eastwards towards Sydney Harbour Bridge (see Figure 2.3). Such harbour views come at a price, however, with penthouse apartments in 'The Point' development selling for AU$2 million. The commodification of harbour views so evident in Pyrmont-Ultimo and the increased aesthetic evaluation of water vistas are themselves a reflection of the ascendancy of water's exchange value over its use value. As Port Jackson became used less and less as a source of economic livelihood and military defence, Sydneysiders have emphasized either gazing at the harbour as an aesthetic object or casting it as a recreational resource. As an aesthetic object the harbour gaze has been invested with several promises. Viewing water has a long-standing association, particularly among bourgeois Anglo-Australians, as a healthy pastime, known for its soothing, calming affects (Lowe, 1982; Drew, 1994). In the post-industrial city, property developers embrace these promises, marketing water views as an antidote for the stress, tensions and confinement of the working day. Equally, the act of gazing upon the harbour is portrayed as a relaxing leisure activity; prospective purchasers are invited to take delight in watching the shifting light on an ever-changing vista of ferries and yachts. However, perhaps most significantly, in Sydney harbour views are above all else a symbol of money and power. Harbour views therefore have significant cultural capital.

Proximity to water and its aesthetic quality are also utilized by residential property developers to suggest that residents are provided with a lifestyle that is closer to nature. Such a fixation with accomplishing a close connection to nature has long been recognized as a prominent trait of the upper and middle stratum of society (Urry, 1990), particularly in Anglo-Celtic Australia following the growth of manufacturing industries in the inner city (Richards, 1994). Suburban growth was partly spawned by the desire to reconnect with nature through the performances of gardening. Interestingly, in Pyrmont-Ultimo the sea has now been appropriated by property developers as a natural symbol and made the object of viewing. Harbour views are purveyed as a mechanism inviting prospective purchasers to combine city living with suburban lifestyle. Interestingly, in Sydney, water vistas, combined with the promise of smaller, human-scale living environments of a 'village', allow professional white-collar workers to live a non-urban lifestyle in the city. Spatial segregation of these professionals still occurs. However, by extending the symbolized natural connections, previously only perceived to be available in the suburbs to water vistas, professionals' environmental needs can be accommodated – within the post-industrial city.

Ironically, the closeness to nature promised by viewing ultimately leads to the romanticized objectification of the water and a division between the viewer and the viewed (Lowe, 1982). The romanticizing of 'natural' elements in bourgeois Anglo-Celtic Australia in the past has led to an understanding of nature as separate from and distinctive from humans; such as wilderness regions (Lane and Waitt, 2001) or the history of zoos (Anderson, 1995). Prioritizing water's aesthetic value over its functional uses and its definition as something natural, opposed to the city, paradoxically reinforces the boundaries between culture and nature along a binary divide.

Conclusion

Pyrmont-Ultimo is Sydney's newest chic quarter, and an integral part of Sydney's inner-city urban renaissance (Vipond *et al.,* 1998). Pyrmont-Ultimo is a geographical expression of processes of social polarization, derived from the occupational and economic restructuring occasioned by de-industrialization and global capital. Social divisions have always characterized Sydney's precincts, however Pyrmont-Ultimo's physical form and demographics are both new. Never before have Sydney's affluent residents chosen medium-high apartment living in the inner city. Unlike previous phases of inner-city gentrification that restored old homes in the 1980s, the majority of inner-city gentrification, creative service sector executives and professionals of the new millennium are seeking to live in new condominiums. Whilst 'charm' is still sought in nineteenth-century cottages, terraces, wharves or bond stores, they must be refashioned as cafés, boutique shops, offices, loft apartments, museums or nightclubs. Convenience underpins their new 24/7 city lifestyle. City West and private property corporations have repackaged Pyrmont-Ultimo to the new urban professionals not only as in walking distance to work, service and play but also prestigious, aesthetic, safe, human-scaled and close to nature. 'Village' living is how developers package and sell these attributes. However, this is an exclusive 'village'. This precinct is fashioned as socially selective by redevelopers through housing costs, style and employment opportunities. Harbour views and maritime heritage are also called upon to create up-market residential, working and recreational spaces and to generate a sense of belonging amongst white-collar professionals within this former industrial precinct. In doing so, marketing strategies give ascendancy to bourgeois imaginings that draw upon either romanticized pasts or lifestyles from elsewhere that both in turn deny the everyday, the local and its histories. Both the physical and symbolic refashioning of Pyrmont-Ultimo as home to Sydney's new middle classes has effectively excluded those marginalized by the process of economic restructuring. Furthermore, as with gentrification elsewhere, long-established residents experience increasing alienation stemming from inadequate consultation during the planning process and from the precinct's contemporary facilities and lifestyles. However, traditional residents are no longer in sufficient numbers to fight unequal power relations with both new residents and property developers.

As Sydney's newest urban chic quarter, Pyrmont-Ultimo exemplifies the social realities of entrepreneurial urban planning policies that prioritize the interest of capital above social justice, wealth creation above redistribution and place image above substance. Such priorities have contributed to processes that wall-out the majority of Sydney's socially disadvantaged from Pyrmont-Ultimo and their walling-in to precincts of extensive state housing or low-priced private rental accommodation, as in Sydney's outer south-western suburbs. Government funding for inner-city revitalization has only exacerbated social divisions within Sydney, beginning at a time of increasing deprivation and disadvantage in the outer suburbs (Orchard, 1999). Entrepreneurial urban policies aimed at 'Building Better Cities' have apparently helped reinforce a socially fragmented Sydney.

Chapter 3

Drawn and Quartered: El Raval and the Haussmannization of Barcelona

Malcolm Miles

Implying a link between seemingly ubiquitous cultural quarters and consumption, Sharon Zukin writes that 'every well-designed downtown has a mixed-use shopping center and a nearby artists' quarter' (Zukin, 1995: 22). Where manufacturing industries have been replaced by service economies or ports have been modernized, cultural development re-utilizes redundant buildings and sites while raising a city's profile in a globally competitive market for investment. But if cultural quarters re-invent a city's image, what is their effect on its human as well as economic geography? Is the aestheticization of space in a cultural quarter a new colonialism in which the needs of a city's own diverse publics are as disregarded as were those of indigenous peoples when Europeans drew lines on the maps of other continents?

This chapter reconsiders the case of el Raval in Barcelona, Spain. The city of Barcelona has a history of innovative planning, from the Cerdà plan of 1859 to the city-wide improvements prior to the 1992 Olympics, and el Raval has three aspects which constitute it as a cultural quarter: a flagship cultural institution, the Museu d'Art Contemporani Barcelona (MACBA); a clustering of small galleries and outlets for cultural consumption; and renovation of the built environment producing gentrification. It is thus an appropriate case through which to relate current to past development. The chapter begins by setting Barcelona's recent redevelopment and the role of cultural consumption in it in a wider European context. This leads into a discussion of the city's policy for cultural tourism and extension of its cultural infrastructure. The ethos of redevelopment in el Raval is then compared with that of Cerdà's 1859 plan for the city's extension (*Eixample*), which is in turn compared with Baron Haussmann's remodelling of Paris for Napoleon III. From this the chapter asks to which of these models el Raval is closest.

Culturally-Led Redevelopment Strategies in Europe

There seems to be an expectation in the minds of city planners, and the new breed of city managers, that prosperity follows culture (in the narrow sense of cultural consumption, from art to fashion and designer beers). This is based on models in the

US where, as Zukin again says, 'Sometimes it seems that every derelict factory district or waterfront has been converted into one of those sites of visual delectation – a themed shopping space for seasonal produce, cooking equipment, restaurants, art galleries, and an aquarium' (Zukin, 1995: 22-3).[1] Rosalyn Deutsche (1988) has drawn attention to the uneven benefits of the aestheticization of urban space in New York, and Zukin notes that not all such schemes have been successful; but art is now a central element in a city's symbolic economy just as the broader cultural industries sector, in which culture and consumption are fused, is seen as key to the economic revival of declining industrial zones. Not all commentators see this as delightful.[2]

Cultural consumption is lucrative. Cultural goods are expensive, and museum visitors and cultural tourists are largely from high-income sectors of society. The economic case for a zone of culture-based consumption is then clear, though the ascendancy of the cultural quarter may also reflect the strength, or loudness, of arts advocacy through the 1980s. In the UK this led to adoption of Percent for Art policies by public authorities, and a widespread commissioning of public art.[3] The case for culturally-led redevelopment was supported by research showing that evidence of an active cultural life was an incentive for corporate relocation, and confirmed by the success of Glasgow as European City of Culture in 1990.[4] The evidence, however, was uneven, and Glasgow's economic upturn may have been at the expense of local cultures.[5] Claims were still made that culture was linked to prosperity, even to a reduction in crime, and the trend continues with a new art gallery in Walsall, and the conversion of the Baltic Mill in Gateshead to a contemporary art gallery as part of a Tyneside cultural renaissance which draws in unprecedented numbers of visitors.[6]

Elsewhere in Europe, redundant industrial and port buildings were (and are) given new cultural uses – such as the Cable Factory in Helsinki, and the recently opened Caixa Foundation gallery for contemporary art in a *modernista* (art nouveau) textile factory in Barcelona. Similarly, the Guggenheim in an industrial area of Bilbao is seen as symbol of the city's rebranding as a cosmopolitan centre rather than a drab gateway to Spain. But this model is by no means universal. European histories of cultural policy and planning through the 1980s and 1990s and their relations to urban economic development are complex, and differences follow political allegiances. While there has been a general drift from an ethos of public administration of arts subsidy within a welfare state to one of business management and arts investment in the context of free-market economics and a shrinking public sector (Bianchini, 1999a), co-option of culture to market forces is not the only possibility.[7] Where left-leaning administrations held power they supported grass-roots cultural expression giving visibility to social diversity. In France under the Socialist government between 1982 and '86, cultural expenditure rose considerably, with Bordeaux, Rennes, Montpellier and Grenoble being particular beneficiaries (Bianchini and Parkinson, 1993). In Rome under the Communist municipality from 1976 to '85, as in London during the period of the Greater London Council between 1981 and '86, resources were devolved to grass-roots cultural organizations in a spirit of radical democracy.[8] Aram Eizenschitz cites the GLC paper *The State of the Art and the Art of the State* (1985): 'Cultural production is to be reclaimed so as to develop community identities and increase choice for the disadvantaged' (Eizenschitz, 1997: 170).

The business turn in the arts, however, has become the dominant condition for cultural development, and emphasizes cultural consumption over production. But it also coincided with an expansion of publicly-subsidized conversion of industrial buildings to artists' studios in areas such as Hackney in London, Prenzlauerberg in Berlin and Belle-de-Mai in Marseilles.[9] These were artist-led initiatives negotiated through the funding system, extending artists' efforts to control their means of production and dissemination, which Raymond Williams sees as a defining aspect of modernism (Williams, 1989).

In some cases the areas in which the studios are situated remain economically depressed, while in others, where other kinds of development and other kinds of occupant have moved in, gentrification has followed. This was the case in New York's SoHo in the 1980s, where artists not protected by rent control were forced out, as now in London's Hoxton.[10] For a young, professional urban class, the consumption of art experience and habitation in an arts district are marks of status, and it is this class which today is moving into el Raval.[11] Esther Leslie's description of Tate Modern is apposite:

> Tate Modern is a brand that niche-markets art experience. Its galleries are showrooms. However, this is still art and not just business. The commodity must not show too glossy a face. The reclamation of an industrial space that provides the shell for the Tate Modern lends the building a fashionably squatted aspect, like Berlin water towers or crumbling arcades that serve as edgy art galleries or music venues for a while ... After religion and industry, the next great force is art. Its powers were to be harnessed to a bit of urban regeneration (Leslie, 2001: 3).

But a cultural quarter requires more than a single institution, and is constituted more by the general re-use of space in a neighbourhood, though insertion of a new public gallery tends to encourage relocation by independent, culturally-validated businesses.

One definition of a cultural quarter is given by Allen Scott:

> In these districts, much of the work of conception and production of cultural products is carried out by small artisanal and neo-artisanal firms, that is, by firms whose basic labor processes range from handicraft skills ... to high-order conceptual activities combined with modern digital technologies (Scott, 2000: 205).

This does not fit SoHo, too narrow in space-use now, but fits cultural quarters in Sheffield, Rotterdam and Manchester's Castlefield, though Scott's emphasis on production ignores the cultural ambience of cafés, bars and plazas where the cognoscenti become postmodern flâneurs.[12]

There are, then, several overlapping strands in a culturally-led strategy for economic development or creation of a cultural quarter: a clustering of cultural industries in a zone slated for improvement, finding new uses for redundant buildings and halting physical decay; insertion of a flagship cultural institution as magnet to private-sector investment, either in a redundant (as with Tate Modern) or new building (as with the Guggenheim in Bilbao designed by Frank Gehry,[13] and MACBA by Richard Meier); and, within a cultural ambience, attraction of consumers to a variety of bars and restaurants which revive the night-time economy while employment in the cultural industries and museum visiting revive its daytime equivalent.[14] For city managers and marketers, a professional group which expanded significantly during the 1980s (Bianchini, 1999a), such factors offer a way to manage change when manufacturing is replaced by less labour- and space-intensive service industries; and they generate media coverage associating a city with advanced consumerism.[15] But in most cases it is an economic strategy which is implemented, seldom one of benefit for cultural producers or likely to promote social inclusion.[16] In these terms, flagship cultural institutions have in common with the architects' studios, media firms, independent galleries, bars, marketing and public relations consultancies, fashion and jewellery design workshops, graphic communication businesses and boutiques which make up a cultural quarter, that they relate to symbolic goods in a city's symbolic economy.[17] That the venues for cultural consumption are within sight of another kind of post-industrial city in abandoned plots is not a disincentive; but if the gentrified city is adjacent but not connected to the tenement city, to use Peter Marcuse's (1989) terms, the contrast draws attention to a variable voluntariness.[18] The inhabitants of the gentrified city or cultural quarter are there from choice, their housing being a statement of their lifestyle; those of tenement city or ghetto are not (Marcuse, 2002). So, are cultural quarters socially beneficial? Or is it, as Mayor Koch put it in New York, a matter of 'If you can't afford to live here, mo-o-ove' (quoted in Rosler, 1991: 35, illus. 44).

Cultural Tourism in Barcelona

In Barcelona, the redevelopment of el Raval through the late 1990s follows adoption of a policy to encourage cultural and business-related tourism by expanding the local (Catalan) cultural infrastructure, as in the new National Theatre (1997, at Plaça de les Glóries), a new building in Montjuic for Teatre Lliure (1999), and MACBA in el Raval. Cultural consumption is linked to architecture but not cultural production, since there is no provision in the city's policies to directly assist artists and performers.[19] The insertion of an architecturally-significant cultural institution in el Raval was, as with Tate Modern in Southwark, London, a magnet for investment in an area designated as upwardly mobile, and has produced visible gentrification as the remaining nineteenth-century apartment blocks are renovated.[20] It has also stimulated an already present cultural tourism. A few minutes walk down narrow side streets from the Ramblas, el Raval retains some of the allure it held for the intrepid tourist for whom to chance on a characteristic bar after mixing with prostitutes, gypsies, north Africans and artists in the dark, narrow alleys once constituted a genuine Barcelona experience.

Authenticity now underpins the city's tourism strategy which, as Dodd (1999) describes, rejects the mass market tourism encouraged by national promotions in favour of cultural tourism.[21] This coincides with a renaissance of Catalan culture – the Catalan language was banned under the fascist regime, as previously under the Bourbons – but is also recognition that upmarket tourists like to think of themselves as travellers, an illusion fostered by simple devices such as displaying information on cultural events and public transport only in Catalan:

> even if the tourists do not use all the attractions on offer, the knowledge of their presence ... will encourage a return visit. [And] because these cultural elements are not built for tourist purposes, business or culturally educated tourists will be more interested in them, because they tend to search for authenticity (Dodd, 1999: 57-8).

This strategy enabled Barcelona's politicians and public officials to invest in a tourist infrastructure which was also a local cultural provision; and to differentiate their strategy from that of Bilbao with its imported Guggenheim. Another somewhat unusual factor is the financial contribution, required by their constitution, of Barcelona's non-profit savings banks to cultural and social projects. It can also be noted that, contrary to the tendency in the UK under the current centre-right administration, in Barcelona (in Port Vell, for instance) the lead in major construction projects is taken by the public sector, which, having taken the creative risk, sells on developments to the private sector at a profit. But possibly *the* driving force of Barcelona's re-invention of itself is the authorities' desire to be rid of the image of an impoverished Mediterranean port city – to become instead a global city. Hence the World Trade Centre in Port Vell; the twin towers (one of which is the Hotel des Arts) and a casino on the new waterfront; and the designation of the working-class quarter of Poble Nou as a knowledge quarter. Extending the succession of themed events, and building on a history of international fairs (Meller, 2001), 2004 will be the year of a World Forum of Cultures.[22] Near its site a mall has been built by a US company, surrounded by high-rise apartment blocks in a landscaped park, Parc del Diagonal-Mar, designed shortly before his death by E Miralles.[23] There was an element of internationalism in the approach to the 1992 Olympics, the second for which the city had bid (the first being the 1936 Olympics which went to Berlin), and internationalism, or international modernism, is evident in the commissioning of large public sculptures by international artists.[24] These are site-general works with sparse relation to the human, cultural, or even physical geographies of Barcelona.[25] The painted steel book of matches by Oldenburg and van Bruggen, for instance, at Parc de la Vall d'Hebron (1992), is red and yellow, the colours of the Catalan flag; and perhaps the central match which stands up with a steel flame amid the others all spent, bent or broken off and scattered on the pavement, might just be an image of resistance. But the point is less the interpretation of the work than its presence as part of the city's claim to a place on an international culture map, and beyond that a transition from *internationalism* to *globalism* (or globalization).[26] Street names such as Plaça Salvador Allende (ousted by a US-backed military coup on 11th September 1973) and Jardins de Rosa Luxemburg, however, tell another story.

El Raval

Leading up to the 1992 Olympics, the city created a large number of small urban spaces.[27] The new buildings which housed the athletes are now desirable middle-class residences, but the emphasis of the wider programme was on public benefit.[28] Does this liberal policy continue, or does the renovation (which includes new public space) of el Raval signify a change of direction, as the change of name from *barri xino* (or *barrio chino* in Spanish) signifies a change of image? The area once housed convents and hostels, and became the site of the first industries within the city's walls and extensive apartment building, when church lands were sold in the nineteenth century. Separated from the gothic city but near the port, the area became known as a red-light district in the 1930s (photographs of which are on show in the Museu de l'Eròtica). In the 1960s and 1970s, cheap rooms attracted students and artists as well as recent Asian and north African immigrants, making the district one of the most ethnically diverse in the city. It also had a reputation for crime, which the whole city now enjoys. Monica Degen (2002) notes the term used by the planning authority to describe its work there: *esponjamiento*, a loosening of the weave referring to selective demolition to create large public spaces at Plaça dels Angels in front of MACBA (designed by F Ramos and associates in 1995) and, spectacularly, a new Rambla del Raval (designed by P Cabrera and J Artigues in 2000).

To create the new Rambla del Raval three city blocks were demolished. At the north end of the cleared space, before it was completed, a vast billboard proclaimed, not in Catalan or even Castilian but in American, PUBLIC SPACE above an image of a plaza lined by palm trees.[29] Now the palm trees grow next to rusty steel lamp-posts which resemble Richard Serra sculptures. Not many people wander in the new Rambla, parallel to the old one but without obvious destinations to either end – directly north is MACBA, but through a narrow street of balconies. There is a plan to build a new hotel, but not all the small galleries which moved to the area in the 1990s have survived.

Where in el Raval new buildings have been inserted, they tend to have either no balconies or only very narrow ones.[30] Public space has been provided in generous measure but the transitional zone of the balcony above the street, ambivalent as extension of domestic and entry into public space, is slated for abolition. Looks triumph over occupation; or in Lefebvre's terms (1991), conceptual space over lived spaces. Degen quotes a former councillor:

> public space resolves two problems in a neighbourhood that apart from having the narrowness of a historic city centre has a second problem ... the function of receiving the residual activities of the city for many years. The permeability, the facility of penetration by the exterior ... the opening of the neighbourhood to the city was a principal [concern] (Degen, 2002: 27-8).[31]

Figure 3.1   Barcelona, El Raval: Typical Street with Nineteenth-Century Apartments and Balconies (Photo: M. Miles)

Figure 3.2 Barcelona, El Raval: Museum of Contemporary Art (MACBA)
(Photo: M. Miles)

The aim is to open up the quarter to clean it. The issue of balconies, in a city where street façades are highly regulated, is not one of aesthetics against utility: the function of aesthetics here is to turn the city away from its history as a Mediterranean port of narrow alleys (even if they are picturesque for the visitor), poverty and prostitution; and from the liberal city represented by the nineteenth-century extension. In place of all that are the clean lines of a northern city. This was not the ethos of the Cerdà plan.

The Cerdà Plan

Idelfons Cerdà's plan for the Barcelona extension (*Eixample*) was approved by the Spanish government in 1859 and by royal decree in 1860. This followed permission to dismantle the city walls in 1854 and repeal of the city's fortified status – which prohibited building within firing range – in 1858. Cerdà's plan was not welcomed by the city's administration,[32] and his writing has since received little recognition in planning history; it nonetheless represents a singular case of enlightened planning, or planning in an Enlightenment spirit of rationality and reform.[33] Rationality produces the grid, which Cerdà saw in scientific terms (Choay, 1997); and reform produces a city based on the needs of the modern citizen for decent housing and networks of communication.

While the grid exhibits contrasting meanings as an urban form,[34] here it translates a human-centred planning ethos into the material fabric of the city, combining the intellectual freedom implicit in rationality itself with practical solutions to the ills of the city's containment within its walls – walls which were signs of the loss of independence.[35] The extension was also, crucially, the means by which Barcelona could expand commercially.

Although it was mainly the middle class which moved to the extension, the Cerdà plan enshrined an egalitarian attitude. Population density in the old city was exceptionally high, with frequent outbreaks of contagious diseases; and for Cerdà the living conditions of the poor were a cause of unrest, as in a strike in 1855 after which the city sought a loan of 10 million reals to construct four new roads as public works projects: Avinguda Parallel, Rambla de Catalunya, Avinguda Meridiana, and Gran Via, all identified by Cerdà in a preliminary plan of 1854. The plan for the extension arose, then, in a climate of economic expansion and social reformism. Cerdà, a professional engineer, city councillor (1854-56 and 1863-66), provincial councillor (vice-president 1873-4) and Progressive Party member of the national parliament from 1851, expresses this duality throughout his writing. As a liberal reformer, he affirms the value of private property ownership while seeking civic intervention in and regulation of the built environment. The grounds of intervention are not aesthetic – he is critical of a previous code which dealt in detail with façades but ignored the buildings behind them (Soria y Puig, 1999) – but of health, social welfare, and public order. He notes in his *Theory of the Construction of Cities* (1859) that while food sales were regulated for hygiene, and industries obliged to respect the needs of health and safety, there was no equivalent regulation of the interiors of buildings:

And let it not be thought that the evils that arise from this enormous void in the code of our municipal administration are insignificant for humanity. Because of it, people find themselves condemned to not live, but die slowly, under the destructive action of the illnesses which arise from the lack of space, shortage of light and the action of damp, all combined with deprivation from the breathable air necessary for our economy. Most of the houses which are being built in Barcelona today have such a layout and capacity that they scarcely give their residents a quarter of the atmospheric air necessary for respiration ... (Cerdà, *Teoría de la construcción de las ciudades aplicada al proyecto de reforma y ensanche de Barcelona*, 1859: 520, cited in Soria y Puig, 1999: 417).

He calls on the men [sic] of art and science to advise the municipality, and proclaims the triumph of humanity over monopoly and exploitation. But Cerdà is not a utopian, describing the overcrowded tenements of the old city as a training ground for communism (Soria y Puig, 1999).[36] His aim was to extend bourgeois society's assumption of health and ease to the whole population. Hence the equality conveyed by the uniform grid[37] which accommodates housing for upper-income families as well as single artisans, with various gradations between.[38]

Each block has a uniform size of 113 metres, with a green central space for use by residents. In the 1859 plan there are also several public parks, and in the 1863 revision a small number of factories, creating a multi-function zoning.[39] Streets are tree-lined, with lighting and benches where porters could rest, and of a uniform 20-metre width of which the central 10 metres are for carriages, leaving half the space for pedestrians. The intersections are chamfered (with 20-metre sides) to create regular, octagonal circuses which ensure efficiency of movement by giving traffic and pedestrians clear sight lines.[40] The network of services and the rationally-proportioned grid remain indelibly, as does the variation of spatial experience within a regular framework moderated by the organic growth of the district with a variety of architectural styles and adaptations by dwellers.[41] It is crucial to see the grid here as a sign of equality, not of land values as in New York; for Cerdà it is not a colonialist inscription of order[42] but denotes social justice thought through in practical ways, including Cerdà's specification of maximum distances between dwellings and schools, food markets, hospitals and parks; and in regulation of minimum interior spaces per dweller.[43]

Not all this idealism survived in the construction of the extension in two phases, from 1860-65 with Cerdà's involvement as technical consultant, and from 1866-74 in a market-led climate when the city council sought to adapt the plan and speculation by credit and real estate companies, buying farmland to sell on or develop themselves, largely erasing its egalitarianism. Cerdà's relation with the city became antagonistic, but in 1874 he became a key figure in the briefly-proclaimed Republic (Meller, 2001). In 1875, after the Republic's fall, he left for Valencia and died within the year. The extension which exists now thus both is (in structure) and is not (in application) Cerdà's. Many of the open spaces within the blocks were built over in the nineteenth century, though some have been reclaimed in recent improvements; and not all the parks were realized. But, as Choay writes: 'Cerdà formulates for the first time the two basic concepts that remain today the operative poles of urbanism:

habitation and circulation' (Choay, 1997: 237). His 1859 plan could be compared with L'Enfant's (1791) plan for Washington DC, described by Richard Sennett as a mix of the social and political reflecting 'a truly republican concept of a national capital: a place in which great power is absorbed into the tapestry of a multi-centered, mixed-use city' (Sennett, 1995: 267); but, beyond that, *Eixample* is an explicitly modern city of service and transport networks, a city of movement and industry as well as domesticity and administration.

What emerges is an emphasis on equality and social justice within a liberal reformist attitude, compromised by the later development of the extension but still in marked contrast to Haussmann's remodelling of Paris for Napoleon III between 1853 and 1870, under a similarly bourgeois but less reformist political, planning, and aesthetic regime.[44]

Haussmannization

Baron Haussmann, Prefect of the Seine, working to Napoleon III's sketch, did not use a grid. He did not use the concept of social justice either, except to abuse it. His 'urban geometers', as he called them, used tall wooden towers to survey the existing urban fabric before measuring out wide streets through the old working-class quarters (Sennett, 1995). The aim was to divide them, while to a large extent displacing the poor to the periphery. The new streets created free-fire zones wide enough for two army wagons to roll abreast, and linked the inner city to the barracks. For Walter Benjamin, 'The true goal of Haussmann's projects was to secure the city against civil war ... to make the erection of barricades in the streets of Paris impossible for all time' (Benjamin, 2002: 23). In place of the old quarters, he provided a new opera house, a market, and a substantial profit to private-sector investors.[45]

Along with the commercialization of space – in the new department stores to serve the consumption of the urban bourgeoisie, and in the glass and iron arcades (though these date from the 1830s to 1860s), which were the subject-matter of Benjamin's unfinished *Passagen-werk* – Haussmann's city is essentially visual while Cerdà's is practical.[46] In Paris looking is the primary act, whereas in Barcelona's extension it was intended to be dwelling. This privileging of visuality is an aestheticization of the city, in one way providing Impressionist painters with views; but, apart from a single-use zoning in which industry and recreation are separated from domestic life and shopping, and neighbourhoods are segregated by class (Pile, Brook and Mooney, 1999), it is in another way a possession. Doreen Massey (1994) writes that visuality offers a detachment which is also a viewpoint of power; and Benjamin notes: 'Haussmann's urbanistic ideal was one of views in perspective down long street-vistas. Before their completion, boulevards were covered over with tarpaulins, and unveiled like monuments' (Benjamin, 1997: 174). The boulevards made walking in the streets more visible, offering opportunities to be seen while affirming an increasingly restrictive climate for women's use of streets.[47] For the poor, too, Paris became a city of exclusion as areas of informal housing were cleared[48] to produce a new vagrancy to which Haussmann, largely responsible for it, reacted with vitriol.[49] David Harvey, citing Zola's *The Kill* (1871), writes of 'Haussmann's wounding slashes through the veins of a living city, wounds that spurt gold', concluding that 'The perpetual reshaping of the geographical landscape of capitalism is a process of violence and pain' (Harvey, 1989a: 193).

Conclusion

The question, for this essay, is to what extent the gentrification of el Raval within a policy for cultural tourism and wider climate of the manufacture of cultural quarters, as discussed above, constitutes a Haussmannization of Barcelona and a rejection of Cerdà's liberal egalitarianism.

In addressing this admittedly speculative and provocative question, it should be remembered that Cerdà is not a revolutionary; his idealism is scientific and applied, his reformism has only a basic sense of social justice in common with Marxism, and had he met Bakunin he might not have been impressed. Cerdà writes: 'In modern cities there is an imperative need ... for internal defense and preservation of public order, the first guarantee of civilized nations, which has obliged the Emperor Napoleon to open up spacious streets' (Cerdà, 1859; *Juicio critico de la exposición de planos y proyectos para la reforma y ensanche de Barcelona*, cited in Soria y Puig, 1999: 133). But this paragraph, in a document the title of which is suffixed by the dates of approval of his plan by royal decree and provincial order, is partly a refutation of rival plans, and notes the rapid restoration of order in Barceloneta (which has a grid plan set out by military engineers) in a disturbance of 1856. It can be put beside the more frequent expressions of egalitarianism elsewhere in Cerdà's writings, and the evidence of the grid and its socially beneficial regulation. To provide all classes with decent conditions of dwelling and ease of movement may have been a means to civic order, but it remains a statement of social justice, and avoids peripheralization of the poor in a fully integrated, networked, and multi-use zoned city. This spirit informs the pre-1992 neighbourhood improvements. But perhaps there it stops? In el Raval, opening up the narrow streets is not the result of an aesthetic judgement, though it is part of a wider aestheticization of space, but represents class and ethnic sanitization. As a planner says, 'people like us are moving in' (cited in Degen, 2002: 28), and self-organized groups have criticized the renovations as concealing or displacing the neighbourhood's problems.

A recent tourist guide describes el Raval today as 'a neighbourhood in the process of gentrification with whole blocks being pulled down, previous no-go areas being transformed into broad boulevards and inevitably, as the district becomes fashionable, house prices going through the roof' (Brown, 1999: 71). It notes the area's appearance in Genet's *Thief's Journal* – frequented by prostitutes, anarcho-syndicalists, and homosexuals – and Orwell's observation in 1936 of posters urging prostitutes to abandon their profession. Paradoxically, as Degen observes, it is often this old el Raval (the *barri xino*) in memory or residual form which visitors and new residents seek out: 'the marginality that the regeneration strategies aim to dispel is precisely what attracts many newcomers to the area'. She writes that 'part of the process of normalising 'marginal' parts of the city is internalising its margins, as commodified sites' (Degen, 2002: 30). Of course, power leaks and Plaça dels Angels is taken over by skateboarders and motorcyclists at night.[50] But renovation – or *esponjamiento* – is instrumental here in gentrification, and not by chance.

To end, the following five overlapping factors might indicate that the recent creation of a cultural quarter in el Raval is on balance closer to Haussmann's oppressive ethos than to Cerdà's liberalism: firstly, an emphasis on visuality and an aestheticization of space; secondly, the insertion of a major cultural institution (for Haussmann it was the opera, here MACBA); thirdly, the clearance of the built environment and driving through of wide streets (though here not connecting anything); fourthly, the opportunities offered for real estate speculation; and fifthly, the anti-social effect of peripheralization of the poor (no longer able to pay the cost of housing inflated by service charges even when rents are controlled). But el Raval is not, in fact, the first case of Haussmann's influence in Barcelona: in 1908, a new broad street, Via Laietana, was cut through the eastern edge of the medieval city to connect the port with the city's new extension to the north on Haussmannesque lines - 'cutting arbitrarily through the built environment' (Meller, 2001: 53). Perhaps, however, the difference between the redevelopment of el Raval and Haussmann's approach is that in el Raval a more dispersed cultural ambience is commodified – a postmodern, multi-faceted and not necessarily coherent experience which absorbs the excitement of perceived danger when hotel concierges tell tourists not to go there at night. Maybe it is a Haussmannization by other means designed to enhance the city's symbolic economy and aspiration to a global status. This is the image reflected in the new façades of concrete, steel, glass, and money.

Notes

1   Zukin may have in mind developments such as New York's South Street Seaport, Boston's Faneuil Hall, Baltimore's Harbor Place, Pittsburgh's Station Square, or Seattle's Pike Place Market. From the 1970s onwards, these schemes sought to bring consumption back to downtown areas, many of them managed by the Rouse Company. Faneuil Hall Marketplace has around 150 outlets. Gratz writes that it 'combines the management techniques of the mall with the ingredients of a small-scale lively marketplace' (Gratz, 1989:317).

2   Hajer sees Rotterdam's regeneration process as drawing on waterfront developments in Toronto, Baltimore, and Boston; he heads a section of his essay 'The tragedy of the American inspiration' (Hajer, 1993: 49, 62-4).

3   The case for public art tended towards indemonstrable claims that art lends places identity and leads to economic recovery. Typical of this advocacy are two Arts Council publications: *An Urban Renaissance* (1989), and *Percent for Art: a Review* (1991) following a two-year round of meetings chaired by architect Richard Burton. Sara Selwood, in the executive summary of a report, *The Benefits of Public Art* (1995), for the

Policy Studies Institute, states: 'None of the cases studied had been formally evaluated by those involved. The specific criteria according to which they might have been evaluated were rarely identified as such' (Selwood, 1995). More generally, bodies such as the Arts Councils in the UK have been seen as constructing an approved taste – Pearson (1982: 103) writes that 'They effect a closure on a process that needs to be open; they demand consensus in a culture and society that is varied and diverse. They appeal to unargued implicit assumptions about the nature of culture and the nature of art. They universalize what needs to be argued from the particular'. See also Pick (1988).

4   This was argued from evidence- and interview-based research by John Myerscough, based on studies of Glasgow, Merseyside, and Ipswich in a report, *The Economic Importance of the Arts in Britain* for the Policy Studies Institute, London (Myerscough, 1988). But a report on private-sector commissioning of art in property development by the University of Westminster (Roberts, Salter and Marsh, 1993) showed that factors such as rent and transport were more important than aesthetics. For an examination of Myerscough's work, see Pick (1988).

5   Eizenschitz (1997: 170-1) writes, citing McLay's *The Reckoning*, published in 1990 by Workers City, Glasgow, that the values of high culture conflict with those of communities: 'during Glasgow's Year of Culture, for instance, its indigenous socialist culture was systematically downgraded'.

6   Bianchini *et al.* (1988) cite two police chiefs, from Boston and San Jose, to this effect.

7   Bianchini writes of a turning away from 'personal and community developments, participation, egalitarianism, neighbourhood decentralization, the democratization of urban space and the revitalization of public social life' towards 'urban economic and physical regeneration' (Bianchini, 1999a: 81).

8   Bianchini and Parkinson comment that politicians in these cities 'radicalized the traditional welfarist objective to promote individual and group self-expression and widen access to cultural facilities and activities for all citizens. Equally common was the use of cultural policy to encourage forms of public life accessible to all residents and not just to the privileged' (Bianchini and Parkinson, 1993: 10-11).

9   For a detailed account of the conversion of derelict sites for arts uses in Liverpool and Marseilles, see Lorente (2000). As Lorente notes, there is a European network of around twenty artists' studio organizations – Trans Europe Halles – with representation from Amsterdam, Berlin, Brussels, Dublin, Helsinki, and Milan.

10   See Zukin (1982). In a later work, Zukin comments 'Artists themselves have become a cultural means of framing space. They confirm the city's claim of continued cultural hegemony, in contrast to the suburbs and exurbs. Their presence ... puts a neighbourhood on the road to gentrification ... In such cities as New York and Los Angeles, the presence of artists documents a claim to these cities' status in the global hierarchy' (Zukin, 1995: 23).

11   Peter Marcuse sums up the appeal of cultural quarters and gentrified bohemias for the new bourgeois class: 'The frustrated pseudo-creativity of their actions leads to a quest for other satisfactions, found in consumption, in specific forms of culture, in 'urbanity' devoid of its original historical content, more related to consumption than to intellectual productivity or political freedom' (Marcuse, 2002: 95).

12   This produces interesting variations and a leakage of the power of capital when specific groups occupy consumption sites in their own ways – see Ryan and Fitzpatrick (1996) on the spatial tactics of users of bars and cafés in Manchester's gay district.

13 Gehry also designed the Temporary Contemporary in Los Angeles, the temporary forerunner of the Museum of Contemporary Art by Arata Isozaki (see Berelowitz, 1994).

14 Bianchini *et al.* (1988: 49) assert that a cultural district revitalizes evening economies, offering 'one place which gives the town a buzz', citing Sheffield.

15 Bianchini and Parkinson write (1993: 14-15): 'Prestigious arts festivals, major sports competitions and other high-profile cultural events were organized by urban policy-makers to support 'internationalization' strategies, and to enhance the cosmopolitan image and appeal of their cities'. They identify Glasgow, Paris, Rennes, Montpellier, Barcelona, and the Ruhr cities where as cultural policy is geared to an expansion of the leisure and tourism industries; Glasgow, Sheffield and Bilbao as gaining improved external and internal perception, while in Frankfurt arts projects have 'acted as symbols of newly acquired elegance, sophistication and cosmopolitanism'; and Montpellier, Nîmes, Grenoble, Rennes, Hamburg, Cologne, Barcelona and Bologna as where cultural policy has provided images of innovation.

16 Gonzalez observes that the Plan General for Bilbao excludes social priorities: 'If quality of life is an interconnected whole consisting of ecological, social and physical dimensions, it must be concluded that in Bilbao the social dimension is not specifically identified ... This is becoming a problem for a considerable number of local citizens (Gonzalez, 1993: 83).

17 Featherstone states: 'goods are used to mark boundaries between groups, to create and demarcate differences or communality between figurations of people'; and, citing Leiss (1978: 19), that goods are doubly symbolic in affluent societies: 'symbolism is consciously employed in the design and imagery attached to goods in the production and marketing process, and symbolic associations are used by consumers in using goods to construct differentiated lifestyle models' (Featherstone, 1995: 21).

18 Marcuse outlines a layered city based on New York, with dispersed and overlapping quarters. He differentiates the gentrified city, the suburban city, the tenement city and the abandoned city, each with class and ethnic associations; and cities of corporate control, advanced services, production, unskilled work and residual sites. While there are parallels in the delineation of the gentrified and advanced services cities, or the residual and abandoned cities, they represent city-wide as well as human and cultural geographies. He deduces that 'A complex pattern of clustering thus characterizes the city' (Marcuse, 2002: 102).

19 Dodd sees this as a weakness: 'There are very few subsidies available for community arts, arts for the disabled or new developing arts, despite great interest in amateur arts associations ... Few plays by new writers get staged' (Dodd, 1999: 61).

20 Teedon writes of Southwark after Tate Modern: 'the area previously (un)known as Bankside has become associated with significant inputs of high-design quality. This in turn has had the effect of reformulating the conception of urban regeneration towards one which aims to be design conscious and architecturally aware' (Teedon, 2002: 56).

21 The policy begins with the establishment in 1993 of Turisme de Barcelona by the city council, the chamber of commerce and Foundation for the International Promotion of Barcelona (Dodd, 1999). As Dodd notes, its work extended that already carried out by the city council in a series of themed annual festivities leading to the 1992 Olympics – 1988 Gate of the Olympiad, 1989 Year of Culture and Sports, 1990 Year of the Arts, and 1991 Year of the Future.

22 Ghirardo comments on the towers: 'Unfortunately the whole complex is dominated by two sky-scraper hotels [one being Hotel des Arts], one by Bruce Graham, senior partner of Skidmore Owings and Merrill ... Completely out of scale with their seven-storey

neighbours, the hotels represent the typical exploitation of urban centers and beachfront property throughout Western cities' (Ghirardo, 1996: 200).

23 For an account of an alternative, grass-roots process, see Remesar and Pol (2000).

24 Commissions included work by Beverly Pepper at Parc de l'Estació del Nord (1992); Richard Serra at Palmera de Sant Martí (1985); Claes Oldenburg and Coosje van Bruggen at Parc de la Vall d'Hebron (1992); and Roy Lichtenstein at Moll de Bosch i Alsina (1987). A work by Basque artist Eduardo Chilida was commissioned for Parc de a Creueta del Coli (1986), and many Catalan artists were also commissioned. A walking guide to the city's redevelopment (Ajuntament de Barcelona, 2001, n. p.) states: 'From the start, public sculpture has been the object of special attention as an essential symbolic element, which characterize [sic] the city. The enthusiastic participation of excellent artists has played a key role in the development of this new culture of urban spaces'.

25 The term site-general, antidote to site-specific, was coined by Brian MacAvera to describe work by Antony Gormley in Derry: 'The whole point about Gormley's work is not that it is site-specific but that it is site-general. The concept is so vague that it will take the *imposition* of almost any roughly analogous situation' (MacAvera, 1990: 113).

26 For similar reasons, Middlesbrough has *Bottle of Notes*, also by Oldenburg and van Bruggen. This is a white and blue, openwork steel bottle, leaning at 17 degrees to the vertical, to commemorate the voyages of Captain Cook; its formal derivation is from previous sketchbook pages relating to a story, 'MS in a bottle' by Edgar Poe (Cork, 1995).

27 Ghirardo remarks: 'over one hundred small interventions in public spaces dispersed throughout the city and around its edges, a modest, inexpensive program to add small urban parks, sculpture and murals to neglected sections' (Ghirardo, 1996: 200).

28 Buildings for the games were in four locations: the stadium at Montjuic, adapted on the 1929 site by Vittorio Gregotti and Correa & Mila (see Ghirardo, 1996: 198-9); at the north-west end of Avinguda Diagonal; at Vall d'Hebron; and at Nova Icária, site of the Hotel des Arts within an Olympic Village on the waterfront beyond Barceloneta, previously an area of docks and rail freight yards.

29 The writer walked through the site in its construction phase in 1999, one sunny Sunday afternoon when families sat on the steps of their apartments looking out at a field of rubble. Degen, on whose research the writer has previously drawn (Miles, 2000), writes: 'a walk through the derelict streets offers a vista of gutted houses and lonely walls that's immediately reminiscent of a war zone ... But if this is a war zone then it's an ongoing conflict, as the ravaged landscape is constantly accompanied by the intense sounds of construction' (Degen, 2002: 24). Degen also describes the *barri xino* in terms like those used by Marcuse to describe the abandoned city: 'it became [a] dangerous, drug and crime-ridden neighbourhood ... Those who could, left the area. Remaining behind were the old, the mentally ill, the unwanted citizens of Barcelona living in dilapidated housing and streets filled with closed metallic shutters' (Degen, 2002: 19). She cites P Villar's *Historia y Leyenda del Barrio Chino* (1996), but her description is perhaps too close here to that projected by the city authorities to justify their intervention.

30 Degen cites a resident: 'this paranoia of architecture to get rid of balconies'; and a local journalist: 'There's the old building with the gas canister on the balcony, an old lady leaning out of the window. It's an old building but it is open because the windows are open, the balcony can be seen ... Next to it you have a stone building with glass and metal, perfectly rectangular, geometric, with automatic doorbells, the windows hermetically sealed, without balconies. They are more interested in aesthetics than utility' (Degen, 2002: 29).

31 Degen uses the term 'worry' but concern seems to make better sense.

32 The idea for an extension was welcomed, and had been proposed as early as 1840, when the city council organized a competition for proposals for the demolition of the walls. The winner was Pere Filip Monlau with ¡¡¡Abajo las Murallas!!! (1840). Further calls for demolition from the religious philosopher Jaume Balmes were published in *La Sociedad*, leading to a commission to map a possible extension in 1846 (Gimeno, 2001). Cerdà's plan was, however, only one of several put forward, if by far the most detailed. The city organized a competition in 1859, in part as an attempt to limit Cerdà's influence on the extension, which was won by Antoni Rivera i Trías with a more radial plan. All the entries subsequently published used a grid of some kind (see Gimeno, 2001; Soria y Puig, 1999).

33 Choay attributes this to the length of (and what he calls redundancy of some of) the text, in two volumes of 800 pages, only part of what Cerdà drafted, and hence lack of translations (Choay, 1997); but his commentary puts the *Teoría* in the company of Alberti and More.

34 To indicate this multi-valency: McEwen relates the orthogonal plan in Greek colonial and port cities to material culture and the concept of appearance: 'if we think of the city in terms of weaving ... the intention made manifest in orthogonal street layouts becomes quite precise. ... *Harmonia*, close fitting, can be a feature of the tightly woven cloth only: a textile with a loose weave ... does not, properly speaking, appear at all' (McEwen, 1993: 83-4). Lefebvre writes on Roman spatial practice (which he sees as contradicting Greek): 'The way citizens "thought" their city was not as one space among others but instead as something vast: the city constituted their representation of space as a whole' (Lefebvre, 1991: 244). In New York, the grid-iron plan was set out in 1811 to divide land into lots of equal size for speculative investment, with little provision for open space until the construction of Central Park in the 1850s. Gandy writes: 'this plan was no more than a cartographic abstraction' (Gandy, 2002: 81-2).

35 Barcelona fell to the Bourbons on September 11th, 1714. Dirges for the martyrs of that siege and its ending are still sung at Fossar de les Moreres, their burial ground near the church of Santa Maria del Mar. The small, triangular plaza was redesigned, with an eternal flame, by C Fiol (1990) as part of the pre-Olympic improvements.

36 Bernard Miller (1977) sees similarities between Cerdà's writing and that of Owen, Fourier, and Saint-Simon.

37 'By distributing with total equality and perfect justice the benefits of "vitality" and of building among all streets and all of the street blocks which bound them, the square grid system has the inestimable advantage of not creating odious artificial preferences' (Cerdà, *Teoría de la viabilidad urbana y reforma de la de Madrid*, 1861; 691-5, cited in Soria y Puig, 1999: 128).

38 In his preliminary 1855 plan there are detached and terraced houses of 180 to 720 sq. m and workers' apartments of 69 to 103 sq. m in rectilinear blocks around a central garden. All housing has at least a minimum standard in terms of space, light, and access to a courtyard. He suggests an element of prefabrication to reduce costs and ensure rents affordable to workers, and produced a detailed study of current wage levels with 333 occupational categories, as well as a study of the minimum dietary standards required for health – met in only eleven of the 333 categories (Soria y Puig, 1999). Later exploitation of the extension, regardless of Cerdà's aim, made most of it a middle-class residential zone. The exception is the working-class neighbourhood of Poble Nou.

39 Cerdà proposed a specific urban block for sites adjacent to railways, in which the two outer of four tracks were for loading and unloading at basement level for businesses occupying the first and second floors, above which were apartments. In his 1863 revisions, Cerdà

includes a 'station of stations' on the site of the old citadel, and an urban transport system of trams and narrow-gauge railways (Tarragó, 2001).

40 In the old city street widths were as low as 3 metres; Carrer Ample (Broad Street) is 10. The ratio of street and open space to built space in the old town is 17-83, in the extension 34-66 (Serratosa, 2001b).

41 Cerdà writes: 'Monotony? Where do these myopic critics find it? In the drawing and only in the drawing, because the short-sightedness of their intelligence and the enfeeblement of their imagination prevents them from seeing beyond the drawing to the reality of buildings already erected. With their variety of shapes, their gardens, plazas, parks, their reality vigorously refutes such puerile accusations' (Cerdà, 1861, *Teoría de la viabilidad urbana y de la de Madrid*, § 702, cited in Soria y Puig, 1999: 180).

42 The grid is conventionally seen as an imposition (from the 1573 Law of the Indies) on the New World. Low (2000) questions this, noting the existence in pre-Conquest societies of grids and open squares to argue that the grid was in fact borrowed by Europeans from conquered societies, adapted in the development of Madrid after 1561 and re-exported to Latin America.

43 In an earlier paragraph (701) of the text quoted in note 41, Cerdà writes: 'First and foremost, the fundamental basis for any technical expert to proceed upon must always be justice, and justice demands, requires, nay, imposes this uniformity and equality ... equal and uniform for all' (cited in Soria y Puig, 1999).

44 In Paris in the 1860s a florid style of neo-classicism informs architecture, public monuments and salon art. In Barcelona it is among the *modernista* milieu around the painter Manuel Milà and his elder brother, the writer Pablo Milà (whose circle met at the Café Nuevo), that opposition to Cerdà was most vicious (Soria y Puig, 1999: 41-2).

45 Short summarizes: 'the scheme consisted in the clearance of the older and high-density housing of the poor and moderate-income population and in their place the construction of broad boulevards, public parks, public buildings, and new shopping areas. The winners were the moneylenders, who made profit from extending credit to the government, the state itself, which pushed broad, easily policed streets through pockets of working-class resistance, and the bourgeoisie of Paris, who saw the city written in their own image and in their own interest' (Short, 1996: 177). This echoes Benjamin in *Das Passagen-Werk*: 'In Paris, speculation is at its height. Haussmann's expropriations give rise to speculation that borders on fraud' (Benjamin, 2002: 23).

46 For an English translation, see Benjamin (2002). For a commentary, see Buck-Morss (1991). For a general introduction, see Gilloch (1996, 2002): 'For Benjamin, the edifices and objects of the metropolis are utopian wish-images, frozen representations or objectifications of genuine wants and aspirations that remain unfulfilled or thwarted. The utopian impulses of long-dead generations lie embedded in the latest products and innovations of capitalist society' (1996: 105).

47 Barbara Hooper writes of Haussmann's 'clearing away of darkness and bringing in of light, straight lines, wide vistas, clean air, and staged theatricality of monumental sights as a regularization of the city ... repeated in the nineteenth-century struggle to control the female body. Ridding the city of pathological spaces by controlling the streets comes to mean ... a ridding of the city of the disorderly, pathological, sexually dangerous female' (Hooper, 1998: 240).

48 An illustration in Pile, Brook and Mooney (1999: 113) shows a group of small dwellings awaiting clearance in Rue Champlain.

49 Benjamin writes: 'In 1864, in a speech before the National Assembly, he vents his hatred

of the rootless urban population. This population grows ever larger as a result of his projects. Rising rents drive the proletariat into the suburbs. The *quartiers* of Paris in this way lose their distinctive physiognomy' (Benjamin, 2002: 23).

50 Degen (2002) notes the city authority's efforts to prevent this by encouraging late-night openings and events.

Chapter 4

Fables of the Reconstruction (of the Fables ...): Lower Manhattan after 9/11[1]

James DeFilippis

> The Corporation will work closely with the private sector to determine a proper market-driven response to the economic and infrastructure needs of Lower Manhattan (Lower Manhattan Development Corporation, 29th November, 2001).

British journalist Robert Fisk began a recent talk in New York (USA) with the statement, 'please don't say the world changed after 9/11'. While of a very different subject matter than Mr. Fisk's talk, this chapter begins with the same plea. And the quote from the Lower Manhattan Development Corporation (LMDC) – which was how it announced itself to the world in its first public statement – indicates that the world of the production of American urban space has indeed not changed. This chapter is an examination of the process of reconstructing Lower Manhattan after 9/11, and how that process has mirrored so many others in the recent history of urbanization in the United States. Unlike the other chapters in this volume, it is about an urban quarter in the process of being (re)constructed. It is necessarily, therefore, a snapshot of a moving target. But that limitation notwithstanding, some very definite observations – about decisions already made – can be advanced at this point about what kind of urban quarter we are going to construct in the newly rebuilt Lower Manhattan. The singular *quarter* is deliberately used here because, despite the fact that Lower Manhattan, like most geographic spaces, is a conflict-laden heterogeneous space with various meanings, definitions and lived experiences, it is being constructed as a relatively singular space for a very clearly defined public.

This chapter will begin by describing the larger context of the production of American downtown urban spaces. Two themes stand out, and will be addressed here: the dominance of entrepreneurial state activities and the prominence of local 'growth machines' within these state apparatuses; and the construction of public spaces and quarters which are inherently exclusionary in their form and intent. I will then describe how these processes are manifest in the reconstruction of Lower Manhattan. Given that the spaces being discussed are not fully realized, the chapter will emphasize the processes involved in their construction. It will discuss how they are being contested by community activists and organizers, and how these contestations – which have been particularly visible and visceral because of the context in which this redevelopment is occurring – have thus far been unable to alter the general trajectory of the development process or the principles governing reconstruction. The chapter concludes with some observations about how these two dominant themes in the American urban geographical and political economy actively work to reinforce each other, and how Lower Manhattan – always a space of iconic significance – in its new form will symbolically and materially reproduce them.

The Entrepreneurial State, Public-Private Partnerships and the Production of American Downtowns

Instead of describing the vast array of downtown development processes in American cities, which is beyond the scope of this chapter, I will only briefly describe four characteristics in the political economy of American urban development which are most important for us here. First, this is an era of intensified economic competition between cities. Economic competition between cities has long existed in the US, but this competition has increased in the last 25 years, and has involved new roles and initiatives on the part of local governments. While there are numerous causes of this increased competition, there is little doubt that because of the increased mobility of capital, cities are increasingly competing against each other to be the destinations for mobile capital – and, it should be added, to maintain the capital already located in places, which might get lured away by cash handouts and tax breaks by other localities.

This increased competition between localities has been heightened by the decline in transfers of money from federal to municipal governments, which has made localities increasingly dependent upon self-generated revenue. Property taxes are most important in this regard, and they are the largest source of local revenue for local governments in the US. An emphasis on land development is therefore structured into the institutional imperatives of American local states.

Second, there has accordingly been a shift in local government from being primarily concerned with issues of the local management of social services to being more explicitly and actively entrepreneurial in its goals and actions. Municipal governments had traditionally been concerned with the provision of the goods needed for social reproduction (or 'collective consumption' as Castells (1977) put it) at the local level. This included schools, health care, housing, public safety, infrastructure, etc. Local governments continue to be involved in the provision of such goods, but they have significantly supplemented this work by becoming more directly involved in the processes of economic development within their localities. This shift, which Harvey (1989b) referred to as 'From Managerialism to Entrepreneurialism', is perhaps the defining characteristic of contemporary urban politics and government. Many researchers have therefore talked about this period as one of a 'New Urban Politics' (NUP).

Third, local politics have become increasingly characterized by a shift away from local govern*ment* and towards local govern*ance*, as more and more activities and functions are performed outside of the specific structures of local governments. This shift, from the public sector to the quasi-public, private, or not-for-profit sectors, has occurred in both the more traditional provision of social services, and the newer, more privatized and entrepreneurial activities of local governance. Social services are increasingly provided by not-for-profit (and, in some cases, for-profit) corporations, rather than the public sector. Similarly, business improvement districts (BIDs), tax increment financing (TIF) districts, and quasi-public local development corporations have emerged in cities throughout the country. These various public-private partnerships functionally remove money from the public sector and place it into unaccountable business- and property-development focused entities that work in narrow geographic spaces – at the expense of the rest of the city. These are, in short, the institutional forms that the 'growth machine' often takes in American cities. As a result of all these changes, the provision of social services and housing have suffered as small, often community-based non-government organizations (NGOs) and not-for-profits struggle to fulfil the roles of local governments.

Finally, as a result of the above transformations, there are growing gaps between the different classes and races in American cities. When the shift of local politics away from social service provision is combined with the decline in industrial employment and the growth in high-paying producer services and low-paying consumer services jobs, we are left with a situation in which American cities are more unequal than they have been since the 1920s. This has led many observers to talk about the emergence of 'Dual Cities' in the US. While this characterization might be a bit too simplistic, and the class and race divisions in American cities are more complex and multi-faceted, there is nonetheless a significant amount of truth in it. But perhaps more important than this outcome is the fact that poverty alleviation, and social justice more broadly, have fallen off the urban political map. Neil Smith (1996) has argued that contemporary urban politics are one of a 'Revanchist City' in which affluent and middle-class people are taking revenge upon the poor people and people of color that 'took' the city from them in the post-war era. The structure of local governments, and the exclusionary production of spaces in American downtowns, certainly support this almost apocalyptic view.

Exclusion, Inclusion and 'the Public' in American Cities

There has long been concern in American urban life about public spaces and public life. Historically, this literature has broadly been in a liberal or civic republican framework of public spaces being important because of their role as spaces in which people could encounter their 'neighbors of all classes'. And while there have certainly been instrumental uses of precisely this kind of 'safety valve' role of public spaces as diffusing urban conflict – as in the work of Olmstead in planning such spaces as Central Park in New York – there have also been more politically critical uses of this framework. Most notably was the work of Jane Jacobs (1961), who lamented the demise of public life and spaces where people could interact informally in a realm of various and continuous activity. But even Jacobs' own work – and particularly her framework of informalized and non-institutional surveillance of 'the eyes on the street', which could have been anything from a neighbourhood 'Miss Marple' in her garden to kids playing stickball in the street – has been instrumentalized into the design of exclusionary and oppressive surveillance, which resembles the panopticon more than the liberal self-governance of Jacobs' vision. The intellectual justification for this oppressive surveillance has been found in Oscar Newman's *Defensible Spaces* (1972), and his framework has become an integral component of how American public spaces are physically designed and built. Ultimately, however, Jacobs' work was right in that the spaces she found so appealing were becoming increasingly rare through the last half of the twentieth century. The irony is that her own work was mobilized in support of their destruction.

It is in this context of the loss of public spaces that much of the literature on public space in American cities over the last 15 years is in what can be termed the 'Disneyfication' school. The public space literature has accurately been described as a 'literature of loss' (Kilian, 1998). Following from Jacobs, this school places its emphasis on the exclusionary design of the built form of contemporary American cities. Perhaps the most significant of the works in this school remains *Variations on a Theme Park*, edited by Michael Sorkin (1992). A few excerpts illustrate the limitations of this school of thought. In his discussion of skyways and underground pedestrian tunnels, Boddy (1992: 93) argues: 'Heretofore streets functioned as periodic reminders and enforcers of the civic domain; the new patterns of city building remove even this remaining vestige of city life'. Leaving aside the fact that streets have never functioned in the manner he describes and have always been exclusionary, Boddy seems to simply equate 'street' with 'public'. Similarly, in her discussion of the history of enclosed malls, Crawford (1992: 106) states: 'As the mall incorporated more and more of the city inside its walls, the nascent conflict between private and public space became acute'. For Crawford, public seems to mean out-of-doors and private means within them. By focusing on design, these authors underestimate the various other social, political and ideological factors that help to define the meaning of a space. Therefore, they conclude we are witnessing the 'end of public space' in American cities.

But while this body of work was developing, a related, and often overlapping, framework for understanding the inherently political and representational roles of public space also emerged.[2] Most notable in this regard has been Mitchell's work (1995), which offers a way beyond this open/enclosed, street/mall, public/private, before/after set of dichotomies by suggesting that there are two competing visions of public space, 'a space marked by free interaction and the absence of coercion by powerful institutions' and 'open space for recreation and entertainment, subject to usage by an appropriate public that is allowed in'. While his dichotomy is also too simple – urban spaces are never completely free from control by powerful institutions, nor do privately controlled spaces go uncontested by those excluded from them – it is a useful starting point to understand how public spaces are produced. Instead of two separate 'visions' of what constitutes public space, Mitchell's typology should be seen as two different poles along a spectrum of different types of public spaces. This spectrum emphasizes social and political control over access, with the normative goal of free, uncontrolled interaction at one end and complete private control over accessibility at the other. The focus on control in this framework allows us to analyse how design interacts with practical and ideological forces that give spaces their meanings. If, paraphrasing Lefevbre (1991), spaces are produced through the complex inter-relations between how they are conceived, perceived and lived, then surely any understanding of public spaces must extend beyond questions of design and directly into the politics of representation and lived experiences. Public spaces are therefore inherently *political* spaces.

Habermas (1989: 68) argued that the public sphere is the 'sphere which mediates between social and the state, and where the public organizes itself as the bearer of public opinion'. That is, the public sphere is the arena in which people express their concerns and questions about the political and cultural contexts of their society. Habermas's conception of the public sphere came from his historical analysis of the coffee houses and salons of seventeenth- and eighteenth-century Europe, but it is clear that these spaces were only accessible to the male bourgeois public. Who constituted 'the public' was decided in this class- and gender-exclusive public sphere and its class- and gender-exclusive public spaces. It was this public sphere that transformed the monarchies of Europe in liberal democracies, but to the women, rural peasants and emerging urban proletariat who were excluded from the spaces of this public sphere, the transformation was a hollow one indeed.

But the politics of public spaces extend beyond the exclusion of the certain people from 'the public'. Spatial exclusion from public spaces serves the dual and inter-related functions of rendering those not included invisible and allowing those included to feel that they make up the entire public. The production of public spaces is therefore dialectically both part of the process of defining 'the public' and an outcome of that process. Given the massive growth in class- and race-based differences in American cities in the last 25 years, the spatial exclusion of large numbers of people from urban public spaces serves a vital political function for local states. Just as the exclusion of women, peasants, and the proletariat from the dominant public spaces of early capitalist Europe contributed to the historic marginalization of these groups, so is the increasing exclusion of poor people and people of color from urban public spaces contributing to the increasing marginalization of these groups now. In short, the very real transformations of downtown public spaces in American cities do not signal 'the end of public space', but a use of space in the redefinition of who constitutes the American public. Nowhere is this more true than in a space with the kind of iconic significance of Lower Manhattan after 9/11.

The Reconstruction of Lower Manhattan

A Brief History of Exclusion and Property Development

While the tragedy that preceded the current reconstruction of Lower Manhattan was unprecedented in the city's history, the exclusionary ways in which reconstruction is being carried out echo past redevelopment – and redefinitions – of the area. Lower Manhattan has a long history of being a space which has been built for and controlled by the city's ruling classes, and one in which the status of real property as a commodity has come together with hegemonic forms of commerce and finance to exclude other forms of social, political and economic relationships. Of course, one can point to the Dutch colonizers 'buying' the land from the Lanape Indians as the beginning of these often violently exclusionary – if also often violently contested – urban development processes. This was followed by the widespread (if largely erased from local history) practice of slavery in Lower Manhattan by both the Dutch and British colonizers. The modern era produced Robert Moses' 1950s displacement of the Syrian immigrant community to build the Battery Tunnel to Brooklyn, followed by the destruction of New York's largest and greatest public market, demolished in the late 1950s in order to make room for the peculiar combination of a modernist planning and design with a post-industrial view of the hegemony of finance capital, the World Trade Center (WTC) itself. After its construction, the WTC and its environs had been an oppressively inhospitable anti-public space with the open plaza being a large and uncomfortable wind tunnel, a tightly controlled underground mall, the towers themselves being purpose-built for finance capital and some recreation for the affluent (such as the exclusive and expensive restaurant of 'Windows on the World').

The period of postmodernity has continued this trend, but with the requisite features of the city itself as a site of consumption for the affluent accompanied by the residential development required for them to consume it at close quarters. The most obvious example was the decision to build Battery Park City – a landfill development on the western side of the lower Manhattan created by the earth removed for the WTC – as a site of upper-income luxury housing, despite the initial plans which had called for a mixed-income community. As a result of the fiscal crisis of the 1970s, the affordable housing that was supposed to be integral to this development would instead be built 'off site' (that is, The Bronx) with revenues generated by the site. Thus the segregation of downtown as a residential space for the affluent became an inherent component of what was actually built. Battery Park City, with its adjacent World Financial Center, has therefore never become the vibrant community many had hoped for when it was first planned. As Andrew Ross recently observed, 'BPC has never shaken off its antiseptic profile as a security enclave where the public are temporary visitors and where the sharing of public space in its riverside park and piazza, while genuinely spirited, still feels like a privilege and not a right' (Ross, 2002: 126). This decision was mirrored on the other side of Lower Manhattan by the local state-driven transformation of South Street Seaport from an open-air museum and park to a privately owned and controlled mall (DeFilippis, 1997). The 1980s and 1990s rather famously brought gentrification to the area, whether it was the 'loft living' of SoHo creeping further south, or new spaces for the affluent like TriBeCa, or the riot-inspiring displacement of low-income residents in the Lower East Side. In short, the gentrification of Lower Manhattan moved south from northwest, north and northeast. Thus, despite its population doubling in the prior 20 years, the median household income in lower Manhattan in 1999 had reached $79,475 – more than twice that of the city's.[3] And in a city where whites are only a third of the population, Lower Manhattan is 66.9 per cent white (US Census Bureau, 2000).

Politics, Process, and Privatization in Lower Manhattan

The current reconstruction of Lower Manhattan involves both the rebuilding of the 16-acre site of the WTC, as well as the much larger redevelopment of all of Lower Manhattan. Both are governed by an almost dizzying web of government – and, more importantly, quasi-government – institutions and funding sources that includes the federal, state, and city governments, and an alphabet soup of public-private partnerships and development corporations. The most important institution in this process is the Lower Manhattan Development Corporation (LMDC). The LMDC administers and allocates the $21 billion of federal money provided for the reconstruction effort, and this is the reason for its centrality in this process. Despite being at the heart of one of the most globally visible planning and development processes that the world has ever seen, its birth was driven by the most parochial and narrow set of concerns imaginable – evidence, perhaps, that despite the implications of the attack at the national and global scales, it was also a very localized event. The LMDC was created out of thin air in the period immediately after 9/11 by the Republican duo of the governor and mayor of New York because they were concerned that a Democrat might win the local elections in early November 2001 (he didn't, and speculation has therefore abounded that the LMDC might be disbanded). As a result of this history, the LMDC is largely controlled by the governor's office, but its board contains several appointees of former Mayor Giuliani. There is only one representative of 'the community' on the LMDC board, and she is from the affluent white community of Lower Manhattan, and distinctly *not* from the Lower East Side or Chinatown that abut it immediately to the northeast.

For all of its powers, the LMDC's ability to control the development of the WTC site is limited because of the privatization of land development that had already occurred there. The land is owned by the Port Authority – itself an unaccountable quasi-public development corporation – and the buildings had been leased to a private real estate developer, who therefore has a significant voice and influence in what will get built there. The current privatized land development process is thus working within constraints that result from the history of a privatized land development process.

Despite the quasi-public sector and private real estate control over the reconstruction process, a dense and overlapping network of civic groups, community organizations, organized labour, planners, architects and artists has emerged to influence the process. Most of these, such as the Civic Alliance,

Imagine NY, the Labor Community Advocacy Network, and the Rebuild with a Spotlight on the Poor Coalition, have emphasized the importance of understanding Lower Manhattan in its citywide, metropolitan and regional contexts. They have thus deliberately tried to broaden the agenda, and to some extent such groups have been able to shape the city's public conversations about the future of Lower Manhattan and the city. But their impact on what will actually be built, and more importantly for what purposes and with what normative frameworks, seems to have been much more limited.

The redevelopment of the site has unsurprisingly attracted the most attention, and has been marked by a series of public events in which public 'input' into what will go there has been emphasized. Most visible of these was certainly the 'Listening to the City' event which took place in July 2002, and at which around 5,000 participants – mostly New Yorkers, but a disproportionately white and professional-class segment of New York – commented on the initial six designs proposed by the LMDC for the rebuilding of the site. The LMDC did not organize the event, which was organized and sponsored by many of the groups mentioned above, but was consulted extensively about it beforehand, eventually becoming a co-sponsor. The LMDC wanted the conversation and input limited to just the architecture of the plans, while the planners and advocates organizing the event wanted the agenda to be much more expansive in both geographic and substantive foci. The day was most striking because of the visceral rejection of the real estate development focus of the plans that had been presented by the LMDC. The plans had to meet several LMDC-imposed design requirements which reflected both the inherent logic of land development as an end in itself, as well as the more immediate contractual requirements that resulted from the private leasing of this land. These requirements included rebuilding the 11 million square feet of office space lost on 9/11; 600,000 square feet of hotel space; and at least 430,000- 600,000 square feet of retail space. Thus the design study had intensive land development built into its requirements. The community and civic groups which had mobilized their members to flood the meeting recognized and directly challenged this. They argued for a much more comprehensive view of the rebuilding process. As the summary that resulted from the event put it:

> Central to this broad view of the rebuilding mission was a desire to ensure that the needs of low- and moderate-income people and new immigrants are not forgotten. The idea of including poor and moderate income New Yorkers permeated 'Listening to the City'; participants repeatedly reminded decision makers to make affordable housing a priority, to promote job-training and development programs ... to provide adequate public facilities such as childcare centers and schools and to take steps to maintain the vibrancy of Chinatown and other downtown communities (Civic Alliance to Rebuild Downtown New York, 2002).

Following the event, the LMDC went back to the drawing board and produced a set of design requirements that mirrored those of the initial plan. The office square footage has shrunk to only 10 million (which itself is probably a function of the vast amounts of vacant office space in Lower Manhattan – much of it owned by the private real estate firm that has the rights to the WTC site), and an increase in the retail space to over 800,000 square feet. Other than these minor adjustments, the revised plans were essentially the same as those that had been thoroughly rejected.

What did change, however, was architecture. The LMDC commissioned nine of the most glamorous architecture firms, or consortiums of firms, to put forward their designs for the new site. The results were spectacular – in the literal sense of spectacles to behold. They were vast and dramatic, and elicited a significant amount of comment in New York's public spheres. There was, to be blunt, *a lot of architecture*. But what was lost in the dominant public reaction to these revised plans was that they were driven by the same imperatives as the initial ones. Having seen both the form and function of its initial plans rejected, those controlling the redevelopment worked to radically change the former, while maintaining the latter. Thus the spectacle of the form of the architecture overwhelmed the questions and debates of its function. And having failed to achieve a narrow discussion at the 'Listening to the City' event, the LMDC decided to use the grandeur of architecture to produce the same overly truncated debate it had always wanted.

Public Spaces in the New Lower Manhattan

Along with the office construction, the plans for the reconstruction also include retail space and some public spaces and facilities. Central among these is the plan for a memorial for those who died on 9/11. As of this time, however, there are few guidelines or plans as to what the memorial should look like, or how it should function. So despite a protracted process of public participation (as theatre) about the office and commercial development, plans for the memorial – which, to many New Yorkers, is the most important part of the new downtown – have been unspecified and taken a back seat. One thing is likely, however, and that is the memorial will construct the attack, which was on the symbols of American financial and military power, as an attack on American freedom.[4] One of the dominant myths of American public discourse in the last decade is that the stock market is the ultimate expression of freedom (which brings with it the corollary that any attempts to regulate it amount to an infringement on American freedom). The memorial can therefore be expected to not only mark the lives lost that day, but also reproduce the ideology of the market as freedom. In this way there is nothing ideologically inconsistent with the (not profit-generating) memorial taking a distant back seat to the nominally free-market driven land development process.

Despite the ambiguity surrounding the future of the memorial, the design requirements have stated that 'attractive public spaces' were important to the future of the area. Given its density of land uses, Lower Manhattan is lacking in significant public spaces, and those governing its redevelopment have recognized this need. The plans' discussions of open space, however, are almost immediately followed by one of security. It states:

> Security is a critical consideration in the planning and design of structures for the World Trade Center site and adjacent areas. Design should emphasize personal security

for visitors to the memorials, office workers, shoppers and area residents. Urban design and architecture cues can be used to define the environment as a secure space ... clear sight lines and good lighting can reinforce the sense that the area is under surveillance (LMDC, n.d.: 18).

It is clear, therefore, that 'attractive' is a code word for 'secure', and Newman's framework of defensible spaces is being employed completely uncritically. The tightly-controlled public spaces that have come to dominate American urban life will here be enhanced by the threat of terrorism – both real and cynically employed – to reproduce the spatial exclusion that is already so much part of Lower Manhattan (and which had been a feature of the underground retail space in the former WTC site). So, as the *New York Times* described it, the rebuilding plans possess 'security precautions at a level not seen since the golden age of castle keeps' (quoted in Marcuse, 2003: 12).

The chosen plan, by the Studio Daniel Libeskind, does include several open spaces, as well as a museum and performing arts centre. The street grid which had been eliminated in the construction of the original WTC is also to be restored, and there will be an emphasis on street-level retail to complement the half-million square foot underground mall planned. But given the lack of public control over the process, the private control over the land and development, the emphasis on defensible spaces, and who will live and work in the area (see below), it is exceedingly difficult to imagine anything other than a narrowly defined 'public' being able to use, appropriate or control this space.

Beyond the 16 Acres

The future of the rest of Lower Manhattan has been similarly deliberately exclusionary of all but affluent professional-class workers and residents. This has been evident in both the economic development monies allocated thus far, and in the kinds of housing currently being constructed with the public sector's redevelopment funds. The resources spent for economic development beyond the 16-acre site have been an almost eerie replication of the practice of local governments giving handouts to large multinational corporations that use the threat of capital mobility to extort money. These handouts have gone overwhelmingly to FIRE (finance, insurance, real estate) sector firms, including $40 million to Bank of New York, $25 million to American Express, $23 million to the New York Board of Trade, and $13 million to Deloitte and Touche. There are no strings attached to these funds, except that the companies have to commit to remain in New York for seven years (*Good Jobs New York*, 2002). Nor is there any evidence that New Yorkers will benefit from these handouts – even the threat of capital mobility seems to be unneeded. As a spokesperson for American Express put it after the company received its $25 million grant: 'Our decision to return downtown, which has been our home for more than 150 years, was not predicated on financial incentives ... Once those financial incentives became available, we chose to participate, as did other companies' (Hetter, 2002: 126).

A significant amount of money for the redevelopment of Lower Manhattan has also been allocated for housing construction, and the uses of this money have thus far aggressively reinforced the vision of Lower Manhattan as a quarter for the affluent. Virtually all of the housing units being constructed with public money are luxury units, which require incomes beyond $100,000 a year (three times the city's median). A limited number of the units (five percent) are designated 'affordable' because they only require incomes of $85,000 a year! Those controlling the redevelopment are thus actively working to ensure that Lower Manhattan, as a space for work and residences, remains a wealthy, professional-class (and overwhelmingly white) quarter; it could hardly be more unambiguous. In this effort, however, support of the community – that is, the white affluent residents of Lower Manhattan – has been enlisted. This community has eagerly embraced a framework of 'nimbyism' and exclusion of affordable housing, and even fought the Coalition for the Homeless's efforts to work downtown. This is striking evidence that the 'growth machine' and 'the community' are not necessarily on opposite sides in the politics of urban development (as they are in Logan and Molotch's (1987) influential framework).

Conclusions

Lower Manhattan is in the midst of a major reconstruction process, which will shape the future of this iconic urban space for decades to come. Unfortunately, it is one which is being driven by the processes of entrepreneurial city politics combining with exclusionary housing development and tightly-controlled public spaces. This chapter has focused on the processes involved, to some extent because that is all there is to report at this time. Given that spaces can be, and are, appropriated and used (and therefore, partially produced) in ways that often run contrary to how they are conceived and built, this is a significant limitation; and it is certainly conceivable that the exclusions will be contested (as they have been throughout the process). But given how little these contestations have been able to affect the process, I am not optimistic that these contestations would yield much beyond limited, pyrrhic victories.

The process was architecture-driven. Architecture, not the goals, ideas, agendas, uses and meanings of the space, was what the LMDC wanted to discuss. This reality was made abundantly clear by its ignoring all of the criticisms that emerged at 'Listening to the City' – except the criticisms about architecture – and having the final design plans based on exactly the criteria that had been rejected. And thus the discussion here has predominantly not been about the built form being proposed or constructed in Lower Manhattan, either on the 16-acre site, or in Lower Manhattan as a whole. Instead, the criticism is that the purposes and uses of what will be reconstructed – office space and cash handouts for the FIRE sector, an underground mall, a hotel, surveillance-heavy open spaces, and luxury housing – preclude the production of public spaces that are inclusive. The spaces being produced not only mark a continuation of the longer-term processes of using space to define the public more narrowly, but actually mark an intensification of those processes. While the decimation of local government finances has furthered and deepened the cuts in social service provision, the ability to make those cuts is reinforced and supported by the construction of new spaces which render invisible those who will feel the impacts of those cuts. In this way, the oppressive socio-spatial production of American cities takes on new and more pronounced forms with each new wave of building construction.

It is a cruel irony that the events of 9/11, which both reinvigorated public life in New York and allowed a glimpse of what a *public* which is inclusive of the city's astonishing diversity might look like, are now the catalyst for the further development of Lower Manhattan which will serve the interests of the FIRE sector, and simultaneously intensify and deepen the class- and race-based exclusions and segregation which dominate America's – and New York's – urban socio-spatial fabric. What is being planned is the built form of the ideology of the market as freedom, coupled with an erasure of the people who suffer at the hands of the market.

Notes

1 With apologies to REM.
2 This emergence was fed by the translating of Habermas's *Structural Transformation of the Public Sphere* in 1989, and Lefebvre's *The Production of Space* in 1991. Together they came to provide two halves to understanding that space is productive and not an inert container of social activity.
3 Defined here as Community Board 1 in New York, which is from the Southern Tip of the Island, to Canal Street, but not the eastern part of Canal Street which is part of Chinatown and the Lower East Side.
4 If you include the Pentagon.

Part 2
Production and Consumption

Chapter 5

Cultural Industry Quarters: From Pre-Industrial to Post-Industrial Production

Graeme Evans

Welcome to the new Bohemia. New underground art collective seeks collaborators, creative involvement, ideas, suggestions, whatever. Phone Dave.

This advertisement was placed in the window of a corner shop off Hoxton Square, East London – 'the capital's trendiest area' – next door to the local osteopathy and massage centre (*The Economist*, 2000). The phenomenon of collective production in 'Marshallian districts' has been evident from pre-industrial artist and crafts-based communities, to contemporary cultural industries quarters in 'post-industrial' (*sic*) cities. The arts and particular forms of cultural production have exhibited this preference, with the clustering of firms and the convergence of production and consumption and related support activities being practised from classical times; in medieval and mercantile societies; to industrial and late-industrial eras, including the neo-Bohemian quarters of cities. The focus on the historical role and impact of so-called *cultural milieu* in the heyday of cities has also been celebrated in major publications (Hall, 1998; Jardine, 1996) and in exhibitions such as *La Ville: Art et Architecture en Europe 1870-1993* (Pompidou, 1994); *Century City, Arts & Culture in the Modern Metropolis* (Tate Modern, 2000); *Creative Quarters: the Art World in London 1700-2000* (Museum of London, 2001); *Paris Capital of the Arts 1900-1968* (Royal Academy, 2002); and the first international conference dedicated to *Creative Clusters* held recently in Sheffield (2002). This West Yorkshire city, long associated with mining, steel and related manufacture, has since the 1980s adopted the Cultural Industry Quarter as one of the prime elements of its urban regeneration strategy (URBED, 1988), particularly in the declining city centre, joined by a growing list of cities which aspire to identify and nurture cultural quarters and the economic and marketing advantages of a critical mass of activities – both consumption- and production-based.

That cultural industry quarters persist in post-industrial cities is arguably counter-factual, given the vertical integration, then dis-integration and post-Fordist dispersal of production to lower cost areas nationally and globally (Harvey, 1989c; Krugman, 1991), and the supposed placelessness of communications technology and new media practice (Backlund and Sandberg, 2002; Braczyk *et al.*, 1999; Castells, 1989, 1996). But, as Gottdiener (2000: 98) claims: 'While the information economy progresses to an increasing degree of disembodied spacelessness, the producers of knowledge still require specific locations or spaces to work. In short, our new economy will function in this respect very much like the old one with persisting need for adequate design of the built environment'. Pratt (2000) likewise suggests that the 'death of distance' is exaggerated, using a case study of new media firms in New York's Silicon Alley to demonstrate that place and space are still important, as is the value of social interaction. The deliberate conflation of symbolic and economic sites for global media headquarter operations has also been observed by Sassen and Roost (1999) in the case of Time Square, Manhattan. They conclude that a cosmopolitan comparative advantage justifies an otherwise high cost and unsalubrious location for the incumbent corporations. This is mirrored in London, where transnational car-makers such as Ford and Nissan have relocated their design divisions to the high-rent Soho area where media, entertainment and specialist services intersperse with porn shops, night clubs, bars and café culture. One downside of this process is that it often leads to the sanitization of these interstitial zones between the core business districts, *beaux quartiers* and retail and entertainment zones, with the result that diversity of use and activity – key characteristics of the longer-established cultural quarters – is narrowed. This also undermines, as with other forms of branding and commodification of residential-based production quarters, the very nature and spirit which brought the quarter into being in the first place. They are a largely organic and chaotic, as opposed to a business or government planning, phenomenon (Green, 1999), and are often influenced by visionary individuals, social activists and entrepreneurs, and groups of artists. Institutional replication on the other hand is less well-placed to capture this energy, which limits the viability of municipal or corporate cluster developments.

The promotion of cultural industry quarters and workspaces by public authorities – national, local and regional (and transnational, i.e. Europe) – has nonetheless gained momentum, not least since local production systems and public sector land-use planning are otherwise seen to be ineffective and vulnerable by government and by economists, geographers and business organizational researchers alike (Borja and Castells, 1997; Curran and Blackburn, 1994; Simmie, 2001). Despite their commonplaceness in retail and leisure consumption – high streets, shopping centres, entertainment and restaurant districts and tourism resorts – in production terms they represent an anachronistic hangover from traditional craft, cooperative and place-based manufacturing, but at the same time a renewed landscape in contemporary art, new media and advanced services production (Hutton, 2000) as part of the resurgent 'cities of culture'. Today, the production of art and cultural goods is decidedly *industry*. Workspaces in cultural quarters wear their industrial re-used buildings with pride: Powerhouse, Gasworks, Leadmill, Printworks, Perseverance Works, Foundry and the Arts Factory are all facility names, whether or not they are actually 'producing' or occupying former industrial buildings (Evans, 2003).

Clusters – Cooperation or Collusion?

Attitudes to close location and cooperative links have also changed over time, with Adam Smith's more cynical perspective reflected in neo-classical economics associated with late-twentieth-century liberal market ideology. Fear of price fixing and uncompetitive behaviour at the cost of the consumer drives this paranoia today: 'People of the same trade seldom meet together, even for merriment and diversion, but the conversation ends in a conspiracy against the public, or in some contrivance to rise prices' (*Wealth of Nations,* 1776). However, the idea behind linking economic change with innovation through spatial configuration was also partly inspired a century on by the work of Alfred Marshall, who first coined the phrase 'industrial district' in 1890:

> The leadership in a special industry, which a district derives from an industrial atmosphere, such as that of Sheffield or Solingen, has shown more vitality than might have seemed probable in view of the incessant changes of technique. It is to be remembered that a man can generally pass easily from one machine to another, but that the manual handling of a material often requires a fine skill that is not easily acquired in the middle age: for that is characteristic of a special industrial atmosphere. Yet history shows that a strong centre of specialized industry often attracts much new shrewd energy to supplement that of native origin, and is thus able to expand and maintain its lead (Marshall, 1925: 287).

Marshall's observation reflects the catalytic effect that a concentration of production activity can have, both to individuals and to organizations. This is similar to some artists' communities, and with formal and informal agglomerations of cultural and other production-based activity (e.g. agricultural and manufacturing cooperatives). In a comparative assessment of innovation in cities (and knowledge and information activity is increasingly conflated with the so-called creative industries – DCMS, 2001), Simmie (2000) argues that the examples of small craft firms in places like Emilia-Romagna, north-western Italy (ceramic tile industry); Mondragon, Basque region; Galicia, Spain (fashion – Zara and Adolfo Dominguez brands); and the high fashion areas of Paris (Scott, 2000), have illustrated the positive benefits of flexible specialization. But he goes on to argue that these should be regarded as special cases rather than presaging a real paradigm shift in production, since they are confined to older, design- and craft-based industries, not representative of the dominant high-technology corporations who are the major players in the new knowledge-based international economy. Notwithstanding this scepticism, interest in clustering effects is prolific within economic and human geography (Portnov and Erell, 2001), with regular articles and sectoral case studies in journals of regional and area studies, planning, urban studies and information technology, and with the cultural industries also warranting special attention (Caves, 2000; DCMS, 2001; Hesmondhalgh, 2002; Kockel, 2003; Lacroix and Tremblay, 1997; Scott, 2001; Verwijnen and Lehtovuori, 1999).

Although not forming part of the traditional economist's and geographer's assessment, the attraction that avant-garde movements can have to a wide interest group mirrors that of other human endeavour once innovation and new ideas –

whether technologically or culturally driven – are disseminated. Avant-garde artists create a clustering effect much wider than the practice and eventual economic spin-offs from their work – they generate social and what today are referred to as lifestyle movements, which include gentrification and even touristic and heritage processes. For instance, the bohème of nineteenth-century Paris formed clusters or specialized districts such as the Latin Quarter and, on the periphery of the city, Montparnasse and Montmartre – centres which provided both the producers and consumers of what would a century later be called an underground, or counter-culture. As Hobsbawm (1977: 347) noted: 'the growing desire of the bourgeoisie to clasp the arts to its bosom multiplied the candidates for its embrace – arts students, aspiring writers ... in what was now the secular paradise of the western world and an art-centre with which Italy could no longer compete'. These alternative cultural quarters also created the foundation of artist colonies which the city of Paris has continued to protect and control through zoning and rent subsidy (although the city now ejects and fines unlicensed street artists). Hall (1998) refers to 6,000 artists in Paris around 1870, a quarter of these in Montparnasse, multiplied by art suppliers, dealers and academics; however, Hobsbawm quotes between 10-20,000 people 'calling themselves artists' in Paris (347), and at this pivotal time in industrial urbanisation, there was also a concentration of bohemian artists in Munich – the 4,500 members of the *Munchner Kunstverein* – and in the city fringe district of Clerkenwell, London, a similar number of craftspeople (which I will return to in more detail later).

The magnetic effect that these bohemian quarters generated also drew an international as well as domestic milieu, as Franck (2002: xii-xiii) writes: 'Mixing languages and cultures, drawing on incredibly diverse sources of inspiration, the Dutch, Polish-Italian, Swiss, Mexican, Scandinavian, Russian ... to name a few, were enriching the century's artistic legacy. In the 1920s the American writers would arrive, as would the Romanian, Swedes, more Russians'. This was of course more than Marshallian 'knowledge and technology transfer' but also a reflection of France's open-door policy in terms of refugees – fuelled by the economic necessity for workers on major building projects and mining, which together attracted Polish and Romanian students, plus many Jewish and other artists and intellectuals fleeing Tsarist persecution. Conversely, Huguenots escaping Louis XIV's anti-Protestant France settled in England in the late seventeenth century, bringing with them craft-based skills and influence in weaving and related trades, as successive refugee groups have done, enriching cultural development and production from Jewish, Bangladeshi to more recent diaspora from eastern Europe, Africa and south-east Asia. The imperative for immigrant groups to cluster in ghettos (Evans and Foord, 2003) has reinforced cultural quarters around intensive production activity, associated with sweatshops, handcrafts and cuisine, as well as arts and entertainment activity such as music halls and festivals. Marshallian industrial districts are therefore only one explanation for clustering effects, which are driven historically, and still today, by social, political and cultural factors, as well as the more obvious economic rationales. The 'economic world reversed' characterized in Bourdieu's (1984) notion of cultural capital is evident in some cultural manifestations which reject established art practice and society, notably avant-garde movements which grew in opposition to the established bourgeois society and cultural values. Cultural clusters can therefore be the antithesis of economic efficiency imperatives for co-location. However, as Wilson (2002) points out in her assessment of the 'mythical' Bohemian phenomenon, in 1920s and 1930s Paris as in other examples, such as London's Soho, Greenwich Village and later in Zukin's artist-led *Loft Living* New York (1982), commodification, gentrification and ultimately heritage tourism succeeded these alternative spaces of exchange and resistance – *from coffee house to café culture.*

Clusters can therefore be seen as examples of mutual cooperation through informal and formal economies of scale, spreading risk in research and development (R&D) and information sharing via socio-economic networks; as reactive anti-establishment action (avant garde, artists' squats); and as a defensive necessity, resisting control from licensing authorities, guilds and dominant cultures, artistic and political. In Sennett's (1986: 266) view, the close physical association by social and ethnic *quartier* can also create anti-social effects, with 'empathy for a select group of people allied with rejection of those not within the local circle ... creat(ing) demands for autonomy from the outside world, for being left alone by it rather than demanding that the outside world itself change. The more intimate however, the less sociable'. Identifying those whom clusters effectively exclude can therefore reveal particular aspects of how and why clusters exist and operate. For instance, a group of graphic designers clustered informally around two north London boroughs (i.e. a social network), formed a Digital Business group, with the aim of maintaining standards in web-based design, then in its very early days. Drawing up a protocol and membership scheme, the group found the need to establish quality standards in their field, which was fast being occupied by what they saw as new media 'cowboys'. As a joint marketing tool which included sharing the cost of stands at trade exhibitions, mutual advice and exchange of technology and knowledge, this group, who otherwise operated in direct competition with one another, used the cluster and local network to effectively control membership of their self-styled group (Evans, 1996).

The more dominant economic (efficiency) factors that contribute to this concentration and proximity include cost-saving in the production chain, cross-trading, joint ventures (e.g. in marketing, IT, R&D, capital investment) and a rediscovery of live-work facilities and the managed workspace within former industrial zones and buildings. Lifestyle and other synergies are also emerging as pull-factors in clusters of firms in both traditional 'pre-industrial' arts (Lacroix and Tremblay, 1997) and in new media services (Backland and Sandburg, 2002). How far these new modes of production encourage or diminish innovation and creativity is a key question (Simmie, 2000), whilst the changing nature of cultural production itself warrants attention as new forms of arts and media replace old crafts, and the profile of artists and cultural producers themselves inevitably changes through technological and gentrification effects.

The attention being paid to the possibilities of clusters today is generally driven by one or more of the following:

- The local response to globalization ('glocalization') and post-Fordist drift, and the resultant growth in micro-enterprises and community businesses (Porter's argument for the benefits of local competition in stimulating more world-class company performance, 1990).
- Industrial economic policies focusing on a declining (and therefore disproportionately important) number of growth sectors and their export potential – notably so-called creative production-consumption industries (see DCMS, 2000; Evans, 2001a; Scott, 2000).
- Capturing (and retaining) new technology and related producer services in new media, through clustering, e.g. the science/techno-park facility (Batt, 2001; DCMS, 2001; Downey and McGuigan, 1999).
- The environmental and lifestyle factors attracting urban professionals to work and reside in inner city/fringe areas through the renovation of industrial and utility buildings into workspaces and consumption venues (e.g. galleries, designer retail, restaurants, clubs) and loft-style apartments (Foord, 1999; O'Connor and Wynne, 1996; Verwijnen and Lehtovuori, 1999; Zukin, 1982).

The support and promotion of local and regional cultural industry production has also sought to redress the imbalance between capital and central production areas which nationally (and internationally, e.g. world cities – London, Paris, New York and Tokyo) dominate and act as an 'unfair magnet' for investment and trade, and for skilled workers and creative artists. Examples in the UK include Birmingham's Jewellery Quarter and the Custard Factory, and similar clusters and regional city networks in Cardiff, Manchester, Liverpool, Sheffield and Huddersfield, Yorkshire (Fleming, 1999), often supported by designated cultural industries development agencies (CIDAs) and regional aid. As Scott (2000: 209) suggests: 'Provided that the right mix of entrepreneurial know-how, creative energy, and public policy can be brought to bear on the relevant developmental issues, there is little reason why these cities cannot parlay their existing and latent cultural-products sectors into major global industries'. Rural economic development has also looked to crafts and new home-based communications and technology employment (tele-cottaging) as agriculture declines, in some respects harking back to the earlier Arts and Crafts movement inspired by Ruskin and William Morris. The support of village-based cultural production is also evident in countries such as Mexico, Thailand and Indonesia (e.g. textiles, ceramics), exploiting both tourist art (Evans, 2000b) and fair trade links (Evans and Cleverdon, 2000).

The resurgence of regional cities has seen a major shift in attitude and pride in cultural development, particularly in centrist countries such as the UK, France and Spain. As Fisher (1991: 6) asserted: 'For years our cultural life, like almost every other aspect of British life, has been hugely weighted towards the south-east. Despite cities like Manchester developing a strong cultural voice, the capital has kept most things to itself, theatres, galleries, television companies, publishing houses, agents, work, and investment. Now other cities are fighting back'. The dominance of cultural production has also been broken in some areas such as music, with New York's US hegemony challenged by the cities of Austin and

Miami, and with film production relocating to Toronto (Scott, 2000). Regional cultural development is also subject to national and globalized cultural hegemony, with artistic directors frequently imported from capital cities, including from other countries. In France, for instance, regional *grand projets* were 'accompanied by an inverse tendency to recruit those with specialist talents and abilities from national level, often [the capital] Paris' (Negrier, 1993: 142). The concentration of cultural mediation still resides, nonetheless, in the cultural capitals and seats of media corporations and government agencies, which also play host to multicultural quarters, the filters for urban cultural and global 'fusion' – an unlikely but palpable comparative advantage: 'The economic and spatial structures of the entertainment industry increasingly call for the specific functions provided by cities. Global cities in particular, are emerging as strategic centres for both consumption and production' (Sassen and Roost, 1999: 153). Traditional ethnic quarters (e.g. Little Italy, Little Germany, Chinatown, etc.) are now the subject of transformation into new cultural clusters through the branding opportunities offered by Banglatown, Little Vietnam, Curry Triangle and so on, constructed localities which are animated and marketed simultaneously as cultural producer (e.g. food, crafts, fashion, music) and consumption places (see Chan, this volume).

The development of a high concentration of cultural workers and facilities for public consumption has also been a familiar aspect of theatre-lands and designated entertainment zones such as in the West End, London, Broadway, New York, Rio's cinema-land, and Amsterdam's red-light district (Burtenshaw *et al.*, 1991), but this can also be seen in 'non-public' cultural activity which focuses on production separate from distribution/dissemination, such as in London's Soho (film/media and music post-production) and California's Silicon Valley(s) (Scott, 2000). At a more local level, versions of agglomeration and cultural industry quarters can be seen (or not, i.e. they are hidden but nonetheless active), bringing together a range of compatible elements in the particular production chain, whether audio-visual, design, crafts, visual arts or producer services based. For example the artisan's villages in the Modena region of northern Italy have played an important part in the area's renaissance since the late 1970s and 1980s, through the flexible production of individual arts and crafts settlements made up of a wide variety of small manufacturers (Lane, 1998). These form a network in which companies are competitive with and complementary to one another, in common with small crafts producers in managed workspaces (Evans, 1990). These producer zones in turn form a 'polycentric grid' throughout the region, which has ensured their competitiveness over manufacturers (e.g. furniture, ceramic tiles) in traditional 'chaotic' areas, such as in East London (Green, 1999). As Scott (2001: 11) maintains: 'The cultural economy of [late] capitalism now appears to be entering a new phase marked by increasingly high levels of product differentiation and polycentric production sites'.

Where cultural producer clusters or industrial districts are long established, their survival and development has also reflected structural changes in production techniques and technology, as well as markets and cultural development in both design and consumption/fashion. This is evident in the profile of cultural production in traditional quarters where 'new media' has replaced print and publishing (e.g. from magazine to website); metalcrafts and weaving have evolved into multimedia jewellery and textiles production; and painting and sculpture is supplanted by media art and time-based film and video installation – a shift from (hand)craft artisan to designer-maker and producer. The continuity has therefore been in the places and spaces occupied for this activity, rather than the precise forms of creative production themselves, although some residual continuity is still evident in the performing arts, metalcrafts/jewellery and specialist services such as instrument makers, costumiers – skills often passed down through the family and which have not been so easily automated or designer-labelled. Where established manufacturing activity requires updating and a more responsive mode to market and consumer demands, secondary or complementary clusters form, which are able to feed the traditional production district and filter design and innovation emanating from art schools and designers. This has occurred in New York (Rantisi, 2002) and the Nord-Pas de Calais region of France (Vervaeke and Lefebvre, 2002), which support a traditional sweatshop design and manufacturing district linked to major retailers, and an inter-dependent but culturally distinct new quarter served by art and designs schools, specialist ('trendy') boutiques and independent designers/makers. The shift in power towards major retailers and the needs of a fast-changing market able to respond to fashion trends, and away from manufacturers, is thus enabled by cultural intermediaries and a number of clusters linking traditional and contemporary, and large and micro-enterprise activity. This multi-cluster system has enabled these areas to maintain their share of national production and minimize the post-Fordist fragmentation of the design, production and distribution/consumption chain. Extended clusters are also evident in areas where over-capacity and rental increases limit further demand from artists and designers, in areas such as Manhattan, New York, and the East End of London, which has resulted in extended communities and workspace developments further east and north of the original cultural quarter.

Mixed Use, *Reclaiming the City*

A particular feature of workspace and site-based regeneration, both new-build and conversion, has been the mixed or multi-use designed development, where a variety of public and private functions take place within a complex, such as arts and entertainment, retail, office and workspace, as well as residential – in what Coupland (1997) optimistically terms *Reclaiming the City*. This contrasts to the Utopian models of modern planning philosophy which ignored the interdependence of everyday activities, recognizing instead that 'Our most enjoyable cities are those which quietly weave together a rich and complex pattern of different uses and activities' (Zeidler, 1983: 9). Artist and small-scale cultural workspace increasingly coexists with housing and light industrial production, which have similarly expanded as a result of contracting-out to 'independent' producer and ancillary services: 'It is after all the artist and not the bureaucrat who provides the catalyst for much change in our city by colonising redundant buildings, informing and challenging the design of the urban environment, and animating the street or square with performance' (LAB, 1992: 26). In London, as in other cities, not-for-profit organizations were first established in the early 1970s (during an earlier property market boom and bust), for example the ACME organization which manages over 460 studios in 230,000 square feet of converted industrial property. These include former meat pie, cosmetics and cigarette factories. In Shoreditch, East London, a former match factory, Perseverance Works, hosts over 50 small firms including a bible factory, model agency and T-shirt printers 'Philosophy Football' (e.g. 'Each succeeds in reaching the goal by a different method – Machiavelli'). As Worpole (1991: 143) observed: 'In addition to the performance-based arts, small-scale workshop production is back on the agenda again both in handicrafts and hi-tech cultural forms such as video animation, computer graphics, electronic music, desk-top publishing'. One almost iconic type of space for cultural production is therefore the artist's/craftsperson's workspace or studio. This long-established mode of production has been a growing feature of post-industrial urban development, but one that has attempted to mediate within a largely inhospitable property and entrenched land-use separation and use-value system (Jencks, 1996). Some cities have however retained stronger provision and protection for artist workspaces (notably Paris and Munich, above), whilst others have developed planning policies which support and recognize the integration of uses, everyday living and the cross-trading/production possibilities and attraction for well-informed consumers and visitors (e.g. Toronto, Vancouver). The attraction and availability, albeit transitory, of former industrial buildings also coincided with the shift to large-scale work by contemporary artists. In SoHo, Manhattan lofts averaged 2,500 square feet: 'The large windows of cast-iron construction flooded each floor with natural light. Freight elevators provided useful access. Rents were affordable. A perfect prescription for artists. The transformation of SoHo had begun' (Grantz and Mintz, 1998: 297).

Quarters where cultural activity and intense production congregates therefore draw on differing rationales which have been on one hand prescriptive, and on the other opportunistic (and sometimes oppositional). The influence of key individuals, whether entrepreneurs, family businesses or artists, is often required to first create and then sustain local networks and facilities, as in the case of artist and designer studio organisations and larger community arts organizations; for example, in London, Omnibus (DoEn, 1987), SPACE (artist Bridget Riley *et al.*) and ACME (1990); the Custard Factory, Birmingham; Artspace in Toronto (BAAA, 1993) and artists' workspace organizations in Philadelphia, Berlin and Stockholm (Evans, 2001a). The economic, social and cultural rationales for their development present quite different political and structural responses to the value of cultural clustering, as Table 5.1 summarizes. They are not, however, exclusive, despite their seemingly oppositional roots, and policy initiatives have looked to capture all of these in conflating social and economic regeneration and environmental improvement through 'culture' (Evans and Foord, 2002). This is seen in government promotion of local cultural strategies and the power of the arts in addressing factors which lead to social exclusion (DCMS, 1999; Shaw, 1999). Particularly in areas of high unemployment, poor health and housing, these areas are often congruent with ethnic minority and new immigrant communities, as well as entrenched older working-class communities whose core employment base has disappeared (docks, manufacturing, printing, mining) and whose skill base finds little value in the new service economy.

Table 5.1 Rationales for Cultural Clusters

Economic	Social	Cultural
• *Industrial District*	• *Neighbourhood Renewal*	• *Avant Garde/Bohemia*
• *Managed Workspace*	• *Urban Village*	• *Artists' Studios and*
• *Production Chain*	• *Community Arts*	*Galleries*
e.g. crafts, media, TV	• *Urban Regeneration*	• *New Media*
• *Production Networks*	• *Collective Identity*	• *Ethnic Arts*
• *Technology Transfer*	• *Arts & Social Inclusion*	• *Local Cultural Strategies*
e.g. Silicon Valley	• *Social Networks*	• *Arts Schools and Education*

The emergence of the less tangible but nonetheless valuable power of networks and networking between firms in various production and creative processes, has generated interest in not only better understanding clustering and the minimization of transaction costs and risks arising, but also the value of social and cultural networks which cultural quarters and shared workspaces can facilitate. These 'untraded interdependencies' (Storper, 1995) and the cultural milieux generating such mutual exchange, are credited with innovation and competitiveness based upon soft factors such as 'shared rules, conventions or knowledge', or 'various forms of socio-cultural identification' (Amin and Thrift, 1994: 14). The benefits of local networking are more valued amongst cultural (and financial) service firms than other sectors (Buck et al., 2003), in part reflecting the creative exchange process, in contrast to more inward and competitive business practices (see Adam Smith versus Marshall, above). Put another way, this is the magic ingredient behind the nature and genesis of many cultural quarters and collective production facilities.

From another perspective, localized cultural activity has been directed at the declining social as well as economic life in urban villages (Aldous, 1992). The Council of Europe's three-year study (1993-6) 'Culture and Neighbourhoods' investigated 24 local areas in eleven cities, hoping to bridge local planning, cultural and community agencies around a micro-spatial focus for cultural development (see Bianchini and Gilhardi, this volume). Neighbourhoods were studied in cities from Athens, Bilbao, Budapest, Copenhagen, Liverpool, Marseilles, Munich, Prague to Vienna, and in some cases served as a catalyst for cultural projects. Several of these cities have subsequently developed major cultural flagships, notably Guggenheim Bilbao, MuseumQuartier Vienna, Euromediterranée international business centre, Marseilles, and Munich's new Pinakothek der Moderne Art, as centres for cultural districts, but evidence of sustained neighbourhood cultural activity through European regional development is less apparent, as are the benefits of these cultural tourism and inward investment strategies to local residents (Evans and Foord, 2000b). Munich in the *länder* of

Bavaria ('Hollywood of Germany') is now associated with 'laptops and lederhosen', with new media and high-tech firms exploiting an expanding film studio infrastructure and its geographical advantage and proximity to Italy and the Mediterranean climate. New industrial activity has however developed in the suburbs through the business park model, rather than in the central urban neighbourhoods, whilst it is Hamburg that now claims one of the highest clusters of audio-visual activity in Germany, building on the concentration of print media (magazines, newspapers) and TV/radio production (Henriques and Thiel, 1998). Despite loss of film production to Berlin and Munich, convergence between print and broadcast media and the growth of independent production witnessed elsewhere has ensured a vibrant cultural production cluster in this second German city: 'a centre of multimedia production has been established, providing both all the necessary facilities and cooperation interfaces for productive activities' (ibid: 19). Meanwhile, in the city of Leipzig in the *Neue Länder* of former East Germany, a new media cluster has developed since reunification, driven by the impact of the Middle German Broadcasting Service, and which is now having a stabilizing effect on an otherwise fragile economy (Bathelt, 2002). Cultural production quarters are therefore not necessarily exclusive or dominated by a single locality, despite the tendency for agglomeration and economies of scale in global production areas such as film (i.e. Hollywood; Scott, 2002). The shift from an essentially internal and specialized market for the range of new media and design products and services covering both creative content and distribution technology, to a more generic concern and demand for image, style and design amongst individual and corporate consumers, has fuelled multimedia clusters in many towns and cities. This is particularly so where they are able to build on an existing cultural production inheritance, even if 'old industry'-based such as printing and manufacturing (e.g. furniture, textiles). As Lash and Urry argue (1994): 'all industrial production, being design-intensive, is increasingly similar to cultural production' (in McGuigan, 1996: 88).

Models of Success?

Critiques of cultural industry clustering and its contribution to economic development and innovation veer between the sceptical, 'special case' (Curran and Blackburn, 1994; Simmie, 2001); the limited historic/heritage district (e.g. Lowell, MA.);[1] to the instrumental (Evans and Foord, 2000a; Foord, 1999), even celebratory (Hall, 1998; Landry, 2000; Verwijnen and Lehtovuori, 1999). The latter fuels city and other authority intervention through property and economic development programmes which seek to create and enhance production zones and facilities, notably managed workspaces – a more functional re-creation of medieval craft guild quarters. This is an extension of industrial relocation and boosterist strategies which have been long employed (Tuan, 1977). However, cultural production linked to consumption, speciality retail and experiential place-making tends to be understated by economists in their assessment of clustering impacts and motivations. Outside the basic supply and demand relationship, the understanding of 'consumption' and 'symbolic goods' is less developed, let alone conceptualized, than 'production' (Fine and Leopold, 1993; Scott, 2001). A typology of cultural quarters may help in distinguishing their organization and effects, if their assessment and promotion is to be at all appropriate to given local situations. A wider review of agglomeration, or at least spatial clustering of cultural activity, therefore encompasses the following, which are not necessarily exclusive:

• Mono-cultural industry production – vertical dis/integration (e.g. TV/film and music post-production and studios, new media, textiles, ceramics);
• Plural-cultural industry production – horizontal integration (e.g. managed workspaces, visual arts, architecture and design, multimedia, crafts/designer-making, performing arts, arts/resource centres);
• Cultural production-consumption – open studios, art markets (e.g. Spitalfields, Whitechapel, London), events/festivals (e.g. festival marketplace waterfronts – Baltimore, Barcelona, Toronto, Temple Bar Dublin, Bankside London – see Marshall, 2001);
• Cultural consumption – retail (fashion, computing/electronics), street markets (antique, crafts, food); arts and entertainment venues and 'quarters' (e.g. museum islands, theatre and cinema lands, red-light districts, restaurants/clubs/bars – Arrigoni, 2000; Evans, 2001a).

The linkages – production and spatial – between these forms include examples of cultural production supporting performing and broadcast arts in proximity to theatres and studios; retail activity linked to wholesalers, studios and exhibition venues as extensions of production workshops (e.g. furniture, fashion, crafts); and festival marketplaces combining live events, retail and exhibitions. Research into formal as well as informal network processes can also understate the importance of lifestyle and the 'hub and spoke' effects between the large number of micro-enterprises who employ less than five staff, and their much larger clients – public (i.e. government) and private – which include creative generators such as universities/arts and design schools, major corporations, TV/media companies, publishing houses, record companies, art houses and museums/galleries.

Small is Beautiful?

The high proportion of small firms operating in the cultural industries also understates their dependence on the larger enterprise. For instance, the contribution to the total turnover of small firms in the UK represented by *one* main client or customer was found to be over 50 per cent, and the *two largest* clients over 80 per cent (Stanworth *et al.*, 1992) – a Pareto effect where a small number of customers (in value and volume) represents a disproportionately high element of the business/turnover (e.g. an 'independent' TV production company working 75 per cent for one commissioning channel). This is particularly prevalent in self-employment and contract secondment of self-employed artists and creative workers in the fields of arts education, live art and film production and music. A session musician in London may work with numerous artists (bands, orchestras), but in only two or three venues or studio locations financed by a handful of record companies or a state funding body, likewise a freelance writer/journalist working for a handful of publications, and so on.

As an indication of the profile of the small firm in this sector, in a recent study of cultural industries in a fast-growing quarter of East London – Spitalfields, now subject of intensive redevelopment – it was found that 62 per cent of firms were sole traders or partnerships and 53 per cent employed three or less people. These were not, however, marginal enterprises, 54 per cent had been in business over 3 years (most new businesses fail within this time period), primarily in the new media sectors of design, fashion/designer-making, visual arts and audio-visual production (CIDA, 1999). From a separate study of multimedia SMEs in London (Evans, 1996), their micro-scale was shown to belie both high profitability and turnover – the choice to remain 'small' was a personal, lifestyle one, not a sign of poor growth potential, a fact which defies normal business and employment growth models. Proximity to others with this perspective led to their co-location, even if ostensibly in direct competition with one another. With such a 'skewed' structure, it is therefore important to better understand the relationship *between* the large commercial firm and public institutions and the micro-level cultural sectors who service them, if we are to more accurately measure their economic and employment profile, as well as their weaknesses and support needs through clustering and other networking (Evans, 2000a). Viewing the cultural industries simplistically as a vibrant, ever-growing independent sector ignores the causes of structural weaknesses which include a shortage of financial capital (working and investment), extreme lack of R&D, low take-up of training and new technology/ICT (Evans, 2001b), and below-average earnings, often necessitating portfolio careers. The mixed economy in much arts practice and cultural production therefore requires a greater degree of close proximity between places of residence, work and production, which in turn supports the hub and spoke relationships and the concentration of cultural activity in loose sub-regional districts.

Recent examples in Canada include the Cité Multimedia in Montreal's soon-to-be-developed industrial waterfront district, and the Liberty Hall complex in Toronto. In the King-Liberty area, a liberal approach to change of use was combined with restoration of building façades. Following the closure of former factories and warehouses, the area provided a natural incubator for small enterprises initiated by artists and designers. Low-rent premises were adapted for studios and workshops, including live-work accommodation, sometimes in contravention of planning controls. By the early 1990s, however, there was a significant policy shift away from the presumption that industry and housing were incompatible in close proximity. Rigid zoning for industrial use in the City Plan proved a structural constraint for the emerging strategies for regeneration. As in the US and Europe, the recycling of brown-field sites and deliberate creation of mixed land-use neighbourhoods on the fringe of downtown, especially those incorporating cultural industries, came to be seen as desirable aims of planning intervention. Flexible leases combined with easy accommodation of physical expansion enabled some to prosper within an artistic community – both resident and mobile. New media industries moved into this area, serviced by bistro-style bars and restaurants. As an employment district, jobs increased from 3,300 to 3,800 between 1995 and 1999. By 2001 new-build condominium apartments in Liberty Village had clearly become sought after. The lifestyle advantages of King-Liberty were being promoted strongly by real estate agencies, with strap-lines aimed at passing longer-distance commuters such as: 'If you lived here, you'd be home by now!', with parallels to Denver, Colorado's *lo-do* area: 'Kiss the Burbs G'Bye!'.

In Montreal a different approach to the development of creative industries quarters is being pursued. The city-region had been a prime manufacturer in textiles and related production, but as this declined, Montreal had not developed a specific design capability (unlike, say, Northern Italy and Scandinavia) which could switch to other forms of creative industry (e.g. new media, designer-making fashion and textiles). The refurbishment of former industrial premises in downtown/heritage districts and waterside areas is therefore being supplemented with new-build premises to house multimedia firms in order to capture this growing activity, as many other post-industrial cities have done. Grants for firms linked to employment encourage growth over a ten-year period, but the rentals and lease/purchase costs are at commercial rates. Labour and skills are being supported, rather than premises, which has been the model elsewhere (e.g. managed workspaces, subsidized rents/flexible lease terms). The logic in Montreal is that if the firm is successful in developing a service or product which will be competitively financed due to subsidized labour costs, income/profits will be sufficient to pay higher rents and over time increase to attain self-sufficiency once employment subsidies end.

The more recent cultural industry quarters have therefore emerged often as part of, or in response to, the urban regeneration regimes operating in post-industrial cities in North America and Europe, including peripheral regions (e.g. Helsinki – Verwijnen and Lehtovuori, 1999), and more recently in developing countries and emerging world cities, particularly those with their colonial heritage intact. Their short shelf-life and/or their reliance on state subsidy arguably limits their case to be taken as successful, sustainable models until established in a post-dependency phase, which has yet to be reached in cities such as Manchester, Liverpool and Sheffield. Market-led examples also include the boom-bust cycle evident in areas such as SoMa, San Francisco (Berger, 2002; Pratt, 2002), which came and went within a frenzied five-year period. Like urban policy and regeneration evaluation, a longer time period is required in order to both map land-use and economic change, and to test whether an industry quarter is robust, or even a quarter at all. A micro-level analysis of cultural producers and land use is presented below, based on an established cultural industries quarter in London – the area of Clerkenwell on the city fringe – host to crafts and cultural production for over 300 years, and new media and design services and residual crafts/designer-making today.

Clerkenwell, City Fringe: Evolution of a Cultural Industries Quarter

The roots of Clerkenwell's formation as an urban settlement, hosting an evolving range of cultural production, skills and knowledge, draw on its topography, its proximity to the City (outside the City walls, avoiding the power and control of craft guilds), a luxury good clientele (Jardine, 1996), and the cultural capital's growing art and design infrastructure (schools/institutes, performing arts venues). The census of 1861 recorded 877 men who were clock and watchmakers, 725 goldsmiths, 720 printers, 314 bookbinders, 164 engravers, 97 musical instrument makers and 20 surgical instrument makers. 1,477 women were milliners/dressmakers, 267 bookbinders and 33 embroiderers (Olsen, 1982). Much of this activity was housed in live-work premises and workshops supporting a resident community which spilled over to a rich mix of support amenities and social exchange – cultural and political. An area for political discourse, Lenin edited a socialist paper and Marx also resided here, celebrated today in the Marx Library Archive.

One hundred years later this cultural industry quarter still maintained over 900 separate arts and crafts-based firms and artists/designers, nearly 50 per cent in the print/design and jewellery/metal craft trades (Evans, 1990). Its proximity to the City of London, centre of this world city's financial district, also made it vulnerable to property expansion in successive office boom periods, and at the same time the decline of light industrial production as relocation to cheaper and less restricted locations followed the loss of manufacturing in furniture, textiles and watchmaking to overseas competition from Italy, Sweden, Switzerland and Japan. Land-use planning liberalization under the Thatcher regime also removed the protection that change-of-use legislation had afforded, allowing workshop space to be re-used for offices and services, exploiting the shop/accommodation form of housing and workspace. Both workshop/studio and local amenities were thus lost to encroaching office development and services such as estate agents and solicitors, with a commuting rather than residential occupier. The social as well as the economic and cultural fabric of the district was thus diminished. Social and economic change has of course been a feature of urban settlement within which cultural and more symbolic forms have adapted and resisted external forces of change. In this case local crafts communities organized in the late 1960s to limit the change-of-use drift and office development, occupying and using the managed workspace model to develop a complex of light industrial buildings, initially despite local planning authorities who had granted planning permission and disposed of their own holdings in the area, but subsequently with support from both regional and local authorities, as the importance of the cultural industries became a policy concern and later, an economic and cultural strategy (GLC, 1985; DPA, 2000). In 1971, the Clerkenwell Green Association was formed, occupying light industrial buildings divided into 100 to 2,500 square foot studio spaces and offering a flexible letting policy with a minimum commitment and notice period. Over a quarter of the spaces were designated for new crafts firms/artists. Five years later the Clerkenwell Workshops were similarly developed, with support of the then regional authority (GLC) and five years on from then, the nearby Omnibus

Workshops (as its name indicates, a former bus works), all providing shared support services and all-inclusive rents.

From successive surveys of cultural industries activity in this area (Evans, 1989, 1990, 2001c), a general decline and both a spatial and cultural redistribution is evident (see the table and figures below). There has been a 40 per cent loss of cultural sector firms and artists/designers in Clerkenwell between the late 1980s to the turn of the new century, confirming the negative effect of the office development/change-of-use regime over this period. One effect of this has been a drift east, to both established, but cheaper and new urban fringe locations, which are now the subject of cultural industry makeovers and gentrification themselves. The subsequent recession and slowdown in an over-supplied office market offered little respite, since the inner urban housing market took over the conversion of workshop and retail premises, as loft living became fashionable for both single/childless professionals and a second (weekday) home city elite. At the same time there has also been a redistribution of cultural activity across this borough, as the proportion of cultural industries has increased in the north around both retail and night-time economy areas, expanding further and higher education institutions ('hubs') and residential neighbourhoods undergoing regeneration, where re-use and mixed-use development has attracted cultural firms to locate at lower rentals. However, only a 14 per cent decline in arts and cultural production in the borough as a whole has taken place over this decade, with the ebb and flow of firms leaving (relocating, closing down) offset by the fact that nearly 30 per cent of cultural sector firms in this borough had been formed since 1990 (during the 1980s, 35 per cent of the total were likewise newly formed). The cultural industries are therefore a dynamic sector with a core of established organizations and a significant proportion of mobile activity, particularly younger art and design graduates and sole practitioners/artists. This is evident in the longer-established managed workspaces noted above, which continue to host firms which have been in situ since they first opened, particularly in sectors such as architecture and design. These firms could long afford their own premises with more upmarket postcodes, but prefer the atmosphere of the mixed-use facility from which they first grew.

Over this decade the profile of cultural production has also shifted, evident from employment occupation data (standard industry classifications) with a sharp decline in traditional jewellery/metalcrafts and ceramics of between 30 per cent to 60 per cent, and in performing/live arts companies, but with increases in weaving/designer-makers, specialist jewellers/engravers and advanced producer services such as agents, consultants and other intermediaries. This distribution can be visualized in the maps below, showing graphically the concentration of cultural production and services in the southern city fringe quarter, but also the distribution across the borough. This has taken place as much due to market forces as any form of intervention or cultural policy, nevertheless greater distribution has been the goal of local and regional arts bodies (GLA, 1990). This comparative survey also revealed structural changes in employment in the various cultural subsectors. In the late 1980s the average number of people employed in the cultural industries as a whole was twelve, a number weighted by the larger printing and publishing firms employing two to three times the number of people in other less labour-intensive

Table 5.2 Clerkenwell Arts and Cultural Industries Survey, 2001 and 1989

Cultural Industry Sector	No. of firms 2001	%	No. of firms 1989	%
Visual Arts/Crafts	164	33	200	21
Design	134	26	254	27
Print & Publishing	67	13	76	8
Youth & Community Arts/Arts in Education	44	9	50	
Services, Agents etc.	34	7	25	3
Performing Arts/Venue	30	6	143	16
Media, Audio-Visual/Film	19	4	131	15
Museum and Library/Heritage	5	-	10	1
Other	5	-	15	2
Total of Borough, 2001	**507**	**29%**	**904**	**41%**

activity. By 2001 the average employment had nearly halved (even in the printing and publishing industry, due to new technology and contracting out) to seven, with the exception of the performing arts which have been less susceptible to new technology and are more subsidy dependent than design- and artist-based production. Another indicator of structure, the balance between full- and part-time employment, also showed an increase in the use of part-time workers, with the full:part-time ratio moving from 80:20 to 70:30 over this period.

Clerkenwell still survives as one of the longest-established cultural industry quarters, reflecting socio-cultural as well as the more obvious economic and land-use/premises change. Its large managed workspace organizations, residual design and jewellery, and growing nightclub and restaurant quarter ironically flourish as its incumbent residential population declines and a smaller but wealthier resident establishes itself, including a higher-income cultural worker (e.g. in design, new media) able to support a growing café culture and property market. The spatial concentration of activity still distinguishes this district as a viable cultural quarter which has survived largely in spite of planning/zoning and economic development policies, and largely without state arts subsidy. As Jonathan Harvey, co-founder of ACME, one of the UK's most successful workspace developers, opines: 'Until very recently artists were treated with some suspicion by local government: at best, as solutions to vacant property problems; at worst with outright hostility ... [ACME's] work has been in spite of, rather than because of local authority regeneration programmes' (in Wedd *et al.*, 2001: 154). These programmes increasingly look beyond the production facility as the solution to employment and wealth generation in inactive areas, valuing visitor-led solutions built around the

Figure 5.1a   Survey of Arts and Cultural Industries in Islington – Selected Sectors (Evans, 2001c)

Figure 5.1b   Survey of Arts and Cultural Industries in Islington – Selected Sectors (Evans, 2001c)

night-time economy, designer-retail and cultural tourism. Production quarters alone are less attractive prospects, since they are seen to create substitution through the distribution of existing activity, rather than the higher multipliers arising from consumption in general and a higher-spending consumer in particular. Cultural production therefore is increasingly threatened or displaced by cultural *consumption* development, as is evident around major cultural facilities such as Tate Modern, with over 100 resident artists evicted as adjoining property 'hope values' were realized; MACBA, Barcelona, standing sterile in this partially regenerated el Raval district, and which has largely failed to create an independent cultural production quarter (Ulldemolins, 2000; Miles, this volume); and most recently the MuseumQuartier, Vienna, which parachuted in two major contemporary art museums, at substantial cost to the state and city authorities, but which denied incumbent community arts and Turkish youth arts groups their place in this complex. Subsidy was also withdrawn by the state to those groups who were unable/unwilling to use the production-consumption formula of this self-styled 'Shopping Mall for Culture' (Evans, 2001a).

The consumption/production relationship also moves closer to what Marx had constructed through *production as consumption*, each arbitrating and mediating one another (*Grundrisse,* 1973), a relationship never more apparent than in today's consumer culture and cultural consumer. Thus, in his view, new forms of production create new forms of response and new possibilities for consumption.

Production districts emulate this in the combination of design and cultural production with retail, arts and entertainment, hospitality and events/festival activity, and in open studios and specialist markets/exhibitions as promotional devices for studio-based artists and designers (such as *Hidden Art of Hackney* (Foord, 1999), Whitechapel Open, Designer's Block, London); in gallery centres combined with semi-open studios such as HarborPlace, Toronto, and in product design shows (e.g. furniture/interiors) in Barcelona and Milan. However, the new cultural quarters of cities increasingly look to the major public-funded *grand projet* as the focus for ancillary and trickle-down effects on smaller cultural firms and suppliers – the already noted MuseumQuartier, Vienna (Waldner, in Sheffield, 2002); Tate Modern, Bankside, London and other millennial schemes (Birmingham, Salford – Evans, 2002), Guggenheim Bilbao, and further afield, the Esplanade Global City for the Arts, Singapore (Chang, 2000) – to name a few (see Evans, 2003; Zukin, 2001). More local neighbourhood quarters, on the other hand, depend on local regeneration and smaller-scale developments which face a harder task beyond the artist collective and volunteer effort of community action, where an internal market may be insufficient to guarantee their viability and gentrification effects may undermine their initial low rental base, as exemplars of cultural industry development in Manchester and East London now experience (Evans and Foord, 2002). Here, in a celebrated East End cultural quarter, 1,000 local jobs a year have been created, but 'the local unemployment level never seems to change. Partly thanks to the success of Hoxton, land values in the area have soared. So locals who do get jobs often have to move outside the borough. The impoverished artists who created the Hoxton experience in the first place have also moved on because of the rise in property prices' (*The Economist*, 2000). Whilst Manchester's inner-city population has increased five-fold over the past five years – like SoHo New York, Clerkenwell, London and boom-and-bust SoMa, San Francisco, before it – gentrification inevitably undermines production quarters through higher land-use values and capital realization. A few salutary quotes attest to this familiar cycle: 'increasing property rents in Manchester are forcing out creative industries' (Manchester Independents, 2003: news @cids.co.uk); 'The artists' squats have disappeared. Turned over to loft-style living, nearly five years after Hoxton was declared London's art hot spot: is it still hot, or has it become the Covent Garden of the East – all gloss and glamour and no grit?' (Renton, 2002: 53). In one of the most extreme cases, and symbol of the dot.com goldrush, the South of the Market (SoMa) area of San Fransisco saw an influx of over 200 companies in a two square mile radius of South Park: 'we were experiencing the highest residential eviction rates in the country, entire blocks were being completely evicted … Rents simply got way too high. A lot of creative people – architects, engineers, and graphic designers – moved out of the area entirely. They were part of the culture of the city, and now they're gone' (in Berger, 2002: 71, and see Graham and Guy, 2002). 'Hot jobs in cool places?' (Pratt, 2002) – with hindsight, no jobs and no homes in ex-places: South Park currently sits as a desolate green space occupied by rough sleepers, surrounded by vacant premises.

Conclusion

The cultural industry quarter models now promoted as key elements of urban regeneration and place-making strategies in cities worldwide, tend to neglect both the historic precedents and the symbolic importance and value of place and space: 'Cultural quarters are a *fairly recent concept*', writes an architect involved in a scheme to develop a creative industries quarter in the old textiles area of Leicester (Ash, 2003: 5). Where they locate and draw on a manifest authenticity and inheritance of former cultural activity and production – whether symbolic or economic through a residual labour market, higher education hubs, specialist skills and locational advantages – evidence suggests a better chance of success. But examples of workspace facilities as putative quarters based on the 'brick and shed' style urban fringe/suburban business and techno-park facility, which lack sufficient indigenous creative talent and a critical mass of production experience, are more remote prospects for achieving cultural quarter status. In particular, a blind faith in new media and high-tech centres as a panacea for local regeneration appears naïve, as several science and technoparks languish under-used and poorly located. Scott therefore sounds a note of warning: 'As the experience of many actual local economic development efforts over the 1980s demonstrates, it is in general not advisable to attempt to become a Silicon Valley when Silicon Valley exists elsewhere' (Scott, 2000: 27).

How cultural industry quarters have evolved and survived in differing political and cultural regimes can offer clues to how and if they may be developed in the future (and more importantly, how existing ones may be supported). Planning and zoning approaches, including heritage-based protection, also bypass or under-value economic and cultural interaction, focusing on the built environment and fabric but ignoring what goes on inside and between occupants and their constituencies, which includes social, educational and cultural networks, clients and users. These are often hidden, existing in memory, as well as in the finer grain of cultural exchange, whether through the production chain, or through informal networks and synergies that create the creative clusters in the first place. Without these externalities, clusters are little more than an arbitrary concentration of economic activity with little value added or comparative advantage to ensure a viable local production system, let alone opportunities for innovation and wider impacts. As well as a focus on the micro-spatial scale, incorporating the anthropological and as well as the architectural structures and identities which underlie clusters (Kockel, 2003), the relationships between production quarters and other economic flows within the city and beyond – between the micro, meso and global production chain that now operates – will need to be explored if clustering is to retain much *cultural* value and distinctiveness. As Knox (1996: 117) put it: 'We need detailed biographies of cities that set local change in global context … to examine the significance of particular cities as sites for the construction of new cultural identities and political discourses and new processes of political and cultural transformation'.

Note

1   This New England mill town and birthplace of the American Industrial Revolution,
     sought refuge from its industrial (textiles) decline and high unemployment in the 1970s,
     running at 15 per cent. This was found in part through its newly-designated urban
     National Historical Park status in 1984, and the relocation of Wang Laboratories' new
     world headquarters, which attracted smaller technology and support firms. 'Old New
     England City Heals Itself' was a *Wall Street Journal* lead article on 1st February 1985
     which contrasted Lowell's success with the failure of Akron, Ohio (Zukin, 1995).
     However, the employment opportunities to the large minority ethnic population have
     been less apparent, and Wang has since closed, leaving Lowell's heritage industry as its
     main asset, with competing cultural tourism destinations fast multiplying in city, historic
     towns and natural heritage sites.

Chapter 6

Supporting the Cultural Quarter?
The Role of the Creative Intermediary

Tom Fleming

You move to a city. You hang out in bars. You form a gang, turn it into a scene, and turn that into a movement (Anonymous artist, Spitalfields, East London 2000).

The last decade has seen the rise and rise of the cultural and creative industries in the UK:[1] as a construct for policy-making and redefinitions of nationhood; as a sector with economic power and a sexy, BoHo, progressive, inclusive agenda; and as a tool for regeneration and renewal.[2] This embrace with all things creative is part gloss and part realization of the regenerative potential of a sector which, though roughly-hewn as a policy construct by the UK government's Department of Culture, Media and Sport (DCMS) and others, does include major growth areas for the UK economy. More particularly, the creative industries sector is often viewed as a key driver in the economic, social and definitional transformation of UK cities and specific urban districts. It is rich with innovation, often underpinned by new technology, focused through research and experimentation, most successful in specific milieux. What is more, it employs many people, makes a lot of money and, significantly, it sells ideas: ideas of lifestyle; ideas of identity; ideas of the city; and ideas of particular places and spaces – districts, locales, neighbourhoods, networks, clusters and *quarters*.

Little wonder therefore that planners and urban decision-makers are keen to attract creative industries activity and to add value to existing creative assets (Bianchini and Parkinson, 1993; Griffiths, 1998). A sector that offers employment opportunities alongside innovative approaches to physical gentrification, and new identities alongside alternative ways of (re)imagining the urban realm, is an alluring prospect for cities and city districts atrophied through processes of de-industrialization, blighted through poverty and polarization, and left enervated by the absence of a civic identity other than that shaded in the negative (Comedia, 1992; Scott, 1997). Little wonder therefore that there are a multiplicity of examples of cities re-focusing their economic development policies through a cultural lens, many of which are directly embracing creative industries development programmes; a significant proportion of these are delivered through a specific spatial construct – such as a cultural quarter, a network, a cluster or a creative supply chain (Ash, 2003; Evans, 2001a; Hesmondhalgh, 2002).

Proliferating processes of creative industries spatialization are at play in UK cities, attaching old places to new meanings through the allocation of cultural quarter status; utilizing the opportunities provided by diverse, unconventional and relatively affordable building stock; and levering new opportunities offered by public and private finance to position cultural quarters as central or relevant to evolving discourses of the city (from publicity information to multiple senses of place) and to the physical core of the city (disconnection and isolation are not desirable if a cultural quarter is to succeed and grow) (see Boyle, 1993, 1997; Gomez, 1998). Some cultural quarter initiatives attend to the multidimensional, place-specific, yet trans-local focus of the creative industries sector to establish dynamic, sustainable, business-focused environments that offer development opportunities for the sector in ways that enhance the comparative advantage of the entire city. Others range from the shallow to the absurd, the products of overly avaricious civic boosterism initiatives, arbitrarily delineated, under-integrated, fabricated, and thus unconvincing.

The Creative Intermediary

The focus of this chapter is not to antagonize the validity of various cultural quarter models or initiatives; nor to problematize the rather broader tendency to herald the creative industries sector (and the freeplay of meanings it evokes) as a panacea for the woes of post-industrial and increasingly inter-competitive cities seeking a way forward or a way out. The focus of this chapter is to engage briefly with that fleeting, fast-moving, diverse and opaque movement that runs through, runs around in, underpins and often ignores the brand, signature, territory, community and construct that hangs above it as the cultural quarter. The focus here is to make a momentary intervention that offers a way of making sense of the creative industries sector and thus the reciprocal, sensitive creative intermediary services established to support the sector through a closeness unusual in public policy intervention. For without this attention to the dynamics of the sector and the intermediaries that endeavour to serve it, the notion of a cultural quarter – that which hangs above – lacks locatedness: it remains a title that refers to a place with little connection to the multiple processes at work in that place.

The role of the new publicly-funded creative intermediary is little understood and rarely explored. The chapter will introduce the role of the creative intermediary through the presentation and problematization of a creative intermediary tool kit that can be moulded to fit the dynamics of the creative industries sector as they are expressed in specifically local circumstances. In this sense, the creative intermediary is introduced as a vital agent of change for the creative industries sector in specific milieux, but requiring of a set of basic characteristics and qualities transferable across places, if the local sector is to be appropriately served.

The chapter is purposefully focused through experience as a basis for model-building. Deliberately, it is relatively reference-free, written instead through my experience as a creative intermediary, in a creative industries development agency in East London, UK, and supplemented through experience of facilitating the development of intermediary services elsewhere through research and consultancy services.

A Case for Intervention?

Creative industries businesses are *in the business* of cultivating meaning-laden products, while the creative industries sector itself and the space(s) it inhabits lead to particular understandings of ways of living, ways of seeing and ways of planning. The sector is understood to thrive when located within creative clusters, perhaps cultural quarters; it is dependent upon informal networks and face-to-face contact; it requires flexible, accessible supply chains; it feels as comfortable in the café as the office. Creative industries businesses inhabit multiple positionalities, traversing between and across the formal and the informal; the local and the non-local; the subsector-specific and the generic; the lifestyle-oriented and the profit-motivated (see for example Evans and Foord, 2000a; Wynne, 1992; Verwijnen and Lehtovuori, 1999). Creative businesses, and the amalgam or sector that they form, are defined through the creative processes that are at their core. The strategies and accidents, projects and experiments that whirr and fizz to articulate this creativity (such as through products, performances and productions) are discrepant, diverse and always in motion, each contributing to new and evolving, even creative senses of place (see Florida, 2002; Landry, 2000; Landry and Bianchini, 1995).

The task for the creative intermediary is to make sense of these processes, identify opportunities, and offer support in ways that enhance and enable rather than intrude and disable. Used here, the term creative intermediary does not refer to the new petit bourgeois professional identified by Pierre Bourdieu as a carrier of media or arbiter of taste positioned between producers and consumers (see Bourdieu, 1984; Bovane, 1990), perhaps as critics or advertising executives (see Featherstone, 1991; Nixon, 1997). It is perhaps closer to Bill Ryan's (1992) and later, David Hesmondhalgh's (2002) notion of the Cultural Manager, operating in an Artist and Repertoire (A&R) and marketing role for an artist, band, company etc., charged with responsibility to make things happen. Yet this is also limited because it positions the intermediary role in a purely commercial context, with a subsectoral focus. In this chapter, the term creative intermediary refers to that relatively new position of a public-sector employee working in a specific locality, across multiple subsectors, with a very broad remit to facilitate and nurture opportunities that contribute to the sustainable and inclusive growth of the local creative industries sector.

A creative intermediary operates, variously, as a gatekeeper (an access point offering generic and specialist support and advice); a broker (between practitioners and providers as a kind of dating agent); an information resource (providing access to knowledge concerning education and training opportunities, employment initiatives and market opportunities); an initiator (calling for gaps in existing support to be filled and defects in provision to be eradicated); a provider of business support (offering planning advice and signposting); and an advocate (operating as a voice for the diverse activities, networks and enterprises of the creative sector in the locality and beyond). The creative intermediary feels part of the sector; the sector is willingly inclusive of the creative intermediary, and yet the intermediary can look the other way, gain the trust of and seek to influence decision-makers, funders, even consumers.

The aim of the creative intermediary, wherever located, is to provide a flexible service responsive to the changing needs of a transforming sector; to keep in touch with the sector and work within it to nurture those networks, harden those clusters, bridge gaps in those supply chains, and make the cultural quarter work. The task is, with reference to the opening quote by the anonymous East End artist, to nurture an optimum structural and creative ecology for the movement to happen, without relieving the movement of its sectoral ownership or denuding it of the very vibrancy and unpredictability that enabled the gang to grow to form a movement. This chapter will therefore act as an open assessment of the potential challenges, even problems, facing the creative intermediary in a sector that requires space for experimentation and independence, that is suspicious of the potentially corporatizing hand of public policy, and that some argue moves too fast to be touched.

Indeed, perhaps the sector is mercifully impenetrable to the meddling hands of policy-makers: it is organic and explorative; it would rather extemporize than follow a narrow path laid down by a prescribed Business Plan. Yet the creative industries sector *is* replete with policy intervention. Policy-makers and academics rightly recognize the economic, social and cultural importance of the sector; and they value the impression the sector can make on the economies, landscapes and identities of their cities. And then they intervene: in walks the creative intermediary.

Three Central Questions

There are now several dedicated creative intermediary support services in the UK. There is, for example, the Creative Industries Development Service (CIDS) in Manchester;[3] the Cultural Industries Development Agency (CIDA) in East London;[4] the Cultural Enterprise Service (CES) in Cardiff;[5] the Creative Lewisham Agency;[6] and Inspiral in Sheffield.[7] There are creative industries development officers or small creative regeneration-focused teams in places as diverse as Knowsley and Brighton, Hastings and Nottingham.[8] There are a myriad of targeted intermediary-led interventions with different emphases in many towns, cities and rural areas, including creative industries training initiatives (from specialized subsectoral skills to business skills), export-led programmes (including trade and inward missions), and network development/supply chain exercises (from open studios to local procurement policies). Each is predominantly public-sector financed (with a heavy reliance on Single Regeneration Budget and European

Structural Funds) and led; simultaneously output and outcome driven (balancing contractual agreements with funders to broader strategic development for the sector); and structurally positioned between the sector and funding authorities (through strategy, intention and/or legal constitution).

Each also, without exception, exists to serve, add value to or even attempt to establish a creative industries sector that is unequivocally shaped through, dependent on, and transformative of the structures, meanings and opportunities of a specific locality (from a city to a cultural quarter). They are thus place-bound. This is in part due to a realization that the creative industries sector is dependent upon strong local networks, clusters and a scene, if it is to flourish (Evans, 2001a; Pratt, 2002). This is partly driven through an attempt to enhance the competitiveness of towns and cities and to achieve comparative advantage in areas beyond the auspices of the creative industries sector (Zukin, 2001). And this is partly linked to a combination of structural, political and funding-regime factors that require regeneration programmes to focus on a specific (and often arbitrarily-constructed) locality (Bianchini *et al.*, 1988).

By drawing boundaries around intermediary programmes in this way, the intermediary faces at times vexing challenges, often due to the narrow foci of funding regimes or the peculiar boundaries of the eligible regeneration area. However, it is appropriate that the energy of the intermediary is targeted within a specific locality, because it is here that networks develop, ideas are formed and products tested. By acting visibly within the local creative industries sector, the intermediary is best placed to gain credibility, build essential knowledge systems, and make connections, both locally and with markets and suppliers that can stretch across the world.

This local specificity therefore provides the context for the three axiomatic questions that require an answer if creative industries intermediary intervention is to be appropriate, bespoke and beneficial to the growth of the local sector:

- Q1: What are the dynamics of the local creative industries sector (perhaps located within a specific cultural quarter)?
- Q2: How best to support the retention and growth of the sector?
- Q3: What therefore is the position and role of the creative intermediary?

The first question requires an answer because without an understanding of the specific dynamics of the local creative industries sector (and these dynamics are different in every locality), any support initiative will be at best ineffective and at worst extremely harmful. The second question therefore seeks a pathway to make a connection between the distinctly local factors (from subsectoral profiles to gender issues; from the availability of affordable workspace to the best place to grab a coffee), and the corresponding need to establish highly bespoke intervention. The third question guarantees that the role of the intermediary is problematized; that the needs, aspirations and growth potential of the sector are imbricated intensely with the operational modalities of the creative intermediary. Each of the questions provides an opportunity to develop the necessary knowledge systems for creative industries intervention to have a relevance to the sector it is seeking to serve; and for the weighting, position, even tone of the intermediary to fit comfortably and move with a sector that refuses to stand still.

Getting a Sense of Place

This section addresses Question 1: What are the dynamics of the local creative industries sector (perhaps located within a specific cultural quarter)? Recent approaches to or applications of place are different from those that preceded them. Today place is not *about* fixity, enclosure and entrenchment. Neither is it necessarily predicated upon collectivity, internal consistency or community. Instead it operates as a transforming and transformative *process*, socially and culturally (re)constructed through networks of social relations which traverse different localities, drawing on links and conflating and mixing with flows from elsewhere. To be local, to be of a place, is also to be trans-local, to have a 'global sense of the local, a global sense of place' (Massey, 1995: 68). Places are thus 'open and porous' (Massey, 1994: 5), distantiated and disembedded (Giddens 1990).[9] Moreover, they are the contested terrains across which multiple identities are ascribed and prescribed; multiple communities are represented/mapped out, re-imagined and transgressed; and for the creative industries sector, multiple creative processes and products are imagined, produced and located.

What, then, for the creative industries sector, is the sense of a sense of place? If we are constantly looking over our shoulders to the places of our past, if we are ceaselessly searching out, performing, objectifying new identities, if our imagined communities are complexly *globalized*, then surely place is inconsequential, a retrograde lapse.[10] Herein lies the paradox: with the bewildering depthlessness of this 'collapse of spatial barriers' (Harvey, 1993: 293) comes a *'strengthening* of local identities' (Hall, 1992: 306), the 'resacralization of place' (Harvey, 1993: 14). And with an 'objectiveness of increasing connectedness' (Robertson, 1995: 113) come processes of re-interpretation, versioning, localized production, consumption and practice. Senses of place, then, are fragile discursive moments of constructed objectification which continue to develop as part of a *process* of negotiation, production and consumption, that is trans-local yet focused through the contested spatialities and interactions of the local – through the (individual and collective) specificity of the *mix*.

The creative industries sector captures and changes these senses of place – these imagined communities and creative alliances; this mix. The sector is constantly transformed through performed social ties and trade connections; through the conflation, re-articulation and contestation of trans-local concepts, technologies, even policy instruments. The hotbed for this activity is local; the nomenclature through which the sector and its social relations are defined can only be understood in the local; and thus the ideas, friendships, partnerships, parties, networks, are all distinctively local, even if dependent upon influences and structures elsewhere.

Charged with providing support services that are responsive to and embedded within a manifestly and necessarily local creative industries sector, and with responsibility to make the most of the comparative advantage – the distinction – that the sector produces, the creative intermediary needs to deconstruct and indeed embrace the multidimensionality of place. This includes, of course, the specific histories of place; the ethnic mix and syncretic cultural forms this might produce; the intricate intonations of class and gender; and the processes through which these characteristics are transforming. It also includes issues specific to the creative industries sector – such as the direction, profile and quality of networks; market knowledge systems; existing skills and skills gaps; finance opportunities; workspace availability; the strength and coherence of cultural quarters; connection to clusters and networks elsewhere; even individual business issues. Without a highly detailed map of the creative economies and cultural histories of the local, an intermediary will lack the knowledge to act appropriately and will be detached from the personal and structural issues that so inform the identities and development processes of the sector.

Yet a dilemma for a creative intermediary is the indeterminacy of where to look to develop these knowledge systems and interpersonal relations. To simply plunge into a local creative industries sector would be bewildering and disheartening, although this is necessary as part of a broader strategy. A practical starting point perhaps is to focus on those defining principles and common issues for the creative industries sector *wherever* it is located, and to seek to discern and appreciate the ways these generalisms are distinctively articulated in this specific locality.

A Networked Economy

The creative industries sector is dependent upon and re-articulated through networks (see for example, Crewe and Forster, 1993; Crewe, 1996; Purvis, 1996). It is a sector that flourishes through connectivity, be it through brainstorming over a cup of coffee with a neighbour; sharing a stand at a trade show for designer-makers; participating in a local wireless project; or actively forming a studio providers' group. This is because at a local level it is a sector made up of many individual sole traders, small companies and organisations, and larger companies dependent upon smaller companies through creative supply-chain relationships. The sole traders and smaller companies rely on each other to enhance their visibility and voice; to share knowledge and thus improve competitiveness; to develop partnerships (that may be project-specific) for the pursing of specific creative projects/products; to raise their profile en masse; and to improve confidence by reducing isolation. The larger (often non-creative industries) companies rely on the sole traders and smaller companies for specific creative services (an increasingly common requirement with the growing appreciation of creativity-led products and services, and the severance of in-house creative teams), and for enhancing the locality in which they are based (such as through out-of-office services and the ambiance they bring).

Networks and their spatial expression – be they virtual, building-based, subsector-specific, formalized, raggedly informal, social or business oriented –

provide the local creative industries sector with its infrastructure and filigree; its sense of place and source of inspiration; and the media for expression, exploration and the translation of ideas into economic reward. The task for the creative intermediary is to make sense of these networks, identify the key components of supply chains, and provide opportunities and initiatives that add resources and infrastructure to existing networks, make connection between those where it is productive to do so, and work in partnership with the sector to facilitate new ones where there is a sector-led desire to do so. This is a role intrinsic to the intermediary's broader task of creative place-building (Goodwin, 1993; Crewe and Beaverstock, 1998).

A Shy Economy

Despite its propensity for networking and dependence on networks, the creative industries sector is not made up of boisterous, dauntless networkers, confident in themselves and promiscuous in the routes they will take to develop ideas and secure business. The sector is distinctive in terms of its relative youth, with a large proportion of very young practitioners, fresh out of college, lacking business skills, weak of voice, unaware of how to articulate their creativity as commodity. It is also a sector with a high proportion of practitioners who are relatively old in years but new to the sector, often developing creative businesses as a second or third career. They can be nervous, unsure of how to develop viable businesses, made hesitant by the general youth and vivacity of the wider sector and the way the sector is (re)constructed as cool, radical, and therefore demographically exclusive. Similarly, it is a sector that is dependent upon yet socially exclusive to a diverse and talent-bulging community sector. There are significant cultural and fraternal barriers to talented individuals and innovative social enterprises endeavouring to develop businesses in the creative industries sector. Indeed, such is the exclusivity of the sector, with its networks limited in their reach, that many highly creative individuals are not even aware of the potential of their talent to be translated as a commercial commodity. The sodality of the creative industries sector, the debarring qualities of its networks, and the absence of a dedicated approach to career path development, all introduce challenges for the creative intermediary striving to stimulate openness, inclusivity and confidence (see Leadbeater and Oakley, 1995).

The sector is also shy because it does not have a coherent, articulate, confident voice. A further challenge for the creative intermediary is to overcome the lingering doubts of decision-makers regarding the value and potential of the creative industries sector, and a belief by many that the sector does not hold together as a range of subsectors underpinned by coherent values, approaches, needs, aspirations and issues. Taken as a whole, there are great disparities between the content, function and direction of creative industries subsectors. There is a lack of awareness, from creative businesses, decision-makers and commentators, of what the sector means, who it represents, how it can feasibly ally divergent sub-sectors, many of which do not consider themselves to be a part of a unified creative industries sector. This is because, of course, it is a policy construct, devised as much for delivery purposes as for nurturing cosy creative communities.

However, it is also a progressive cultural concept. With creativity at their core, there is scope for highlighting the connections between subsectors as divergent as film and graphic design, theatre and new media. This is not just because of potential supply-chain relationships between subsectors (although these are important), but because of what these sometimes discrepant subsectors can bring to a specific locality (from a cultural quarter to a nation). The ways creative businesses and activities indulge themselves with the cultural distinctiveness of the places and spaces of their creative (re)production, and the ways they then imbue places with notions and feelings of creativity that far outstrip the relatively basic development of creative products, require that they are approached as a whole (with targeted subsectoral intervention). This also requires that they are understood and supported as operating within a broad and diverse creative place as part of a creative industries sector that serves and continually reinvents that place.

In this sense, the creative industries sector refers to different things in different places. The task for the creative intermediary is to articulate that difference to decision-makers as a local strength that is directly economically productive (it is a fast-growing sector), and absolutely vital for engendering creativity across communities towards creative senses of place. The task for the creative intermediary is thus to make the case, have the sector taken seriously, and thus raise the necessary investment and infrastructural support for the sector to fulfil its potential.

A Knowledge-Reliant Economy

Creative industries businesses are key knowledge producers, with a major influence over patterns of economic production and consumption, plus an energetic role in recreating senses of place and identity (from Britishness to Mancunianness).[11] They are also intrepid knowledge consumers, unbridled and exuberant in their search for new information, ideas and technologies; unbounded in their capacity to experiment to develop new concepts, forms and thus knowledges. However, this creative knowledge exploration often distracts from the search for practical knowledges; from opportunities, assistance and tricks that will help them to translate their creativity into commodities that sell.

Most creative industries businesses are not fulfilling their potential to become profitable businesses. There are fashion designers with great ideas but little concept of the market for these ideas; there are furniture designers showcasing prototypes at inappropriate trade shows; there are musicians peddling demos to every record company listed, as if this will work. For a knowledge-rich sector, creative industries businesses in any locality are remarkably under-informed.

This is due to the absence of dynamic, inclusive networks, which are excellent ways to stumble across vital knowledge or can be used to channel targeted and specialist information (such as how to develop export markets if you are a designer-maker) (see Castells, 1996). It is an outcome of the shyness and isolatedness of much of the sector, in particular sole traders. It can be linked to the low business aspirations of many creatives (even a lack of awareness that their skills and products are potential commodities), many of whom are doing what they do for reasons of lifestyle. And it is due to the absence or failure of dedicated information, business support and advisory services for the creative industries sector, established to produce and enhance knowledge systems – of markets, competitors, skills/training options, even the best place to go for a high-quality yet affordable reprographics service. The creative intermediary thus has another challenge: to be a provider of and signposter to knowledge that will enhance the competitiveness of the local creative industries sector, to make the sector aware of its potential, and to improve the confidence of the sector so that it utilizes knowledge in productive ways. The creative intermediary must manage information, keep abreast of what is happening, know where to go and who to talk to find things out (things that are often very specialist), and ensure therefore that the networks are bristling with knowledge.

An Economy Founded on Risk and Trust

A sector that thrives through its innovativeness and is deliberate in its efforts to experiment, is a sector familiar with the notion of risk (Raffo *et al.,* 1999). Yet exercised risks are too often extended into business strategies, partnership arrangements and non-contractual relationships. The informal, often social-driven networks that are so important for the knowledge systems of the creative industries sector, are carried into transactions and deals often based on little other than alcohol-inflated trust. There is a dilemma where the camaraderie and kinship necessary for a flourishing local creative industries sector leads directly into hasty and under-informed decisions that have a business cost and invidiously compromise the ownership of intellectual property.

The challenge for the creative intermediary is to provide information (from markets to business practice) to ensure that risk is exercised in a more strategic context. The challenge is also to mediate the interpersonal dynamics of the sector, warning businesses against hasty and under-informed decisions, providing contractual templates, and maintaining a presence to ensure that projects and partnerships are monitored. But the greatest challenge here is to find ways of introducing businesses to each other (and thus passing a judgement on who can work together), formalizing partnerships where there are critical levels of risk, and intervening to provide essential business knowledge before any commitments are made; yet also allowing the sector to promiscuously network and to develop its own codes and laws of trust, and letting it be known that to succeed, creative businesses/projects may first (and several times thereafter) fail.

An Evanescent Economy

Creative businesses are luminaries of many local economies. Not because they are the biggest businesses or the even the most inclusive, but because they produce meaning-laden goods and forms that provoke opinions; they connect to and (re)create identities around and through which consumers assemble, negotiate and contest. Yet while the sector itself may maintain a high profile, it is in a state of perpetual transformation: new businesses emerge, old businesses close down or move away, retained businesses change and change again their products and approaches. A sector that is in the business of creating meaning is vulnerable to the vicissitudes of a cultural politics of taste, which has direct material implications for business growth (or the lack of it). Some businesses are able to change, yet many creative businesses are fastened to a singular creative approach/style/form that suffers if the market moves away. In addition, many creative subsectors – such a fashion or film – have a market interface that is seasonal or for which there is a considerable lag between the initial idea and the opportunity to sell it.

It is important therefore that creative intermediaries saturate the local sector with information on trends and markets; seek to secure relevant showcase opportunities for innovative market-leader companies; and maintain the profile of sectors while they are hidden in tenebrous studios and offices, so that by the time the lights go on, a welter of market expectation has formed. Once again, the creative intermediary is assigned a duty that requires looking many ways all of the time.

Living and Breathing the Sector: Positioning the Creative Intermediary

This section addresses Question 2: How best to support the retention and growth of the sector? and Question 3: What therefore is the position and role of the creative intermediary? The creative intermediary and/or creative intermediary service (such as an agency) might therefore be conceptualized as a network builder and facilitator; a confidence primer; an advocate and champion; a knowledge resource and research agent; a broker; an opinion former; a representative; a presider over catalysing processes. In short, the challenge is to do everything that can be possibly done to keep the movement going and to do it, wherever possible, in ways that secure the independence and sense of ownership of local creative businesses. For this to be achieved, intermediary services work most effectively when they are positioned and inflected in ways that complement the practices, lifestyles and lexicon of the local creative industries sector. A network will be empty of participants if it holds no resonance for the sector; just as a business support service will be avoided if it provides inappropriate information or presents a disconnectedness to the sector it is supposed to serve. A successful creative intermediary service abides by, engages with, and feels a part of the cultures and proclivities of the creative entrepreneur. To do this requires a change of approach and emphasis according to location and client. However, just as there are common factors connecting creative industries businesses in different localities (see Hesmondhalgh, 2002; Louise, 2003; O'Connor and Wynne, 1996), there are operational characteristics necessary for the creative intermediary service to adopt if it is to complement these common factors. These are elements of the creative intermediary tool kit.

Accessibility

A creative intermediary and/or intermediary service is approachable, within reach. Unlike many of the traditional business support agencies, and certainly at variance to most local authority departments, accessibility is paramount. This refers not just to the capacity of the intermediary to visit individual businesses or make appointments at short notice. It refers to the *culture of support provision*. This includes the clothes an intermediary wears, the language employed, the level of formality and familiarity, the acceptance that there are many ways of addressing a project or problem. The creative industries sector is dependent upon distinct processes of risk and trust, and thus the relationship between client and intermediary must be formulated through a process of creative partnership, where solutions are identified and targets drawn in anticipation – through trust – that each party is investing similarly in the risk, and that each party feels comfortable in the relationship.

Flexibility

Allied to accessibility, a creative intermediary and/or intermediary service has the in-built capacity to be responsive – to opportunities, barriers, and dilemmas. Working across a range of subsectors, each made up of individuals and businesses with complex profiles, the intermediary must be absolutely ensconced in these individual and collective narratives if support provision is to have any relevance to this transforming landscape. The strategies of the intermediary must range therefore from one that accommodates new ideas and is willing to pursue them in partnership; to an acceptance that a technique of support provision (such as a nascent network for a specific subsector) is not operating successfully, thus necessitating an alternative approach. The true test of this flexibility is if a previously unseen creative business with a set of entirely idiosyncratic characteristics and issues approaches the intermediary, and the intermediary is able to work with the client to identify opportunities or create them if they do not presently exist. To be able to do this for the whole local creative industries sector, simultaneously making connections with markets and supply chains elsewhere (not to mention decision-makers and funders), is flexibility indeed.

Knowledge-Rich

Creative businesses are knowledge-reliant. A creative intermediary service must therefore be a provider of knowledge (from market knowledge to a database of affordable workspace); a researcher of knowledge (for the type of knowledge demand is always changing); and a signposter to knowledge (knowing where to locate knowledge is as important, given that there is of course too much to know at once). Knowledge services might therefore include that which is carried in the head of the intermediary (such as a deeply engaged understanding of the way markets work or of funding sources); accessible library services (with trade press and funding directories); on-line directories (often used to underpin a network);

signposting (to specialist knowledge sources or other businesses); and research (finding out information to which there is no obvious path).

Of equal importance, however, are the skills of the intermediary in translating these knowledges to provide practical market value or project development expertise. This in itself requires a specific strain of knowledge. Locating a potential funder or investor is unproductive if the knowledge of how to reach, court and convince is absent. Similarly, knowledge that there is a potential market for a specific product in a distant place is fruitless without the knowledge systems requisite to reach the market with the message, entice the market, and carry out the necessary production and distribution processes. An intermediary that carries these knowledges or knows how to access them is a significant asset to the local creative industries sector. If these knowledges are absent, then it is incumbent upon the intermediary to develop skills programmes to ensure they are developed somewhere in the local creative milieu.

Explorative and Entrepreneurial

A local creative industries sector consists of multiple innovating, probing, experimenting, often boundary-crossing individuals, businesses and projects. Such processes are the foundations of creativity. Each creative process presents new practical challenges – from identifying markets to reaching them; from finding appropriate spaces for showcasing or expressing the product to securing the funds to do so. These in turn are translated as challenges to the creative intermediary, and because they are unconventional challenges, the response of the intermediary is necessarily explorative and always entrepreneurial. An intermediary service might thus explore finance options that vary from the norm; it might seek to bring together a partnership or collective (as a small and focused network) to lead a project; it may attempt to bring into use a redundant building for a specific performance or longer-term tenancy. All the time, the creative intermediary must be learning, listening to the sector, eavesdropping on discussions elsewhere (in the local authority, at the regional development agency), and experimenting with this knowledge to support initiatives that might focus on an individual artist, or on an entire sector.

Persuasive

The creative intermediary is therefore sector-focused, accessible, flexible, knowledgeable, explorative and entrepreneurial: like the sector for the sector. Yet the creative intermediary is also an interface and translator – between the creative industries sector, the processes and flows of policies, funding regimes, training programmes, and any other opportunities or impediments that have a resonance for the local creative industries sector. This requires that the creative intermediary secures partnerships with decision-makers and public/private-sector investors to ensure that funding, workspace and other initiatives are beneficial to or even targeted towards the creative industries sector. It requires that the creative intermediary acts as a representative of and advocate for the sector, thus necessitating the establishment of trust with both the sector and those with the power and resources to influence it. It requires therefore that the intermediary comfortably traverses between spaces that are formal and informal; institutionalized and proudly independent; inherently bureaucratic and haphazardly systems-less. It requires that the creative intermediary wears a suit for at least some of the time.

Efficient, Systems-Proficient and Numerate

Creative intermediary support services are predominantly public-sector funded. This requires an attention to issues of accountability, output counting, number crunching and intense management scrutiny. The creative intermediary is required to balance flexible embeddedness with the local creative industries sector with the painstaking, often meaningless monitoring processes and inflexible payment procedures insisted upon by public sector programme managers. These output-heavy regimes, though often devised for programmes in other, more traditional sectors such as construction, place enormous pressure on the creative intermediary to serve a sector while inflicted with administrative misery. This extends further the skill-sets required within an intermediary support service, and can work to undermine the credibility of the service within the sector it is seeking to serve (see Verwijen, 1999).

Challenges: Corporate Narcissism or Local Sensitivity?

Creative intermediary services are undertaking some progressive and effective work in support of the local creative industries sector and creative communities across the UK. It is often the creative intermediary service that organizes the open studios event; provides specialist business advice surgeries; undertakes trade missions; manages the fashion design network; introduces one business to another. It is the creative intermediary service which coordinates the activities that add legitimacy to the cultural quarter. From Hidden Art in Hackney[12] to Bristol's bid to be European Capital of Culture in 2008,[13] it is creative intermediaries who lead the way. Opportunistic, proactive and responsive, the task of the creative intermediary is to identify, pursue and implement projects and programmes that are absolutely in tune with the development needs and potential of the local creative industries sector. That in part explains the divergent models, structures and subsectoral emphases of creative intermediary services in different places. It also explains the need for intermediary services to invest as much energy focusing on model-building, delivery structure, staffing profiles and other in-house organizational issues, as on understanding the cultures, practices and processes of the local sector.

The manifold and diverse roles incumbent on a locally sensitive and tailored creative intermediary service require that the service look as carefully at itself as the sector it is seeking to serve, because without this matching of structure and delivery with need, the local creative industries sector will be inappropriately supported, under-supported, even harmed. This is a cultural process as much as it is structural, because for a creative intermediary service to gain the trust of creative businesses and organizations (and thus be in a position to offer support), it must be able to operate across a range of cultural paradigms and maintain a cultural credibility across different creative communities. There is thus a necessary level of corporate narcissism and self-absorption, which might be understood as an iterative process of evaluation and (re)action. However, there is also a danger that creative intermediary services, in their efforts to be at one with the sector and snuggle up to its social and cultural communities, can become intoxicated by a vanity that affords the public-sector service with the same glamour as the creatives at its door.

Creative intermediary services are not and cannot be as progressive, dazzling and voguish as large parts of the creative industries sector. They must be explorative, flexible, resourceful, entrepreneurial; but they cannot reach the untrammelled, giddy latitude of a fast-moving and diverse sector of highly creative businesses. Nor should they believe this is possible. For all of their sentience and fine-grained responsiveness, creative intermediary services remain public-sector structures with attendant issues of accountability, the need to reach outputs, and political expectations; as well as a range of demands from potential beneficiaries with agendas that may lie outside of the remit of the service. The creative intermediary service must find a way of supporting the diverse needs of multiple subsectors with highly disparate needs, all within a very limited budget. The service must balance acutely-targeted intervention to a more generic support approach that caters for larger parts of the sector. The service must develop links between a creatively rich yet information and expectation poor community sector, and a socially/ethnically exclusive creative business sector. The creative intermediary service is thus stricken by a burden of representation that exists even before the crushing weight of public sector accountability (and the inflexibility and corporatization therein) is added.

There are many activities and measures that the creative intermediary service cannot and should not pursue. There are many things that the creative intermediary service cannot and should not be. A service that is over-stretched and functionally dispersed, and that imagines itself to have the glamour and fleet-footedness of its client businesses, is as ineffective, erroneous and shallow as many cultural quarter constructs. If the gang is to turn into the movement, then it is as much as task of the cultural intermediary to limit its service; to let the sector lead; and, for the long-term development of the sector, to *learn to let go*.

A cultural quarter requires legitimacy and ownership from resident businesses and communities: it needs to make sense to them. The creative intermediary has a prominent role to play in *making the quarter work*, and this is achieved by creating opportunities for the sector to claim space and make place so that the quarter is understood as a compelling, distinctive, transforming milieu for which they can stake a claim. In this way, creative businesses can find room to contest the meanings, boundaries, internal dynamics and external links of the cultural quarter, but at least they accept that it or at least some kind of spatially expressed local creative movement *actually exists*.

Notes

1   Referred to in this chapter as the creative industries for reasons of continuity, not for reasons of pedantry: a descent into that irksome definitional impasse has hindered the development of policy and academic debate for too long.

2   A 2003 conference led by Demos, BURA, RICS and English Partnerships, focusing on creativity and the future of UK cities (see www.bura.org.uk/events). With keynote speaker Richard Florida, the conference seems to elevate the significance of creativity as an (if not *the*) essential baseline for a city's comparative advantage. However, by attaching nebulous straplines such as BoHo, strong arguments are trivialized and cynics mobilized. Just as there was a counter-culture to the Cool Britannia tag, BoHo Britain is a term likely to distract and antagonize rather than focus and galvanize.

3   See www.cids.co.uk

4   See www.cida.co.uk

5   See www.cultural-enterprize.com

6   See www.creativelewishamagency.org.uk

7   See www.inspiral.org.uk

8   See Louise, 2003.

9   As a means to discuss the ways in which space and time are increasingly compressed, Giddens identifies two related processes – distantiation and disembedding. Distantiation refers to 'the conditions under which time and space are organized so as to connect presence and absence' (1990: 14); while disembedding focuses on the disjuncture of social relations from their local contexts and their relocation and restructuring 'across indefinite spans of space-time' (21). The local and the global are thus caught up in a dialectical swirl that prioritizes neither and emphasizes their mutuality and inseparability.

10   Here this refers to the constant syncretism, creolization and interchange of cultural consumption and performance (see for example Hannerz 1987, 1990, 1996), rather than to one global, homogeneous, *mass* culture. This is similar to what Roland Robertson configures as 'the scope and depth of consciousness of the world as a single place', establishing place as an *aspect* of globalization rather than something which prefigures or opposes it (Robertson, 1995: 30-35).

11   Halfacre and Kitchin, 1996; Haslam, 1999; Milestone, 1996 and discuss the power of new cultural forms in the (re)construction of new Mancunian senses of place.

12   See www.hiddenart.com and Foord, 1999.

13   See www.bristol2008.com

Chapter 7

Popular Music, Urban Regeneration and Cultural Quarters: The Case of the Rope Walks, Liverpool

Abigail Gilmore

This chapter examines the development of a 'creative quarter' in the city of Liverpool, UK, which formally began in 1997 and had its official opening in 2002. I discuss the role and involvement of the local popular music sector in this process of quarterization. I argue that the 'local musical spaces' which were favoured within this process are organized around particular music activities and music businesses which fitted with the dominant model for the creative quarter, and which were anchored to music consumption and the night-time economy in particular. These dominant forms reflect an ongoing relationship between the local music sector, local authorities and policy-makers. This context of public-sector involvement in cultural industries policy includes a complex range of discourses employed in the relationship between the local music industry and the city. This been constructed through conflict over the connections between music, local economic development and city image, described by Cohen (2002: 263) as a 'political battlefield'.

The continued development of cultural quarters as a popular focus for culture-led regeneration in the post-industrial city demands a critical approach to the quarterization process, not least since there are more examples and models for implementation in existence from which to learn. However, the evaluation of the 'success' of cultural quarters is problematical. Firstly, as a relatively recent formalized technology of urban and cultural planning, they lack longevity, leading to the sense that 'only time will tell', coupled with a lack of critical distance. Secondly, and in tension with the first problem, they are not fixed and cannot be summed up with a teleological account, but are best seen in relational terms (Amin and Graham, 1999) as sites for the dynamic sets of flows, practices, networks and nodes which thread through their materiality. Regeneration is a fluid, ongoing, uneven process, rather than a single achievable state, which makes the parameter-setting for an appropriate evaluation period difficult: at what point does a cultural quarter start or end diachronically? Thirdly, and most importantly, there is a range of perspectives and interests that need to be taken into account in their assessment, which adopt different frameworks and definitions of 'success', and which variously include or exclude the interests of different social groups, including politicians and policy-makers, communities of place, identity and interest, residents, economists, tourists, place-marketeers, audiences and creative practitioners.

The initiative which resulted in the Rope Walks Quarter (formerly known as the 'Duke Street/Bold Street' area) in Liverpool attempted to take on board past lessons and satisfy the many diverse groups with interests in the area, through an 'integrated action plan' developed in 1997. I want to consider the plans for this cultural quarter as a way of thinking about how music (and most notably in this case popular music/music defined by its proximity to industrial production) is inscribed by the regeneration process in the production of the cultural quarter and the wider city, and how the interests of local music industry practitioners are represented. Suffice to say, this is not an assessment of the Rope Walks Quarter's success but an opportunity to consider music's place in urban regeneration in relation to a particular, situated initiative.

Popular Music and Regeneration

In the general context of arts and culture-led urban regeneration, music is represented as particular sets of cultural practices, which can take on a number of useful roles. Musical performances, events and products may attract visitors, project and express local identity to a wider market and encourage consumption of place at a more or less local level – through the musical legacies mediated through cultural tourism, or the constructions of place in exported product (songs, tunes, styles and stars). Music as a creative industries subsector, with a typically complex and protracted production chain and set of business practices, is also considered in terms of its role in wider economic and skills-base development criteria, and has a history of involvement in social regeneration through initiatives and projects aimed at social inclusion and community development. However, music, in particular popular music, also creates problems for urban regeneration, through its evolving, dynamic and elusive qualities which prove hard to capture and relate to initiatives geared to improving public realm and built environment, through its audibility and its potential to disrupt public space, and through its ties to youth culture, risk, rebellion and disorder.

For the purposes of thinking about cultural quarterization as a technology of regeneration I want to distinguish between music consumption and production in relation to place. The former includes music venues, museums and centres as flagship projects, and the regulation of public (and semi-public) space in relation to noise and soundscapes (for example, with entertainments licensing and busking controls, and the use of music scenes and stars, local consumption practices and the notion of local sounds or musical styles in place-marketing and cultural tourism). The latter emphasizes the networks, strategies and conditions for the business of music creation, reproduction, distribution and retail and how the 'local' provides for these activities in competition with other industrial centres of production and within the context of the global music industry. Identifying a discrete division between consumption and production is somewhat artificial, given their inconnectedness and the importance of consumption to the production of place, but I want to employ them heuristically as polar distinctions to allow for consideration of the homology between music and the dominant models for cultural quarters.

Popular music performance has long been associated with regulatory cultural policy, from state intervention into the freedom of street musicians to concerns over the moral and physical safety of pubs and music halls in the nineteenth century, exercised through licensing reforms (Bailey, 2002; Crump, 1986; Hoher, 1986). Proposals for public entertainments licensing reform in England and Wales, tabled through the 2000 White Paper *Time to Reform*, which devolves licensing decisions back to local authorities and re-defines what constitutes public performance, are currently re-invoking debates over the rights of musicians and the general public to hold performances in public space. At stake is a fine balance between producing animated city centres and sustainable night-time economies, and regulating the behaviour of musicians and music audiences.

Music tourism and the presentation of music heritage sites, routes and purpose-built visitor attractions has expanded in recent years to become a more visible (if not audible) part of the cultural/visitor economy in cities, with a number of new flagship developments based around celebrating and exhibiting musical production associated with place, with varying degrees of success. The Experience Music Project in Seattle and the Rock and Roll Hall of Fame in Cleveland have been lauded, whilst the National Centre of Popular Music in Sheffield was damned prior to opening, closed less than a year later, then damned further. Birmingham's cultural renaissance and regeneration have been variously attributed to Simon Rattle, the City of Birmingham Symphony Orchestra and the 1992 Year of Music (Bailey, 2002), and Vienna's House of Music presents an interactive account of music's importance whilst contributing to the place marketing of the 'proverbial capital city of music'. There are countless other city initiatives which aim to exploit local music for tourism purposes, including the expansion of festivals from local celebrations to commercial operations geared to producing optimum impact from visitor economies.

New emphases on cultural production and profits in the economic turn of cultural policy have allowed a new respectability for popular music in the UK. As part of the embrace of creative industries by policy-makers from the mid-1980s onwards, the music industry, and most notably the recording industry, has been heralded for its export value and for helping to position British creativity on a world stage (Brown, O'Connor and Cohen, 2000). Recent studies have looked at the contribution of popular music to economic development, both in the context of creative industries auditing and economic impact studies (see for example, Dane, Feist *et al.*, 1999; Towse, 1993) and in terms of cultural policy issues and debates (see for example, Brown, O'Connor and Cohen, 2000; Cohen 2002; Cohen, 1991a; Shank, 1994).

So music consumption and production has an uneasy relationship to urban regeneration, and I want to think about how both perspectives – consumption-oriented and production-oriented – are represented in the story of the regeneration of a 'creative quarter' in Liverpool. Much of the material presented here originated from research conducted for a project on music policy and local economic development, which coincided with the consultation and planning exercises for the Rope Walks Quarter.[1]

A(nother) Creative Quarter: From Industrial Zone to the Liverpool Rope Walks

A frequent observation within the regeneration process of the Rope Walks is that this particular area has had more regeneration plans then anywhere else in Liverpool. This is not without reason. The area of 37.3 hectares designated as what was to become the Rope Walks Quarter had, in 1997, a socio-economic profile that included high levels of unemployment (in excess of 30 per cent in the overlapping Duke Street/Cornwallis Pathways area); low skills and educational attainment levels; very low residential levels within the Quarter itself (between 100-200 people); poor communication and transport links; and high crime rates. As the planning process began, there was a degree of migration of small businesses from the area, and a negative external image – low morale within resident businesses and problems of litter and public disorder – which were perceived to be spilling over to the main shopping and working area of the city centre.

The designated area was a densely-packed zone of warehouse buildings, retail and industrial units, laid out in a narrow grid system stretching downhill towards the centre of the city and its main large-scale retail area. It contained many of the right ingredients for regeneration as a quarter: built heritage assets, traces of its industrial past (the centre for rope making and supply to the shipping industry; merchant warehouses and residences), cheap (in some cases free) workspace for artists, musicians and other creatives, licensed venues, pubs, clubs and bars that stretched back into Liverpool's musical past, secret spaces – courtyards, alleys and squares – and seeds of organic activity filling these places. Despite a feeling of intense, burgeoning dilapidation manifest in litter-strewn streets and derelict buildings, and 'dead zones' where at certain times of the day and night particular spots were un-peopled/unsafe, at the beginning of the regeneration programme the area was an existing centre of creative and cultural activity. Cultural production and creative industry – specialist retail, exhibition and studio space, recording, rehearsal and performance facilities, design businesses, media production companies – had been present in the area for some time, reflected in the will to capitalize on indigenous cultural activity found in previous plans for regeneration.

In 1958, the area was first designated as a predominantly industrial zone in the City Development Plan; this was reaffirmed in the 1966 City Centre Plan and 1972 City Centre Plan Review. In 1987, Liverpool City Council formally acknowledged the cultural heritage importance of the area defined by Duke Street and Bold Street and in 1988 the Duke Street Conservation Area was established, encompassing over 80 listed buildings. In 1989, a City Council-commissioned report first labelled the area a 'cultural district'.[2] It recommended design-led regeneration, based within the development of design production in the city from crafts and cottage industry towards larger-scale production within manufacturing. It was supported by the research of Comedia and the Centre for Urban Studies, Liverpool University, into the role of design in local economic development. The report suggested that there was an insufficient infrastructure to retain the design talent present in Liverpool, particularly developed through fashion and design courses at the city's colleges and universities, and that this talent was lost or drained away from Liverpool. It also suggested there was insufficient awareness of the potential of profit in design on the part of manufacturers. The report recommended strategic development of the design sector, including a number of initiatives and institutions that would underpin the design community as part of a 'production oriented "cultural district"'. The 'Duke Street/Bold Street' area was seen as the ideal location because of its arts, craft and design businesses and restaurants, bars and live music venues, its status as an under-used urban area and the potential for cross-subsidization including European monies, funding from the Urban Programme and private investment, potentially from Irish banks.

The City Council produced an action plan in 1990, assembling all existing plans for the area and instigating a new partnership between the London developers Charterhouse Estates (who had begun to buy up the Council's freehold interests in the area in 1989) and the City Council. This proposed a 'Creative Industries Quarter' in the Duke Street conservation area, and launched a programme to establish the 'cultural district', combining residential, office, speciality shopping, restaurants, arts venues and workspace for crafts, design, fashion, electronic music and the media. Expected outputs from the ten-year programme were investment of more than £100m into the area and the creation of 2,500 jobs. Comparing the programme to other quarter initiatives then in existence, such as Merchant City in Glasgow, Little Germany in Bradford, and the Cultural Industries Quarter in Sheffield (a visit by cultural practitioners and policy makers to the CIQ to look at best practice had been funded by the City Council in 1989), the plan aimed to situate cultural industries at the heart of the physical regeneration of the area, and as a flagship development in the Council's cultural policy-led regeneration strategy.[3]

By April 1990, Charterhouse had acquired around 350 properties (comprising 75 per cent of the building stock) from the Council at cut-price cost of £8 million, thus effectively transferring the area (and with it the responsibility for regeneration) from public to private ownership. They held a three-month exhibition-based consultation exercise, inviting the local communities to view the plans for the Creative Industries Quarter, which included a performance venue and managed workspace development and proposed an 'equity lease-plan' which would involve selecting prospective tenants from the creative industries. These tenants would then be offered a share in the increase of value by virtue of their 'sweat equity'. The programme emphasized that regeneration for the 'quartier' should be creative industries-led, anchored to organic development and nurturing existing conditions for creative practice, having debated the problems with large-scale physical redevelopment which might have priced out existing businesses from the area: 'Outlandish as it might seem to us now, we must be concerned that the area does not go too far up market, and become a devalued caricature of its previous self. We can benefit not by racking up rents unduly but by inserting new buildings at enhanced levels of return'.[4]

However, in 1992 Charterhouse went into receivership, the land stock was purchased by Frensons (the majority holder at 150,000 sq ft) and Rosemary Duke Street (a joint venture between Cruden Construction, Tweeds and the Dean of Liverpool) and the plans for the area dissolved. The consequences of this episode were profound, as residents and businesses were frustrated, disappointed and disillusioned by a company coming from outside Liverpool and promising great change with no positive outcome. Frensons, the new majority land-holders, made little apparent move to redevelop the area, leaving buildings to decline, amidst reports of money laundering and illegal trading in property. Land acquisition in the area became even more problematical: knowledge of who actually owned what became obscured, and the City Council proved reluctant to buy back the land under Compulsory Purchase Orders, citing pressure on public funds, or to place renovation orders on property which might have made it cheaper to acquire privately.

In 1993, Merseyside was awarded European Union Objective One status and became England's first Objective One area, initiating a five-year programme with the potential for £1.25 billion investment, comprising £630 million European funds matched by UK Government and other funds. In 1994, a further study was conducted on the Duke Street/Bold Street area to consider the feasibility of progressing regeneration, identify funding packages and examine the lessons that could be learnt from the previous years.[5] It prepared the ground for the Rope Walks regeneration scheme, initiating and advising discussions between English Partnerships and the City Council over the structure and accountability involved in the joint venture.

The mid-1990s saw a convergence of expanding bar culture, post-Militant recovery, Objective One status and a cumulative history of urban regeneration programming, strongly anchored in arts and cultural assets-led approach piloted in the regeneration of the Albert Docks, but characterized according to some observers as a story of 'missed opportunities' (Parkinson and Bianchini, 1993). From the perspective of image-led urban regeneration, many of the desired elements for fostering a thriving cultural quarter close to the city centre were already in place.

The Planning of Rope Walks

The consultation and planning process for Rope Walks began with a history of repeated attempts to initiate regeneration by public-private partnerships which failed before they reached the stage of implementation, leaving a legacy of mistrust and unease for local communities encouraged to join in yet another quarter-based regeneration programme. It also took place in the context of growing rhetoric around and an expanding funding base for regeneration and economic development led by the arts and cultural industries, through the priorities of funding streams and organization of enabling bodies designated by Merseyside's Objective One status.

Plans for the city centre also reflected local will to trade on arts and culture for regional investment, including the quarter itself, the nomination of 24-hour city status, and investigation into the feasibility of further arts, media and culture-based flagship projects, including a National Centre for Contemporary Popular Music following the creation of the Liverpool Institute of Performing Arts in 1993.[6]

The consultation exercise for what was initially called the 'Duke Street/Bold Street Creative Quarter' took the form of a series of workshops, planning weekends and public meetings to which local communities were invited, facilitated through a consortium of consultants led by the Building Design Partnership (who were responsible for master planning and producing the action plan). Mapping and scoping research was also commissioned by the accountable body, the City Council in partnership with English Partnerships, and community consultation through the City Council and the Duke Street Cornwallis Partnership. A range of communities of interest was represented in the process, including the Chinese community (from Chinatown which borders the area), visual artists groups (of which there were a large number using the studio space in the quarter), community arts and education groups, environmentalists and alternative businesses (for example, the Liverpool Cycle Centre, and the alternative bookshop News from Nowhere), some bar and property owners, and members of the Duke Street Cornwallis partnership. Very few local residents were present at the planning stage. In terms of representation of the local music industry, this was dominated by Cream, the local club night turned dance music empire, that made considerable input into discussions in public meetings. Also present was the owner of the Jacaranda, a Merseybeat coffee bar frequented by The Beatles and later an anarchist squat in the 1970s. But in general the music-related businesses in the area – of which at the time there were over 70 (out of the 400 businesses located in the area) plus 12 music venues – were largely silent.

Specific reports were drawn up on the management of the night-time economy and the potential for digital networks in the quarter, based on consultancy managed by the Manchester Institute of Popular Culture, who acted as advisers on the cultural industries, the night-time economy and information technologies. This involved consultation with businesses in the area and recommended as one priority action the temporal zoning of licensing in the quarter.

The consultation and planning outcomes recognized two distinctive features of the quarter in terms of arts and cultural activity. First was the extent of activity in the area: it already had critical mass to some degree, centred around the bars, clubs and venues in the area, of which Cream was the most notable. Second was the degree of daytime activity that was dependent on and intimately related to the night-time economy, such as specialist retail providing for night-time economies (for example clubwear and record shops, music managers, promoters, agencies and cultural businesses, which used the bars and clubs for networking and promotion).

The recommended approach for the regeneration programme was a tripartite 'integrated' approach, weaving together business support, training and employment to provide for human resource and softer outputs, a development programme comprising a bundle of projects and initiatives which would be supported in their search for funding, and a public realm programme. It was proposed that these aspects would be linked into the vast network of public and voluntary agencies on Merseyside, through contact with the enabling agencies and partnerships established in the 'Pathways' community development areas designated in Objective One. A new partnership was set up to oversee delivery of the programme, linking together these groups, and including representation at board level from English Partnerships, Liverpool City Council, private-sector developers and the voluntary sector.

There was however no specific cultural industries strategy included in the action plan, despite the flagging up of creative and cultural industries within the consultation exercise and within marketing for the regeneration initiative. As a result concerns were raised over the overall commitment of the local authorities and English Partnerships to the cultural or creative aspect of the quarter, and the planners were criticized for prioritizing the public realm aspects of regeneration, in part because this element was easier to progress in funding terms since it was not so reliant on the complicated monitoring mechanisms for softer outputs. The responsibility for strategic development of the cultural industries was devolved into three elements: firstly, the Merseyside Arts Cultural and Media Enterprise (ACME), the 'umbrella' arts coordination organization which had recently been approved for Objective One funding; secondly, the physical development projects devised by private developers linked to arts and culture and supported by the action plan; and thirdly, linkage to the somewhat mysterious Media Factory, a proposed development in Chavasse Park at the northwest boundary of the quarter which never materialized.

The action plan was approved for £16 million from the European Regional Development Fund and £1.7 million from the European Social Fund in July 1997, with a total project cost of £71 million including £30 million private sector investment. Forecasts for the application to Brussels estimated between 800 and 1,400 jobs directly resulting from the scheme, with projected estimates of a further £28m private-sector investment creating 700 more jobs. The following year the quarter was renamed Rope Walks as a result of local competition.

Early reactions to the planning process indicated a mistrust of regeneration programmes, particularly for those who had been present through the previous feasibility studies and consultation exercises. Developers were concerned that the wait for the programme to be ratified and then implemented would hold up projects that were already happening organically in the area and that were not being taken into account. The lack of definitive plans for arts and cultural activity within the action plan has also led to concerns that arts and cultural industries were being left behind, or that the lack of awareness of specific needs for the cultural sector and structures to deliver services to them would lead to a flattening out of activity or transformation to a 'boutique area'.

At time of writing, five years on from the planning process, some tangible outcomes of the regeneration initiative can be seen. These include the opening of key flagship projects such as FACT, a media centre opened in March 2003, and the Tea Factory, a mixed-use development by Urban Splash. Various public realm improvements have been made, including a new gateway to Chinatown, the opening up of squares and thoroughfares, and crucially renovation of building stock has created more living space in the area as well as the development of rental office units. However, staggered funding deadlines from disparate sources and continued reticence of private owners to sell on or the City Council to release property from private ownership through Compulsory Purchase Orders, has engendered delay to physical developments and training programmes. Private landlords have also been too slow to take up funding opportunities released by the regeneration scheme for maintaining and upgrading buildings. Some aspects of physical development have attracted particular controversy, most notably the demolition of the Casartelli building, a Grade 2 listed eighteenth-century wine warehouse first heralded in the Comedia report but left derelict to the point that it was dismantled for safety reasons in 2001, prompting enquiry from the English Heritage Historic Built Environment Advisory Committee. A number of buildings and terraces have suffered significant decline, as they stand empty.

There have been conflicts and grievances aired by groups and communities in the area, for example complaints from the Chinese community about continued exclusion from access to resources. Those groups requiring the cheap space once in abundance in the area have, as predicted within more vociferous moments within planning meetings, been those that have suffered: many of the visual artists, who first voiced these concerns during the consultation process, have been forced to move out of the area as buildings have transferred hands, and campaign continually for funding to cover increased rents.[7] Rehearsal space, including the Holmes Building (used by 1990s Liverpool bands including the Farm and the La's), has been taken over for private development: in the case of the Holmes Building and nearby Maggs Antiques Building by breweries, quick to take advantage of positive encouragement for night-time economies through the granting of liquor licences. As the commendation of the public realm development and flagship projects is coupled with the thriving creative sector in city marketing literature, it appears many of the fears of gentrification and transfer of creative semi-public space to private hands are being realized.

Liverpool – Music City

Liverpool's music scenes and buoyant musical economies have been celebrated in a growing literature, most recently by Du Noyer (2002), and anthologized by various Merseybeat historians and research conducted by the Institute of Popular Music (Cohen, 1991b; Cohen and McManus, 1991; McManus, 1994a and 1994b). This has included the documentation of links between music and urban regeneration (Cohen, 1991a, 2002) and more broadly to place-marketing and tourism, identity and structures of feeling (Cohen, 1991b; Du Noyer, 2002), chiefly through The Beatles, and more latterly through the uncovering of its musical past and present to roll out the focus of attention on the Fab Four to the role of successive waves of successful Liverpudlian music scenes, bands and acts. The Beatles industry, including heritage sites (the Cavern Quarter, John Lennon and Paul McCartney's family homes), merchandise, written and verbal narratives and anecdotes delivered by a host of Merseybeat contemporaries, themed cafés and shops, two annual festivals, Magical Mystery tours and a rather derided Beatles Experience, is worth an estimated £20 million to the local economy. Tourism research has situated music events and sites at the core of the tourist experience on the basis of volume, with the Mathew Street festival attracting 250,000 visitors in 2000, Creamfields the third most popular paid admission event in the same year, and an estimated 600,000 visitors brought to the city solely on the basis of their interest in The Beatles, making up nearly half the number and economic impact of estimated cultural tourists to the area.[8]

City marketeers and local authorities are well aware of the popular cultural cachet to be had from being the place of origin for such globally lucid and mobile cultural product as The Beatles. Although perhaps a little jaded in the British context, where popular music histories are complicated by closer proximity to local music scenes and styles, it is a hugely important marque for the global marketing of the city. The supporting literature for the city's UK Capital of Culture 2008 bid states: 'Mention Liverpool, almost anywhere in the world, and it's recognized straight away – "Beatles" and "Liverpool or Everton FC" or more recently "Cream" are the quality brands that the people of the world associate with our city'.[9]

The Beatles dominate, but more 'knowledgeable', situated music tourism has been developed and encouraged by Mersey Tourism, informed by music maps, listing guides, websites and city promotional flyers, highlighting the traces of key protagonists in the 'Liverpool sound' at different stages in the city's music story and guiding visitors through the plethora of clubs, bars and venues. The city is also a centre of popular music research and education, with the flagship Liverpool Institute for the Performing Arts, the Institute of Popular Music at Liverpool University – including the UK's first MA in Popular Music and MBA in Music Industry Management – Liverpool John Moores University, Liverpool Community College and various community-based projects and training initiatives, including those orchestrated through the Liverpool Music Action Zone led by the Merseyside Music Development Agency (see below).

There is a history of relations between Liverpool music industry and city policy-makers which highlights the role of the local industry in economic development, as part of the broader strategic approach for arts and cultural industries in the city and surrounding region. A number of reports and studies have been carried out, and initiatives mooted and developed, to try to strengthen the relationship between support for local musicians, businesses and services and growth of the local cultural economy. These have attained various levels of implementation; the most notable, as documented by Cohen (1991a, 2002), include City Beat – a failed proposal to establish a City Council-run music management and production company; Music City – which advocated amongst other initiatives the development of a Liverpool Institute for the Performing Arts; the Merseyside Music Industry Association (MMIA) – a local trade association established as a democratic company to represent and lobby for the interests of music industry members in the context of local policy-making; and the Merseyside Music Development Agency (MMDA), launched in 1998, which was awarded £1.12 million funding through the Objective One programme in its first year.

The MMDA grew out of the somewhat painful marriage of a production-oriented cultural industries development model, creating subsector 'enabling agencies', which was espoused by arts consultants advising a partnership of public-sector bodies on arts and cultural industries development strategies on Merseyside, and the wishes of the local music industry as represented by the MMIA. Since its launch the MMDA has been clouded in controversy, primarily with regard to the accountability and representativeness of the executives of the Agency and their interests in grant awards; however, this is a not uncommon accusation within the 'dependency culture' fostered by the history of public funding for the city and region, particularly when attempting to bridge the needs of the private sector. It was also something that the Development Agency steering group had worked hard to avoid in their constitution but fell privy to in any case. The Agency has established a number of different elements under its umbrella, under various configurations, including a platform for music partnerships in the city, networking activities and proposals for business incubators. In 1999 it commissioned an economic profile of the music sector on Merseyside, which surveyed music businesses and the live music sector. It found that the value of the music industry in terms of private-sector growth finance to the Merseyside region was almost £1.9 million, with music industry producing an aggregate turnover of £45.8 million, with £6.5 million of this figure originating from the live performance sector.[10]

Music industry development from within, or in partnership with, the public sector has therefore been fraught. As the often-cited observation by Bianchini (1999a) notes, in an 'age of city marketing', cultural policy is more at ease with using cultural development as an imaging exercise, by showcasing local economies and cultural assets to attract investment and raise the profile of the city and region in a global competitive context. In the case of Liverpool 'music city', this has taken the form primarily of appropriating the brands built through indigenous cultural activity into broader marketing campaigns. The Beatles and Cream stand as positive markers for the city, as heritage assets facing tourist markets, presiding over policies that support contemporary production.

Other cultural sectors in the city are equally if not more important to city imaging as the music sector. Football weaves its own magic through the global network of fans, and continues as the preferred vernacular *language* in business, policy and music circles in the city. The successes of the Liverpool Film Office in attracting film production to the region through marketing the city as a location, and of Mersey TV in continually drawing on local resources for its independent productions, has given extensive access to the aesthetics of the city, even when it acts as a stand-in for elsewhere or an un-named cityscape representing degenerated but sentimental 'northern-ness'. Selling Liverpool as a location for film is rooted in the city's built heritage and assets – the dramatic vistas of the skyline, the Georgian and Victorian architecture, a tradition of production-oriented arts advocacy in the region, and the will of the local authorities to invest in this approach, funding the first municipal Film Liaison Officer in the early 1990s. The reputation of Liverpool spoken word – plays, comics, poets and actors – is also called on as currency for external perceptions of the city's innate creativity, although the parlance of 'Scouse' – a dialect, sense of humour and ethnic identity – has more problematical connotations, associated with the stereotypical media representations of 'Scousers' as tracksuit-wearing thieves, gangsters and drug addicts.

Music in the Rope Walks Quarter

Mahtani and Salmon (2001) describe 'local musical spaces' as territories in which communities of taste organized around music practices operate. They are spaces which contribute to and draw upon 'place-based networks of creation, production and consumption', which resist the pull towards the homogenization of musical product by the global music industry, and which allow for expression of place and local identities (Mahtani and Salmon, 2001: 169). Importantly, consumption practices and resources are as much part of this space and place construction as those associated with production.

The area designated as Rope Walks constitutes a number of overlapping local musical spaces. When the process of regeneration for the Rope Walks area finally began in 1997, music consumption in the regeneration area and the city centre was profligate in evidence, complex in its associations with various styles, genres and musical communities, and ripe for picking in urban regeneration terms. The city's night-time economy was expanding in terms of the bars and clubs which featured dance music as their idiom, complemented by a network of live music venues to cater for a variety of audiences and musicians, from the post-Britpop surge of new rock bands to established touring acts, as well as local jazz and hiphop scenes, karaoke nights and covers bands, heavy metal and Irish folk scenes. Cream, the 'superclub' born of a local club night in 1992, was poised for global domination, running its own DJ agency, opening up a London office and winning numerous dance music industry awards as well as the accolade of the City Council and tourism agencies for its role in attracting students to Liverpool, and beginning its expansion into overseas operations through compilations sales and festivals.[11]

The night-time economy of the quarter was dominated by the dance sector, anchored to Cream, and supported by a number of other clubs and bars. Nightclubs in the Rope Walks area were not operating in isolation from each other, from wider aspects of the local dance scene or from national and international trends. The rise of dance music in particular in the 1990s, and its legitimization as mainstream youth culture, emerging out of illegal warehouse raves and onto city centre streets into the spaces left by past trends and genres, has suited the city's sociable reputation, and the club scene has won over 'outsiders', drawing clubbers from outside the region 'up North' and earning its own title for the sub-genre of 'Scouse House'.[12] Although the dance scene in Liverpool, from its movement from illicit events in the derelict dockland buildings on the outskirts of the city to the city centre, has been perceived as relatively narrowcast and dependent on the success of Cream, in the late 1990s dance music and club culture were diversifying in part in reaction to the dominance of mainstream house music, which was criticized as symptomatic of the flattening out of dance music through large-scale corporate intervention in the post-acid house years.

This was taking place at a local level in response to Cream, and within the club itself. The smaller clubs and bars running dance nights in the regeneration area were operating in part in competition with Cream and also in reaction to the perceived homogenizing effect of the superclub. Smaller, less well-resourced club nights had to work their programming around Cream's (there was rumours of contractual agreements between venues and the superclub that banned hiring promoters of conflicting events for the same nights of the week), but could work to fill the spaces provided by those critical of corporate dance music. This resulted in a growing diversity of musical styles, which was also influenced by the student presence in the city, bringing in new preferences from outside the region and encouraging demand for alternatives to the more mainstream dance music associated with Cream. In turn, Cream differentiated itself from smaller 'local' clubs, claiming superior status as a taste-setter that introduced new styles from outside the parochial. Commenting on their decision to focus on resident DJs employed exclusively on their books, the Head of Communications at Cream claimed their resource-strong status as a superclub which took control of their DJ artists allowed them to experiment with new sounds and educate their audience, who were distinguished from other club-goers by their numbers (the venue had 2,000 capacity) and their draw from outside the Merseyside region.

Other music styles and genres have also been fostered within the narrow streets of the quarter. Although the larger capacity venues in the city are situated outside its boundaries, there are a number of smaller venues that provided gigs for local and touring bands, some specializing in particulars genres such as jazz, funk, rock and indie. The proximity to the universities, colleges and the Liverpool Institute of Performing Arts, and the availability of cheap drink and student discounts, meant these often catered for student audiences as well as locals. As with many university towns, there are tensions between local people and students; some pubs and bars are more 'Scouse' (and hence less student) than others, particularly towards the centre of the city. The delineation between indigenous musical practice and that of the 'outsider' students is, however, becoming more eroded in the area, as popular music students from these nearby institutions promote gigs, run club nights and perform in the quarter. The quarter's streets and venues offer a contested terrain for audiences, promoters, music genres and styles, and also eras – there are some 'heritage' sites from bygone times still staunchly operating, for example the Jacaranda, and the Blue Angel, a sixties haunt visited by Bob Dylan and Judy Garland.

The music industry's presence in the quarter is not only defined by night-time consumption. Music businesses and services associated with management, recording, production, promotion, product design, instruments, distribution and retail are also clustered within the area. The Parr Street Studios complex houses management and production companies, recording studios and accommodation for recording musicians. There is a cluster of specialist, locally-owned record shops, including Probe, established in the 1970s and a central part of Liverpool music scene as a wholesaler, distributor and record label throughout the 1980s. Probe moved up from Mathew Street in the 1990s, following its redevelopment as the Cavern Quarter. Nearby, 3 Beat, a label, management company and record shop, has taken a similar role in the local dance music scene: it is part of the Liverpool Palace complex, an old furniture warehouse developed in 1989 as a mixed-use development with a strong presence of music businesses, by Tom Bloxham (who went on to found Urban Splash).[13]

The businesses at the Liverpool Palace are very aware of music scenes surrounding them and of the benefits they bring to their businesses. The record shops provide information on local music acts, events and personnel formally – through record promotion and flyers – and informally through personal knowledge and contact. The Palace acts as a resource centre for music scene participants, through promotional flyers for events, as a meeting place and venue, through its emphasis on young creativity and entrepreneurialism, and a critical mass of products and commodities, images and styles. There is a degree of transparency between production and consumption of music and music-related commodities encouraged by the visibility and proximity of activity in the building.

The clustering, organic or otherwise, of music businesses within a designated 'creative quarter' is not necessarily enough to keep them within the local music industry. Some have left, echoing prevailing concerns within music's longstanding relationship with the city (for example, the management company of an internationally successful Liverpool band based in the quarter, which could no longer delay moving to London to be closer to industry contacts). There has been a 'rhetoric of the local' (Cohen, 2002) within music policy and the local industry which is concerned with taking steps against the abandonment of the city by popular musicians and music businesses, usually for London and usually at the point of departure for greater success (typified by The Beatles leaving in 1964), and which Cohen argues was a main impetus for policy initiatives aimed at harnessing their potential for economic development and preventing the 'haemorrhaging' of talent and money from the city.[14]

That success as the reason for leaving the city should be castigated in local discourse is not a marker through which to evaluate the success or otherwise of the possibilities of creative quarterization for fostering the music industry – far more poignant and problematical are the stories of businesses that left or closed due to lack of support from creative industries development or through gentrification and rent-raising. However, the prescription of loyalty to the city which features so heavily in music industry and cultural policy discourse provides some background to the debates inscribing the recent closing of Cream's weekly club night at the venue Nation in the quarter (discussed below), and the superclub's particular stance on their relationship to the city. The company has consistently pitched itself in public relations as allied, but not anchored, to Liverpool:

> Cream's pitch has always been it is a Liverpool-based company that works world-wide. It is not a Liverpool club. It has never said it is a Liverpool club. The Buzz is a Liverpool club, it caters for a Liverpool market, it advertises within Liverpool. We don't really advertise formally within Liverpool, we advertise nation-wide and world-wide ... I think Cream has always perceived itself differently to how other clubs would perceive themselves, because they were Liverpool clubs, catering for a

Liverpool market. Cream always saw itself as a Liverpool based business, but was catering for a world market.[15]

This has not prevented criticism of their actions, defined as a betrayal of the city:

Yes, it will be sad to see the end of Cream, but the most annoying part of this is that the people who made the money out of the whole venture ... chose the same week that the Judges for the Capital of Culture visited the city to drop the bombshell. Good to see that James [Barton, founder of Cream] stays loyal to his roots.[16]

In terms of the relationship between music businesses and the regeneration process of Rope Walks, Cream have dominated throughout. As the success story of the area and of Liverpool for the 1990s, the superclub was very visible in the public consultation of the regeneration programme. The consultation team were invited to visit the club over the Planning Weekend, and its contribution to the area in terms of profile, visitors and employment was recognized and referred to frequently in the planning and feedback reports. The club's importance and its impact on the area was reflected by reference to part of the quarter as 'the Cream Zone' and to the aspirations of the children's planning group to building a 'Kiddies Cream'. In public meetings and in the final action plan, the club was prioritized in the public realm plans for the surrounding Wolstenholme Square, including discussion of hotel development, so that visitors to the club would not be disrupted. As one of the consultants for the planning process commented, 'I'm sure they [the clubbers] would like somewhere nice to queue'.[17]

Figure 7.1 Nation, the Venue for the Nightclub Cream in the Newly Developed Wolstenholme Square (Photo: A. Gilmore)

Cream has had experience in and produced good results from creating close relationships with a range of different agencies in the city, from joining the Chamber of Commerce to liaising with the police and the public sector over licencing and drugs issues. They credit themselves with changing licensing policy in the city to allow for 6am licences, for creating good practice standards for safe clubbing and for generating respect and investment for the city, for example through drawing young people to the city as weekend tourists and as students, and through the Challenge award for best Millennial celebrations following the Creamfields event at Pierhead. Moreover, they have incorporated their role in the consultation for the Rope Walks initiative into their own marketing rhetoric, claiming at a recent conference on cultural tourism held in the city that they were directly responsible for the instigation of the cultural quarterization process.[18]

This hubris is not without basis since the Cream brand, with its connotations of youth, club lifestyle, urban cultural tourism and entrepreneurialism, has been heavily invested in symbolically, if not materially, throughout the regeneration scheme by the planners and their partners. Cream, as the epitome of the night-time economy in the area, been consistently referred to in Rope Walks (and other city-centre) marketing literature, and also features as the landmark for the south of the city centre in promotion for Tea Factory retail and leisure units produced by Urban Splash:

> They've created an aura that goes beyond the nightclub. Hughes's and Barton's ambitions for Cream are awesome and global. 'We want to be the best youth brand', says Barton (Alvarez, 1997).

The explanation for Cream's prominence can be attributed to a number of reasons, not least their public relations prowess and awareness of local structures of city governance and policy-making, as well as their profile and success in drawing visitors in from outside the city. In the landscape of other music businesses and activities, of other 'local musical spaces', Cream is also distinguished by particular characteristics which make it more appropriate for use as a technology of regeneration. As Zukin comments, reprising her work on the artistic mode of production as the role of artists in fostering cultural consumption:

> Visual representations are hegemonic in both our sensual experience of cities and contemporary consumer culture. So it is not surprising that visual artists have a key *productive* role in creating and processing images for the urban economy (Zukin, 2001: 260, original emphasis).

The visual aesthetics of Cream – embodied in its logo, the visibility of the night-time economy and its physical environment of designer bars, clubs and clothes – and the adept brand-building that has been part of establishing a successful superclub, are far more likely to coincide with desires of regeneration planners to project Rope Walks as a dynamic, fast-moving, contemporaneously relevant, globally-connected consumption-based creative quarter than other less visible, more production-oriented elements of the music industry or musical landscape that can be found within the quarter. They are, in part, homologous with what Degen (2002) terms the 'aesthetic strategies of regeneration' – clean, strong lines, reflective surfaces, open spaces. Despite the successes of Liverpool rock bands throughout the 1990s, many of them with strong links to the Rope Walks area, and the continued presence of a variety of genres and styles represented in businesses and venues there, (corporate) dance music presided over the regeneration process as the metaphor for inner-city creativity. Similarly, new media and digital arts are more synonymous with the projection of global post-industrial urban chic than good old-fashioned painting; little wonder media centres are prioritized over the studio needs of visual arts groups.

Cream ended as a regular club night in July 2002, engendering much mournful debate amongst clubbers, and speculation as to whether this again heralded the end of dance music's grip on youth culture (Perreti, 2002). The brand Cream lives resolutely on, however; the decision to close the club night was quickly justified in business terms as Cream continued their expansion rhetoric, citing the desire to continue diversifying vertically, into new territories through the success of their Creamfields festival events overseas, and horizontally, in terms of setting up media production operations. Having situated themselves as loyal to the city but always outward looking, a global brand that just happened to be good for its place of origin, this was in part an exercise in brand preservation, a necessary re-invention in the face of global market forces.

Conclusion: Cultural Quarters, Popular Music and Urban Regeneration

The Rope Walks Quarter is not the only cultural or creative quarter in Liverpool with strong musical connections; the city has also the Cavern Quarter, its own designated music heritage zone. This concentrated Beatles-themed quarter contains some extraordinary public art representations of the group as well as the reconstructed Cavern club, a rock wall of Merseyside fame, a number of bars, pubs and clubs which feature live music, and shops including the Cavern Walks arcade. It is dominated by commerce, having been established through a partnership of the private-sector concerns in the quarter, and provides a focus for Beatles tourism in the city. Another quarter, established around the time the Rope Walks initiative began, is the Hope Street Arts Quarter, steered by a committee with strong connections to the Royal Liverpool Philharmonic Society. The ethos of this quarter is community-arts based. It is guided by the principles of small-scale community-arts development and capacity building, delivered in partnership with institutions within its geographical (and cultural) scope such as the Philharmonic, the Everyman Theatre, Unity Theatre and the Metropolitan and Anglican Cathedrals, who can offer 'intellectual capital' training for local communities.[19]

Figure 7.2 Mathew Street, the Cavern Quarter, 'Birthplace of The Beatles'
(Photo: A.Gilmore)

Rope Walks is distinctive therefore as a major public-private initiative, which is primarily property-led, attracting large amounts of European funding and which is committed to an integrated approach including creative industries support and development, in recognition of the existing activity in the area. Levels of actual support for cultural production remain unclear, as public realm concerns have continued to be prioritized, not least because of problems over land-ownership and dilapidated buildings, and the night-time economy based around music, in particular dance music, has been sustained so far into the process. In relation to musical spaces and music industry, the quarter initiative reflects some of the characteristic issues for (public-sector led) cultural policy and regeneration which attempts to capture organic popular cultural activity. These are associated with key issues relating to dynamics and discourses of music industry activity in relation to those of public-sector cultural planning.

The first of these is concerned with the tensions between entrepreneurialism and cultural policy, embodied by the case of Cream and their relationship with city planners. This relationship has been characterized by Cream's own interventions into the planning process in order to service the right conditions for their business, and the careful preservation of their profile in order to maintain ascendancy. No waiting around for the criteria of funding programmes to be announced is evident within this relationship, rather the dictate that music business as defined by the market calls the shots; as Cream stated recently, the difference between local authorities and private sector 'is that private sector know what they want and got what they wanted. We know what our agenda is, the City doesn't'.[20]

The second is around the necessary messiness of popular culture and fears that as cultural tourism-based regeneration advances so spaces for creativity recede. One of the first measures to be taken when preparing for cultural tourism is the removal of messy environmental factors such as flyposting and skateboarders. In Liverpool, when the judging process began for the city's bid for the UK Capital of Culture 2008, it was announced that fines for these activities were to rise to £2,500 and £500 respectively; before the judging panel's second visit teams of City Council employees were seen on the streets removing posters. In the Rope Walks Quarter, the newly-furnished public squares rub up against poster-strewn crumbling walls, and broken glass from night-time revelry lies at the feet of buskers and *Big Issue* sellers. During the planning meetings, there was talk of the 'celebration of dereliction', which described the prescient concern that too much development would change the grain of the area. Five years on, the patina of local musical spaces remains in the area, defiant or oblivious to processes of gentrification which may yet pose a threat.

Thirdly, there is the associated issue of production-oriented versus consumption-oriented models for cultural quarters, and which model offers the optimum conditions for creative industries and cultural development. For example, Moss (2002) discusses the problems associated with the production-oriented Cultural Industries Quarter in Sheffield, which lacked the mixed economy favoured by a more 'integrated' approach between consumption and production. The Rope Walks Quarter subscribes to an integrated action plan, but appears to favour consumption and public realm concerns. Popular music is clearly a strong driver for consumption in the area and is championed as such, but given scant attention or specific resources targeted towards production other than the (private) development of rental space in the quarter. The local music industry has, with the exception of Cream, been disengaged and distanced from the regeneration process, operating in the context of a complex and ambivalent relationship between the local music industry and city cultural policy, which has inured many to the lure of public-sector initiatives.

Figure 7.3 Flyposting in the Rope Walks Quarter (Photo: A.Gilmore)
The text of the poster proclaiming 'This is Culture' encourages others to make copies and paste them throughout the city, in protest against the recent increasing of penalties for flyposting

Finally, there is the tension between dynamism and heritage when attempting to capitalize on local musical scenes, products and spaces in regeneration. A quality of the music industry reflected by the diversity of popular music scenes is its cyclical nature and the importance of being able to invent and re-invent new trends, styles and products for consumption. The progressive waves of musical product from Liverpool (and other 'music cities') reflect this, but when music becomes part of the cultural tourism resource then some aspects of music history are open to being taken out of circulation, frozen in time and preserved in marketing discourse aspic. The museumization of popular music has proved problematic, as Liverpool has discovered with the heritagization of The Beatles, and creating tourist products and sites from recent and contemporary popular culture instantly runs the risk of legitimizing or denying the subcultural elements which constitute its attraction. This is perhaps another reason that Cream pulled out of the Rope Walks Quarter – to avoid their own museumization: as one quip remarked in an internet chat forum on the closure of Cream at Nation: 'good riddance to bad rubbish!! flush the loo when you're finished mr lennon or they might put ur POO on display'.[21]

The quarterization of Rope Walks has thus far provided conditions for local music spaces, including production and consumption, to survive in the broader context of the global music industry; how much they are altered, threatened, supported or exploited by the continuing regeneration process remains to be seen.

Notes

1   'Music Policy, the Music Industry and Local Economic Development', funded by the Economic and Social Research Council, conducted by the Institute of Popular Music at Liverpool University and the Manchester Institute of Popular Culture at Manchester Metropolitan University. I would like to thank and acknowledge the Economic and Social Research Council and my colleagues on this project, Sara Cohen, Adam Brown and Justin O'Connor, for which I was Research Assistant from March 1997 to March 1998.

2   August 1989, *From City of Imagination to City of Design: A design strategy for Liverpool,* Comedia.

3   The City Council published its Arts and Cultural Industries Strategy in 1987, encouraging the role of arts and cultural activities in the economic development and social regeneration of the city and establishing the Liverpool City Council Arts and Cultural Industries Unit. For more extensive accounts of the history of arts and cultural industries policy in Liverpool see Cohen (1991a, 2002) and Parkinson and Bianchini (1993).

4   *Creative Industries Quarter, Liverpool, Bridewell Area, Development Strategy,* Charterhouse Estates Limited, May (1990: 17).

5   *Duke Street/Bold Street Regeneration Study for English Partnerships and Liverpool City Council,* October 1994, Drivers Jonas Llewellyn-Davies Campbell Reith Hill.

6   *Ambitions for the City Centre: Liverpool's Draft City Centre Strategy for the Next Five Years* (Planning and Transportation Service, LCC, 1996).

7   For example, the Arena artists group, based in the area since 1984, who have held art auctions to raise money for the Arena Survival Fund, along with Lottery grant applications, in order to remain in their building on Duke Street.

8   Figures from *Visitors to Merseyside 2000*, North West Tourist Board; Strategic
     Regeneration Framework, Liverpool Vision, 2000.

9   *Liverpool: the World in One City*, bid document for UK Capital of Culture 2008,
     produced by the Liverpool Culture Company.

10   *The Hidden Economy: An Economic Profile of the Music Sector on Merseyside in 1999*,
     produced by the Merseyside Music Development Agency.

11   In 1996, rumours began of a survey conducted by Liverpool John Moores University on
     reasons for student recruitment. A figure of 70 per cent of students who claimed they
     came to the city to study because of the location of Cream was cited, and consequently
     used in city marketing, in discussion of the state and role of superclubs (Alvarez, 1997)
     and in advertising for the superclub itself. In his book *Liverpool: Wondrous Place*, Du
     Noyer cites Jayne Casey, Head of Communications for Cream as the originator of the
     myth: she 'simply made it up' (Du Noyer, 2002: 206).

12   A classification for the type of 4-beat dance music favoured in Liverpool clubs, which
     according to Du Noyer echoes previous traditions in the city towards melodic, anthemic
     tunes and away from more industrial or ambient sounds (Du Noyer, 2002). The term is
     attributed to Liverpool dance music record label 3 Beat, and continues to have currency,
     with its own websites and web dictionary definition: 'a form of house music,
     unbelievably bouncy!' (www.urbandictionary.com).

13   Urban Splash, the northwest property development company, has sizeable investment in
     the quarter, having completed Concert Square, an apartment, bar and club complex,
     which was the first such development in the quarter in 1993. The Tea Factory, due for
     completion in 2003 and similarly with apartments, rental units and bar, was identified as
     a major project early in the planning for the Rope Walks initiative, the site having been
     acquired by the developers two years before the scheme began. Bloxham was elected
     onto the Rope Walks Partnership board in 1997 but resigned in 1999.

14   See Cohen 1991a and in particular 2002, where she discusses how this rhetoric impinges
     on local musicians' and music practitioners' relationship with the 'local' industry and
     produces distinctions of success and 'making it', loyalty and betrayal in relation to a
     dominant geographical framework.

15   Jayne Casey, interview with author.

16   Jane, Liverpool, BBC Radio One website discussion group, 7th August 2002,
     www.bbc.co.uk/liverpool/talk/cream_talk.shtml

17   Simon Bedford, Building Design Partnership, 'Making it Happen' seminar, Liverpool,
     19th May 1997.

18   Jayne Casey, Head of Communications, Cream, speaking at the Cultural Impact
     conference, LIPA, Liverpool, 31st July 2002.

19   Hillary Burrage, Cultural Impact conference, LIPA, 31st July 2002. For example,
     community education about length and format of classical music concerts and the
     encouragement of personal audiences with orchestra members.

20   Jayne Casey, Cultural Impact conference.

21   Wendy, Ipswich, BBC Radio One website discussion group, 7th August 2002,
     www.bbc.co.uk/liverpool/talk/cream_talk.shtml

Chapter 8

Quarterizing the City: The Spatial Politics of the Joyce Industry in Dublin

Stephanie Rains

The large and increasing cultural tourism market within Dublin, Eire, has many of its origins in, and is still mainly centred around, a utilization of James Joyce's fictional representations of the city. While a wide variety of other attractions, including the national museums and art galleries, several theatres and more recently a number of restored buildings, have become important attractions in Ireland's capital, Joycean references still abound within advertising and branding for the city, and some of its longest-running tourist ventures are crucially centred around Joycean themes.

The use of popular or well-known fictional characters and their creators as the basis of cultural tourism has been successfully adopted in many cities or regions, varying from the marketing of Wessex in England as 'Hardy Country' to the museum established in Keats' house on the Spanish Steps in Rome. What this chapter will address with reference to the 'Joyce Industry' in Dublin is the specific way in which the creative connections of a city or region are utilized in order to present an alternative historical as well as artistic discourse to tourists. In particular, there will be an analysis of the ways in which the Joycean tourism industry has been used as a method by which the colonial, Anglo-Irish cultural and material identity of Dublin has been reclaimed and rehabilitated under contemporary postcolonial and postmodern conditions.

The chapter will also discuss the ways in which Joycean readings of Dublin's material fabric and cultural identity function in order to provide a highly specific variation upon the concept of a 'cultural quarter', which escapes the physical boundaries normally defining such an area in order to represent the entire inner city within the construct of Joycean imaginings. This form of representation within Dublin cultural tourism is therefore strongly grounded in the spatial fabric and history of the city, relying as it does upon the intimately embedded cultural meanings of its architecture and urban design.

However, as Michel Foucault (1987) argues, it is important to resist an 'architecturally determinist' approach to the design of urban spaces and buildings. Just as such planning cannot be, purely by its nature, a force for liberation, it also cannot be fundamentally repressive either. The actual function of architecture and planning is ultimately determined by practice:

> That is not to say that the exercise of freedom is completely indifferent to spatial
> distribution, but it can only function when there is a certain convergence (Foucault,
> 1987: 247).

In other words, in the exercise of power relations, neither the schemes of architects
and city-planners nor their interpretation by later organizations such as tourist
authorities are incontestable, because their structures and infrastructures are always
vulnerable to practices of resistance on the part of individuals and the wider
citizenry. Foucault describes his vision of the effect created by these resistant
practices as one of 'heterotopias'. This indicates a description of public or social
spaces which are differently used by different groups even to the extent of creating
oppositional symbolic meanings for those spaces. Therefore, Foucault argues,
although architecture and city planning can provide a system of 'canalization' of
individuals' patterns of circulation and a 'coding of their reciprocal relations'
(1987: 252-3), it can never be deterministic of these patterns or relations because of
the possibility which always exists for the population to engage in resistance
practices. The nature and power of these urban practices envisioned by Foucault
was explored further by Michel de Certeau – with particular reference to the
'rhetoric' of walking, an advancement of that classic urban manifestation, the
flâneur – which will be explored in detail below. Defining these practices as those
of the 'everyday' in opposition to or at least subversion of the perspectival
'official' practices embodied in urban architecture and city planning, de Certeau
argues that:

> one can follow the swarming activity of these procedures that, far from being
> regulated or eliminated by panoptic administration, have reinforced themselves in a
> proliferating illegitimacy, developed and insinuated themselves into the networks of
> surveillance, and combined in accord with unreadable but stable tactics to the point of
> constituting everyday regulations and surreptitious creativities that are merely
> concealed by the frantic mechanisms and discourses of the observational organization
> (de Certeau, 1993: 156).

The colonial, and later postcolonial, city is a particularly clear site for an
investigation of the extent to which such heterotopias and rhetorics can be
produced through a set of resistant practices within hegemonic spatial structures.
In particular, within the context of this chapter, is the issue of the ways in which
the 'panoptic administration' of a colonial city reveals not only the resistant
strategies of its colonized inhabitants, but also the ambiguities inherent to the
expression of difference, in which the ambivalence of imperial identity is repressed
in order to produce a stable administrative and physical urban text. In the later,
postcolonial context, the ways in which this imperial legacy can be accommodated
within a new 'official' discourse, and the extent to which this process of
hybridization is a liberation or threat to the practices of the 'everyday', are also
important areas of discussion regarding tourist interpretations. Before discussing
the 'Joyce industry' in detail, however, it is first necessary to examine the role and

nature of heritage-based tourism in a postcolonial context, in order to delineate its very specific uses and difficulties.

Dublin's Urban Heritage

The first point which needs to be considered is the approach to the concept of the city's history which an emphasis upon 'heritage' both works from and then continues to reinforce. While all constructions of history are necessarily selective and hierarchical commemorations of the past, the notion of history as 'heritage' privileges certain events and sites above others, according to a very particular set of criteria. Primarily, these criteria are based upon the concept of an inheritance of 'value' from the past, which can be projected across both the present and the future through preservation and appropriate interpretation. As Ashworth and Tunbridge argue: 'Heritage not only automatically poses the question "whose heritage?" but, even more fundamentally, can only logically be defined in terms of the market' (Ashworth and Tunbridge, 1990: 25). It could be argued, however, that in the case of Dublin's heritage industry, the question of 'whose heritage?' is in fact equally as important as the concept of the market, mainly because, as a direct result of the city's history as a seat of colonial administration which later became a national capital, that market is very largely determined by questions of identity and ownership of the heritage concerned.

The ways in which the material fabric of the city is converted into heritage locations for visitors suggests a delicately and only recently negotiated method of rehabilitating Dublin's colonial and Anglo-Irish history in a way which both appeals to the tourist market and is acceptable to the city's inhabitants. The necessity of achieving this balance between promoting a version of heritage which appeals to the international tourist market by delineating 'this space' from all other spaces within the global system, and at the same time working from a selection of local (or national) history with which the inhabitants feel comfortable, is made particularly difficult in a postcolonial city whose cultural and material fabric is a direct link back to a colonial past.

Dublin's contemporary architectural, social and political history is, above all else, grounded in its eighteenth-century position as the power-base of the socially elite Protestant Anglo-Irish Ascendancy. During that century, the Ascendancy acquired and anticipated ever-greater independence from direct English rule, and against that anticipation they invested in and speculated for the material development of Dublin as a capital city to rival London. Thus the urban design, public buildings and formerly residential housing of what is today the city centre are predominantly Georgian in style, including many of the finest surviving examples of Palladian and neo-classical urban architecture in Europe.

The eighteenth-century development of the city, followed by its stagnation during the nineteenth century as the Ascendancy's hopes of greater independence were dashed by the 1801 Act of Union, ensured that within the Catholic nationalist canon of Irish history, both the city and its inhabitants were generally characterized as anglicized and unrepresentative of an essentialized Irishness. Instead, the rural

West of Ireland and its inhabitants were valorized as embodying the spirit of national identity which motivated the struggle for political and cultural independence, and Dublin, despite remaining the national capital after that independence was achieved, consequently experienced something of a crisis of status and representation within the nationalist era of the early to mid-twentieth century.

Due mainly to the severe financial constraints under which the new Irish government operated after Independence in 1922, the colonial government buildings which they inherited in the capital city were inhabited and utilized more or less unchanged from British rule, even including Dublin Castle, a particularly feared and loathed symbol of colonial occupation. Despite or perhaps because of this practical necessity, the Georgian fabric of the city was regarded by the new and successive administrations with suspicion at best and frequently with open distaste. Little if any official protection was afforded to the city's historic infrastructure, and during the coming decades considerable amounts of it were destroyed and replaced with no specific reference to a heritage which was regarded as having no relevance to the majority of the Irish people.

Aside from the more crucial social and political effects of Dublin's highly-specific history as a colonial and then postcolonial capital city, its history and status have also had a significant impact on the ways in which it has been represented within tourist discourse. A strong emphasis upon the history of British occupation and the Anglo-Irish tradition, whilst it would probably be of great interest to many tourists, and is amply illustrated by much of contemporary Dublin's remaining structures, would not have been generally acceptable to the majority of the indigenous population or, significantly, to the systems of national power and government symbolically and literally represented within the city.

It is in this respect that the development of Dublin's heritage tourist industry through the strong literary connections of the city becomes extremely significant. As Ashworth and Tunbridge describe, the model by which urban heritage is developed for a tourist market follows the combination of a 'site', distinguished by the intrinsic features of a building or area, and a 'marker', which is a directional guide for the visitor to outline the context in which the experience is to be consumed. The result, they argue, 'is the 'sacralization' of space, where a site whose physical characteristics may be unremarkable, or even indistinguishable from others, is endowed with value by the process of *enshrinement*' (Ashworth and Tunbridge, 1990: 25). And as Ashworth and Tunbridge stress, this process of enshrinement can follow a site's creative or imaginative history as easily – or in Dublin's case, perhaps more easily – as it can follow political-historical events.

Dublin's Literary Heritage

Thus, as Victor Luftig describes, Dublin's Georgian Anglo-Irish architecture is marketed to tourists as the Dublin of 'Sheridan, Joyce, Shaw, Wilde, Synge, Yeats and O'Casey' (Luftig, 1996: 142), linking it to a creative rather than historical past.

While these associations do not avoid the complications of Dublin's ambiguous position in Irish national history – as the varied social and political backgrounds of this selection of writers show – they would appear to present a version of the city's heritage which is more acceptable to the national sense of identity through its operation at a metaphorical or even mythological level than other interpretations of the urban structure might be.

It is notable that this method of presenting the city to tourists through literary and fictional references has a considerable provenance in Dublin, and one which interestingly appears to pre-date the rise of a more general cultural tourism. Throughout the 1950s and 1960s, a large number of short promotional films were made in and about Ireland, designed to attract tourists to the country. In these films, largely though not exclusively funded by Bord Fáilte (the Irish tourist authority), Dublin featured regularly, most often appearing as the arrival point of tourists, particularly those from Britain.

However, the city itself is the specific subject of several films, such as *See You At the Pillar* (1967) and *Autumn in Dublin* (1962). In most of the films which show Dublin in any detail, it is represented as being relatively unmodernized for a European capital city, with a relaxed pace of living and convivial social life being emphasized. *See You At the Pillar* is a particularly interesting example of the way in which Dublin's urban status is downplayed, with the commentators, Anthony Quayle and Norman Rodway, engaging in a banter of literary quotes associated with the city, so that the accompanying images of the streets appear to be literary illustrations rather than shots of a contemporary city. Dublin's anglicized history, architecture and culture is conspicuously avoided where possible in these films, which concentrate instead upon its role in the national struggle for independence and its place in contemporary Irish cultural production. *No More Yesterdays* (1967), for example, describes Dublin as 'once a city of violence, now a city of culture'.

So, although Dublin's position as a large and urbanized centre is unavoidably present within these films promoting it as a tourist location, its attractions are very selectively represented in order to avoid a concentration upon Ireland's colonial history, and to reinforce the image of the country as being removed from the modernized existence from which it was presumed most tourists would have come. This is also achieved, to a considerable degree, by the reliance upon evocations of a fictive and literary Dublin, even at a time when a specifically cultural tourism had not begun to develop.

It is in this context that the most popular and most emblematic feature of Dublin's heritage tourist industry, the '*Ulysses* Walks' based on the routes taken in James Joyce's novel, becomes particularly significant, not only to the tourist perception of the city, but also perhaps to the ways in which it is used by its contemporary inhabitants. *Ulysses,* as an account of Dublin as a 'living' city, seems to have provided a particularly useful way for the city to represent itself on the international stage in contemporary terms precisely because it provides a way to emphasize the international importance and historical position of the city which caused a previous Irish nationalism to reject it as a cultural model. As a novel which positions Dublin as an exemplar of a city within a modern international context, *Ulysses* can now be used as a way of emphasizing national pride in its culture and history. In other words, despite the ironies of Joyce's work being adopted as a source of national or local pride (given his uneasy relationship with the nationalism of his own time), the recognized cultural importance of *Ulysses*, along with the work of many other Irish writers, has become a contemporary vehicle for establishing an Irish 'cultural' empire on the international stage largely to replace the 'spiritual' empire of earlier nationalism.

There are several principal forms which the Joyce industry takes in its appeal to tourists in Dublin. Of these, the '*Ulysses* Walks' are probably the best known. As can be seen from the map (see Figure 8.1), these follow a number of the routes taken by Leopold Bloom within the novel, between them effectively cauterizing the city centre and creating a cultural 'key' to the entire inner city, through which an otherwise general impression of Dublin can be read by the wandering tourist. Only one of the walks, that which leads from the James Joyce Centre on North Great George's Street up to Eccles Street, is a guided walk, for which the tourist pays to join an accompanied group. All of the other routes shown on the map (which is sold by the James Joyce Centre) are to be followed independently by the tourist.

Another route taken by Bloom, that of his lunchtime walk between the offices of the Evening Telegraph Office and the National Library, is marked into Dublin's material fabric through the embedding of bronze plaques, bearing engraved illustrations and short *Ulysses* quotes, at strategic points in the city's pavements. It is interesting to note, in passing, that these plaques were laid as part of Dublin's 1988 Millennium celebrations, commemorating 1,000 years of its city status, and they have remained as one of the more permanent and tangible features of that year's programme of events. Thus, once again, the city's actual history is displaced or at least intertwined with its fictional half-life.

Joyce and his alter-ego, Leopold Bloom, also appear in the popular 'Literary Pub Crawl' advertised to tourists, and sponsored by Jameson Whiskey. This tour moves through some of Dublin's more noted pubs, particularly those closely associated with famous Irish writers such as Joyce, Beckett, Behan and Kavanagh, accompanied by actors reading from the relevant writer's work. While Joyce himself spent too much of his life living outside Ireland to be closely associated with many pubs as a patron, his writing is suffused with references to Dublin's landmark bars, and so his contribution to the Jameson Pub Crawl is mainly through Bloom's fictional drinking experiences.

Joyce as a Dublin Commodity

The extent to which the perceptions and interpretations of Dublin evident within Joyce's own work connect in themselves to ideas of 'heritage' which are useful in the city's contemporary engagement with the cultural tourism industry are also worth considering. His creation of the archetypal flâneur Leopold Bloom perhaps

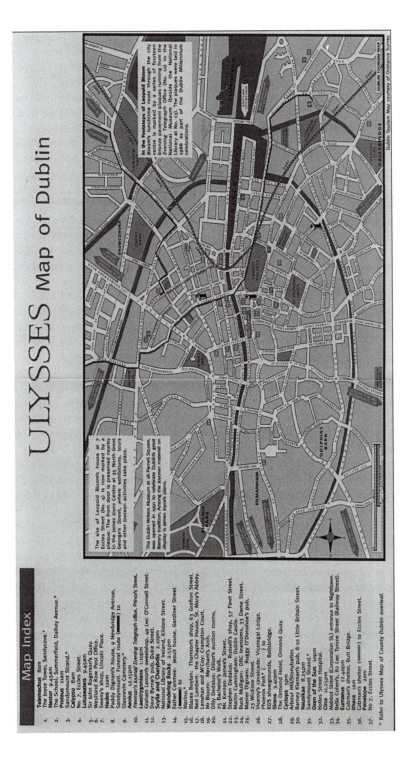

ULYSSES Map of Dublin

Map Index

1. **Telemachus** 8am
   The Joyce Tower, Sandycove.*
2. **Nestor** 9.45am
   The School, Summerfield, Dalkey Avenue.*
3. **Proteus** 11am
   Sandymount Strand.*
4. **Calypso** 8am
   No. 7, Eccles Street.
5. **Lotuseaters** 9.45am
   Sir John Rogerson's Quay.
6. **Westland Row Post Office.
7. Sweny's shop, Lincoln Place.
8. **Hades** 11am
   Paddy Dignam's house, 9 Newbridge Avenue.
   Sandymount. Funeral route (━━) to
9. **Glasnevin Cemetery.* to
10. **Aeolus** 12.15pm
    Freeman's Journal/Evening Telegraph office, Prince's Street.
11. **Laestrygonians** 1.10pm
    Graham Lemon's sweetshop, 49 Lwr. O'Connell Street.
12. Davy Byrne's pub, Duke Street.
13. **Scylla and Charybdis** 2.00pm
    National Library of Ireland, Kildare Street.
14. **Wandering Rocks** 2.55pm
    Father Conmee: Jesuit house, Gardiner Street
    (━━) to
    Marino.*
15. Bachelor's Walk.
16. Blazes Boylan: Thornton's shop, 63 Grafton Street.
17. Ned Lambert: the Chapter House, St. Mary's Abbey.
18. Lenehan and M'Coy: Crampton Court.
19. Mr Bloom: Merchant's Arch.
20. Dilly Dedalus: Dillon's auction rooms,
    25, Bachelor's Walk.
21. Mr Kernan: James's Street.
22. Stephen Dedalus: Russell's shop, 57 Fleet Street.
23. Martin Cunningham: Dublin Castle.
24. Buck Mulligan: DBC tearooms, 33 Dame Street.
25. Master Dignam: Ruggy O'Donohoe's pub,
    23 Wicklow Street.
26. Viceroy cavalcade: Viceregal Lodge,
    Phoenix Park* (━━) to
27. RDS showgrounds, Ballsbridge.
28. **Sirens** 3.40pm
    The Ormond Hotel, Ormond Quay.
29. **Cyclops** 5pm
    Barney Kiernan's pub, 8-10 Little Britain Street.
30. Arbour Hill/Stonybatter.
31. **Nausikaa** 8.25pm
    Sandymount Strand.*
32. **Oxen of the Sun** 10pm
    Holles Street Hospital.
33. **Circe** 11.25pm
    Mabbot Street (Corporation Sq) entrance to Nighttown.
34. Bella Cohen's, 82 Lwr. Tyrone Street (Railway Street).
35. **Eumaeus** 12.40pm
    Cabman's shelter, Butt Bridge.
36. **Ithaca** 1am
    Cabman's shelter (━━) to Eccles Street.
37. **Penelope** 2am
    No 7, Eccles Street.

* Refer to Ulysses Map of County Dublin overleaf.

In the Footsteps of Leopold Bloom
Bloom's lunchtime route through the city centre is marked by a series of fourteen bronze pavement plaques running from the *Evening Telegraph* Office (No. 10) to the National Museum (beside the National Library at No. 13). The plaques were laid in 1988 as part of the Dublin Millennium celebrations.

The site of Leopold Bloom's house at 7 Eccles Street (No. 4) is now marked by a plaque. The front door is preserved nearby in the James Joyce Centre at 35 North Great George's Street, where exhibitions, tours and other Joycean activities take place.

The Dublin Writers Museum at 18 Parnell Square, was opened in 1991 to celebrate Dublin's great literary tradition. Among the Joycean material on display is James Joyce's plans.

Figure 8.1 *Ulysses Walk* (Based on Ordnance Survey Ireland by Permission of the Government Permit No7618, Copyright Ordnance Survey and the Government of Ireland)

presages, in Bloom's extended and highly observant movements around Dublin, both the tourist's own necessarily impressionistic and sensory relationship to their destination as well as their unusually lengthy exposure to the experience of operating in public spaces.

In interpreting Dublin's colonial history for modern (or postmodern) tourists, the journey around the city of Leopold Bloom also provides a useful method of 'marking' the city as a 'site' by being, above all else, a representative of the 'common man'. Thus centring the experience of Dublin upon Bloom in his perceptions as well as his physical movement allows the city to be represented historically from the position of that 'common man' rather than the more frequent 'great man' version of history, which in Dublin's case would involve an emphasis upon Anglo-Irish and English history. So the very breakdown of authorial position and metanarratives which the novel itself achieved is also reflected in its use in breaking down colonial metanarratives of history to present the contemporary and historical city to the tourist in a way which projects a locally acceptable version of its heritage. Joyce's use of a classical schema for his novel also introduces an interesting new perspective from which both visitors and inhabitants may choose to view the eighteenth-century Anglo-Irish *neo*-classical architecture of the city.

The fact that the Joyce industry's greatest emphasis is upon retracing the steps of Leopold Bloom and Stephen Dedalus' fictional journeys around Dublin therefore allows the contemporary tourist who undertakes this 'heritage experience' to become a kind of postmodern flâneur, directed by the original experience of an archetypal modernist flâneur, but receiving and actually creating an essentially postmodern version for themselves. This process, which is one of the formative guides to experience for many visitors to the city, raises questions about the way in which the material and cultural fabric of the city now acts as a structure of power over individuals, as well as about the ways in which this power is resisted and subverted.

On one level, the prescribed routes and destinations of significance laid out by the '*Ulysses* Map of Dublin' are a supreme example of the 'canalization' of individuals by spatial structures described as a system of power by Foucault (1987). Within the novel itself, Bloom's wandering throughout the day of 16th June 1904 is structured by errands and the effects of chance encounters. The routes and destinations which he chooses thereby create the fundamental experience of a flâneur, the (relatively) privileged view of city life gained through the disinterested wanderings of an observer who is free to be directed mainly by his own desires. The present-day tourist, however, rather than recreating the spirit of Bloom's experience by exploring the contemporary city in the same way, is instead directed to recreate the physicality of Bloom's journey, presumably without significant deviation from the prescribed route, as though these particular trajectories were of significance in themselves. This is emphasized by the brass *Ulysses* plaques set into the pavements around Dublin. Tourists are invited to follow this route without reference to the ironies inherent in this situation; that, on the one hand, the 'Joyce's Dublin' which they are exploring has largely disappeared – or has been moved – and on the other hand, that they are charged for the privilege of participating in one of the few fundamental freedoms of modern urban experience – that of walking in the city. The fact that much of the city described in *Ulysses* has been demolished or at least completely changed, is largely a result of the very lack of appreciation of its structures and history which prevailed until it was 'rehabilitated' by the tourism industry. Most significantly, No. 7 Eccles Street, Bloom's home and the starting point of the novel, was demolished in the 1970s. Its front door, however, is now exhibited in the '*Ulysses* Tea Room' at the James Joyce Centre on North Great George's Street. So Joycean tourists who choose this method of exploring contemporary Dublin begin by inspecting the displaced door of the non-existent home of a fictional character, before beginning a journey through the city guided as much by buildings or landmarks which no longer stand as by those that do. Their experience of the contemporary city, therefore, is deeply 'canalized' by the novel, whereas it is doubtful whether their experience of the novel is significantly enhanced by their physical encounter with present-day Dublin. As Helen Meaney argues:

> Joyce's Dublin defies mapping and tracking; it exists only in his work, as his unique construct, his singular endeavour to build, in Stephen Dedalus' words, 'eternity's mansions out of time's ruins' (Meaney, 1997: 8).

A similar reading is given by Michael Malouf (1999) of the Joycean design of the last Irish £10 note (a design in circulation between 1993 and the introduction of the Euro in 2002). The note featured a drawing of Joyce's head superimposed over a topographical representation of Howth Head on one side, and the head of Anna Livia, along with excerpts from *Finnegan's Wake*, superimposed over a map of Dublin on the other side. Such 'canonization', Malouf writes, occurred as part of Ireland's Celtic Tiger economic embrace of globalization and free-floating signifiers under contemporary capitalism. He argues that:

> Significantly, by choosing a passage that ends in a specific, historically-verifiable location, Howth Castle, the designers engage with the 'annotated' aspect of Joyce that is so valued by academics and tourism. In completing the montage ... they activate an image of the artist as an authenticating and authentic-making figure (Malouf, 1999: 5-6).

Malouf goes on to argue that such representations serve to commodify Joyce to both tourists and residents, along with the use of his work as a 'literary Baedeker' for Dublin.

'Walking in the City'

However, what such readings of the experience of Dublin by Joycean tourists fail to take into account is their own creation of what de Certeau terms a 'rhetoric' of walking. He argues that it is inadequate to judge the paths of urban walking only by what can be inscribed onto a map as paths, directions and trajectories. This is in fact a critique of the entire process of mapping as a totalizing system of knowledge, which therefore renders non-existent what it cannot register. Mapping, he argues:

> has the effect of making invisible the operation that made it possible. These fixations constitute procedures for forgetting. The trace left behind is substituted for the practice. It exhibits the (voracious) property that the geographical system has of being able to transform action into legibility, but in doing so it causes a way of being in the world to be forgotten (de Certeau, 1993: 157).

So, in the case of the reconstructed routes of Bloom and Dedalus through Dublin, those who follow the maps are, within the structure of knowledge allowed for by geographical mapping, operating within a (capitalist) system of power which is 'canalizing' their movements and therefore their experience. However, as de Certeau makes clear, the following of these routes is only a fraction of the actual experience of walking, the rest depending upon, as he refers to it, the rhetoric or style of operating which the walker adopts. While the features of a journey taken which can be represented on a map, such as direction and route, can be thought of as the norm of movement in the city, the style in which it is done, and which cannot be mapped after the fact, also includes the symbolic meaning which the walker derives and creates from their path.

This essential feature of moving through a city allows the walker to subvert the strictures of behaviour and response which are demanded of them, and to do so in a way which is individual and largely unobservable. Thus not only does the follower of the '*Ulysses* Walk' through contemporary Dublin become again a flâneur who is freely moving through the cityscape guided only by a map which is fictional in more ways than one, but they are also, necessarily due to their contemporary surroundings, actively aware of the fictional or inauthentic nature of their actions in following the path of an imaginary character during a vanished moment of time. As such, they know, as John Urry describes, 'that there is *no* authentic tourist experience, that there are merely a series of games or texts that can be played' (Urry, 1990: 11). In Urry's words they are acting as 'post-tourists' or perhaps more accurately in this context, as 'postmodern flâneurs'. And in composing their own experiences of the city, even as they supposedly follow the 'authorized' maps, such walkers are also resisting the officially prescribed uses of urban space, thereby creating Foucauldian 'heterotopias' of the city streets.

Because of the influence of Joyce's symbolic Dublin upon the actual contemporary city, the power of proper names, which always shape the imaginary as well as actual structure of a city, is particularly strong. De Certeau describes their function as:

> Disposed in constellations that hierarchize and semantically order the surface of the city ... these words ... slowly lose, like old coins, the value engraved on them, but their ability to signify outlives its first definition (de Certeau, 1993: 158).

The first definition of most Dublin street names is quite clearly drawn from their colonial origins, with examples such as Mountjoy Square, Ormond Quay and

Dawson Street being named after their Anglo-Irish founders or prestigious figures of the colonial administration. The bilingual street signs of the last century, which attracted Donald Horne's attention as a 'reminder of the "Irishification" of Ireland that began in the 1880s' (Horne, 1986: 110), are clear examples of the cultural nationalists' understanding of the power of naming upon the symbolic meaning of place. This was reflected again in 1991 when Dublin was European City of Culture, and there was a proposal – strongly resisted and rapidly defeated – to re-name the city's quays in order to remove their more obviously colonial names. In a postcolonial context, such re-naming is not unusual, but as Colm Lincoln points out: 'For Dubliners these names are not merely suggestive of the city, they are Dublin – the means by which the city is known and orally constituted' (Lincoln, 1993: 225). This argument is, in effect, claiming the hybrid identity for Dubliners which the postmodern and postcolonial is seen to offer. Again, *Ulysses* appears to play an important role in facilitating this location of identity by Dublin citizens within the proper names of the city, by having provided that symbolic link between the imaginary and the actual city which also draws the tourists. It is in this way that the 'marking' of the 'site' of the heritage-city, through a process of 'enshrinement', also has a powerful impact upon the citizens of Dublin. By enshrining Dublin largely through the work of James Joyce and other writers, rather than through colonial history, and creating a heritage within which Dubliners can locate themselves, the city's proper names have acquired a complex layering of meaning, described by de Certeau as giving them:

> [T]he function of articulating a second, poetic geography on top of the geography of the literal, forbidden or permitted meaning. They insinuate other routes into the functionalist and historical order of movement (de Certeau, 1993: 159).

Indeed, de Certeau argues that walking through city streets, guided by these multi-layered proper names, as well as landmarks which represent unmappable personal and collective memories and associations, provides a contemporary substitute for pre-modern systems of knowledge such as legends and myths.

The crucial subject of the power of proper names in urban imaginings and identifications also raises the concept of 'cultural quarters' as they are generally conceived and enacted. This normally entails the marking of a clearly bounded 'site' within a city area as specifically if not exclusively enshrined for the production, circulation and consumption of cultural activity. It is significant, for a discussion of the impact of Joycean heritage upon the cultural imagining of Dublin, to consider that the city does have such an area, in the form of the Temple Bar 'cultural quarter'. The *ad hoc* development of this formerly rundown part of the city centre into an area of artistic activity was formalized by the 1991 Temple Bar Renewal and Development Act, with the stated aim of converting it into a specific cultural quarter for the city. It now contains a large proportion of Dublin's arts institutions, and is a crucial centrepiece among the capital's tourism attractions. The extent of Temple Bar's commercial success within the heritage and tourism industries as a site of cultural consumption, and the impact that this has had upon its original function as a site of cultural production, has been discussed more fully elsewhere, by Lincoln (1993), Walker (1996) and Rains (1999), among others. However, for the purposes of this analysis, it is important to consider the effect, in spatial terms, that a formally-constructed cultural quarter has had upon the presentation of Dublin's complex urban history. Such 'canalization', it can be suggested:

> risks a homogenizing tendency which can equate Temple Bar with Soho or similar districts in any other city in the world, but is simultaneously risking, through its uncritical acceptance of the notion of cultural hybridity, the incorporation of a contemporary cultural imperialism within its postcolonial identity ... Therefore in the process of projects developed in one locality being replicated within another, the non-specific characteristics of such development may be uncritically read as cultural hybridity when in fact they are a cultural monotony distinguished only by geographical variety (Rains, 1999: 13).

The longer-established, but actually less formal development of the Joycean walks, trails and commemorative sites remain as Dublin's most prominent cultural tourism competitor to Temple Bar's cultural quarter. By contrast to Temple Bar, the Joycean trails 'quarterize' the city they traverse, rather than being 'quartered' in a geographically-contained region whose contents can and are strictly controlled. Instead, the '*Ulysses* Walks' and similar trails criss-cross the non-touristic city centre, most significantly including large sections of the north inner city which few tourists would normally encounter, and which will reveal to them a version of Dublin life in frequently stark contrast to the stylish prosperity so conspicuously displayed in areas such as Temple Bar. In their relative lack of formal structure and geographical containment, such tourist activities allow for a far greater application of 'rhetoric' on the part of participants, who will establish a relationship with the city's material fabric based largely upon interpretation or even a kind of free association.

This interpretation of cultural tourist trails and routes through a contemporary city is also reflective of an approach to urban culture and memory discussed by Kevin Wheelan in his analysis of Joyce's own imaginative mapping of Dublin. Describing the influence on Joyce's work of the Italian Enlightenment philosopher Giambattista Vico, Wheelan explains that:

> Vico believed that memory involved imagination, ingenuity, even invention: 'Memory thus has three different aspects: memory when it remembers things, imagination when it alters or imitates them, and invention when it gives them a new turn or puts them into proper arrangement and relationship.' That understanding informed Vico's distinctive style: not the linear, discursive method favoured by the mainstream enlightenment but a spiral of connectivity, a recursive, clotted, elliptical matrix. The influence on Joyce is clear ... it is within this expansive Viconian sense of memory that we should locate Joyce's engagement with his native city (Wheelan, 2002: 77).

Wheelan goes on to point out that not only do Joyce's own narratives (including *The Dead*, as well as the more obvious example of *Ulysses*) work from an understanding of Dublin's historically developed 'quarters', but also that a touristic-historic interpretation of the city was already established at the time that Joyce was writing. Wheelan cites both a 1899 book entitled *Memorable Dublin Houses*, a guide to 'over one hundred city houses with literary or historical connections', as well as the trail of statues, execution and burial sites through the city laid out and enthusiastically followed by processions and visitors in 1898 to commemorate the centenary of the 1798 Rebellion.

Building on a similar conception of the unmappable, internal associations between urban landmarks and individual memory or experience, Hegarty and Stone's 1997 Nissan Art Project installation, *For Dublin*, placed pink neon quotations from Molly Bloom's soliloquy at strategic points around the city. Commenting on their approach to the project, Andrew Stone argued that:

> If you talk about these two factions who tend to claim Joyce, Irish academia and Irish tourism, I'm quite interested in that in relation to the way that I've found English things to be claimed in very much the same way (in Clancy, 1997: 10).

His partner, Frances Hegarty, explained that:

> We started off looking for pieces from *Ulysses* which were very non-specific ... But then, when we got to Dublin, all that changed. We really had to take on references to Joyce, bronze plaques, and trails for tourists to follow, from physical landmarks on the city to guided history and literary tours (in Clancy, 1997: 10).

The installation therefore worked from and spoke to the established quarterization of the city by Joycean references, and sought to interrogate that system through their work. Examples of the installations included the line 'it'd be much better for the world to be governed by the women in it' emblazoned in pink above the portico of Dublin City Hall, and 'I wouldn't give a snap of my two fingers for all their learning' inscribed on the walls of Trinity College on Nassau Street.

Following several reviewers' reservations about this art work as having acted merely as an addition to the commercial tourist structures using Joyce, Malouf suggests that *For Dublin* may have strayed too close to a mimicking of advertising style, and that 'it blurred the line between authenticity and commodity and as a result arguments about what this installation did to the "real" Joyce prevailed' (Malouf, 1999: 8).

Aside from missing the fairly obvious humour contained in the installations, such analyses also appear unwilling to grant similar agency and application of 'tactical engagement' to contemporary visitors to the city that most critiques of Joyce's own work ascribe to his representations of practices such as commodification and modernity. As one reviewer of the *For Dublin* installations, at least, recognised:

> They ... play with notions of James Joyce as he is used by academia and by the 'heritage' industry. The quotations are placed to play with the idea of cityscape. They play with the *Ulysses* text: Bloom sold advertising, for instance. Above all, unlike

statues or fountains, they respond to what we bring to them ourselves (O'Faolain, 1997: 16).

This analysis may underestimate the power of postmodern flâneurs (including resident Dubliners with non-touristic agendas) walking the Joycean trails to bring their own interpretations to statues or fountains, which function as the imaginatively imbued landmarks described by de Certeau. It does, however, allow for the extent to which official structures, however commodified, are likely to be subverted and undermined through the actual practices of their consumption.

Conclusion

The central feature of postmodern and postcolonial culture for this analysis of its effects within Dublin has been the experience of 'hybridity' and its relationship to the structures of power and agency which operate upon the city as a text. The breakdown of metanarratives within postcolonialism, and of spatial and temporal barriers within postmodernity, are widely perceived to have opened up contested spaces such as the city of Dublin to an eclecticism and 'hybridity' of form and culture which supposedly cauterizes the hierarchical spatial power structures of modernity. Therefore, the complex and painful relationship to the space and form of the city which was established under a colonial system is believed to be resolved through the newly-established relationship between the local and the global, with its apparent freedom from hierarchies based upon the concept of 'centres' and 'peripheries'.

Certainly, as is clear from an examination of processes such as the development of heritage tourism and urban regeneration, these postmodern and postcolonial processes have allowed for a symbolic re-figuring of the city's material forms and their relationship to its cultural history. The effects of this development should not be underestimated, particularly the changes in concepts of 'centre' and 'periphery', and those of local identity and agency.

Perhaps the most important theoretical conclusion of this analysis has been the recognition of the importance of spatial form and positioning in the production of cultural identity, as well as the extent to which that constructed space remains always open to methods of re-interpretation which ultimately operate beneath formal structures of power. The modernist approach to space was that it was, in Foucault's words, undialectical and fixed (cited in Harvey, 1989), merely operating as the inert ground for time's creation of meaning. Therefore the site of a city such as Dublin was regarded as acquiring meaning only through the 'creative destruction' of its politicized re-modelling during the eighteenth century and also, perhaps, through the decline and demolition of this infrastructure during the nineteenth and twentieth centuries. While not denying the power of such processes, it must also be acknowledged that the cultural identity of the city of Dublin has been equally affected by its operation as a space in itself, both within and outside the 'canalization' of official structures of power.

The city's experience of colonialism was one which was deeply rooted in the politics of space. The imperial project was fundamentally grounded not only in 'geographical violence', but also in an intimate understanding of the way in which power operates at the point of relationships between specific spaces. This process created the 'centres' and 'peripheries' upon which colonialism was dependent, and at a periphery such as Dublin produced cultural identities and modes of operation which were based upon this hierarchical ordering of space itself. This was reflected again in the cultural nationalist inversion and re-ordering of this spatial hierarchy, which continued to marginalize Dublin.

The city's contemporary experience of postmodernity and postcolonialism is also based in the operations of a spatial ordering, in which those earlier spatial barriers are broken down and individual spaces are re-categorized by concepts such as 'hybridity'. Michel de Certeau's examination of cultural operations which act beneath official structures of power, and therefore have the ability to subvert or even avoid them to some degree, is a vital reminder of the lack of totality which all spatialized structures of power exhibit. However, an important conclusion which this study draws from such processes is that they still represent and create spatial hierarchies of power, rather than producing the heterodox equality which is sometimes claimed.

The often ignored politics of spatial power are perhaps unconsciously revealed in the theoretical metaphors which are necessarily involved when analysing the cultural themes covered by an analysis such as this. 'Sites' or 'quarters' of cultural action are 'explored' and 'mapped', while issues of agency and power are 'grounded' and 'positioned'. So the language of academic analysis and the actual practice of tourist activities such as those discussed above display a notable similarity which is rarely highlighted but which should be examined in order to study the spatial influence upon cultural identities.

Part 3
Identities, Lifestyles and Forms of Sociability

Chapter 9

Nottingham's *de facto* Cultural Quarter: The Lace Market, Independents and a Convivial Ecology

Jim Shorthose

There is ample evidence that the Lace Market area of Nottingham, UK, is recognized as the cultural quarter of the city. As such, it stands as a good example of urban regeneration through cultural development (Rogers, 1997), and of the general proposition that 'cities are good for us' (Sherlock, 1991). In this chapter I will draw a picture of cultural activity in the Lace Market, the contribution it makes to the quality of life of the city and the general importance placed on it by local residents. Specifically, I shall point to the scale and vibrancy of the creative industries in the area.

These points stem largely from survey work carried out by the Cultural Policy and Planning Research Unit (CPPRU) between February and April 2000.[1] These specific findings can be situated within the context of more general points about cultural development and its positive contribution to urban quality of life (Landry, 2000; Seed and Lloyd, 1997). The CPPRU surveyed the commercial sector of the creative industries in the Lace Market, which is comprised of approximately 200 micro-businesses. It also surveyed a random sample of the general public in the Lace Market, who use the area largely for cultural consumption and socializing. As we shall see below, these surveys have yielded some illuminating findings about the current perceptions of the creative producers and consumers alike towards the importance of cultural quarters. There is clear evidence from this research, both on the density of cultural production and consumption, and on the perceptions of the city's population, that the Lace Market as the cultural quarter of Nottingham is seen as a very positive contribution to the life of the city as a whole.

Before discussing these points however, I want to discuss the processes whereby this cultural quarter came about. The Lace Market is a *de facto* cultural quarter. It became the cultural quarter not through a process of planning and policy-making, but as something that has grown 'organically' over the years. This organic growth of the Lace Market as a cultural quarter has come about through a process that was informal, unstructured and do-it-yourself (D-I-Y). Many of the cultural activities that have carried this process forward have been developed through the temporary and unstructured creative relationships and networks that make up the independent sector of creative practitioners. Independents are the individual artists, freelancers, sole traders and those temporarily employed in the creative industries. The networks they live and work in are best characterized as an *ecology* of interdependent relationships and flows between independents, and between them and other cultural organizations and businesses in the area. It differs from the formal economy of official organizations and structured working relationships. These informal processes have been the catalyst for the organic growth of the Lace Market as a cultural quarter. It is for this reason that an analysis of the independent sector and this ecology of interdependent relationships takes up much of this chapter. Below I shall provide a detailed account of the everyday operation of this ecology.

This analysis of the independent sector stems from two sources: firstly, the CPPRU survey mentioned above, in which we conducted semi-structured interviews with 39 independent creative people who have either a spatial or cultural relationship with the Lace Market area; secondly, it also stems from participant observation. I am writing this chapter from the perspective of someone who has taken part in the independent creative ecology of the Lace Market for the past 15 years. So although this account does refer to empirical research, it is also something of a personal account. My active participation in the independent ecology enables me to offer insights into its more informal and interpersonal aspects. This is vital, as the creative processes of this ecology are often carried by hidden, spontaneous, temporary and fragile networks. Often the best and most exciting creative work develops out of these kinds of partnerships as likeminded people collaborate and share ideas in and around the Lace Market. As will be discussed below in more detail, anyone who has this organic relationship to the ecology will readily be able to identify the places where this happens and the people involved. I do not think it too romantic to call the Lace Market a 'cultural village' where creative people congregate and share their interest, knowledge and skills. It does often feel like a place where everyone knows everyone else. For instance, much of this activity tends to be in the Broadway Media Centre. This institution, whilst ostensibly just a cinema, is much more. It operates to facilitate these kinds of clustering activities. It is often referred to as something like the 'community centre for creative people'. But more of that later; first some basic descriptions and history.

The Lace Market

The Lace Market is a fairly distinct area to the east of Nottingham's city centre. Throughout the nineteenth and most of the twentieth century, the Lace Market was an industrial area made up of textile factories. Architecturally, it is comprised of many large nineteenth-century, four-or five-storey factory and warehouse buildings. By the 1970s, however, the Lace Market was becoming just a fairly rundown area to the east of the main North-South shopping axis in Nottingham.

The informal redevelopment of the area has been happening over the past 20 years. By the 1980s many of the vacated former industrial spaces were 'lost spaces' (Tranick, 1986) and were being used by the independents. The relatively low cost of these spaces made the Lace Market the natural home for artists' studios, independent production spaces and the more alternative bars and clubs. Anyone familiar with the Nottingham of the past 20 years will remember G-Force, an independent fashion design and retail operation, and The Garage, a nightclub. Both were born in the Lace Market area and became 'cultural institutions' of the independent scene throughout the 1980s when there was little else of cultural note in the Lace Market. G-Force is still there. During the 1980s the Lace Market's main thoroughfare going eastwards away from the City centre became the place where the independent retail spaces were often situated.

Figure 9.1 Broadway Street, the Lace Market (Photo: J. Shorthose)

There have been some formal cultural developments since the 1980s that have resonated with the independent networks and helped them form. The first half of the 1980s saw the birth and demise of the Midland Group, an arts centre and photographic gallery in the Lace Market. Just before its demise, it created a bar that was on its way to becoming a key networking site for the independent community. Another major component in the cultural history of the Lace Market over the past 10 years that has filled the void left by the Midland Group has been the growth of the Broadway Media Centre. The Broadway began operating as a cinema in 1990. However, the key developments of the Broadway, as far as the cultural quarter was concerned, continued happening throughout the 1990s through a process of organic growth that is still continuing today. In 1992, Intermedia, a film and video resource centre that also runs courses in film and video production, took up residence on the same site as the Broadway. In 1993 the Broadway opened a café-bar that has since become the centre of independent creative networking and clustering. The Broadway's role in the informal processes and networks is being recognized and brought into a more strategic plan for Nottingham's creative industries. The Broadway has plans to develop a more formal and dedicated Creative Industries Business Centre and is negotiating with the Regional Development Agency and other strategic civic bodies.

All this independent activity meant that throughout the 1980s and 1990s, the Lace Market developed its own distinctive character and alternative, independent culture. The creative producers and retailers who made this process happen tended to define themselves in terms of their difference from the rest of the city. Historically, there was a certain D-I-Y feel about much of this creative activity. This could easily be overstated and is rather intangible, but it exists nonetheless. There is a history of this community trying to hold its own independent annual festival. Several times the independent producers and retailers have tried to form a Traders Association to pursue their own development agenda. Given such a history, people who occupied the Lace Market share an intangible and nascent feeling of community.

Today, many of the independents can no longer afford to be physically based in the Lace Market, but the feeling of a creative community persists. It now comes more from a cultural relationship to the creative community that occupies the area, and a shared sense of ownership, rather than any physical presence. It persists despite the fact that some of the independent creative activities that historically occurred within the Lace Market have been priced out by recent redevelopment.

Recent cultural and infrastructural developments have begun to change the area, as the Lace Market goes through a soft cultural gentrification. Recent commercial and residential developments may be attenuating the Lace Market's distinctive alternative character. The residential developments that are currently happening in the Lace Market have quickly brought lots of up-market residences. The old warehouses which were once independent studio spaces are currently being turned into expensive 'loft living' residences. Many new chain-bars and restaurants have moved into the area, with the consequence that the alternative character of the place is less than it was. One sign of this is the pronounced shift in the Lace Market area from being a largely day-time economy to a night-time economy.

The Independent Creative Community in the Lace Market

The Lace Market is still however the cultural habitat of many independent creative producers. There is a growing recognition of the significance of the independent sector in the creative industries (Leadbetter and Oakley, 1999). However, there is no easy and 'water-tight' definition of an independent. Indeed, one of the defining features of the independents is their 'portfolio careers' and migration between different sectors of the creative economy. They do different things at different times. This will mean engaging in paid commercial work, teaching and community-based work as much as following their own creative inspiration. Having said this, there is a clear distinction to be made between the approach taken by an outright commercial entity at one end of the spectrum, and independents at the other end. A working definition of the spectrum of differentiation between commercial and independent sectors could be characterized by the following features:

Commercial Sector	Independent Sector
Formally registered as a business	Not registered as a business
Formally registered for tax	Not registered for tax
Employs staff	Individual or informal group
Established & dedicated business premises	Use of home/temporary space
Standardized product or service	Creative uniqueness and aura
Profit maximization	Quality of life maximization
Funds from commercial investment	Personal or public funds
Formal organizational structures	Network membership
Routinized division of labour	'Portfolio' career

These distinctions are not exhaustive, and to some extent they mirror distinction of ethos as much as operation. They also mirror distinctions one could make between different subsectors of the creative industries. However, the 'definition' of an independent above does give some indication of the way they work in the Lace Market's ecology.

Thirty-nine interviews were carried out by the CPPRU on the independents in the Lace Market. The selected findings show that the independent sector perceive the Lace Market as the cultural quarter of the city, and as such view it as a valuable site for cultural production and consumption. They occupy and relate to the Lace Market as their 'natural habitat':

- 82 per cent of this sector rated as 'important or crucial' the Lace Market as a 'platform' for display, performance, promotion and sale of their 'product';
- 72 per cent of these respondents felt 'fairly strongly/strongly/very strongly' part of a creative community or social network;
- 60 per cent rated belonging to this creative community as 'important or crucial' for them;
- 65 per cent felt this sense of creative community membership came from their social networks (14 per cent felt it came from being part of a specific studio group, 13 per cent felt it came as a consequence of living and working in a specific part of Nottingham).

Clearly a combination of working, socializing and having access to a wider social network accounts for almost all the feelings of being part of the creative community of the Lace Market. As we shall see below, this process, which is social and cultural as much as professional and practical, can be described as a convivial ecology. Such a process is qualitatively different from orthodox economic relationships and working practices. It has significant implications for the way the independent creative community comes together to work and exchange. It can be seen as evidence of a 'social capital' network (Putnam, 2000). Although the CPPRU survey of independents indicates a higher level of preparedness to relocate than those in the commercial sector, the majority of respondents indicated a keenness to stay in Nottingham. For a combination of professional and quality of life issues, such as being part of this creative ecology, most independents felt resistant to the 'talent drift' towards London.

The strong feelings of membership of an informal creative community mean that flexible networks of interdependent members grow. This is what makes the creative community analogous to an ecology of interdependent species rather than a formal economy of structured relations of exchange. It is this D-I-Y process that has led to the Lace Market as a cultural quarter growing organically. It is to the details of this process that I now turn.

The Convivial Ecology of the Lace Market's Independent Creative Community

This ecology could be said to exhibit features characteristic of conviviality. Ivan Illich refers to conviviality as 'the autonomous and creative intercourse between persons, and the intercourse of persons with their environment ... I consider conviviality to be individual freedom realized in personal interdependence and, as such, an intrinsic vale' (Illich, 1973: 11). Building on this, we can suggest that a convivial approach to the world is characterized by the following features:

- A focus upon practical 'ends' rather than mistaking 'means' for ends. In this way it can be characterized by a 'substantive rationality' rather than a 'formal rationality' (Weber, 1978). A value placed on everyday life, rather than some other approaches whose focus is more on culture-for-money.
- An articulation of alternative everyday lives for people and the choices they can make.
- A focus on the 'existential resources' that people need to sustain their independence. 'Existential resources' are the resources necessary for the translation of 'capabilities' into successful action (Sen, 1999; Seve, 1978); for example, resources such as free time (Gorz, 1982, 1989, 1999), free space (Tranick, 1986), convivial technology (Illich, 1973; Scumacher, 1974), convivial organization (Held and Pollitt, 1986; Hirst 1986) and the 'social capital' (Putnam, 2000) that come from membership of cultural networks.
- A focus on what people can do for themselves through 'freedoms as process' (Sen, 1999), rather than understanding cultural development as the 'arrival' at an abstract and officially pre-ordained stage of cultural progress.
- Cultural production and everyday life are seen as an on-going journey. Like Buddhism, the quality of the journey is more important then the 'arrival' at a prescribed stage of development (Schwarz and Schwarz, 1999).

- A value on what Sen (1999) has called the more 'friendly' approach, rather than the hard-edged and 'cold' approach that sees culture as a 'luxury' that can be 'dealt with later'.
- An underlying logic of 'intermediateness' and 'appropriateness' (Schumacher, 1974), which wants to steer a path between either-or solutions.
- A focus on the practicalities of what works in specific contexts, rather than focusing on the abstract and the universal.

These are some of the defining features of a convivial approach. Whilst these features are an abstract formulation, and are often only at best a vague sensibility for the independent ecology in question, they are revealing nevertheless. The notion of conviviality helps to account for the cultural atmosphere within the ecology of independent creative practitioners. It is to a large extent through this process of convivial ecology that the cultural life of the area grew 'organically'. It was largely a D-I-Y approach reminiscent of this conviviality that characterized the independents' ecology that led to the Lace Market becoming the *de facto* cultural quarter. This convivial ecology, made up as it is of informal networks, differs from more orthodox, structured professional relationships. As such it is characterized by a substantive rationality more than by a formal rationality. The operation of the ecology is convivial in that the everyday networks of creative partnerships are characterized by symbiotic links and a clear self-reflexivity concerning practical interdependence. It is characterized by a 'friendly' and sociable approach to work. We can also point to the high value placed on independence itself and the joy gained through doing things in alternative ways with access to 'existential resources'. We can point to how the orthodox distinction between work and social life ceases to hold any meaning for many of these people. Rahnema (1997) has referred to a 'vernacular society' that exhibits some of these convivial features. He refers to the 'organic consistency' that leads to networks of social and cultural bonds forming an 'immune system' for the community in question. He also shows how productive activities and relations in 'vernacular societies' are thoroughly embedded in cultural values and meanings, rather than in orthodox settings where abstracted notions' productive efficiency is held to be paramount. The conviviality at work within the independent ecology echoes this 'organic consistency' and cultural embeddedness.

Such factors are important for an understanding of the social and cultural underpinnings of the ecology and the motivations of the creative individuals who make it happen. The specific details of its everyday operation are as follows. It is made up of *informal and unstructured creative relationships* between the independent artists and micro-businesses that occupy the area. These relationships are intermittent, and are in no way formalized through contractual agreements. They are often as much social relationships as purely economic ones. Friends and acquaintances congregate to produce creative work through these clusters. Things often happen in an unplanned, haphazard and flexible way.

This means that the ecology (and the creative partnerships that make it up) is often a hidden ecology. Orthodox statistics on employment, job creation, turnover and investment are largely inappropriate for understanding this hidden ecology. The informal nature of many of the creative partnerships means that many of the independent creators do not rely on their creative work as their main source of income. Many earn their money through other means such as casual working. This is not to say that their creative work is not the main focus of their working life, just that they often adopt supplementary means to pay the rent. Often such income is re-invested back into their creative work as self-financing is the only option for many. For instance, of the 22 people who worked in the Broadway Media Centre's bar and kitchen in 2000, Joff and Haydn are both designers and have recently formed a micro-business; Niki is a painter; Ben is a performance artist; Jacob is a painter; Shona is a musician; Sara C is a weaver; Ollie is a painter/graphic artist who met Haydn and Joff at work and has recently joined the team; Sarah O is a painter; Matt is an actor and Tristan is a film-maker.

Another key feature of the hidden nature of this ecology is the *migration* that takes place amongst the various independent projects and micro-businesses. Individuals will not be employed by an employer in any orthodox sense, but are often more likely to come and go, in and through various projects, groups and events. To try to pin this movement down in any orthodox sense is to ask the wrong types of questions, as the ecology does not operate in this way. Being part of the ecology is a more important long-term 'existential resource' than 'getting a job'. There is a fluidity to the operation of the ecology that differs from identifiable structures of employment and financial relationships.

The creative ecology of the Lace Market is also defined by a *cross-sector symbiosis*. Often people with various interests and skills from various art forms will come together simply to bounce ideas off each other, to learn from each other and to trade favours. The creative ecology of the Lace Market is made up of these social relationships as much as professional and work-related relationships. It is common to find out that someone knows someone else who can help you, who has the right piece of equipment that you could borrow. It is often as important to know people as it is to develop the skills or borrow the funds when it comes to developing a creative project. For instance, the 'village' nature of the creative community in the Lace Market often means that one's collaborators and the informal trading with them becomes the most vital resource one can have. This often leads to collaborators becoming friends as much as professional colleagues. There are clear elements of a 'social capital' network in this.

Given this cross-sector collaboration and the migration between projects and groups, independents often develop *portfolio careers or ways of working.* This entails that they will be willing and able to take on different roles and jobs at different times. This is often down to material survival as much as conviviality. However, it is the basis of a felt independence and a self-consciously alternative approach to creativity and work. Many independents are willing to accept relatively high job insecurity for this sense of independence and excitement in new projects.

The Broadway Media Centre forms a *key place* for the convivial ecology. The Broadway runs various outreach and educational programmes. It offers courses in film appreciation and sometimes operates as a venue for local groups. Over and above this, however, The Broadway has grown in an informal and organic way along with the ecology as a whole. It is now recognized by the ecology members as the natural habitat of the creative ecology. This started when the place was redeveloped the early 1990s. These redevelopments included a café-bar. This quickly became a 'community centre' for the creative community of the Lace Market. The informal process of collaboration, the discussing of ideas, the forming of partnerships, the trading of favours around creative projects all tend to get sparked off in The Broadway bar.

This has happened in a way that included both an unplanned growth and a 'light touch' from The Broadway's management. The substantive rationality, 'appropriateness' and friendly approach adopted by The Broadway's management in these respects fits very well with the general conviviality at work in the ecology. The management of The Broadway have also been responsible for some other planned developments that have contributed to its role as a key place for the ecology. The most important of these has been the development of *incubator space* for individuals or groups of film-makers. This has given these individuals valuable access to time, space for production, technical resources and a venue for showing work to enable them to develop their creative potential. It has also contributed to the vibrant and collaborative air of the centre.

At the time of writing there are currently seven independent groups or micro-businesses working in these incubator spaces (Ammunition, Crow, Vital, Trampoline, Angel Delightmare, Zizko and Live Air Magazine). There are other associated individuals occupying these incubator spaces producing film and video work, providing space for twelve independent film-makers. The Broadway stands as a model for the potential to consolidate creative activity and to stimulate more.

Creative Industries in the Lace Market

This convivial ecology of the independent sector has been responsible to a large extent for the early development of the Lace Market as a cultural quarter. It is these processes that have given the area its character and distinctiveness. As a result of this, the Lace Market has seen lots of cultural development in recent years and it is currently very vibrant.

It has attracted lots of bars, clubs and restaurants. The retail, cultural services and tourism sectors within the Lace Market have developed. So currently there is a vibrant cultural consumption aspect to the area. However, cultural production within the Lace Market has also grown over recent years. The Broadway Media Centre has already been mentioned and is growing to meet the expanded needs and capacity of the area. It is currently developing plans for expansion to house up to 40 micro-businesses, offer business support, germinator and incubator spaces. The Broadway also houses the East Midlands Screen Commission, and Intermedia, a film and video resource centre, which is also part of the complex. The Lace Market is also home to Dance 4, a major dance studio and performance venue and national dance agency. The Lace Market Theatre and the Co-op Arts Theatre are located in the area. Along with this, New College Nottingham has recently relocated their art and design faculty to the area. EMMedia, a regional film development agency, has also recently located within the Lace Market. A new ice stadium, which is a venue for major gigs, is another significant cultural development. So in terms of large, often publicly funded, cultural organizations, the Lace Market is very vibrant.

In the commercial sector there are now 168 businesses in the Lace Market that are active in the creative industries. This is 40 per cent of the total number of businesses located in the Lace Market, and they cover most of the creative industry subsectors. These commercial outfits range from well-established architectural practices with national reputations, to newly-formed micro-businesses run by newly-graduated students, and range from long-standing design and retail firms to new small studio groups of artists and designers.

There is clear evidence that these cultural producers are self-reflexive about the benefits of being located in the Lace Market and its importance as the cultural quarter of the city. CPPRU research on the scale and vibrancy of the creative industries in the Lace Market surveyed 99 (59 per cent) of the 168 creative industry businesses in the area. Selected results from this survey give a clear indication of this. For example:

- 67 per cent rated as 'important to crucial' for their business their location in the Lace Market;
- 61 per cent rated as 'important to crucial' for their business the capacity for meeting and networking with suppliers, collaborators, competitors in the Lace Market;
- 70 per cent gave a 'very good to excellent' rating to the Lace Market as a location for combined business and social interaction;
- 74 per cent rated as 'important to crucial' for their business the attractiveness of the built environment;
- 60 per cent rated as 'important to crucial' for their business the range and quality of restaurants, pubs, clubs and cafés;
- 57 per cent rated as 'important to crucial' for their business the heritage quality of the Lace Market;
- 50 per cent rated as 'important to crucial' for their business the proximity of arts and cultural institutions.

This perception of the Lace Market and its importance as a cultural quarter is shared by the general public. In a survey of users and consumers of the Lace Market, we found the following:

- 91 per cent of users agreed that it 'adds vitality to the city centre area';
- 68 per cent rated it as a 'safe environment';
- 90 per cent rated it as 'good for socializing';
- 94 per cent agreed that 'its heritage quality makes it an attractive place'.

So there appears to be clear evidence of a general agreement that the growth of the Lace Market has been and is a positive addition to the life of the city. This research clearly shows the positive intangibles or 'externalities' for the urban economy of such cultural development. It suggests that the quality of social and cultural life, the general cultural atmosphere, the attractiveness of the architectural heritage, the proximity and critical mass of cultural organizations and safety are all highly valued by producers and consumers alike. This general addition to the quality of urban life is as much the defining feature of the Lace Market as any one specific cultural development. It is the general cultural atmosphere and sense of shared belonging that gives the Lace Market its cultural character. These 'externalities' stem from unpriced effects and unintended consequences of the everyday cultural activities of the creative ecology and the general doing of culture, more than being a result of a cultural master plan. Such 'externalities' are in actual fact more accurately seen as the 'internalities' of the general functioning of the ecology of the Lace Market's creative community. Remy Prud'homme has written:

> Most, if not all externalities, have a geographic dimension. They involve neighbours. They occur in cities. Indeed, externalities are of the essence of cities. They explain the growth of cities: people and enterprises get together in order to benefit from positive externalities, also known as agglomeration economies ... Cities can be analyzed as bundles of externalities. And urban policies could be defined as measures to increase positive externalities and decrease negative externalities (Prud'homme, 1995: 732).

As was suggested above, a defining feature of this kind of process, as it applies to the Lace Market as a cultural quarter, is conviviality. As was implied above, conviviality means both a process of practical interchange and a general cultural sensibility that combines to enable and encourage people to work in a way that is different from the formal. Although the initial catalyst that led the Lace Market to become the city's cultural quarter was the independent sector, the creative ecology that now exists in the Lace Market includes interactions between independent, commercial and subsidized cultural organizations. It continues to grow and be vibrant because of this convivial diversity of interaction.

The Sustainability of the Ecology

To uncover this hidden ecology is to enable more effective identification of its needs and more effective stimulation of cultural production to sustain a healthy ecology. To uncover the everyday operation of the creative ecology may contribute to the development of more imaginative policies for this stimulation over and above simple funding-oriented strategies. It is clear from our research on the independent ecology that cultural production could be stimulated through facilitating the needs of the community as a whole rather than relying just on the funding specific short-term projects.

For example, independents have identified the need for targeted infrastructural developments. Our research on independent visual artists in the Lace Market area highlighted the perceived need for a 'Broadway' for their art form. When surveying the opinions of the independents creative in the Lace Market, many express the need for more affordable production space and better outlets for creative work. Comments like the following were common:

- 'A creative centre or gallery, like the Custard Factory, is needed in the area to stimulate creative work';
- 'More gallery and studio space is needed to create a cultural centre';
- 'More space for production';
- 'It would be good to collaborate in an artist-generated joint project. But we need a dedicated building for a gallery, at the local level. We need the investment in a centre'.

This need for a gallery space at an 'intermediate' or 'appropriate' (Schumacher, 1974) level for local artists came up often. Nottingham is not that well served in this area. It has good gallery spaces that tend to operate at the (inter) national level, which take in invited work. It also tends to have various bars and restaurants which exhibit artwork within a retail space. Something in between – a professionally-run, dedicated gallery for local artists – is needed. This is not just for commercial reasons. Many independent artists leave their ideas at the conceptual stage as they are unwilling to spend money on production knowing that there will be nowhere appropriate to show their work. These painters, sculptors and installation-makers pointed out that it would actually stimulate more cultural production and help consolidate the creative ecology as a whole. It was also suggested by our sample that, as with The Broadway, such a gallery should include a café-bar, to offer another place for the informal clustering to take place, and to become a key place for the ecology. The idea of incorporating incubator spaces for production, rehearsal or studio spaces into such a place was also warmly received. In our survey of the independent sector, whom we have seen above rate a relationship to the Lace Market very highly, only 20 per cent have studio space in the Lace Market, and 31 per cent cited the high costs as the reason why they do not have studio space. Studio spaces within the area could only add to the vibrancy and conviviality of the ecology.

When it comes to training and advice about business and markets, our independent sector survey produced some mixed findings:

- 59 per cent of respondent rated training generally as either only 'poor or average' (17.9 per cent rated it as good);
- 46 per cent rated training in business management and planning as either 'poor or average' (23 per cent rated it as good);
- 48 per cent rated training in marketing as either 'poor or average' (13 per cent rated it as either 'good or very good').

Qualitative research on the independent sector confirmed these findings. Comments like the following were relatively common:

- 'We need more support for the business and marketing side of things';
- 'More business courses would be good';
- 'There should be advice from people – people who know the business side of things'.

There would seem to be some scope for improvement when it comes to the provision of training in business development and marketing for independent creative producers. It would seem that an 'arts centre' model could fill these gaps and provide the practical, technical and business support needed, as well as providing another key place for the ecology to inhabit. To pursue the ecological analogy, such an 'arts centre' is needed as a keystone species is needed in a natural environment, as a central species to allow for the healthy development of the ecology as a whole.

This is but one example of the possibility of a 'convivial cultural policy' approach to development that sees the ecology as a whole and works to sustain it as a whole – an approach that embodies the features of conviviality as described above. It is clear that the creative community that inhabits the Lace Market represents a large pool of creative talent across all the arts forms. It is clear that this community, whether in the form of independent creative individuals or micro-businesses, has gone a long way to creating the Lace Market as the cultural quarter of the city. It is clear that this adds to the vibrancy of the culture of Nottingham as a whole and to its cultural distinctiveness.

However, despite the cultural life of the Lace Market continuing to be vibrant, the current cultural developments represent something of a double-edged sword. The current large-scale retail and residential developments in the area are in danger of changing the nature of the area that initially attracted such investment. The alternative, D-I-Y and convivial nature of working, living and interacting in the Lace Market's creative ecology is threatened by such corporate development. I have been a part of this ecology for around 15 years, and I get the impression that things are still very vibrant, that people are as enthusiastic and creative as ever. I get the impression that the ecology of informal creative partnerships is as healthy as ever. Gentrification is, however, changing the nature of the area. The direct spatial relationship that many had to the Lace Market is no longer affordable. The creative ecology of the Lace Market is on a cusp. With some imaginative and convivial planning and institutional support the creative community in the Lace Market is ready to evolve further. Because the ecology of the Lace Market revolves around lots of informal, temporary partnerships it is fragile. It is however made up of lots of creative individuals who are keen to develop their careers in the creative industries. They are often very self-motivated and talented people who could become key creative professionals for the future of the local and regional economy. Some infrastructural support for this fragile hidden ecology of creative people could be a vital stage in consolidating and developing the Lace Market as a cultural quarter. Without this, the creative ecology is in danger of losing its habitat and thereby its vitality. If this happens it is possible that the creative ecology in the Lace Market will lose the identity that it undoubtedly has. If this happens the city may lose its cultural quarter, and will lose a valuable cultural and economic resource. A little now could go a long way in the future.

Note

1 The Cultural Policy and Planning Research Unit carried out research for the project 'Clustering ... Incubating ... Networking: Consolidating the Value Production Chain in Nottingham's Cultural Quarter' in 2000. This report is not yet in the public domain.

Chapter 10

Quartering Sexualities:
Gay Villages and Sexual Citizenship

Jon Binnie

The origin and development of gay villages up to the 1990s represented something new under the sun (in the UK at least), with (amongst others) the notable development of Old Compton Street in the West End of London, Manchester's gay village and a 'gay district' in Birmingham city centre. The clustering of gay venues into specific districts of the city is, of course, nothing new in the UK – for instance see the development of the 1970s Earl's Court gay scene in London discussed in Jonathan Raban's *Soft City* (1974). Gay villages have existed in the sense that gay districts within cities have existed for decades. However, what was new in the 1990s was the making visible of such spaces within the mainstream media. In cities such as Manchester, UK, these are even being actively promoted in order to produce meaningful liveable cities and to contribute towards a cosmopolitan or European mode of urban experience (Binnie and Skeggs, 1999). But can every city have its gay quarter? Such a vision suggests the homogenization of gay identity and space. In this essay I argue that strategies to promote gay villages face a number of obstacles, as evidenced by problems associated with and conflicts within existing gay villages.

The notion of there being such a generic entity as a 'gay village' is itself problematic. The singularization of this term is significant and implies a homogenization of such spaces – that they share common characteristics with similar districts in other cities. Here I am minded of Nigel Thrift's (2000) warning about one city fitting all. Are such spaces the same across the world? Here we are treading on debates on queer globalization – whether we can speak of the globalization of gay identity and space. The literature on queer globalization has been dominated by discussions of transnational queer mobility and tourism. The perception that gay districts share common characteristics based on gay identity is of course reproduced within these spaces. The sense that these spaces are linked to other spaces is reproduced through material culture – the designs, symbols and iconography, but also through events such as pride marches and Mardi Gras. How we can make progress in theorizing such districts without misrepresenting them or reproducing stereotypical notions about gay affluence has long been a concern of mine. In terms of place promotion it is evident that gay villages have been primarily promoted through gay media – guidebooks, the internet and word-of-mouth. It is a considerable understatement to say that the state has tended to shy away from consciously promoting such spaces.

Within modern gay liberation politics and their spatial manifestation, gay identity could only be expressed within certain spaces and places. Modern homosexual identities map neatly onto modern gay spaces (such as gay villages). The idea of a gay village suggests the universalization of an American spatial model of gay consumption; even the label 'village' recalls Greenwich Village in New York. Gay villages represent a modern solution to the problem of sexual difference: the notion that Other sexualities can be contained and regulated within specific quarters of the city (often overlooked, non-respectable or heterotopic spaces). These can be seen as sites of resistance against the oppressive structures of heterosexual society. Of course such spaces have not uniformly used by all sexual dissidents. Many – not only Marxists and lesbian feminists – have long dis-identified with the commercialism of such venues and their celebration of artifice, conspicuous consumption and superficiality.

Promoting Gay Villages

The notion that gay villages should be promoted has been a highly controversial one. Let's just stop to think for a moment about the very term 'promotion'. 'Promotion' is a highly emotive term when linked to the question of sexuality in the UK. The promotion of sexuality brings us immediately to Section 28 of the Local Government Act (1998), which sought to forbid the promotion of homosexuality as a 'pretended family relationship'. The idea that city authorities should be promoting gay villages is therefore inevitably controversial. In an earlier essay on the promotion of Amsterdam to the US in order to attract international gay tourism (Binnie, 1995), I argued that such promotional campaigns were seen to be highly risky in reinforcing an image of the city that could equally deter business. The Amsterdam experience would appear to suggest that we cannot take for granted the promotion of gay villages; it is still highly contested. The promotion of such spaces *as* gay spaces is highly symbolic of gay inclusion – spaces the city is proud of showing to the rest of the world. In this sense promotional strategies demonstrate gay inclusion within 'advertising citizenship' (Cronin, 2001). Conversely, promoting such spaces would appear to reflect the flip-side of urban pride – namely shame. Elspeth Probyn (2000) has written on the question of shame within the context of the Amsterdam Gay Games. Her discussion of shame is important when considering what is *not* promoted within these promotional campaigns – i.e. the parts of gay culture that remain invisible, the ones that such campaigns disavow as shameful. As Dereka Rushbrook reminds us: 'gay urban spectacles attract tourists and investment; sexually deviant, dangerous rather than risqué, landscapes do not' (2002: 195). In promoting gay spaces to a wider tourist market it is inevitable that this will have some normalizing and disciplining effect.

But before going on to examine these questions in more detail, it is important to trace the relationship between urban governance and sexual citizenship in order to provide a context to my argument. I seek to examine the relationship between urban governance and the 'games of citizenship' traced so eloquently by Nik Rose (2000). I discuss the relationships between the development of gay districts and the urban basis of sexual citizenship: what role does the local state play within their production? The development of gay spaces has tended to take place without much in the way of active local state intervention policy-making. Gay villages have often been the unintended passive recipients of policies to promote cities more generally. What should the role of the local state be? In Manchester, for example, we have seen the local state actively promoting gay space as a cosmopolitan symbol of Manchester's aspiration to be seen as a European city.

Urban Governance and Sexual Citizenship

Debates on entrepreneurialism, city promotion and urban governance have centred on promotional campaigns based on a neoliberal ideological framework. The main focus of these debates has been on neoliberalism, entrepreneurial governance and the socially exclusive (as opposed to inclusive) nature of these policies. Kevin Ward (2000) has argued that such campaigns perform an ideological function in cementing neoliberalism within urban governance. Such strategies reflect the changing role of the local state – the emphasis is on promoting entrepreneurialism as opposed to redistribution. Ward (2000) and Bryan Robson (2002) have both criticized such policies, arguing that they are informed by a neoliberal agenda that fails to address problems associated with social exclusion in the city. It is argued that the vigorous promotion of city-centre living based on the development of upmarket consumption spaces has produced very real exclusions of the urban poor from the city (Mellor, 2002).

In terms of policy-making and attempts to promote or develop gay villages, what is significant about these spaces is that they have grown 'organically' without much in the way of conscious place promotion or investment (at least until very recently). They have tended to be located in parts of the city that were seen as beyond the control and active policy-making realm of the state. These spaces are of course regulated – policed and subject to planning controls, so in that sense they were subject to state intervention.

The development of Manchester's gay village took place within a wider discourse around the 'Manchester model' of urban regeneration – the Manchester script that has to be ascribed to. In this way, the Manchester model of becoming an erstwhile cosmopolitan and European city has become enabling and empowering in helping to shape a sense of entitlement by many users of (and those with a vested interest in promoting) the gay village that they do have a stake. The key to the 'success' of the gay village has been the production of a de-sexualized consumption space where an asexual non-threatening (especially to women) gay identity can be enacted. In this sense asexual gay identities and asexual 'mainstream' ones are converging. Gayness is used as a resource to attract women as consumers into the space; effeminate gay men are used to normalize the behaviour of heterosexual men (Binnie and Skeggs, 1999). However, this consumption space is threatened in a number of ways (see below).

Another issue to consider here is the way in which sexuality can be configured within these debates on urban governance. What is difficult is to link together the literature on governance and regeneration with the material on queer space. There are other powerful discourses at work in the production of gay villages, which means that their development cannot be simply read as another site of spectacle. For instance, witness the considerable level of *emotional* investment in spaces such as the gay village and the sense that these spaces are owned collectively by lesbians and gay men. Another concern is the way that the production of new consumption spaces is seen in terms of spectacle. Critiques of spectacle often fall prey to notions of false consciousness and fail to acknowledge other ways in which new modes of urban spectatorship may being formulated (for instance within a non-heterosexual framework). It is clear that criticisms of the spectacle are often framed within heteronormative frameworks – for lesbians and gay men, being told that the consumption of others is a form of false consciousness is difficult given the lack of opportunities for queer urban spectatorship. Of course, simply because consumption is being done within a non-heterosexual framework does not make it essentially liberatory or outside a system of exploitation and inequality.

Rose's (2000) work provides one solution for integrating questions of urban governance to the questions of embodiment. Debates over the desirability of such promotional campaigns as in Amsterdam can be seen as what Rose terms the 'games' of citizenship. Rose argues that 'in contemporary games of citizenship, citizenship is no longer primarily realized in a relation to the state' (2000: 108). He examines how citizenship relations are embodied in everyday material practices. In particular he is concerned with examining active citizenship and the demands and responsibilities of the citizen associated with 'Third Way' politics: 'games of citizenship today entail acts of free but responsible choice in a variety of private, corporate, and quasi-public practices, from working to shopping' (2000: 108). Rose argues that the consumer is now encouraged to take an active role in regulating and managing consumption through asserting their rights, for instance by participating in focus groups. In this context, gay consumers of gay villages could simultaneously be seen as producers of spectacle for straight observers, their duties being to conform to an accepted and 'respectable' notion of gay identity.

The fact that cities should be proud of such spaces is a positive one, but it is also problematic – what is being promoted here? Promotion can also be seen as a form of regulation. What is being promoted is a very safe form of exotic difference in order to attract mobile capital, most particularly in the form of international tourism. As Rose writes on the games of citizenship, pleasure and city promotion:

> The city becomes not so much a complex of dangerous and compelling spaces of promises and gratifications, but a series of packaged zones of enjoyment, managed by an alliance of urban planners, entrepreneurs, local politicians and quasi-governmental 'regeneration' agencies. But here, once more, urban inhabitants are required to play their part in these games of heritage, not only exploiting them commercially through all sorts of tourist-dependent enterprises, but also promoting their own micro-cultures

of bohemian, gay or alternative lifestyles, and making their own demands for the rerouting of traffic, the refurbishment of buildings, the mitigation of taxes and much more in the name of the unique qualities of pleasure offered by their particular habitat (Rose, 2000: 107).

Debates on sexual citizenship have been characterized by the conflicts between those in favour of strategies of assimilation versus those who insist on the rejection of heteronormative values. In *The Sexual Citizen* (2000), David Bell and I showed that in studying debates on marriage, military and the market, arguments on both sides contained problematic elements. Like all forms of citizenship, claims for inclusion reproduce exclusions (e.g. 'bad' promiscuous gays, those who do not wish to fight for their country, politicized lesbians, those who do not conform to the couple format). One of the main arguments of the book was that each of these debates has a spatial dimension. In particular we put a lot of emphasis on the city as the prime site for the materialization of sexual identity, community and politics. In *When Men Meet* (1997), Henning Bech similarly argues that the city is the home of the homosexual, the key site for (sexualized) encounters with strangers. Cities offer anonymity, publicity and visibility, thus enabling cruising as queer urban spectatorship. Bech argues against simply framing the city as the blank canvas for the operation of sexualities; cities enable the performance of dissident sexualities:

> The city is not merely a stage on which a pre-existing, preconstructed sexuality is displayed and acted out; it is a space where sexuality is generated. What is it about the city that stimulates? Surely that altogether special blend of closeness and distance, crowd and flickering, surface and gaze, freedom and danger (Beck, 1997: 118).

Consumption is now central to how citizenship is defined, and the management and disciplining of the self occurs through choices we make as consumers. The growth of visibility of lesbians and gay men associated with the gay marketing moment and the development of the pink economy discourse has facilitated the articulation of rights claims; but it has also spawned debate about the nature of the freedoms won and the exclusions produced. We also need to be ever aware of the limits and myths of the pink economy discourse (eloquently examined in Badgett's (2001) *Money, Myths and Change*), rather than simply letting it drive the promotion of gay villages.

Inclusion and exclusion have been framed around distinctions between gay villages and queer counterpublics. It is argued that gay villages – commercial spaces – are bounded territories whereas queer counterpublics (e.g. spaces for public sex such as public toilets and cruising areas) are potentially more democratic and are not subject to commodification; they constitute a counterspace to those who disidentify with the increasingly asexual gay village. However, there are very real problems with seeing such queer counterpublic spaces in utopian terms. While not bounded, these spaces exclude on the basis of gender, so how truly queer are they? How can they be seen as 'more queer' given that they are so clearly gendered? The fragility and ephemerality of queer space has also been evidenced by the attacks on public sex (e.g. Giuliani's zoning laws in New York

City – the 'cleaning up' of Times Square). Does the 'Disneyfication' of such spaces make them safer?

The publication of Richard Florida's book *The Rise of the Creative Class* (2002) has brought questions around the role of gays in urban regeneration to the fore. Florida constructed indices of creativity in US cities. He argued that cities where gays were located seemed to offer greater dynamism in the creative and cultural industries. Thus for Florida, the creative class is linked to the 'gay index'. Florida's argument suggests that cities shown to be open to gays are also open to enterprise. However, Florida's data was based on lesbians and gays in same-sex relationships. This points towards the disciplining and normalizing aspects of sexual citizenship; inclusion within the discourse around enterprising gay couples reproduces its own exclusions.

Bounding Gay Villages

The quartering of cities is essentially concerned with drawing borders around parts of the city and marketing and reproducing their distinctive identity. In examining the bounding of gay space, Shane Phelan argues that we need to think critically about borders and the bunkering of queers into safe bounded spaces:

> Our job is to continue to question boundaries, to open ourselves to the change we say we seek. Making our communities into armed camps is not good politics; rather than shoring our borders to prevent infection, we must work on infecting the body politics with the dangerous virus of irreverent democracy (Phelan, 2001: 132).

Phelan's argument behoves us to look at the forms of exclusion that operate within such bounded spaces and the citizenship practices that operate to exclude Others. Here we are not so much thinking about sexual citizenship involving inclusion and exclusion of sexual dissidents within 'straight space', but rather thinking about forms of queer citizenship and how inclusions and exclusions operate and pertain within a queer framework. A queer (as opposed to gay) perspective on space and citizenship acknowledges and promotes inclusivity – as opposed to the exclusivity of gay space. Thus the emphasis is on drawing attention to the traditional gendered exclusion (the exclusion of women from male-oriented gay venues); discrimination against bisexual and transgendered people; exclusions on the basis of disability; and the whole racial economy of the commercial scene.

However, there are arguments now against the somewhat utopian claims of queer inclusivity within sexualized space. If everyone is welcome to the party and if queer is about the 'fucking of boundaries', then what are the consequences of this for these spaces? Attempts to police the boundaries of identity within gay spaces are in this context seen as backward and reactionary – as un-queer. But it is commonly-held perception that gay spaces are becoming diluted and that the only spaces that are actually maintaining a same-sex clientele are the ones where entry is regulated and controlled. The irony is that the greater public visibility of gay spaces (which in a sense reflects greater inclusion at a symbolic level) has gone hand in hand with the destruction of such spaces as 'Other spaces'. They have now become *same spaces*, integrated into the urban fabric and normalized.

Gay districts are subject to a number of threats. Spaces that developed in the 1970s and 1980s appear tired and dated for example, somewhat like museums of gay culture. This poses a crucial question: how can dynamic and sustainable spaces be maintained without losing their distinctiveness? The main threat to gay villages, however, is commonly seen as homophobic hate crime. However, some attempts to curb city-centre crime create other problems. For instance, in Manchester much of the violence in the city centre is alcohol related. In response new by-laws were introduced banning drinking in public places within the city centre. This led to considerable conflict and controversy surrounding Manchester Mardi Gras in 2002. The event was threatened with cancellation because of police attempts to limit the area of the village where drinking would be permitted. The organizers – an association of businesses in the village – initially cancelled the event because they felt this boundary was too tightly drawn. The cancellation provoked a storm of protest, conspiracy theories and allegations of police homophobia. Public meetings were hastily arranged and activists even planned to march on Manchester Town Hall to demand a change of thinking on behalf of the Council and the police so Mardi Gras could take place. In the event the situation was resolved and a scaled-down Mardi Gras went ahead. The intensity of the reaction to the initial cancellation of the event suggests a level of emotional investment and ownership in the gay village.

In terms of the games of citizenship outlined by Rose, what of the games of citizenship within such spaces? Gay villages produce exclusions and these are well documented (Binnie, 1995; Binnie and Skeggs, 1999). Can boundaries be progressive? What forms of entitlement operate within gay spaces? Another major challenge to the gay village is the threat of gentrification and assimilation. The gentrification associated with gay villages means that queer counterpublics are displaced. Also significant are attempts to re-brand space as gay. For instance see David Bell's (2001) discussion of visibility within Manchester's gay village – the bar Prague V and its notorious sign 'This is a Gay Space. Please Respect It', which represents one of the most bizarre examples of misplaced promotion: to a gay consumer this sign advertises the very real straightness of such a space.

One form of exclusion that has recently been the subject of controversy within the UK has been the exclusion of gay men themselves from such spaces. A campaign and website set up by an activist in Brighton has sparked controversy, specifically in the attitudes it expresses towards women. It is significant in asserting a view that sexualized male-male spaces have become diluted and invaded by straight women. The view is articulated that women change the nature of the space as being a space for men to meet socially and cruise one another for sex. While the views of the website could easily dismissed as simple misogyny and biphobia, I think this would be erroneous; they reflect widely-held and serious concerns about the decline of public spaces where men can meet men for sex.

Queer Counterpublics and Post-Gay Spaces

Writers such as Henning Bech (1987) have suggested that the homosexual as a distinctive species is in decline. While this may be true, it is evident that homophobia is not in decline. In fact the greater visibility and publicity accorded to homosexual culture has meant that homophobia has greater publicity. We are simultaneously witnessing the loss of distinctiveness of a homosexual identity – identity based on a lifestyle separate from the heterosexual mainstream. If gay identity is based on conspicuous consumption, designer labels and cosmopolitan consumption spaces, we are all gay now (even lesbians). Gay men could once claim some notion of sovereignty of these as areas that we had authority and knowledge of. In a sense, then, the massive growth of 'lifestyle TV' has meant that gay men are losing this sovereignty. This of course may be no bad thing – lifting the gay man's burden and responsibility to know about design and how to fashion a lifestyle. This is the nearest thing to liberation that we can claim in these times.

While gay spaces have in many senses become normalized – integrated into the fabric of the city as opposed to being detached or separated from the main consumption spaces of the city – then other parts of the city have become detached and separated and seen as Other spaces. In this sense we can trace a subtle but significant change of emphasis within discourses about homophobia which in turn have consequences for how we envision sexualized space within the city. The framing of homophobia is being used to re-articulate urban formations of race, class and gender. Moreover, challenges to queer counterpublics and post-gay spaces come from gays themselves – for instance in the resistance to the attempts to control and limit Mardi Gras within Manchester; also attempts to re-gay spaces, as in the Brighton website.

From Gay Villages to Homophobic Spaces

Of course it is great that homophobia has become a subject of policy-making. It has long been the aim of activists that homophobic crimes should be taken seriously by the authorities. Any activist has to celebrate the fact that the police are increasingly devoting resources to targeting hate crimes against lesbians and gay men. The discourses around homophobia have changed – a new typology of homophobia is emerging in which homophobia is now seen as deviant, as a lack of respectability. Homophobia is now seen as residing within specific neighbourhoods and deviant spaces – as having its own urban (and rural) geography. In this sense one fears that the geographies of sexualities will come to focus on abject whites, examining 'their' spaces as reservoirs of homophobia. Homophobia will come to be seen as a form of deviance associated with deviant spaces. Thus in the changing discourses around race, class and gender, there will be less concern with gay villages as safe spaces from heteronormativity and the straight mainstream, and more with the mainstreaming of a safe, containable, non-threatening asexual gay identity. This will mean that the spatial focus will be on spaces that represent a threat to this normalized asexual mainstream 'bland' of straight and gay lifestyles.

Gays were once seen as a 'cosmopolitan' threat to the nation-state – associated with spies and a lack of loyalty to the state (Binnie, 2004). Now they are recast as symbols of cosmopolitan identity and space. Ulrich Beck (2002) speaks about the 'friends and enemies' of cosmopolitanism. The white working class has now become constituted as one of the enemies of cosmopolitanism, reflecting their distance from being legitimate political actors (Haylett, 2001). In addition, Bryan Turner's essay on 'cosmopolitan virtue' suggests that working-class and rural areas constitute a particular kind of space which may lie outside the commodifying ambitions of the cosmopolitan gaze:

> those sections of the population which are relatively immobile and located in traditional employment patterns (the working class, ethnic minorities and the under classes) may in fact continue to have hot loyalties and thick patterns of solidarity. In a world of mounting unemployment and ethnic tensions, the working class and the inhabitants of areas of rural depopulation may well be recruited to nationalist and reactionary parties. Their worldview, rather than being ironic, becomes associated with reactionary nationalism (Turner, 2000: 141-142).

Turner's corralling of non-cosmopolitanism into specific types of space is significant. If we are to trace the cartography of homophobic spaces, we must be attuned to the class, race and gender basis of homophobia. In the turn of public discourse to construct homophobia as a form of deviance from liberal tolerance, a number of things get unsaid. The main thing that is not said is to acknowledge middle-class homophobia and squeamishness about queer bodily performances (even the term 'performance' suggests a domestication of queer flesh). These become invisible in the rush to label and brand certain practices and spaces as homophobic. It is clear that certain bodies and practices will have to bear the burden of homophobia. The making invisible of middle-class homophobia has gone hand in hand with the adoption of consumption practices previously associated with gays – most notably homemaking and interior design. In a sense these have become de-gayed – it is no longer considered a deviant thing for straight men to discuss home interiors.

Quartering Homophobia, Queering Governance

The concern with homophobic space as deviant will become the major transformation in terms of the politics, representation and geographies of sexualities. Homophobia is associated with anti-cosmopolitanism; with nationalism and fixity. Thus we can trace the shifting spatialities of homophobia, for instance in the attempts to fix it in place compared to the (fictional) mobility of queers. The normalization of a tacit support for anti-homophobic policies has undermined the distinctiveness and urgency of lesbian and gay politics, communities and cultures. This of course does not mean the end of homophobia, or that we should complacently assume that support for gay rights is wider than it is in practice. However, if one accepts the social, cultural and political transformations that took place in the 1990s, these have to a certain extent undermined the original basis (and need) for the development of gay districts in the first place.

Can gay districts be promoted? They work as spaces because they are *not* promoted – they have developed outside the framework and remit of cultural strategies. The history of such spaces suggests that they are highly ephemeral and not particularly sustainable. In many instances they stagnate, and gentrification inevitably leads to their displacement. Gay villages cannot be promoted in the sense that many of the reasons that underpinned their origin and development no longer pertain. Many of these reasons (like the homosexual as a distinct species) have disappeared or are disappearing.

The place promotion of gay villages is highly contested, to say the least. Should such spaces be promoted? If gay districts or urban villages can be promoted, then *what* is being promoted within such spaces? It could simply be argued that such spaces are promoting marketized identities within a neoliberal framework. But condensed into the notions of gay pride and straight tolerance, what about the identities associated with shame? What should be a progressive response to the narratives of heterosexual invasion articulated by many gay men? While the Brighton example demonstrates very real misogyny, surely legitimate concerns are being articulated here. It can also be seen as a form of resistance to the disappearance of sexualized spaces where men can meet men away from the normalizing heterosexual gaze. What is dangerous is that attempts to 'authenticate' same-sex spaces will inevitably exclude.

How can queerness be promoted by the state? Can the anarchic nature of queerness be officially sanctioned and promoted? The whole underlying reasons behind the energy and excitement associated with the development of gay spaces and identities have somewhat subsided and dissipated. It is ironic that exotic difference is annihilated, thus spoiling the transgressive pleasure for the erstwhile cosmopolitan. It is inevitable that homophobia will be tied to the abject Other while middle-class homophobia remains unspoken. Queerness cannot be promoted by the state. The paradoxes of state intervention mean that states that possess the 'best' policies towards lesbians and gay men have weak, less dynamic lesbian and gay cultures.

So, should sexualities be quartered? As long as homophobia exists, then people will desire spaces where they can come together and share a common identity based on resistance to homophobia. And to end, one last question – what would it mean to speak of a heterosexual quarter?

Chapter 11

Finding Chinatown:
Ethnocentrism and Urban Planning

Wun Chan

British planning and urban policy-making has long had an engagement with Chinese culture. The status of this relationship, however, is one that is difficult to pin down, as what often arises is a sense where Chinese culture is held, on one hand, as a source of inspiration and, on the other, in contempt. Yet perhaps one way that it is possible to make sense of this uneven, fractured acceptance of difference is through considering an essay entitled *Of Grammatology as a Positive Science,* by Jacques Derrida (1976). As way of summary, one of the main points of discussion in this essay is a dossier collated by Madeleine V. David, in which Derrida questions the conditions in which a grammatology is possible. In his reading, Derrida cites three 'prejudices'. They are the 'theological prejudice', the 'Chinese prejudice' and the 'hieroglyphist prejudice'. Read together, they demonstrate an ethnocentric appropriation of the other which, Spivak (1999: 280) suggests, comes 'from the appropriate ideological self justification of an imperialist project'. Simplifying somewhat, the theological prejudice takes it for granted that writing has transcended from the hand of God. This prejudice considers writing as a given and, in doing so, relegated a science of language as unnecessary. However, according to Derrida, it is with the legibility of non-occidental script that Western philosophers began to accept the possibility of a multiplicity of writings, thus fracturing the theological prejudice as a universal writing system. Derrida's argument then goes on to discuss Leibniz's praise for Chinese script via Descartes. The argument posed here is that Chinese writing offered a blueprint – but only a blueprint – for a philosophical writing (or what he called 'Characteristic') that was able to make up for 'a lack' of a 'simple absolute', which Derrida tracks to the logos of a Judaeo-Christian God. In other words, Derrida's observations concern the way a de-centring other, in the form of a Chinese writing, becomes understood by Leibniz as a 'domestic representation' and, furthermore, mobilized to re-centre a logocentric position. For Derrida, this ethnocentrism reiterates throughout the twentieth century:

> The concept of Chinese writing ... functioned as a sort of European hallucination. This implied nothing fortuitous: this functioning obeyed a rigorous necessity. And the

hallucination translated less as ignorance than a misunderstanding. It was not disturbed by the knowledge of Chinese script, limited but real, which was then available ... The occultation, far from proceeding, as it would seem, from ethnocentric scorn, takes the form of an hyperbolical admiration. We have not finished verifying the necessity of this pattern. Our century is not free from it; each time that ethnocentrism is precipitately and ostentatiously reversed, some effort silently hides behind all the spectacular effects to consolidate an inside and to draw from it some domestic benefit (Derrida, 1976: 80).

In this chapter, I consider a number of examples in which a similar structure of appropriation and ethnocentrism reiterates through the planning discourse. What I demonstrate is that different forms of Chinese culture, although held in great esteem by British planners, have repeatedly been cited throughout the twentieth century to consolidate an inside, and that this functioning operates through the elision of other, less desired, but nonetheless available forms of identity. I make this claim through drawing out three examples from the planning archive on the relationship between urban planners and Chinese culture. These examples are Patrick Abercrombie's (1943) seminal planning text, *Town and Country Planning*, Peter Hall's 'Enterprise Zones' and Birmingham's Chinese Quarter.

Patrick Abercrombie and a Chinese Prejudice

In *Town and Country Planning*, Abercrombie famously outlines his criteria for planning practice. As is well known to planners, these are practices that refuse 'laissez-faire' and, as he is keen to stress, they are also practices of inter-relations:

> The touchstone of what constitutes a planning scheme is this matter of relationship, the accommodation of several units to make a complete but harmonious whole (Abercrombie, 1943: 11).

One of the relationships that Abercrombie seeks to discuss is, of course, between town and country. On this he draws from example after example to suggest that they represent 'opposite but complementary poles of influence' where each unit becomes formative of the other. For Abercrombie, the implication of these relations is that there is no such thing as 'natural growth' but instead a planning history where it is possible to detect the 'conscious' intervention of 'mankind' [*sic*] in '[moulding] his environment' (*ibid.* 10). Here Abercrombie, like many contemporary thinkers, challenges the orthodox idea that towns are the opposite of nature. Yet importantly the crux of his argument is that if England is to be planned successfully, the connections between town/country and 'nature'/'man' must be handled carefully, especially in light of protecting England's emerging National Parks and when 'wild country' comes within reach of a large population. In his case, the solution is both 'a code of conduct' and a planning practice that he draws from China in the form of Feng Shui.

According to Matless (1993: 174), by drawing upon Feng Shui, Abercrombie's work casts a doubt on 'the view that attention to nature and spirituality and attention to the modern metropolis are and have been entirely separate concerns'. Rather, following Cosgrove and Gruffudd, Matless instead suggests that the appropriation of Feng Shui or 'a rural environmental philosophy in its most spiritual moments cannot necessarily be placed in an anti-modern field' as the 'modern' lies alongside environmentalism (*ibid.* 175). Quite clearly, Matless reminds his reader of Abercrombie's point on the formative relationship between different 'units', which blurs a distinction between nature and culture. However, another way that this dialectical process can be read is by recognizing that 'the Chinese' have become selectively accommodated along a longer trajectory of English planning and, furthermore, are conjured to address the concerns of population and nationalization in inter-war Britain. In this respect, like Leibniz's 'Characteristic', Abercrombie's 'Feng Shui' is located as a domestic representation and reconstructed to fit easily amongst its syntax. The pertinence of this assertion becomes clearer on considering the narrow scope in which 'The Chinese' appear in Abercrombie's work:

> The Chinese, faced with the intensive use of the country, have, as already mentioned, evolved a definite system, the practice and aesthetic of Feng Shui, for the purpose. Whether in the present political welter of that country any vestiges of the system remain, is uncertain; but we might well follow their example in attempting to formulate and act up to some definite principles of conduct. The Chinese landscape, evolved under Feng Shui, is probably the most elaborately composed that has ever existed; but it has remained country, for unlike the Greeks whose city policy dominates Europe, the Chinese have always looked to the country as their home (Abercrombie, 1943: 229-230).

> The professor of Feng Shui ... is placed in a position of extreme power. We can hardly anticipate a practice based upon such esoteric principles ... But it should be possible to evolve a system of landscape design which will be authoritative enough to prevent brutal outrage on the one hand and a misguided attempt at a bogus naturalism or faked antiquity on the other (*ibid.* 231-232).

If read against the grain, what becomes evident in Abercrombie's account is that he draws from 'the Chinese' not their revolutionary actions, even though there are spectres of an unsettling Chinese population. Nor does he gather a Chinese urban landscape, even though Abercrombie tells his students that country is constitutive of town and, conversely, that town is constitutive of country. Instead he praises the Chinese according to a planning system that can deal with 'the density of population per square mile' and in the way that Feng Shui provides 'Local administrators' with 'absolute powers' (*ibid.* 21). That the background of these claims is coloured by an upsurge in feeling that British planners required greater autonomy and should decentralize British cities is far from incidental here. For these domestic politics – which were instructive to the Barlow Commission and the Greater London Plan – mark out the parameters in which Feng Shui becomes accepted and understood. So what is possible to detect in Abercrombie's discussion of Feng Shui and, more broadly, Chinese culture are domestic issues where he makes available the blueprint of Feng Shui to define the necessary corrections and demonstrate the inadequacies of British planning. In this regard, Abercrombie does not import Chinese culture wholesale, but defines it according to certain national conditions. As I now exemplify, Abercrombie's Feng Shui simply marks a precursor: the limited admiration/appropriation of an idea of China reiterates with more contemporary forms of urban planning, albeit with different domestic registers.

Re-Centring the City Centre: Birmingham's Chinese Quarter

'China' as referent hides the hybrid of Chinatown, hidden in its turn from the culturally unmarked Anglo (Spivak, 1999: 332).

In the following sections, I further consider an ethnocentric history of consolidation with reference to urban planning and, in particular, the development of Birmingham's Chinese Quarter. The period which I re-focus this exposition coincides with a governmental revaluation of the city's local and global assets. One of these assets can be identified as multiculturalism, another a select migrant in the form of an ethnic entrepreneur. However, before I discuss these particular features and characters, it is worth outlining the ways in which Birmingham's planners had understood the city prior to their formal introduction. Such an insight brings to the foreground a number of 'lacks', deficits and inadequacies in the cityscape that repeatedly delimit the parameters around which the city's Chinese Quarter was acknowledged by urban planners. To untangle my claim I make a number of steps. Firstly, I broadly describe the planning priorities surrounding the Central Area District Plan (CADP) (Birmingham City Council and West Midlands County Council, 1980a, 1980b, 1981) and, secondly, I examine the much-maligned monument of the Inner Ring Road.[1] These two steps are crucial if we are to understand the emergence of the city's official cultural quarters in the late 1980s.

Hit by rising inflation, hikes in oil prices, competition to its manufacturing sector and subsequently unemployment, like many cities Birmingham began to restructure itself in the 1970s (Beazley *et al.*, 1997; Cherry, 1994; Spencer *et al.*, 1986). Perhaps the most spectacular features of the restructuring took the form of large-scale flagship developments that were intended to broaden the city's economic base (Lister, 1991; Loftman and Nevin, 1996a, 1996b; Smyth, 1994). These included the building of the National Exhibition Centre (NEC) and later the International Convention Centre (ICC). However, closely affiliated to the amelioration package were a series of smaller aesthetic schemes, including the re-establishment of public art and the conservation of a number of fragments from Birmingham's industrial past, that were provided with public support under the proviso that they would 'have a profound effect upon our appreciation and confidence in the area' (CADP, 1981: 1). In government circles and indeed planning, such 'appreciation and confidence' was undoubtedly wrapped up with attracting footloose investment and business tourism (see CADP, 1980a, 1981; Fretter, 1993). The somewhat idealistic, but all too familiar, hope was that the planning authority's taste in symbolic capital would transform into economic capital or, at least, a form of competitive advantage (see Bianchini, 1990; Harvey, 1990; Zukin, 1991). Certainly these narratives were not specific to Birmingham. Yet what becomes apparent is that even though the image enhancement schemes of the CADP never included any mention of a Chinese Quarter, let alone multiculturalism, it is possible to note how its schema became translated into the Quarter's planning. Moreover, it is possible to note how the antithesis of Birmingham's remarketing strategy, which involved tackling the image of the Inner Ring Road and inner city, became an element that preoccupied the Quarter's plans.

Birmingham's Inner Ring Road and the Areas of Potential Change

There is perhaps no better monument that intersects the fluctuating history of Birmingham's post-war planning than the Inner Ring Road. Designed by the architect James Roberts and built of pre-cast *in situ* concrete, the road conjoined seven major junctions with 4.8 miles of dual carriageway, encompassed four underpasses, two flyovers, five bridges, one twin tunnel and covered 52 pedestrian subways as well as 20 public conveniences and 45 shops (Cowles and Piggott, 1974). When it was opened in 1971, the road was officially named the Queensway and, in a similar vein, it was acknowledged to be the 'jewel in the crown' of the region's public developments (Cherry, 1994: 199).[2] Such grand and monolithic gestures were indicative of Birmingham's attempt to demonstrate its support for the local (and then flourishing) automobile industry. However, even at its conception, support for the road was always far from absolute. Despite the fact that the Deputy City Engineer and the Resident Engineer declared that the road had 'improved the environmental quality of the area' (Cowles and Piggott, 1975), its Corbusian structure was dismissed as lacking 'architectural distinction' (Birmingham City Council Planning and Architecture Department, 1996a). In addition, the road itself was said to be a magnet for pollution and its subways were criticized for being a nuisance for the elderly, as well as being prime spots for crime and disorder (Birmingham Development Department, 1989). Indeed, by the 1980s the dismissal of the Queensway became common currency in the local urban discourse. For instance, the CADP associated the road with a multitude of uneven, yet mostly depreciative, signifiers such as 'drab and inhuman', 'gloomy, dirty and dangerous', 'monotone', 'unfinished', 'unattractive', 'particularly unpleasant' and also one of lack:

> Areas which lack visual interest lie between New Street and the Hurst Street area and New Street and Broad Street and at the northern end of Corporation Street. These not only form barriers between entertainment areas but are also unattractive areas in the City Centre both by day as well as by night (CADP, 1980b: 50).

Interwoven into these claims about the road's aesthetics were others that concerned an alteration to its function. The first Highbury Initiative (Birmingham City Council, 1988) – a delegation of academics, architects, planners, management consultants, landowners and government officials – argued that the city should shift the Queensway's emphasis to encourage pedestrianization through building treelined boulevards and by re-routing the city's motor traffic to the Middle Ring Road.[3] They hoped that these measures would release commercial expansion from the city centre and moreover relieve Birmingham of a number of 'leftover spaces' dotted around the inner city (*ibid.* 10). In the draft of the CADP, such leftovers roughly matched what were provisionally called the six major 'areas of potential change' (see Figure 11.1). The argument and intention behind these, which can be tracked from at least the 1975 Survey of City Centre Land Use, was that the Queensway had opened up 'residual land' that needed to be brought back into compatibility with the city centre, and that this 'residual land' offered the space where the city could redefine itself as an international centre. The 'general philosophy' of the CADP states the remit clearly:

> The general philosophy of the Plan acknowledges that during the 1980s the overall pattern of land use will remain stable and that it is the 'areas of potential change' that offer the opportunities for achieving the objectives of the Plan. In them there is room to accommodate those activities which will enhance the City Centre as a regional centre in particular, office uses or cultural activities. However, vacant sites will not be retained indefinitely ... as it is equally important to the aims of the Plan that sites should not remain unused for unduly long periods, thereby giving the City a run-down look (Birmingham City Council and West Midlands County Council, 1980a: 9).

In short, the 'areas of potential change' signalled an aesthetic revaluation of the relation between the city centre and its margins, as well as a reworking of the connection between upper and lower circuits of capital. The suggestion was that these areas were somewhat 'vacant' or 'backwaters' of Birmingham and that they now should be given an enhanced value, whether symbolic or of use, to support Birmingham's search for a new service sector. As outlined in the CADP, this included the enhancement of a consumerist style of urbanization through an expansion of leisure facilities and, in particular, a need to address the 'absence of a well defined restaurant or "eating out" area in the city centre' for the corporate visitors to the NEC (CADP, 1980b: 45). The solution, however, involved finding a suitable site for the establishment of 'a major entertainment zone' and to court joint funding with property owners, occupiers and civic organizations to build 'a better environment' (CADP, 1980a, 109). One of four sites that became identified was the Hurst Street area of potential change:

> In recent years, the area of Hurst Street/Smallbrook Ringway has naturally developed a role as a major entertainment and specialist service trades zone. The Hippodrome Theatre, which is now being refurbished, can serve as the focus for general environmental and physical improvements in this vicinity, including limited pedestrianisation, improved car parking and the facelift of frontages (*ibid.* 114).

Within the different documents that make up the CADP, it seems that from being labelled as an area lacking visual stimulus, Hurst Street was called a naturally-evolving major entertainment zone. Only three years later, planners would also call it a Chinese Quarter, despite the fact that it housed a heterogeneous ethnic population and a number of Birmingham's gay and lesbian businesses. This emergence coincided with the populating of urban policy with the over-valorized figure of the ethnic entrepreneur.

Urban Policy and Ethnic Entrepreneurship

> Some people have felt swamped by immigrants. They've seen the whole character of their neighbourhood change. Of course people can feel that they are being swamped. Small minorities can be absorbed – *they can be assets to the majority community* – but once a minority in a neighbourhood gets very large, people do feel swamped (Margaret Thatcher, 25th February 1979, cited in Solomos, 1993: 97, my emphasis).

Throughout the 1960s to early 1970s, there were a number of changes to governmental discourse that trace the emergence of ethnic minorities in urban planning. Some of the most significant of these shifts occurred with the introduction of the Urban Programme and under Section 11 of the 1966 Local Government Act, which was initially oriented towards social and educational provision, albeit with varying degrees of acknowledgement of race and ethnicity. However, a period between the mid-1970s and the mid-1980s marked a more exaggerated, if not more decisive, turning point in terms of the level of governmental recognition afforded to ethnic and racial differences. For instance, these were times where the larger and more left-leaning local authorities incorporated elements of equal opportunity thinking into their development plans (Davies, 1996), and a time when racial discrimination was formally recognized as an urban problem (HMSO, 1977). On another relevant plane, the Royal Town Planning Institute worked with the Commission for Racial Equality to reconsider planning practices, and it was agreed that a 'colour-blind perspective' should be replaced by an acknowledgement of 'ethnicity' in urban plans (RTPI/CRE, 1983). Undoubtedly, some of these actions were instigated as a response to social protest and, in particular, to unrest in 1981 (Home, 1982), and some of them were by-products of the Race Relations Act of 1976.[4] But coexisting with what has been coined 'the struggle over the politics of representation' (Hall, S., 1996) was another macro-political shift that culminated in an increased valuation of entrepreneurial forms of governance (Harvey, 1989b). Simplifying somewhat, this shift became underwritten by the hegemonic themes of national duty, self-interest, competitive individualism and anti-statism, which promoted the rolling back of the managerial state, contractualization, the reconstruction of service provision as an entrepreneurial practice, and public-private partnerships. With respect to British planning, the turn in the agenda did little for equal opportunities and its attempts to

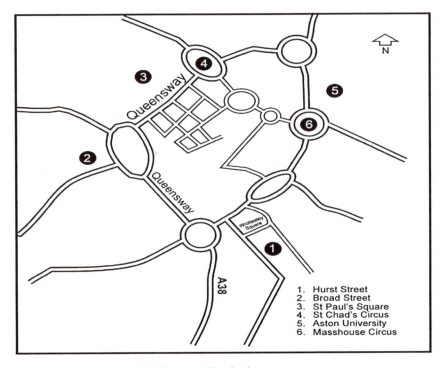

1. Hurst Street
2. Broad Street
3. St Paul's Square
4. St Chad's Circus
5. Aston University
6. Masshouse Circus

The Six Areas of Potential Change, Birmingham

Figure 11.1 Birmingham's 'Leftover Spaces' (CADP, 1980)

tackle socio-economic disadvantage amongst minority groups (Thomas, 1994). Yet I would also suggest that the dispersal of these regulative trajectories, along with the increased recognition of cultural differences, began to share an affinity, if not valorized, a policy formulation of immigrants, or at least some elected features of them, as a potential node of regeneration. As way of example, Peter Hall's address to the Royal Town Planning Institute in 1977 marks the influence of, or hijacking by, these interwoven trajectories. In this speech Hall suggested that to reverse urban decline in the inner cities, one strategy that planners could adopt would be the 'non-plan' (Hall, P., 1977 cited in Hall, P., 1982: 417). More specifically for Hall this meant that they should reduce governmental bureaucracy, eliminate taxation, free the migration of labour and affirm entrepreneurial immigrants to 'recreate the Hong Kong of the 1950s and 1960s inside inner Liverpool or inner Glasgow' (*ibid.*). Four years later, he re-drew this model:

There is yet a further strategy. It is to recognize that in the period when inner city innovation did flourish, it did so to a remarkable degree with the aid of newly-arrived groups of people who brought with them a strong entrepreneurial tradition. The same might happen again, if we attracted small businessmen [sic], with capital and expertise, to settle and establish small workshops and trading centres. Thus we might begin to emulate the drive and enthusiasm of emerging centres like Singapore or Hongkong [sic]. Witness, in the second half of the 1970s, the development of London's Tottenham Court Road as a rival electronics trading centre to Hongkong's [sic] Nathan Road (Hall, 1981: 122).

Although Hall (1982) argued that such a solution was only a 'model' to face up to 'real economic prospects' and insisted that he was a social democrat, unsurprisingly these proposals became easily appropriated by neoliberals who cited Hall's 'non-plan' in their formulations for urban policy. One snag, however, was that with the Conservative Government's commitment towards immigration controls, it was not so much immigrant entrepreneurs who became celebrated, but ethnic entrepreneurs. Subsequently, the Enterprise Zones in which Hall's ideas are accredited brought exemption from rates, development land tax and industrial training levies, but dropped the elements that involved the free migration of labour and the encouragement of immigration (Hall, P., 1996). Nevertheless, other schemes were either re-focussed or constructed to enhance the employability and business skills of ethnic minorities. The Urban Programme in the 1980s along with the Ethnic Minorities Business Initiative and the Ethnic Minority Grant are clear examples of this (see Moon and Atkinson, 1997; Munt, 1994). Furthermore, with reference to the West Midlands, the County Council's Economic Development Committee also took a number of additional steps along these lines. One such step involved the establishment of a Business Advice and Training Scheme to 'assist ethnic entrepreneurs'. Another involved commissioning the writing of various reports to explore different avenues that ethnic minority groups offered in broadening the regional space-economy. In the mid-1980s, these reports included: 'The West Midlands Food Industries', which saw the 'ethnic food market' as a potential means to access overseas markets: 'opportunity for food exports (e.g. halal meat to the Middle East as some West Midland abattoirs are already doing)' (Wiggins and Lang, 1985), and the 'Directory on Ethnic Minority Businesses' (Birmingham Enterprise Centre, 1986), which according to Councillor Albert Bore would 'assist inter-trading' and 'benefit the local economy'.

There is little room to discuss the beneficiaries of the Enterprise Zones here (see Massey, 1982). What is worth underscoring is that ethnic minority enterprises were not new to Birmingham: a handful of 'Chop Suey Houses' had been opened prior to 1960 and ethnic minority businesses had existed in the city as early as the 1930s (Sutcliffe and Smith, 1974).[5] Rather, it was that they had now become enlisted and rationalized as a node of regional regeneration and, furthermore, served as a means to re-visualize the city's connection to different international circuits of capital. As the 1997-2000 Economic Strategy for Birmingham suggests, one of the intentions of Birmingham's Economic Development Partnership (1997: 6) would be to '[build] on the unique advantage that our multi-cultural City gives in international trading arenas'. I think that the case of the handover of Hong Kong to China in 1997 provides another example of the sort of advantages and connections that Birmingham was pursuing.

Hong Kong 1984 to Birmingham 1997

The Joint Declaration between Britain and China in 1984 exacerbated expectations of both emigration and capital flight from Hong Kong (see Cuthbert, 1995; Lin, 1998). In 1994, per capita gross domestic product was higher in Hong Kong than in Britain and Australia (Smart and Smart, 1996), and a number of countries, particularly those around the Pacific Rim, re-regulated their immigration and urban policies to cash in (see Mitchell, 1993, 1998). In Britain, the governmental response, although not clear-cut, was one that promoted a conditional form of settlement that was clouded by self-interest (Parker, 1995). The British Nationality (Hong Kong) Act of 1990, for example, made available 50,000 passports to heads of household and their families according to a points scheme that favoured Hong Kong's corporate, professional, public service and military elite. Other attempts to solicit the dispersal of this financially-affluent polarity of transnational labour were conducted in the West Midlands, where the Development Agency flagged the presence of an existing British Chinese population to attract prospective investors to inner city areas (*Financial Times*, 29th May 1996). Similarly, in Birmingham the local government response played upon a suggestion that around 5,000 post-1984 Hong Kong migrants would arrive in the region and that they would be a source of investment for the city's financial recovery. For this reason a delegation of City Council officers was temporarily located in Hong Kong and a series of conferences were held between senior city councillors and the Birmingham Chinese Society. In one of them, a spokesperson for the Chinese community echoed the views of Margaret Thatcher on immigration and its assets. More precisely, he stated:

> There will be a lot of confused people arriving here. It could put an enormous strain on existing services. I would like Birmingham to have a policy to encourage people to come here. They are not poor refugees. They are nearly all professional, well-educated people, many of them with capital to put into starting businesses. They could be an asset to the city. We are developing a Chinatown in Birmingham as a tourist attraction and it will be a lot more successful if there is a good-sized Chinese community here (Steve Yau, Birmingham Chinese Society, cited in the *Birmingham Post*, 19th June 1991).

A number of points can be made here. Firstly, as Davis (1990) with respect to multiculturalism in Los Angeles and Lin (1995) with respect to Houston's Chinatown argue, the marketing of ethnic diversity provides place entrepreneurs with a forum to negotiate their standing in the city. In Birmingham, like many Western cities, two contingencies that define a similar speaking position have become the features of capital investment and/or value to the tourist industry. Not incidentally, in return for these investments, these business people receive local government support to mobilize their labour and to endorse Chinatown.[6] This relationship might be called a 'regional class alliance' (Harvey, 1985: 140). Secondly, if these agents have become co-opted by local government as players in the city's regeneration, quite clearly they are not subaltern. As Spivak (1999: 310) points out, the entry into the 'circuits of citizenship' is also an insertion 'into the long road to hegemony'. However, it should not be forgotten that such an enculturing and appropriation of multicultural difference does not imply that the eradication of a subaltern subject. For, as with all forms of hegemony the above familial pact, which favours affluence and embraces particular gendered relations, this cannot be thought of as an absolute. Instead, the favouritism acts like a political closure whose syntax cannot help but reveal the repression of an emergent heterogeneity, which is conjured here as the marginal, constitutive figure of the poor refugee. There are undoubtedly other identities amongst them, but one question that this perhaps raises is whether these borderlines are going to be re-figured in the light that the city promotes itself as an international meeting place.

Translating the CADP into Birmingham's Chinese Quarter

With the advent of the Birmingham Unitary Plan of 1993, one group of ethnic entrepreneurs, the Chinese business community, became increasingly highlighted in the planning archive. However, their presence and their potential economic contribution was surrounded by a number of descriptive parameters that delimit the planning of the Chinese Quarter. Often, these limits appear in an interwoven fashion, but for exposition they might be identified as: Birmingham as a motor city, attracting business tourism and building support for the NEC through consumption services, and 'addressing the city's aesthetic lack in the inner city. As alluded to above, such themes are repetitions of the agenda of the CADP and, as such, they indicate that the introduction of the Chinese Quarter is like a translation, repeating a similar domestic agenda that previously had little interest in celebrating multiculturalism. My claim might be elaborated upon if we take a number of examples.

The Chinese Quarter and Birmingham's Roads

The introduction of Birmingham's Chinese Quarter in the local government archive is not so much a rupture from previous 'colour-blind' approaches to planning, but instead becomes discussed through reiterating a number of established 'problems' that have been acknowledged in Birmingham's cityscape. One of these 'problems' includes addressing 'the physical barrier created by the Queensway' (Birmingham City Council, 1992), together with fixing the 'disjointed' and 'insensitive' character of post-war development (Birmingham City Council Planning and Architecture Department, 1996b). Here the Chinese Quarter acts as a means of embellishing the city's roads through street furniture and cultural motifs:

- To continue to promote the Chinese 'Theme' within the area, including signing and the provision of a Chinese Arch, adjacent to the Arcadian;
- To promote enhanced pedestrian accessibility and integration, by the introduction of a normal street junction, with surface pedestrian crossing at Hill Street/Hurst Street;
- To establish a pedestrian priority Square, adjoining the Hippodrome Theatre and Arcadian development, in conjunction with a traffic management scheme for Hurst Street. (Birmingham City Council, 1992: 17).

Like the 'areas of potential change', the Chinese Quarter together with its pagodas and gateways becomes entangled with the city centre, its roads, its conference halls, its hotels, its leisure industries and, moreover, deferring the sights of the monolithic building projects of the 1960s and 1970s. One redevelopment scheme, Birmingham's pagoda, located on a roundabout above the Inner Ring Road, was granted European Funds for the reason that it purportedly '[improved the] environmental infrastructure' and could help to stimulate up to '£75million of private sector investment in the locality' (Application to the Birmingham Integrated Operational Programme for a Chinese Gate, Smallbrook Queensway, 1994).

China Court and Business Tourism

Vital to the emergence of an official Chinese Quarter in Birmingham was the redevelopment of two wholesale warehouses; one formerly called the Lawrence Brothers premises and the other a former property named Bayliss House. For the Development Department, the conversion of these properties provided the 'basis for the establishment of Chinese Quarter [*sic*] in the City Centre' (PA: 920/16) and marked the start of a period when planning began to overtly act upon the economic potential of the Chinese community. Given the outline of the CADP, it was not inevitable that a Chinese Quarter would be focussed around these premises or its immediate surroundings. For example, the CADP had deemed this area as available to a mixture of uses and the Lawrence Brothers building, whilst being considered difficult to let, was exposed to different interests in the early 1980s, all of which were acceptable to the Development Department. Nevertheless, the proposal that particularly excited planners was known as China Court. Initially proposed by Fullwell Service Limited, this development sought to convert the Lawrence Brothers premises into a complex consisting of a restaurant, casino, nightclub, shop units, wine bar, cafeteria, dance studio and offices. Put together, these facilities were described to the local press by the City Planning Officer as a 'comprehensive leisure complex with a genuine Chinese flavour' (*Birmingham Post*, 10th May 1983). However, although the development was, and continues to be, contingent upon Chinese people, the establishment of this flavour became overseen and gathered legitimacy by estate agents and planners who drew attention to particular inadequacies in Birmingham's City Centre. For instance, the developers and the planning authority each repeated a view of China Court as a 'unique' attraction to the United Kingdom that would particularly appeal to conference visitors and enhance Birmingham's image as 'an International Centre' (PA: 920/19/1C). China Court, it seemed, made the necessary corrections to the features that had been identified as somewhat lacking in the CADP, including the lack of a spectacle in the Hurst Street 'area of potential change' and the lack of a well-defined eating out area. Moreover, the second phase of the development was discussed primarily in terms of the lack in the City Centre of specialist retailing:

> The proposed development lies in the Chinese Quarter and Markets area and is wholly consistent with the need to promotes its tourist potential. *The development should create additional specialist retailing which is currently lacking in the City Centre* and should complement the adjacent China Court (Development Department Memorandum from Planning Division to City Centre Group, 9th April 1990, my emphasis).

Wrottesley Square and Spectacle

In 1984, a local Chinatown atmosphere was still in its infancy and, moreover, doubts arose over the level of private-sector commitment for China Court. In response, the City Centre Co-ordinating Steering Group and Business Development Officer sought to reassure Fullwell Services Limited through proposing the redevelopment of an area called Wrottesley Square. This particular square had previously served as an area for car parking, but as the Principal Business Development Officer pointed out, it provided 'an opportunity to extend the 'Chinese' theme' through 'a design scheme' that potentially could have accommodated 'dancing, displays, wrestling etc'. At an estimated cost of £80,000, the design itself was to include 'a traditional Chinese paving module', 'an ornate canopy', street nameplates with 'English names and Chinese equivalents' as well as a 'decorated gateway' or 'Heaven Gate' with 'murals of dragons etc.' (Letter from the Principal Business Development Officer, 20th March 1984). On closer inspection, however, it also included what might be described as a domestic outline.

Throughout the mid-1990s, the process of introducing what were called 'multi-cultural names' for Birmingham's roads was a controversial affair because of claims by local politicians that they were 'the height of politically correct lunacy'.[7] Still, what is interesting about the sign for Hurst Street – as devised by the West Midlands Public Art Collective on behalf of the West Midlands County Council and Birmingham City Council (Figure 11.2) – was that it functioned 'as a sort of European hallucination' (Derrida, 1976: 80). For although a rough etymology of Hurst Street would find that the street was previously known as Hurst Hill and named so, according to McKenna (1986), in 'old' English because this was a wooded hill, a reading of the Chinese equivalent indicates a failure to engage with Chinese language and the failure of what Spivak (1999: 334) calls 'national identity sharing'. For although the middle character of the design can be interpreted in Chinese script as meaning 'son', the other two ideograms may be translated as, to paraphrase Jameson (cited in Spivak, 1999), some dead letters or material signifiers, which are not disturbed by the possibility of actual knowledge of Chinese script. In short, it would seem that the Chinese Quarter could be signified without Chinese language itself.

Conclusion

Like Abercrombie's Feng Shui and Hall's entrepreneurial model, planning in Birmingham has supplemented the CADP by soliciting a 'Chinese prejudice'. In all these cases, it is not that the planner brings to the agenda a 'new' configuration. Nor is it that the planning discourse has significantly altered its limits. It is that with times of uncertainty a 'non-occidental' blueprint has been made legible to fit

Figure 11.2 The Design for the Hurst Street Nameplate

in with the structural objectives and deficits of planning practice. With reference to Birmingham, whilst Chinatown may allude to multicultural difference, the planning discourse accommodates it, and understands it, along a narrow syntactical chain that includes issues of aesthetics and dereliction, together with the ideals of financial investment and the business tourist. These have become the dominant, yet narrow, vectors that reiterate through the understanding of Chinatown by local planners. Lying outside these understandings are entities that are not accounted for, however. These include an actual knowledge of Chinese writing and, not least, the refugee. It would seem that if Birmingham is to consider itself multicultural, then, there is a need to consider this planning orthodoxy and demonstrate a commitment to the other.

Acknowledgements

I would like to thank Cheryl McEwan, David Parker and Adrian Passmore for reading early drafts of the chapter. All responsibility and each mistake, it should go without saying, remains mine.

Notes

1   From now on referred to as the CADP.
2   Although building began in 1957, Queen Elizabeth II only officially opened the Inner Ring Road on 7th April 1971. The Council had intended that only one section of the Ringway, between Holloway Circus and Great Charles Street, should be named 'Queensway'. However, as the Queen was not told this information, she pronounced the entire Inner Ring Road 'Queensway' (McKenna, 1986).
3   In March 1988, Birmingham City Council and the Birmingham City Action Team convened the Birmingham City Centre Challenge Symposium, also known as the Highbury Initiative. A second symposium was held in September 1989. Each symposium resulted in the establishment of an organization – City 2000 and the Birmingham Marketing Partnership – to promote Birmingham as a place of business tourism.
4   Section 19A of the Race Relations Act of 1976 made it 'unlawful for a planning authority to discriminate against a person in carrying out their planning functions' (cited in Thomas and Krishnarayan, 1994: 6).
5   John Wong, in the City Sound Archive (C367), describes the Chinese restaurants that existed prior to 1968 as selling chop suey rather than genuine Cantonese cuisine. Although the first 'Chinese' restaurant (Hua gu lou) in Birmingham opened in 1952, Wong argues that it was not until the Happy Gathering opened in 1968 that genuine Cantonese food was available in the city.
6   As one of the key agencies that seek to represent the Birmingham's Chinese community, BCS readily solicits local government money. In the mid-1990s this included a Community Development Officer who was assigned by the Economic Development Department to meet some key targets that endeavoured to mobilize Chinese labour. These included: establishing an Employment Resource Centre, developing business advice, delivering vocational training, the promotion of Chinese catering businesses and the promotion of the local Chinese Quarter as a tourist attraction. The Community Development Officer also organized seminars on the possible arrival of Hong Kong immigrants.
7   See *Birmingham Evening Mail*, 19th January 1995.

Part 4
Rethinking Neighbourhoods/
Rethinking Quarters

Chapter 12

Rethinking Neighbourhoods:
From Urban Villages to Cultural Hubs

Chris Murray

Following the inception of the Urban Villages Forum (UVF) in the UK during 1992, championed by HRH The Prince of Wales, there has been a sharp rise in the number of mixed-use developments characterized by the term 'urban village'. This chapter explores what the origins – and the reasons for the popularity – of this 'village in the town' concept might be, making a critique of current practice. In particular, the need for clearer thinking about social, economic and particularly cultural factors in urban village-style developments is highlighted; issues of particular importance as we enter the first phase of the UK Government's Sustainable Communities Plan (ODPM, 2003) which sets out a spending programme of some £30 billion over the next three years, much of it on housing. This chapter proposes an agenda for action that builds in these factors to the planning and design of neighbourhoods from the outset. The aim is not to dismiss the work of the UVF, but to build on experience in creating truly liveable neighbourhoods.

What is an Urban Village?

Although the term urban village was probably coined by Taylor (1973), it has only come into common usage since the publication of the 1992 UVF report; their 1995 report (Aldous, 1995) suggests six key characteristics of urban villages. They should: be small, neighbourhood size; combine residential with work, retail and leisure units; aim to be self-sustaining; mix different social and economic groups; have efficient transport and be well designed; and be well managed. I begin by providing a critical commentary on these tenets.

- *Size: It must be small enough to allow people to know each other, but large enough to support a range of facilities and businesses.*

Typically a population will be less than 5,000. The essential question of density was not vigorously explored by the UVF. If the population were less than 1,000, this could be seen as more of an 'urban hamlet' than an urban village. There has not been sufficient consideration regarding optimum size and density in relation to the particular urban environment. How many people are needed to really make a neighbourhood work?

A change in density can have surprising results. Social attitude surveys have consistently found that 'trust' amongst urban communities has steadily declined over the last thirty years. The reverse is true in communities of high density where a high number of social interactions take place between the same people. Put simply, the better we know people, the more we trust them and density is a factor in this.

• *Mixed usage: Residential, commercial, retail and occasionally public buildings are all included and combined in the UVF concept.*

A major omission here is any mention of cultural facilities (sports, arts, leisure, social, community, learning) and the cultural usage of space. It is as if all people do is go from home, to work, to the shops, and back again. It sounds obvious, but the mix of uses has to respond to the needs of the local community and the context in which the neighbourhood sits. It is not possible to have a formula that is rolled out in the same way in each development.

• *Maximum possible self-sufficiency: Including maximum ratio of jobs to economically active residents, live-work spaces and a consideration for the 'balance of usage'.*

Self-sufficiency is here seen by the UVF to be the responsibility of the individual, home working and spending locally; but successful neighbourhoods are living, vibrant organic entities, not a collection of isolated individuals. I have visited several outlying housing estates suffering multiple deprivation where the central issue is their location. Five miles might as well be fifty when the facilities you really need are all in the city centre and the transport is no good. The concept of a self-sufficient neighbourhood needs a complete rethink. Public authorities do not and never will have the resources to duplicate facilities like health, education and transport endlessly in neighbourhoods situated away from the centre. Real self-sufficiency is not about working from home and living above a grocer's shop, it is about making places that work within and respond to a larger urban context.

Bianchini and Schwengel (1991) make a compelling argument that economic sustainability in the post-industrial age is closely linked to the cultural identity and distinctiveness of an area. Attracting inward investment, business relocation, developing creative industry clusters and cohering new or diverse communities all turn on the axis of identity and local culture, requiring a more thoughtful approach; urban issues are cultural issues and neighbourhood planning needs to recognize this.

• *Social and economic integration: A variety of residential and commercial tenures that make it easy for people of different income levels and wealth to live and work in proximity.*

The approach has merit, but in reality has been difficult to achieve. This issue reflects the point above; people with money can get to the facilities they need, others cannot. Without careful thought a two-tier system will develop very quickly, with one group facing outwards for their additional needs, and another facing inwards, effectively trapped.

• *Transport and design: An 'attractive and civilized environment' with good transport links, good public transport, minimum car usage and a priority for pedestrians and cyclists.*

Transport is given a rightly high profile by the UVF. However, it is very unclear what is meant by an 'attractive and civilized environment'; it is an insufficient reference to the importance of design at neighbourhood level, not simply in aesthetic terms, but in relation to fitness for purpose and functionality. The human need to influence and shape the space around communities is perhaps given most expression in neighbourhoods, both positively and negatively.

• *Management and control: To ensure that the urban village concept is achieved and endures.*

There is an attempt here to hand control over to the local community, but in a fairly unsophisticated way. The lesson has been learned from evaluation of recent regeneration projects; this is no easy thing. The capacity of a community to take control of its environment, to manage change, to formulate and achieve high aspirations needs to be cultivated. People require skills, resources and support to do this; an urban village residents' association is not nearly enough.

According to the UVF, the urban village concept was developed as a response to the 'bland and monotonous developments of the 1960s, 70s and 80s' (Aldous, 1995). It is clear from the limited literature the UVF produced, that the movement sought also to deal with social issues that are 'caused' by particular urban environments. There are similarities between the aims of the UVF and those of the Banlieues '89 experiments in France, masterminded by Roland Castro and Michel Cantart-Dupal (see Bianchini and Torrigiani, 1995). However, whereas the Banlieues projects embraced culture and looked to the future for solutions, the UVF, although they did perhaps have an implicit cultural position (i.e. it is not valued), were in many respects backwards-looking, nostalgic for the past and their literature appears to proceed from a standpoint which is anti-urban. Towns are described as 'places which alienate and threaten, which pollute and cause stress, in short, places to get away from' (Aldous, 1992: 36).

This contrasts sharply with the French position because the UVF had no conscious cultural policy; did not refer to the role of culture in urban development; did not involve the cultural sector or practitioners in their developments; and did not appear to wish to engage with contemporary culture in any sense. The literature refers to 'quality of life, socio-economics, cultural, leisure and educational pursuits' but makes no suggestion for their attainment other than through very basic design features and mixed-use tenure. There is an assumption in the reports that a different kind of development will simply produce a better social environment with people who are more appreciative and behave accordingly.

The Commission for Architecture and the Built Environment (CABE) and others have generated significant evidence that better design can achieve substantial social change: better housing; properly functioning public buildings; schools that enhance learning; and hospitals that promote recovery. The UVF literature does talk about good design, but there are two concerns. Firstly, there is no definition of what this might mean and the lack of examples leaves one unconvinced. Secondly, good design is essential, but needs to be supported by a commitment to develop and cohere a new community, particularly if it is economically and demographically diverse. Public participation should be a given. Castells (1972) has described how the 'marking out of space', the planning and designing of space by one group for use by another, will always reflect the dynamics between the two and will be an expression of the aims of the dominant group. The implication is that an approach should be integrated, participative and not simply architecturally led.

Things have moved on and the Urban Villages Forum has developed its ideas and evolved into the Prince's Foundation. CABE is vigorously campaigning for better quality urban design, and architecture centres are developing new, challenging and innovative models of community participation. Nevertheless, the concept of a village-style neighbourhood in an urban context persists and it is worth exploring the origins and potential of this.

The UVF saw mixed-use development of this kind as a solution not only to planning problems but also to 'social troubles'. The use of the village as a model form of development to plan not only space, but society and behaviour, is by no means a new phenomenon. Perhaps as a response to mass urbanization in Britain during the industrial revolution, a nostalgic note from the past of the dispersed rural communities, synthetic village environments (dubbed 'model villages') were developed by landowners seeking on the one hand to provide better living conditions and on the other to control and influence behaviour amongst their employees. Social problems are in this context seen to be exclusively urban (as opposed to rural), and there is a massive assumption supporting the British/English notion that villages and village life are somehow inherently superior to urban form and existence, which is worthy of investigation. Interestingly, this 'anti-urbanism' can be seen in popular culture, for example *Coronation Street* or *EastEnders*, where localism and a community which has a village-style supersede and in fact blot out the broader urban context.

Any attempt to understand the popularity of urban villages and the current movement has to begin by examining the history and development of the ideas which have led to the positioning of the village in such a central and particular way within the British psyche – British because, as I will illustrate, the particular view of village life which has perhaps been distilled within the urban village movement is peculiarly British, even English, and is not expressed in the same way elsewhere in Europe.

Other urban-based 'alternative village' movements and developments have taken place since the last war (e.g. Christiania in Copenhagen), and this is not without significance. As Hans Mommaas (1997) has argued, one of the influences of globalization, particularly through media and communication technologies, has been a 'greater localization' of interests, politics and cultures. Mommaas explains that the result of globalization (and with it an awareness of other cultures that was not previously possible) has not been an homogenization of cultures, as was suspected, but rather an intensifying of national and regional cultural identities in an expanded 'cultural marketplace'; the Scottish becoming more Scottish, the French more French. Identity and culture are equally important at the neighbourhood level.

No community can be successful or sustainable without catering for and raising the expectations of a cultural life for that community. People come together to create and participate in a cultural existence as much as to get a roof over their heads or a job. Communities share joint projects to use, celebrate, claim or appropriate the physical and psychological space around them. This element of village life (i.e. its unique and local cultural existence relating to shared projects and experiences) does exert a strong nostalgic influence, simply because it reflects such a basic need, but other imagined aspects of the village also provoke a sense of loss – closeness to nature, lack of stress, proximity to family, sense of stability and continuity – and it is difficult to set these in any order of priority.

Culture in this context should be seen as 'way of life' activities that enable communities and individuals to differentiate and identify themselves. However, it is important to distinguish between 'culture' as a unifying code for the whole of a community, and culture as it exists in cities, which is a complex mix of values and identities. The 'unifying code' or some kind of monoculture is perhaps what we imagine existed in villages and is again a potential source of nostalgia which seems attractive when trying to grapple with the complexities of present-day urban cultures.

The principles which guide all urban village developments are missing a big trick; cultural factors have not been properly considered, and this is a basic flaw. Urban villages are, in a real sense, neighbourhoods, where developing a distinctive 'way of life' and being able to participate as cultural players within a cultural entity is important not only to the success of that community, but to the success of the town or city in which that neighbourhood exists. As described in the *Culture and Neighbourhoods* series (Council of Europe, Volume 2, 1997: 96), neighbourhoods are places where unique cultural mixes and events take place that influence the development of that city and can be regarded variously as the 'nightmare' or 'critical conscience' of a city, or alternatively as an engine for social change.

A more positive attitude to urban living is developing in the UK and we are beginning to see cities as organic rather than simply urban machines. It is clear from the evidence brought together in the *Culture and Neighbourhoods* series, published between 1995 and 1998 by the Council of Europe, that neighbourhoods are equally cultural entities. It is therefore essential that cultural factors are considered in the planning and development of any neighbourhood.

Perceptions of the Village in the English Psyche

Views of village and rural life are littered with stereotypes. English urbanites hold one of two views on their rural counterparts: 'a serene, idyllic existence, enjoyed by blameless Arcadians happy in their communication with Nature; or alternatively, it is a backward and isolated world where boredom vies with boorishness, inducing a melancholia and a suspicion of incest' (Newby, 1979: 13).

On the whole, I would argue that it is the first view that persists, and that the second view is in fact woven into the first and regarded as part of its charm. Recent studies have suggested that in England, as in other countries, the rural environment was often the most harsh, with the most poverty, the worst housing and, as a result, the greatest unrest (Wells, 1990). It was, in fact, in contrast to its image of a rural idyll, often the scene of violent protest, class conflict and even revolution.

The Model Village Movement

Founded by wealthy industrialists, the new aristocracy of the industrial age, model villages were the first suburbs, often built close to the workplace. However, several examples (Saltaire, Bournville) involved the relocation of the workplace into a more rural environment. Many of these villages still exist and continue to exert a profound influence over twentieth-century planning, such as Bournville, the Cadbury garden village, begun in 1879. Although these developments were humanitarian in their expressed aims, there was perhaps a darker side: 'The industrialists who founded these villages, and those which came after – Saltaire, Port Sunlight, Bournville, New Earswick – were often non-conformists, self-made men with strong social consciences and a sense of moral responsibility – sometimes touching on despotism' (Darley, 1978: 18).

Certainly, the influential views of the time regarding society and humanity, from Darwin to Dickens, were changing, and the possibility was considered that people were shaped by their environment, and that government had a responsibility to provide the right kind of environment to produce the right kind of people. The flip-side of such a libertarian view is, of course, that society can be controlled and engineered in a very specific way. The village was the chosen vehicle for these social experiments. These ideas were to be influential in the Town and Country movement and the development of England's New Towns.

Suburban Utopias

> The British yearning for country living and the invention of a countryside substitute –
> the Anglo-Saxon suburb, one of our most significant cultural exports – has led to an
> overwhelming desire to live in a single detached house with a garden (Adam, 1998: 2-
> 3).

The suburb is the setting for many of the great American horror films of the seventies and eighties*: Halloween; Nightmare on Elm Street; The Stepford Wives; Friday the Thirteenth*; and others. This is not the case in Britain, where horror film of the same period, particularly the Hammer films, focuses on isolated rural locations or inner-city settings: *The Ghouls; The Haunting; Village of the Damned;* and *An American Werewolf in London*. Maybe the English fascination with these places is part attraction, part repulsion; our collective psyche locates horror and terror there as easily as nostalgia and comfort.

Utopias are generally thought to be forward looking, but Relf (1993) asserts that there are two kinds of utopian impulse. The first is regressive and is basically a search for the 'lost love object', impossible perfection, an 'idealized image of desire'. This is in contrast to the progressive impulse for utopia, which is forward-looking, does not reference the past, but risks surprise in the hope of something fundamentally new, but unknown and therefore challenging:

> Like the hero Shevek in Le Guin's *The Dispossessed,* Bolch says that we can come
> home, but it must be to a place we have never been before, located in the *future*, rather
> than the *past* unconscious. Only thus can the desire for utopia work progressively, to
> pull the present forward, towards the better future state (Relf, 1993: 128).

Body of a City, Mind of a Village?

Villages certainly have cultural importance in the rest of Europe, but are not viewed from such an anti-urban position as in England. Elsewhere, like Kuala Lumpur in Malaysia, a kind of reverse principle is operating. The city has rapidly extended to literally swamp a series of villages, swallowing them up whole within a few years. Through improved transport the city extends itself into the heart of the rural hinterlands. It is not uncommon for even low-paid workers to commute for two hours to work each day. The values of the city and the villages it has 'digested' have been carried by commuters into the depths of the hinterland. Brookfield (1991) suggests that these commuters literally have 'the body of a village, and the mind of a city'. This is not totally convincing. Many people turn to the cities for employment to support families 'back home', and the city is seen as anything but comfortable. However, turning the argument on its head may help to explain the importance of the village in England.

In the UK, the expansion of cities took place in a completely different set of circumstances, before transport that allowed such feats of commuter endurance. People moved to cities from rural areas in the industrial age, uprooting or leaving families behind. Often, fairly large groups from the same village or area might be housed in close proximity. People moved into cities and took the attitudes, values and customs of the village with them. It can be argued that this mentality still exists in some respects, and is part of the reason why the village maintains such a strong place in the British psyche: we perhaps have the 'mind of a village in the body of a city'.

The Alternative Village

The idea of the village has now turned full circle. Moving from a self-sustaining community of near equals in the Neolithic period, to a hierarchical feudal serfdom for the last few thousand years, it has once again become the blueprint for a community of equals. These new village communities are not the same as the communes of the 1960s, but are intensely organized, structured and viable living (and sometimes working) environments, where residents participate in some form of commonality. This can be politically or ideologically based, or it can simply be to do with quality of life and environment. Not all of these communities could be regarded as successful, or even healthy, yet many have endured for a significant period of time.

Christiania is an alternative community situated in the heart of old Copenhagen, Denmark. It has been described as a village (Bray, 1980) and does have features in common with some tenets of the urban village movement, although the idea of any similarity would be anathema to the UVF: 'It is not a pretty place, it is not a neat alternative to existing life that could be packaged and sold like a ski resort or retirement villages, and its members include madmen, addicts and criminals as well as constructive and balanced people' (Bray, 1980: 2). However, Christiania endures despite periodic attempts to close it down or clean it up. The fact is that Christiania offers its residents a choice, allows them to develop a culture, to experiment and take risks in looking for a new direction: 'as an experimental place where modern city and social planning precepts have been ignored or rejected, this settlement offers a glimpse in the other direction' (Bray, 1980: 14).

'Owning' Community Space

Christiania is an old fort. The space was taken over by a community group. It was appropriated from the dominant group, and it is worth considering that this kind of act empowers the community, creates ownership. Beyond the survival value of communities, this is what brought people together in the early Stone and Bronze Ages – these community projects, working together to clear land, to build, to settle and grow food. It is the origin of cities. How much more difficult this must be when a space has been designed without public participation to reflect a particular ideology and to influence behaviour – spaces designed by, it has to be said, people who will never live in them.

The effort of appropriating such a space can develop into a negative cycle; people making a mark to change it no matter what the collective cost (vandalism), or simply choosing not to engage (decay). The point is that, if we accept that there is an inherent human need to appropriate space and make it ours, and that this coheres and empowers groups to act for the collective benefit, then it is clear that this can never happen whilst spaces are designed for people to live in without reference to them.

The Social Mix in Urban Villages

A feature of the urban village blueprint is the mixing of high-and low-income bracket housing. This is essential. Social housing, affordable homes, cannot be stuck on the margins, ghettoized. Integration is, however, problematic without other interventions. The result might otherwise take one of two forms: the gentrification of the area and the eventual removal of lower-income households to cheaper accommodation; or abandonment of higher-income earners and a negative cycle of decay. Gentrification, although mainly viewed as a beneficial process and often described as regeneration, can occasionally be described as an attack on less powerful players in the city arena.

The Urban Village as a Neighbourhood

The urban village is an attempt to re-imagine the neighbourhood. The concept seeks to address inequality and to make environmental and social improvements. However, the notion of villages in the city, in the form advocated by the UVF, is problematic for three reasons: it is historically associated with utopian control; it is associated with nostalgia and Arcadian myth that can be regressive; it is underpinned and inspired by a peculiarly English attitude to urbanity.

The urban village concept expresses a series of social aims, both explicitly and implicitly, and seeks to achieve these through mixed usage. In keeping with past initiatives, it does not recognize the importance and particular features of community identity and culture that are essential to creating a successful and liveable environment. Yet the neighbourhood has the potential to be the most exciting and influential of all environments. Provision for cultural needs helps to develop and sustain communities, but local communities also have a function in sustaining and developing the culture of societies as a whole. It is at the margins that innovation often occurs: the blending of cultures, the expression of individual identity, alternative lifestyles. 'Cool Britannia' packages and sells popular culture on a global level, but much of this product originates 'on the street', in neighbourhoods. In order to achieve the potential of neighbourhoods to become 'cultural hubs', coordinated action is required.

Towards an Agenda for Action

English village life as we imagine it may simply be an illusion, an urban conception. British cities do, to some extent, mirror villages, with their separate neighbourhoods, separate houses as an ideal, separate gardens. This is by no means a universal feature of cities in Europe. The questions that need to be asked are: what elements of urban village development and ideology are positive; what can be salvaged from the exercise, what can be used?

Interesting in its visionary, pre-election stance, *Whose Cities?* (Fisher and Owen, 1991), written in conjunction with the Labour Party, contains original ideas about possible urban futures. It proposes that culture has a special role, not just in generating debate, but in keeping those debates open, keeping the idea of limitless possibilities on the table. In reference to urban villages, neighbourhoods, or any other planned urban form, it is vital that this idea is not lost, that we question, investigate and probe our rationale and the possibilities we have rejected or not even considered in attempting to progress the debate and find solutions.

Another important point made in *Whose Cities?* (1991) is in a short essay by Tim Hilton, 'Arts schools and urban culture'. Hilton argues that something special is taking place in art schools and that planners, urban designers and architects could benefit from a training that included a period working in or alongside an art school. The connection between art and architecture has always been a strong, if at times awkward relationship. What is proposed by Hilton for architecture is close to a Bauhaus model. Where he departs from this is in his assertion that urban planners and artists are brought together in their training. This is given almost as a throwaway idea, but it seems startling, radical and exciting. Hilton goes on to explain why an art school education is important, because it produces 'people who as art students learned to think independently and creatively and who in their maturity are disinclined to be governed, want to make what they will of their own lives, and take a keen, critical interest in the newness of things' (Hilton, 1991: 130).

What kinds of new futures could be imagined if we could look forward to a point when this description could be applied to town planners? Historically, this has occasionally been the case, where planning – for example during the industrial revolution – was a core factor in designing-out disease and creating better quality of life.

Eduardo E. Lazano (1990) sets out an agenda for action that mirrors and builds upon the multi-disciplinary approach suggested above. Lazano argues for plurality, for a new and positive approach to urbanism – falling in love with the city again – in a way that reflects community-wide objectives. Lazano advocates a fusion of disciplines and discourses – architecture, social sciences, history, design, planning – to produce a synthesis of the best available approaches to get the right solution. Courses on housing, transportation and the community should all be linked. Studios and workshops should be set up that provide real professional practice experience for people in training, which should be complemented by work on the coalface, out in the community. Seminars should be offered to all involved in developing cities in any way, offering insights into the 'cultural and political frameworks of the urban metropolis'.

Castells (1972) tells us that urban form always reveals its hand, always gives the game away and cannot, in the end, pretend that it does not reflect the social order or system of the day: 'Urban space is structured, that is to say, it is not organized randomly, and the social processes at work in it express, in specifying them, the determinisms of each type and of each period of social organisation' (Castells, 1972: 142). Does this mean, then, that improvement is impossible in urban design and planning unless improvement first takes place in society as a whole? In one sense it can be argued that this is true, and that as Foucault (1988) has pointed out, utopian architecture cannot, in itself, create the conditions of a utopia. Actually, what is needed is a two-pronged approach; improving the condition of urban form and planning must go hand in hand with an attempt to progress the wider social issues. In considering solutions, we should recognize that there is a rising tide of evidence and opinion that favours a central role for culture in neighbourhood renewal.

Eight Key Objectives

I have examined the downside of our current approach to mixed-use development, our regressive nostalgia for village life and the lamentable lack of cultural provision in urban development as a whole. There has been a recent paradigm shift in thinking away from bricks-and-mortar solutions towards design quality and a more culturally-rooted, community-focused regeneration, considered as a process and taking, broadly speaking, a 'cultural planning' approach. How then can these factors be brought together to add cultural value, to perhaps re-invent the urban village concept?

Recognizing Neighbourhoods as Central to the Success of the Whole City

The potential of neighbourhoods to act as cultural laboratories should be recognized, maximizing their contribution to the development of societies as a whole and helping cities to learn and grow as cultural entities. As described in *Culture and Neighbourhoods, Volume 1*, the neighbourhood is 'the basic locus for spontaneity in social relationships, the primary meeting place, the charismatic terrain par excellence, the successor of the village in urban space' (Moles, 1995: 6). This recognition should be expressed in policy at a local, regional, national and international level. In particular, the interrelatedness of the various neighbourhoods – and other players in the life of a city – must be represented in the city centre; this is the place by which the world judges your city.

A Cultural Planning Approach

The urban regeneration programmes of the 1990s often did not achieve their objectives due to their narrow focus on physical and economic regeneration and an output evaluation culture. It was not an integrated approach to urban renewal and did not fully account for social, political and, importantly, cultural factors within the renewal process: 'The idea of 'cultural planning', which has been discussed since the early 1990s in North America, Australia and Europe is a possible alternative to both cultural policy-led urban regeneration strategies and traditional cultural policies' (Bianchini and Ghilardi, 1997: 83).

It is important to state that cultural planning is not the 'planning of culture', but rather a culturally-focused approach to urban planning and policy-making. As such, cultural planning differs from traditional approaches to cultural policy, and has the potential to impact on neighbourhood renewal in more a positive way, for two important reasons. Firstly, cultural planning takes a broader, reconceived and postmodernist view of what constitutes 'culture', 'cultural production' and therefore 'cultural resources'. In a neighbourhood context this can include local jokes, myths, communal spaces, youth culture and pubs as comfortably as local history, archaeology and architecture. Secondly, cultural planning adopts a *territorial* rather than *sectoral* approach to a given project or remit. It seeks to work across cultural, professional and other barriers.

A Multi-Disciplinary Approach to Neighbourhood Development

As described above, this is a central feature of the cultural planning approach. There must be a fusion of disciplines. Better design is absolutely essential and is the foundation for change. But we need to re-imagine the neighbourhood not just as a better designed physical space, but also as a symbolic space where people can exercise their rights, express their diversity. Only in cooperation with a range of disciplines can design be at its most effective in this situation. The 'participative planning' model adopted in Florence – a city known for its medieval cultural attractions, but facing real social exclusion at its margins – provides a signpost: 'Participation creates a higher level of collaboration between administrators and those who are administered. Projects of participation are often complex, intersectorial projects. This nature obliges interdepartmental co-ordination and makes mediation between centralized government and citizens active' (Paba and Paloscia, 1999: 375).

The range of disciplines is fairly unlimited but might include those that are concerned with the development or pathology of individuals, communities and societies and those that are concerned with the environment.

Community Ownership

As well as community involvement in design and build schemes, it is essential that provision is made for appropriation and ownership of space, both physically and psychologically by the people in a locality. Ownership is a complex issue; striking a balance between rights and responsibilities, giving people a stake and a real voice are all essential. This means that devolution of responsibility must go hand in hand with training, support and capacity building; we cannot just leave people to it. In addition, the space that is developed needs to give a positive message to internal and external audiences about value. Denmark has, of recent years, witnessed an urban revolution. City living is more popular than ever, and usage of public pace has moved from 'passive' to 'active': 'Though there was not in Denmark a tradition for public life, the Danes, when gradually given the spaces and the opportunities, have over the years developed a remarkable new culture of using the city intensively' (Gehl, 1999: 247).

There are elements that can be 'designed in', but we also need projects that enable ownership, through activity or through structural changes. The answer may, however, lie not so much in technical or functionalist solutions as in a more innovative approach to the use of planning regulations, allowing people to adapt spaces to new uses, to colonize and revitalize abandoned areas.

Legislation for Localized Control of Developments

There is compelling evidence, as above, that development at neighbourhood level should be undertaken by a public/private sector partnership of a small scale, relevant to the local environment and with significant community representation. The new Urban Regeneration Companies, Urban Development Companies and other Special Purpose Vehicles outlined in the Sustainable Communities Plan represent positive change. Independent organizations with strong links to local, regional and national agencies, they have significant community representation, but are able to act in a way that avoids becoming entrenched in local politics.

Creative Neighbourhoods

As Jerker Söderlind (1999) describes, the arts and other cultural disciplines have a central role to play in urban renewal. Harnessing this creativity can transform our approach, generating new neighbourhood spaces and breathing new life into old environments. Examples are plentiful: Temple Bar, Dublin; Mosebacke, Stockholm; Central Milton Keynes; Christiania, Copenhagen; Greenwich Village, New York; and Kreuzberg, Berlin: 'Artists could play a more active role in city renewal and planning than today. Cultural production and other small scale business represent an unused potential for regenerating city life – in old industrial areas as well as in socially segregated housing areas' (Söderlind, 1999: 337). Artists tend towards flexible, open-minded approaches; innovation; critical and questioning methods; and people-centred solutions. Artists also have a role in facilitation and keeping the debate open.

Education and Training for Neighbourhood Development

The Urban Task Force report stated that England should become the world leader in urban development training and skills. A new approach needs to embrace not only the built environment professions, but those engaged in social, economic and cultural renewal. As discussed above, it is clear that cultural factors, and an approach to neighbourhood development which has culture at its heart, have a better chance of succeeding than those development programmes which are purely construction and economy based. This means that the training of all those involved in the planning, design and delivery of local (neighbourhood) urban developments must be overhauled.

Additionally, a number of basic skills issues threaten our ability to deliver quality neighbourhoods. People are not joining the built environment professions in sufficient numbers. Some colleges have reported a fall of up to 30 per cent in enrolment for courses over the last five years (e.g. planning). Black and minority ethnic groups, disabled people and women are grossly under-represented in these professions. The skills of the professions as a whole are not up to the task of basic urban regeneration, let alone the renaissance we so badly need. The Sustainable Communities Plan has set aside £17 million over three years to take on this immense but vital challenge.

Conflict Management

As a final note, it is important to accept that there are conflicts in urban environments which may not be immediately resolvable, which we will always need to work at and which form part of the 'urban condition'. Difference, diversity and conflict do not need to go hand in hand, but they may be an important component of the exciting cultural fusion that neighbourhoods can and do produce, which is vital to the life of cities. Whilst conflicts cannot always be resolved with any finality, they can be positively managed. There are professions and people equipped with skills in this field that we need to connect with in developing new ideas for the way we create and manage neighbourhoods. The implication for policy-makers is clear. Whilst conflict may not be completely abated, this is not a rationale for doing nothing. Conflict may be minimized by the targeting of resources at the most disadvantaged groups, areas and individuals.

Conclusion

In conclusion, the urban village model has been shown to be problematic in a number of respects. However, it represented a considerable step forward from previous approaches and does recognize the importance of localized policy and planning, moving on from the often disastrous housing solutions of the last thirty years. If we accepted, broadly, the kind of agenda for action that has been outlined above, then the possibilities for localized developments that not only meet their stated objectives, but that produce new, surprising, and perhaps unpredictable outcomes, would be promising. Untried methods provoke fear and a risk of failure, but the evidence to support a quality-design, culturally-based approach to local renewal and the creation of new neighbourhoods is growing. It is something that our European partners are leading on, leaving us to meander in their wake. We spend a great deal of effort on trying to find models of good practice that give comfort to those of us attempting to innovate, but perhaps the model is not quite out there yet. What is out there is the opportunity: massive housing expansion, a huge programme of housing renewal, a once-in-a-century opportunity to do it differently from the outset.

So can we look forward to a new kind of urban development, something that is not regressive, might be currently unknown, but which builds on the experience of the best the UK and the rest of Europe has produced? Or will we once again find ourselves, ten or twenty years down the line, paying the massive price for a penny-pinching timid approach? Only by taking a leap into the dark can we change our urban future, our neighbourhoods, taking them out of the cycle of the 'urban problem' and rethinking them as special, individual cultural centres that are the life's blood, the atomic nuclei of cities. Personally, I find the possibility of a new and different future urban form that I cannot imagine – one that generates ownership, that meets need, that can adapt to change, that has quality at its heart – immensely exciting. Particularly when one considers the alternative; a backwards-looking, low-cost, traditionally-planned approach, relying on the limited imaginations of a few volume house builders creating 'more of the same but different'.

Chapter 13

Red Lights and Safety Zones

Maggie O'Neill, Rosie Campbell, Anne James, Mark Webster, Kate Green,
Jay Patel, Nasreen Akhtar and Waheed Saleem

Walsall South Health Action Zone (HAZ), UK, commissioned the research on which this chapter draws, having identified street prostitution as a significant issue for residents in terms of their well-being and community safety. The challenge to the research team was to consult with residents, sex workers and statutory and voluntary agencies over a period of ten months to get as clear a picture as possible of the major issues, concerns, experiences and ideas for change. Baseline data was collected and analysed through a sex worker survey, client survey and short questionnaire on pimps and pimping that some probation officers completed. Residents were interviewed through focus groups, at home and in local businesses. Representatives from the major statutory and voluntary agencies were interviewed. In addition, the researchers accompanied the SAFE project outreach service, Streeteams outreach service, Addaction and SAFE drop-in and they also conducted their own independent outreach.[1]

The area in which street prostitution takes place is defined historically as a 'red-light area'. In Walsall, the red-light area is also a vibrant residential area. The red-light area is a contested site that includes visible evidence of the social, economic and spatial dynamics of prostitution, alongside local development and regeneration. The area is a cultural space and a site of both consumption and display marked also by evidence of the shifting responses to prostitution, traffic calming and CCTV cameras. Residents have contested their spaces and their right to live without the display of street prostitution via resident action, street patrols, and demands for research and strategic management.

Strategic management of prostitution involves a 'critical infrastructure' of citizens, social relations and sociability that includes the police and other agencies as well as residents, local businesses and sex workers themselves. In order to manage prostitution in any area there is a need to maintain a sense of relative stability and containment. In Walsall it is unthinkable that prostitution might move to other areas.

The history of political involvement through neighbourhood democracy in Walsall is interesting and provided a sound basis for the development of the research this chapter is concerned with. Mark Whitehead (2003: 278) draws upon Lefebvre to analyse neighbourhood politics in Walsall, and describes the town thus:

over the past twenty-five years the town has become something of a cause célèbre in the politics of neighbourhood. Walsall's notoriety stems from serious attempts which have been made by the local Labour group to implement radical forms of neighbourhood democracy. Beginning in the early 1980s with the implementation of neighbourhood offices, these reforms culminated in the mid-1990s with an attempt to devolve the whole of the local authority into locally administered neighbourhood councils.

Whitehead focuses upon the struggles for neighbourhood reform, especially the ways that the neighbourhood is defined and used by social groups in the town within the context of New Labour's use of 'neighbourhood' through schemes such as New Deal for Communities, Sure Start, and the Neighbourhood Renewal Fund. 'Whether it is in terms of social disadvantage, racial exploitation, crime, urban regeneration, or issues of democracy and participation, the neighbourhood is providing the British government with a supple scale within which a flexible geography of state intervention can be legitimated' (Whitehead, 2003: 280). Health Action Zones could be added to Whitehead's list; it was Health Action Zone monies that were used by the residents to commission the research on which this chapter is based. Lefebvre's analysis of the way space is produced includes spatial practice; representations of space; and representational space. Spaces of resistance are played out dialectically through all three categories, from the third area – representational space.

It is our contention that 'Working Together to Create Change', a participatory action research approach to prostitution in Walsall, is an example of the representational appropriation of neighbourhoods by the inhabitants themselves as an oppositional political movement to re-appropriate and re-draw their neighbourhood space. In the process of this work they/we developed greater understanding of the scale and politics of the neighbourhood, but also particular issues, both ideological and material that surround the sex work economy.

The process of writing this chapter necessarily involved many voices, and multiple voices do not produce a seamless univocal text. With this in mind the main person responsible for each section is identified alongside the title.

Urban Villages? Welcome to Walsall (Mark Webster)

Travelling south on the M6, the rolling hills of Cheshire give way to Staffordshire and the Potteries, and before you have had time to reflect on the changing landscape, the red brake lights ignite on the cars in front and you grind to a halt. Traffic backing up for miles, tempers fraying, you look around you for some clue as to what might have happened. Welcome to Walsall; once the heart of the industrial revolution, now the home to DIY superstores, out-of-town shopping and first division football.

Walsall, like many other areas, is less one place and more a succession of places. Layers of industrial history and hundreds of years of inward migration have created a town that is at once parochial and yet international; a place full of contradictions. Once the home of the British Empire's leather industry – it still makes the bridles for the Queen's Cavalry – and later the Empire's smelting shop, Walsall nowadays has a little more trouble defining its reason for existence. While its jobs have ebbed away over the last 25 years it has seen its levels of industrial-related disease replaced by illnesses associated with poverty: high teenage pregnancy rates, catastrophic levels of smoking-related cancers, higher than average levels of coronary heart disease and very low household incomes. No one would call Walsall an attractive place, and yet despite its problems it is also a place full of gritty determined people, who do things and get things done; who innovate and create. It has more self-help groups and voluntary associations than almost any other comparable conurbation; people get together to campaign, to help each other, to have fun, to talk, or just to socialize. Despite successive attempts to redraw its architectural history with bulldozers, tower blocks and concrete, it still retains a heritage of Georgian terraces, quiet ginnels and back lanes. To the north, postwar housing estates form a buttress between the West Midland Conurbation and the Staffordshire countryside. To the west stretches Wolverhampton, to the south Dudley and West Bromwich and to the east, Birmingham. Nestling in the northern hub of the Black Country, Walsall is both one town and a metropolitan area that encompasses five others, Darlaston, Willenhall, Bloxwich, Aldridge and Brownhills, each with their own separate cultural identity and heritage.

Walsall is also an important centre for the Black Country sex trade. The roads leading out of the centre of town and heading south and west towards West Bromwich and Darlaston have gained a reputation as areas in which it is possible to pay for sex. As a result the communities traversed by these roads, Caldmore, Palfrey and Pleck, have become the unwelcoming host to the area's red-light industry. When I first moved to Walsall thirteen years ago I automatically gravitated to Caldmore (pronounced Carmer with an accompanying guttural sound that starts somewhere in the chest and is expelled through the nose). There was something definitely exotic about the place: down at heel, multicultural, and a touch bohemian. Caldmore is the first of the urban settlements you will come to on the road out of Walsall to West Bromwich. As recently as the nineteenth century it was considered to be outside of the town and the town's charter refers to it as part of 'The Foreign'. Indeed, because of its red-light reputation and distinct community, the rest of Walsall still refer to it in a manner that suggests that to visit Caldmore is to take your life in your hands. An old Elizabethan manor house that was once a pub and now serves as social housing stands on the crossroads at the centre, overlooking a triangle of grass called somewhat misleadingly Caldmore Green. During daylight hours, a bustle settles on the Green with people going about their business, visiting the sari shops and mini markets, and on leisurely summer afternoons people of all ages sit or hang around in groups passing the time of day. At night the Green takes on an altogether different character (See Figure 13.1). Fast-food eateries and Balti restaurants stretch up Caldmore Road. Groups of men hurry home from the mosque. Women standing on corners peer questioningly into the windows of cars cruising through or ask male pedestrians if they want 'business'. The speed bumps – *sleeping policemen* – ensure that essentially all drivers become kerb crawlers, and the humps raise the eyeline of inadvertent drivers so that they have to meet the gaze of the women eye to eye. Police vans patrol ominously whilst hurried transactions take place in shadowy doorways and back alleys.

That the drugs and sex industries have had an important impact on Caldmore is undeniable, indeed they are very important components of the present-day economy of Caldmore. It has been argued that along with fast food, Baltis and Indian textiles, they form the core of inward cash investment to the area. Accordingly the drugs and sex trades have come to be an important political football that is taken out at election time or when the police want to be seen to be *doing something*. The point remains however that there is very little political will to actually tackle the problem, because to tackle the problem would mean having to swallow a lot of uncomfortable truths. Despite the regular three-monthly 'crackdown', many local people feel that the authorities already operate a tolerance zone in Caldmore, Palfrey and Pleck, albeit unregulated and against the will of the local community. The fact is that drug dealing and prostitution have to happen somewhere and while the police and local politicians are content to ignore the real causes it might as well be allowed to happen here. Containment is the order of the day. As soon as the street life threatens to drift into more well-healed adjacent areas prompting the appearance of letters in the local press signed 'Disgusted of Highgate' (name and address withheld), you can be sure that the headlines will soon read *Walsall Police in Crackdown on Vice* and Walsall Magistrates Court will have another busy Monday morning.

A barely discernable shift has happened in recent years, however, that threatens to break this cycle. Walsall has started to regain some of its confidence. A towering new art gallery dominates the city skyline and this outward sign of cultural regeneration is echoed throughout Walsall's surrounding communities. People are getting together to look at formerly intractable problems and are using creative methods to put forward their own creative solutions. In Caldmore four years ago an arts project brought people from all communities together to redesign and rebuild the Green. The project, called *Dreaming the Green,* resulted in a piece of urban enhancement that has been universally acclaimed and which has confounded the critics who said that it would not last ten minutes. Similarly creative methods have been at the centre of the consultation around prostitution that has valued the voices of the local community and sex workers alike, as well as involving the ideas of local agencies and public bodies, looking for new solutions and valuing the voices of everyone. Such approaches challenge the existing power balances and create new agendas that are more difficult to ignore because they actually contain the voices of local people putting forward solutions to the problems in their own communities. Things do not change overnight but projects like these start a process that does not end when the Chief Inspector of Police or the Director of Public Health slaps a weighty report into his bottom drawer. Once involved, people stay involved, and the ideas keep bubbling to the surface in the most unlikely forums. In the case of Safety Zones in Walsall, the actual changes so far have been small, but change will happen, and we will find that the very authorities that opposed us will start claiming the ideas as their own. After all, nobody likes to be left out in the cold when the real party gets going.

Figure 13.1 Panoramic Image of Caldmore Green at Night (Photo: Kate Green)

Creative Consultation: Participatory Action Research (PAR) and Participatory Arts (PA) (Maggie O'Neill)

The process we used for the research was premised upon the principles of Walsall Health Action Zone: inclusion; participation; valuing all local voices; and community-driven and sustainable outcomes. These principles are embedded in the research method of Participatory Action Research (PAR). PAR was originally developed with communities in Columbia, Nicaragua and Mexico by Paulo Friere and Orlando Fals Borda,[2] and subsequently used by Maria Mies in Cologne working with women experiencing domestic violence.[3] Research is conducted *with* communities and groups, not on ('subjects' of research) or for them (on their behalf). For Orlando Fals Borda, the sum of knowledge from both participants in the research and academic researchers allows us to acquire a much more accurate picture of the reality we wish to transform. PAR seeks to develop action or praxis (purposeful knowledge/change) by working with groups to achieve certain aims or outcomes generally agreed by all.

Participatory Action Research

Participatory Action Research aims to involve communities themselves in the research process and to produce research that can inform policy development in order to improve the quality of life of communities. This research also consolidates and builds on the history of community participatory appraisal work in Walsall and specifically the South HAZ area. Using PAR methodology the research sought to develop a strategic action plan to look at ways of managing prostitution in the borough through consultation and collaboration with all those involved and affected by prostitution: residents; community groups; women and young people involved in prostitution; statutory and voluntary agencies. To this end, the researchers worked with a group of community co-facilitators to help progress the research. The research team was committed to principles of community governance and partnership development that are at the heart of the principles underpinning Walsall South HAZ. Involving local communities is vital to ensure the sustainability and progress of the research outcomes, in order to take the recommendations forward.

The research team and the authors of this chapter are committed to research that develops partnership responses to prostitution; includes all those involved, thus facilitating shared ownership of the development and outcomes of the research; uses innovative ways of consulting local people, for example through community arts workshops; and has processes of monitoring and evaluation built in to the research outcomes.

The consultation research involved partnership working across a number of groups and agencies: the researchers from Staffordshire and Liverpool; residents and representatives of Caldmore and Palfrey Local Committees; Walsall Community Arts team and Walsall Youth Arts. Outcomes include a report, 'Working Together to Create Change'; an art exhibition, 'Safety Soapbox'; and a pamphlet published by the community, 'What You Told Us about Prostitution', for the community, ensuring that the outcomes of the research are not shut away in a drawer, but kept alive and on the local agenda.[4]

Participatory Arts and Walsall Community Arts Team

Participatory Arts has its roots in social and cultural movements which aim to create opportunities for ordinary people to have access to the means to participate in the processes which generate culture. It stems from the belief that everyone is creative and everyone has something to say. The catch-all description for this activity in Great Britain and Ireland is Community Arts. Although the practice of Community Arts takes many forms, the underlying philosophy of all Community Arts work is that is that everyone has the right and the capacity to participate equally in the arts. Sometimes described as Cultural Democracy, this philosophy has now been widely embraced by local authorities, Regional Arts Boards, and many independent arts organizations as a fundamental principle governing cultural work (see Landry, 1995; McGuigan, 1996).

What is unique to community arts/participative arts projects, however, is that people work together on projects with a common goal and purpose. It involves them taking an active part, often working with an arts worker to learn new skills and help them identify the most effective ways of doing what they want to do. A project could be anything from a community show to a book, a mosaic to a set of postcards, but nearly always it will provide the medium to give voice to some common concern or cause for celebration. Because the process is highly consultative and collaborative, participative arts projects provide a unique way of consulting with people in a non-threatening, non-hierarchical manner and present the results in a way which reflects the richness of opinions and ideas.

Walsall Community Arts Team was set up as part of the Leisure Services Department of Walsall Metropolitan Council in 1989 following a Cultural Audit which indicated the need to foster locally-appropriate arts activities. The team now has eleven members and works in partnership with local people and local agencies to develop arts activities which meet local needs. In 1999 the post of Arts into Health was created within the team in partnership with Walsall Health Authority to specifically work within the Walsall HAZ to identify and set up community arts activities with local people which would contribute to the ten-year health implementation plan (The 'HIMP') which aims to make Walsall a 'Healthier Place to Live, Learn and Work'.

PAR and PA involve a commitment to research that develops partnership responses to developing purposeful knowledge; includes all those involved where possible, thus facilitating shared ownership of the development and outcomes of the research; uses innovative ways of consulting and working with local people; and facilitates change with communities and groups. PAR and PA are directed towards social change with the participants. PAR and PA are interventionist, action-oriented and interpretative. The local community instrumental in commissioning the research, feeling that they were already living in a zone of toleration (see Figure 13.2). They wanted as clear a picture of prostitution as possible with a view to addressing the emerging issues and developing change.

Residents' Voices: Creating Social Change (Anne James)

Strong feelings about prostitution, particularly in Caldmore, resulted in the resident representatives on the Local Committees (Caldmore, Palfrey and Pleck) and the South Health Action Zone Steering Group raising the need for action to reduce the resulting tensions. Previous attempts to cut prostitution in this part of Walsall had been unsuccessful, so if change was to be made an objective approach was vital.

To ensure the collection of accurate baseline data and gain a full understanding of the issues, research was commissioned. Local people were involved from the start and so were active in selecting the researchers and later with the research itself.

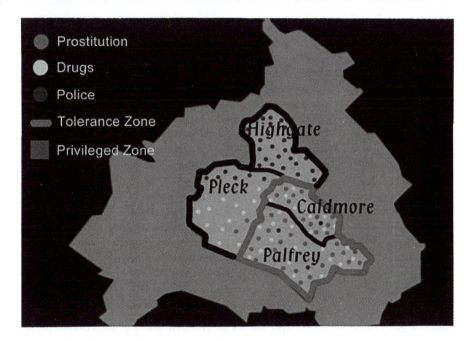

Figure 13.2 Tolerance Zones

Some 150 individuals attended a public meeting held in November 2000. Future plans to deal with prostitution in Walsall were expounded and the process the research would take was explained. Following the consultation phase when researchers gleaned issues important to residents, sex workers, Walsall officials and anyone involved with people affected by prostitution. focus groups were held in various parts of the area and interested local residents, shop workers and businesses owners/proprietors were invited to attend. In-depth interviews were carried out and ethnographic work conducted. Information was collected verbally from anyone wishing to contribute and written submissions were received.

Living with Street Prostitution

'I am angry, I feel we are the victims' – a resident.

Research findings from the residents fell into six categories:

Changes in the dynamics of prostitution through time. Street prostitution had increased over the past five years; women working in prostitution were on the street longer, were more dispersed, were working irregular hours and more young underage girls were seen, the residents observed. This increase had led to a growth in kerb crawlers.

Perceptions of community safety. Most residents raised issues about the safety of their locality, including fear of going out after dark; an increase in traffic especially at night; harassment from kerb crawlers (documented by residents of all ages); female residents being approached for business; men fearing their wives and daughters would be accosted at night; fear of the health risk from discarded needles and used condoms; fear of pimps.

Some residents saw the increase in women working in their locality as being drug related. Higher levels of crime generally were seen to occur in the area due to the prostitution: 'I think there's more chance of ... rather than violence against you yourself on the streets, there's more chance of your home being raided, broken into in that way, than the safety aspect. I think there's a greater degree of break-ins' – a resident. On the whole residents were uncomfortable about pimps but reported their involvement in a range of violent acts against the women. They were fearful of reprisals from pimps if they intervened: 'they're very dangerous people, very, very dangerous people'.

Specific concerns about street prostitution and examples of how people are personally affected. Residents related many of their experiences of 'living with prostitution' in their neighbourhood: 'I have been approached loads of times ... I was attacked once getting on a bus by two girls who thought I was stealing their beat'. Many residents were worried about children picking up condoms and needles or viewing acts they were too young to see. Describing her worst experience, one resident said, 'say your kids wake up in the middle of the night at three o'clock, four o'clock in the morning and you hear them screaming and shouting and swearing, that's the worst one'.

Dissatisfaction with responses from the authorities. There was a concern for the reputation of this neighbourhood of Walsall. The locals felt that if prostitution transferred to more prosperous areas of Walsall, the authorities would move in and stamp it out. So they could not understand why nothing was done in their locality. None of the authorities in Walsall responded effectively, the residents said, and they were unanimous in wanting all the agencies to work together to overcome the difficulties they were suffering. They demanded to be involved with the authorities in making decisions.

Routes into prostitution and concerns for the women and young people involved.
There was a concern that young people were led into prostitution. However a few
residents were so angry about how their own lives were being affected that they
had little sympathy or understanding of the difficulties encountered by the women:
'We know it is bad and vicious ... we know they are beaten ... but I have had
enough ... I have no sympathy left'. Residents cited involvement in drug use and
abuse, poverty, single parenthood, youth offending, running from 'broken homes'
and a response to local authority care as routes into prostitution. Concerns focused
on the pimping of vulnerable young women and the demand for prostitutes by
punters.

Community responses and pragmatic possibilities for change. The residents
understood that prostitution would never be obliterated so wanted it properly
managed. Most were in favour of the setting up of a safety zone away from their
homes and local businesses. The traditional punitive ways of dealing with street
prostitution have not worked, so they perceived a safety zone initiative as a
sensible and practical way of containing the situation to the benefit of both
residents and sex workers: 'if they are going to do it they may as well do it in a
safe place, a safe area, where they are not, you know, disturbing anyone else and
then they'll be safe themselves'. Other suggestions emerged:

• There were mixed feelings about Residents Action and Patrol Groups as a way of
  preventing street prostitution. Some felt involvement in these activities would put
  their families at risk.
• More help for drug users, a stronger focus on deterring men who pay for sex and
  a sustained programme for dealing with the pimps were proposed.
• The residents highlighted the need for opportunities for better education,
  prevention or reduction of risks for the women involved as well as a programme
  for young women to reduce the numbers going into prostitution.
• Many residents wanted the negative media publicity about their area to be
  reversed. A change of emphasis towards the men was suggested: 'Don't blame
  the women, look at the men' (resident, public meeting).
• Many residents wanted a change in the law as a way to control prostitution. The
  licensing of brothels may lead to a diminution of street prostitution. A zone of
  toleration (safety zone) was also suggested as a possibility.

Safety Soapbox: Safety as a Key Emergent Issue (Maggie O'Neill)

As the research progressed the research team became aware very quickly of the
pressing issue of 'Safety' for residents and sex workers. As described above,
women working on the street are very vulnerable to violence, assault and verbal
abuse. Young people and older residents expressed their fear and insecurity about
public space and especially their harassment from kerb crawlers. Overwhelmingly,
in the focus groups and in-depth interviews with residents, they expressed their

concerns about lack of safety on streets, especially after dark, and a fear of crime; much of this is linked to drug cultures – drug abuse and drug dealing. With the support of Walsall Youth Arts and Walsall Community Arts Team, consultative arts workshops were organized for residents and sex workers to express their concerns, and to depict their hopes for change in visual form using photography and computer arts. Kate Green (the arts worker/workshop facilitator) coined the title 'Safety Soapbox' for the arts consultation process. Three groups were involved in the Safety Soapbox consultation: sex workers, residents and specifically young residents. Visual representations can often have a much more powerful effect than words alone, and feed into local and national social and cultural policy.[5] In representing social research in visual/artistic form we hoped to reach as wide an audience as possible, facilitating better understanding of the experiences of the local community (including residents and sex workers) and ideas for changing or managing the current situation.

Making Visible People's Experiences and Ideas for Change

One aim of the consultation research was to show that collaboration (with local committees, agencies, residents, women and young people involved in prostitution) produces rich understanding and social texts (report, strategic action plan, exhibition) that can be useful to the wider community, including local and national policy-makers. Furthermore, in this collaboration between participatory research and participatory arts, our understanding of prostitution is enriched by the experiences and ways of seeing of all those involved – residents, statutory and voluntary agencies, women and young people involved in prostitution. The arts have a vital role in processes of regeneration, communication and building communities. The combination of PAR and PA offers the opportunity for:

- *Reflection* and provides opportunities for people to work through issues/discuss/create a piece of art that makes visible their concerns/ideas/responses. This process is:
- *Transformative*. In creating a piece of work that makes visible concerns, ideas, future possibilities, art works bring something new and tangible into the world that contributes to a better understanding of an issue. The arts process:
- *Adds value* at lots of levels. At the level of the participant (community member/ citizen), the arts are a way of engaging, consulting and involving people in decisions and planning for the future of their community. And finally such work is:
- *Sustainable*. The arts support innovation and experimentation in local communities and have a vital role to play in processes of community development, social inclusion and creative regeneration.[6]

Seven art workshops were arranged for each group (residents, young residents, sex workers), making a total of twenty-one sessions overall. In addition Kate accompanied Maggie and Rosie on street outreach to get a feeling for the issues concerning women, and to encourage women to take part in the arts workshops. Kate also produced some artworks on the basis of her experiences. The next section highlights the main concerns of the three groups concerned: the residents, the young residents, and street sex workers.

Safety Issues

It was agreed by all those who took part that pressing safety issues are: sexual health; drugs; racial equality; violence; and fear of violence and mugging. The key issues for young people resident in Caldmore revolved around feeling unsafe on the streets because of harassment from kerb crawlers and a general fear of crime against them. Two young people talked about carrying knives as protection. Two other young people mentioned friends who were approached to work as an escort and as a prostitute. The seriousness of some of the issues emerging from the voices and artworks of the young residents also reflect the concerns expressed by older focus group residents on behalf of young people.

For young people the major issues include being mistaken for a prostitute, getting propositioned by kerb crawlers, being hassled by pimps, and generally feeling insecure and afraid. They also showed awareness and concern for the situation for street sex workers and had ideas for changing the situation. As described earlier, people were personally affected by their experiences. Some of those taking part in the arts workshops were worried about the impact of prostitution on their children. Residents were also concerned for the safety of sex workers and the factors that may have led them into street prostitution. Key issues that emerged for women working on and off street revolved around their lack of safety on the street and the endemic levels of violence against them: 'One bloke tried to ammonia me ... he was telling me I was going to give him a blow job for a fiver ... he drove past and squirted ammonia at me ... it went in my hair and down my coat luckily'.

For some women, protecting their families (especially their children), from the knowledge of what they do was experienced as very stressful, as it led to them leading 'double lives'. For other women, attempts to do something other than prostitution were frustrated by people's attitudes towards them, and the fact that as a 'common prostitute' you have a criminal record. Attempts at change for some women were also frustrated by lack of self-esteem, economic necessity, drug use, and homelessness caused by fleeing violence at home. The major issues for women emerged as: a wish to be seen as ordinary and avoid derogatory stereotypes; the stress of leading a double life; fear of violence; dangers and difficulties of street work; health issues; dangerous punters; attempts to escape and barriers to exiting; the skills developed in their work; and the effect of fines.

A clear emerging theme in the interviews, survey and focus groups with residents, local businesses and sex workers, as well as representatives from various statutory and voluntary agencies, was the possibility of creating a zone of toleration. The idea of a zone of toleration quickly evolved in the process of the research to be defined as 'a safety zone'.

Figure 13.3 'I'm Not Safe in the Outside World'

Red Lights and Safety Zones: A Way Forward (Rosie Campbell)

The majority of residents living with street prostitution consulted in the course of our research, together with agencies and sex workers, supported the idea of what was referred to as a 'tolerance' zone. What do we mean by tolerance zones? In our research it was clear that when people talked about zones there were differences in what they were imagining. The majority were referring to street zones, non-residential areas where street soliciting is allowed but in a controlled and regulated manner, between specific times, in a specific place. This is what street zoning has meant in the Netherlands and is the definition we use here. In Walsall individuals varied in their understanding of how such zones might be organized and managed. Some individuals when referring to tolerance zones were actually suggesting that prostitution be tolerated in some sort of indoor premises. Hence some people were imagining legalized, licensed or otherwise regulated off-street systems. From a policy point of view zoning and legalization have different implications (see O'Neill and Campbell, 2002; Visser, 1998). Here we focus on the zoning of street prostitution.

Community Views in Walsall

The majority of residents supported the establishment of a street zone. Most of these residents held the view that a pragmatic approach was needed and that street zones offered the potential for 'managing' prostitution and improving the quality of residents' lives. Many residents felt existing approaches were not working and the street zone route should be explored. Some felt strongly that it was time to try more radical approaches to the regulation of street prostitution. Whilst politicians debated zones, communities and sex workers bore the brunt of unsatisfactory law and social policy. One resident who had lived in the area most of his life stated:

> 'I've been here over 60 years, I lived here when I was a kid and the White Hart pub was known then. Prostitution was an overflow from the centre. The women go to the pubs and the trade was there. I remember a meeting 25 years ago just like this in a hall on Corporation Street. The people are fed up now. Residents say provide some zone, an industrial estate, like in Utrecht or Belgium, 25-30 years on we want a rest from it now' (resident attending the public meeting).

Yet there were some reservations and cases of clear opposition. The main concerns and reasons for opposition reflect many of the common 'myths' about zoning. These include assumptions such as:

- It would not be possible to identify and agree an area.
- Clients would not go there for fear that they would be identified.
- It would encourage and increase in the street sex trade.
- If one area alone such as Walsall adopted a zone it would be a magnet for sex workers from all other West Midlands areas.
- It would become a 'lawless' area with drug dealing, pimping and other crime thriving.
- There should be moral opposition: it would condone prostitution and for some the exploitation of women. Some residents favoured only policy measures that attempted to abolish prostitution and involved ongoing criminalization.
- Zoned areas would be unsafe for sex workers: sex workers would not go there and it would be unsafe.
- Ghettoization: it could compound the social marginalization of sex workers by confining them to specific areas.

In Walsall many of those in favour felt such concerns could be overcome through ongoing consultation and careful planning, particularly in relation to where the zone was sited and how it was organized, policed and managed.

The Police

The *Birmingham Post*, 4th October 2002, reported calls from a Chief Superintendent in Wolverhampton for zones of tolerance. He expressed the view that in his area the police had done all they could to address the problems associated with street prostitution, reporting that they had targeted sex workers, clients and pimps but they hadn't got 'very far', and hence a more radical move should be considered. The majority of officers consulted in Walsall made it clear that if politicians took the lead, or there were changes in the law that enabled zoning, they would have no opposition to being involved in policing and managing such zones with other agencies. At the National Vice Conference 2002, the ACPO (Association of Chief Police Officers) led on vice, outlining possible principles for an ACPO policy on prostitution. They stated that ACPO do not support tolerance zones as the police must be seen to enforce the law and cannot abrogate certain aspects of the law. Only if there was a legal change could ACPO change their policy. Despite the official ACPO position, police in a number of cities in the UK have been involved in visits to the Netherlands, in *de facto* zoning, or are developing policies of strategic enforcement. National policing policy seems to be out of step with thinking at grassroots level.

Sex Workers

The majority of sex workers consulted in Walsall supported the idea of a tolerance zone. Some were cynical about the possibility of them ever being 'left alone' by the police. It was difficult for many of the women to imagine a different situation; certainly few women were aware of the organization of zones in the Netherlands, where zones are policed for the safety of the women and health and welfare advice and support are available on site.

Issues for Consideration

• Siting a zone: If Walsall and other areas pursue the policy of strategic enforcement or formal zoning, then clearly, careful consideration should be given to the issue of location. The experience in other areas is that finding a suitable site is difficult although not impossible and that location is crucial to the success of a zone.
• Safety of sex workers: The key concern for those working with sex workers and for sex workers themselves is that if sex worker needs and rights are not considered then street sex workers may be forced into areas that are unsafe and isolated (such as industrial or dock areas). Hence, not only would the women be segregated but they would be pushed to areas where they were vulnerable to robbery, physical and sexual assaults, other forms of exploitation and were out of touch with supporting agencies. The intention of zoning should not be to ghettoize sex workers; zoning should take on board the safety and welfare of sex workers, as well as attempts to reduce nuisance to residents.
• Part of a multi-layered package: zoning or strategic enforcement approaches should not, and rarely do, take place in a policy vacuum and, if adapted in other areas, need to be part of multi-layered strategies which much more proactively address issues such as the commercial sexual exploitation of children and pimping.

- Ongoing management and consultation: It is important not to see zoning as an easy answer to street prostitution. Contrary to some popular thinking, the Dutch model of zoning and the use of strategic enforcement, far from being laissez-faire approaches, involve a considerable degree of ongoing management and regulation and demand a high degree of joint inter-agency working (Campbell *et al.*, 1996; Visser, 1998; Van Doorninck, 1999).

Political Support and the Need for Change!

> In dealing with prostitution, the government and the councils that run Britain's cities are pulling in different directions (*The Economist*, 2000: 35-36).

This seems to be the case with regards to zoning in some local authority areas, and what is clearer is that government (central and local) is often at odds with many local communities. In Walsall there was little political support for zoning amongst ruling Labour councillors and the local Labour MP. At a public meeting held in November 2000, the local MP expressed his views on zoning; these included:

- 'It will not work, people will not go down to an area which is dangerous';
- 'It raises questions about where they should be. If it's a disused industrial site, who's going to clear it up afterwards and the idea of forcing women to isolated, dark areas is not attractive';
- 'I think that tolerance zones may appear to be an attractive option, but I don't think it is'.

There have been no signs from government that they will consider initiatives or changes in the law which would give local agencies such as police, councils and health authorities more confidence and scope to trial strategic enforcement, street zoning or regulation of off-street premises. Government statements do not support approaches that they class as involving the 'liberalization' of prostitution (*The Economist*, 2000: 35-36). Hubbard's (1999: 144) analysis, which points to the principles of local accountability as valid in guiding local policies, offers a modicum of hope for those who wish to trial street zoning: 'the idea of geographically-selective decriminalization remains a distinct possibility in Britain and elsewhere as principles of subsidiary and local accountability head towards the top of the political agenda'.

So is it likely we will see more local authorities go it alone in response to demands from local communities and growing evidence? Will Walsall be one of these areas? Many residents consulted in the course of this research expressed despondency about what they saw as an existing legislative framework and government position which offered little scope for immediate action or alternative policies and changes to the current regulation of street prostitution: 'I felt quite despondent after the meeting as it was changes in the law and that takes forever! So I felt little nothing would be done to alleviate what we face. Today, now, this minute we want something done' (focus group respondent).

High-level political support and leadership at a municipality level would be required for formal zoning in the UK. Politicians need to review the evidence and consider zoning as a viable option rather than dismiss it out of hand, basing policy on actual evidence and not assumption. Central government needs to consider zoning as a feasible and legitimate policy option. Much can be learnt from the Dutch political pragmatism which has enabled zoning in the Netherlands. Policy-makers in the UK should take a pragmatic, evidence-based approach to the development of managed areas for street prostitution. Any decision to move in the direction of zoning requires a co-ordinated process of consultation and detailed planning.

Conclusion

Our research, embedded in PAR and PA, has developed, in consultation and partnership with the local community, a range of text-based and visual outcomes (and also led to high-profile news reporting, including a report in *The Big Issue*.[7] Many of the recommendations contained in the report have been actioned, and local residents have ensured that the issue is kept on the local agenda, that it is not forgotten. The Caldmore area was defined by one of the participants as a tolerance zone where the police manage a process of containment (see Figure 13.2).

The ongoing process has to involve the participation, and take on board the needs, of all groups. The policy of developing tolerance zones is controversial, but in Walsall has majority support from residents affected by prostitution and from street sex workers, and so needs to be given serious consideration. Our research indicates overwhelming dissatisfaction with existing policies and laws on prostitution which fail to address violence against sex workers or residents' and community concerns, and which contribute to adverse circumstances for sex worker services addressing drugs, health and safety needs. Politicians should ultimately be accountable to local people.

Residents and sex workers are part of the local community. They are asking for change and for new approaches, specifically zoning. Through participatory action research they are engaging in a process that makes the social relations of power associated with the organization of neighbourhood space visible; and in so doing are representative of how resistance emerges around forms of subjectivity (class, race, gender, sexuality) that are marginalized in and through space (Bell and Valentine, 1995).

Notes

1   The terms of reference of the consultation research were:
    • To assess present policy approaches to prostitution in Walsall.
    • To produce a baseline of information from which integrated programmes of action can be developed to more effectively address street prostitution.

- To consult all those involved in, and affected by, street prostitution in Walsall in order to identify their key concerns and problems. These groups include: residents, businesses, sex workers, and statutory and voluntary sector agencies presently involved in 'managing' prostitution and providing services for sex workers.
- To include those involved in and affected by prostitution in the research process in order to facilitate shared ownership of the development and outcomes of the research; to learn from shared experience; to further develop understanding of the issues; and to make recommendations on the basis of the data gathered.
- To consider policies which would improve community safety, for example ways of improving the safety of sex workers and the wider community.
- To provide an action plan outlining a multi-agency strategic approach, which would more effectively 'manage' prostitution and which considers the concerns of all those involved and affected by prostitution. A focus will be on partnership responses to prostitution.
- To consider the feasibility of seeking alternative approaches to street prostitution, such as 'street' or 'safety zones'.

2   PAR as a methodology emerged from the World Symposium of Action in Cartagena, Colombia, in 1977. Participatory action research was defined as 'vivencia' necessary for achieving progress and democracy. Thus it is a research methodology and a philosophy of life (see Borda, 1999).

3   See O'Neill (2001).

4   Additionally, further research focusing upon young women and routes into prostitution from care is in the process of development.

5   See Webster (1997). See also second edition of this text (2003).

6   The Safety Soapbox artworks are included in the Home Office Toolkit on 'Prostitution' (authored by Campbell and O'Neill) available on the Home Office website. The aim of the toolkits is to provide local Crime and Disorder Partnerships with:
- guidance on the processes needed to identify, develop, implement and monitor/evaluate solutions to tackle prostitution;
- information on how to make the best use of resources to tackle locally-identified problems and national priorities relevant to tackling prostitution;
- examples of good practice and promising approaches for tackling prostitution;
- A bibliography of existing relevant material;
- information which will be accessible in multi-media form e.g. via the Internet/website, CD ROM and in print, and produced in such a form as to maximize the ability for updating or revising content;
- a mechanism for practitioners to report on success/failure/new approaches.

7   For a fuller account and analysis of this aspect of the project see O'Neill, Campbell and Webster (2002).

Chapter 14

Re-Discovering Coketown

Phil Denning

This chapter will address regeneration initiatives with respect to former industrial European neighbourhoods that are closely connected to the development of urban areas, e.g. mining, steel and textiles. There is evidence of the same policy trajectories in the United States (McNulty, 1999). For reasons of space alone, this chapter will focus on coal mining and steel communities.

It is possible to point to numerous examples of considerable *physical* investment in former industrial sites in the UK, such as Sheffield (with the Meadowhall complex), Gateshead (the Metrocentre and the new Baltic art space), Doncaster (The Earth Centre) and Rotherham (the Magna complex). This activity is mirrored in Europe. Examples can be found in the Ruhr valley in Germany (in the industrial culture park around IBA Emscher Park), in Lille and around St Etienne in France, and in the Netherlands in both Rotterdam and Amsterdam. In the US, the same activity can be found in the so-called 'Rust Belt' cities of Detroit, Pittsburgh, Ohio and Pennsylvania.

There will be an explicit focus in this chapter on *communities*. As Ashwin Desai (2002) stresses, communities are by their very nature multi-dimensional and multi-layered. Communities are not just sites of work but also of love, childrearing, illness, celebration, mourning, cooking and praying – as well as crime, drug and alcohol abuse, prostitution and isolation: in short, the culture of lived lives.

The chapter will attempt to address the question of how regeneration practitioners in Europe can begin to offer a broader repertoire of knowledge and practices that go beyond physical regeneration. I want to argue that there is a need for more effective approaches that should address the wider needs of (increasingly integrated) societies and particularly those who are amongst the most socially excluded and deprived. To begin to address this and offer a contribution to the research and the wider debate, I will address three main points in this chapter.

Firstly, I want to begin to sketch an outline for future research that links the cultural planning approach to heightened environmental and historical understanding in the process of regenerating former industrial communities. I will draw primarily upon the work of environmental historian John McNeil (2001) and his exploration of the environmental aspects of what he terms the 'Coketown-Motown' cluster across Europe and the United States.

Secondly, I will argue that if we are to understand the more complex dynamics of social and technological change and community development over time, then we in Europe need to creatively link cultural planning to neighbourhood development (see Bianchini and Parkinson, 1993). I want to suggest that this linkage will be key to understanding the nuances of regeneration that will hopefully lead to a more creative, sensitive and positive relationship between communities and professionals in the process of regeneration and renewal.

Lastly, I will argue that, far from being left behind by the regeneration activities, deprived communities, and particularly former industrial communities and neighbourhoods who were primarily engaged in mining and steel, are instead key agents of change. They actively engage with this process of change and the underlying theory, but from their own perspectives and for their own aims. I will compare and contrast the benefits and costs of 'top-down' regeneration programmes in Scotland, Hungary and Germany with 'bottom-up' community-led developments in the community of Craigmillar in Scotland.[1]

Coketown and the Boom Period – the Experience of Craigmillar

Craigmillar is a conurbation of local authority housing estates built after 1930 in a period of industrial re-location and central city slum clearance and located on the south-east of the city of Edinburgh, Scotland. It is an area that has steadily been positioned from the late 1950s as existing on the periphery, both geographically and economically. However, it was not always peripheral. Coal has been dug from the ground in the Craigmillar area since the Middle Ages under the supervision of the monastic estates for the purposes of both heating and in the production of sea salt on the nearby tidal estuary of the Firth of Forth. This coal and salt was sent to the Netherlands, Scandinavia, the Baltic countries and England.

The Craigmillar housing estate was built on the land around and incorporating the nineteenth-century mining and mill villages of Newcraighall, the Jewel and Niddrie. These are adjacent to the other south Edinburgh mining village of Gilmerton and the nearby county of Midlothian with its numerous pit villages that were all under the ownership of the Ancram family as the Lords of Lothian. The early residents extracted what existed beneath their feet. The geology of the central belt of Scotland comprises a significant coalfield, in turn part of much larger coal and oil-bearing strata that stretch across Europe and into the North Sea.

The development of this European coalfield was part of a general and rapid expansion of the mining industry in the nineteenth and early twentieth centuries. Mining on an industrial scale of extensive seams of fossil fuels such as coal for energy produced the 'Coketown cluster' identified by the environmental historian John McNeil (2001: 306), named after the fictional town in Dickens' 1854 novel *Hard Times*.

These communities were 'boom towns' that grew rapidly and which also produced materials (literally the hills of slag waste), profits and human misery on a scale that shocked contemporary observers such as Dickens and Zola. At the same time, the boom led to bust as many of the coal seams proved too narrow or uneconomic to mine in the longer term. The landscape of Europe is littered with examples of 'ghost towns' connected to the mining of both coal and lead that remind us that the decline of former industrial communities has a long history.

The Coketown clusters produced an 'energy revolution' as much as an 'industrial revolution' as Europeans and North Americans gained access to huge reserves of photochemical energy locked within coal seams that in turn powered their steam and oil engines. The development of these clusters and the energy they produced materially altered the energy use and standards of living and wealth of European and North Americans on an exponential scale.

McNeil states that Coketown produced coal not only for fuel but also for the production of initially iron and steel and later for electricity and other industrial-chemical products for both growth and export in industries such as automotive (developed in factories that are christened 'Motown' by McNeil), cement, chemical products etc. These products make up the GNP or the wealth of nations.

The lifetime of the cluster was not long. McNeil states that the Coketown fuel complex was both displaced and replaced in the second half of the twentieth century by oil, gas and nuclear based fuel forms. With the replacement of coal as the main energy source and the break-up of the Motown cluster, male employment collapsed. With the decline of the Coketown cluster came a focus on regeneration of the places.

Coketown and its Aftermath

In this section, I want focus on three Coketown clusters and analyse the different approaches to physical regeneration that have been applied. I will compare and contrast the approaches used across Europe. The three clusters are the Forth Valley (incorporating Craigmillar), the Ruhr Valley in Germany and the Odz Valley in Hungary.

Forth Valley

As Edinburgh expanded in the eighteenth, nineteenth and twentieth centuries, it did so by incorporating outlying villages (including those in the north, east and west) into the city jurisdiction. This is usual in terms of urban growth in the UK and beyond. What is unusual is that Edinburgh (a national capital) incorporated in the early decades of the twentieth century fully-fledged industrial mining communities with their own folkways, identities and perspectives on life.

Craigmillar and the other mining communities of the Forth Valley demonstrate all the features of a one-time coalfield community boomtown in terms of rapid growth and decline. It sent its product across the globe via rail links to a major river port. The area saw significant employment growth in the period 1890-1960 as people came to the area for work. Like the rest of the Forth Valley mining communities, Craigmillar suffered decline from the mid-1960s as the Jewel, Klondyke and Newcraighall pits all closed. The aftermath of the miners' strike of 1984-85 saw the closure of the Bilston Glen 'super pit' just twenty years after it opened. In the period 1965-1985 Craigmillar lost 10,000 male jobs. By 1990 the area had become one of Scotland's most disadvantaged communities and was thereby designated for regeneration. Following various stops and starts, the architect Piers Gough was approached by Edinburgh City Council to develop a regeneration master plan in 1998.

It is notable that the Craigmillar master plan, 'A New Beginning' (City of Edinburgh Council, 2000), does not mention this *industrial* background at all but addresses the *social* problems directly. This is not surprising since the main physical evidence of the mining industry (such as winding gear, waste heaps, rail lines and coal docks) had been demolished, abandoned and/or grassed over long before the arrival of Piers Gough and his team of regeneration consultants. The limited remaining evidence of the industrial past on the surface in the Craigmillar and Newcraighall mining neighbourhoods is to be found in the housing stock from the turn of the century – the miners' row.

The master plan presented its vision for the area as a 'new beginning', with the provision of new houses, employment and amenities. The plan envisaged the destruction and demolition of the majority of the housing stock from the 1930s, to be replaced with a blend of social and private housing (with private homes at prices upwards of £250,000 adjacent to Craigmillar Castle – Edinburgh's other, less famous castle), with better transport links to the city centre and more shops. It can be argued that this master plan is an example of 'top-down' planning in that it was never open to public competition, nor were the changes envisaged ever voted upon by the public of Edinburgh or the residents of Craigmillar. Lastly, it is highly selective in what is included and what is excluded – in this case the recent industrial and social past of the area.

Without communities such as Craigmillar, Gilmerton or their counterparts in the Forth Valley, the mining industry and the vital fossil fuel it supplied for industrial/social growth, Edinburgh (let alone Craigmillar) would not have grown. The heavy industrial past and the role of fossil fuel extraction in powering urban development is not acknowledged in the master plan and remains to be acknowledged and written by planners and developers. It must be stressed that the impacts of Coketown on both the environment (water courses, subsidence and despoliation) and the human residents is still being felt.

The Ruhr Valley

In 1850, the Ruhr Valley was agricultural. Less than sixty years later, it was the main coal and steel producing area of Germany. The area and its associated cities of Dusseldorf, Essen, Duisburg, Köln and Dortmund had major industrial and financial strategic significance to the German state after unification in 1870. These flowed from both its role in production of steel for internal use and export and in armament production, particularly through the giant companies of Krupps and Thyssen. Although the Ruhr Valley industry suffered declines in production in the mid-1920s and in the immediate aftermath of World War II, for the majority of the twentieth century it has undergone major growth (Bruggemeir, 1990).

This growth was not without cost, however. The coal strata that lie beneath the valley are high in sulphur content. Burning this type of coal in blast furnaces led to major environmental pollution of both the air and the Ruhr and Emscher rivers. By the 1960s this pollution damage to the environment of the Ruhr Valley was beginning to appear as a political issue and featured in the campaigns of Willi Brandt for the post of West German Chancellor. With the rise of the Green Party in the 1970s and its election successes of the 1980s and 1990s, the clean-up of the industries of the Ruhr began in earnest. At the same time the West German coal and steel industry began to decline. This was partly due to the replacement of coal as a fossil fuel energy source and also the worldwide collapse in the steel market as new competitors began steel production in the Far East.

The State of North Rhine Westphalia responded in 1989 by creating the International Building Exposition (IBA) at Emscher Park. The focus of this decade-long project was to create a comprehensive regional planning scheme working with the cooperation of seventeen municipalities. The IBA's mission was to facilitate the re-use of these former industrial sites and communities as a new network of regional parks underpinned by ecological planning principles. There are two overarching principles. The first is to re-design the concept of the International Exhibition (previously used to present industrial products and innovation) but with a focus on ecological restoration of a former industrial area. The second is to create a 'park of European significance' and to road-test new approaches to redevelopment and regeneration of a former industrial area. A central tenet behind the 120 projects was the element of open competition in terms of design and approach.

As a result, there was a key difference between the German and the Scottish approach. In the Emscher Park development, no effort was made to destroy the industrial buildings of the Coketown complex. Instead the buildings were to be adapted for re-use as recreational facilities and work sites or remain and be re-designated as industrial heritage in a park setting similar to medieval or Roman remains. While this German approach appears to offer a considerable contrast to the Scottish case study at a superficial level, there are significant connections. This is also a 'top-down' initiative being generated by the local *Länder* and with an autonomous structure to deliver the project. IBA is very much a 'master plan' of the local state, led by a key individual (the director of Emscher Park) with limited community input to the development of the projects (Landry, 2000). What regeneration of a former industrial area looks like when these similar contextual elements are missing will be explored in the final case study, from Odz Valley in Hungary.

Ozd Valley

Ozd (population 145,000) is a small coal mining and steel city in north-eastern Hungary. Prior to the collapse of the communist government in 1989, this area was one of the main sites of industrial production in Hungary. The Hungarian steel and coal complexes did not long survive the end of the Cold War and the collapse of the global steel market. From 1992 to 1999 the mining and steel industries collapsed, until male unemployment in Odz reached 40 per cent by 1999 (Grayson, 2002). This collapse posed particular problems in three main ways.

The first is environmental. Odz is located in a river valley and the land contains 'brown' coal (coal with a high percentage of lignite). The area is not only a Coketown but a 'smoke town' as well. The damage caused to the wider society again related to pollution of air, watercourses and land and their impact on local populations. This pollution, whilst obviously noticed by local residents and farmers, was not recognized by the central state.

The second challenge lay in the fact that other infrastructure was not present. The existing NGOs and other environmental groups were emphatically not local community groups. As Tausz (1990: 300-301) comments: 'The totalitarian political system did not tolerate autonomous organizations, nor even live communities ... local organizations, communities were replaced everywhere by the local units of centralized organizations'. These organizations and the related infrastructure all vanished with the end of the communist government. There was no alternative in place, thus the region lacked local organizations and the social capital these supply (sweat equity, commitment to a common good, trust, reciprocation, etc.) in order to address problems of rapid de-industrialization.

The third challenge lay in the nature of the workforce employed in the mining industry. The work of mining coal is dirty, dangerous and of low social status. In the Odz Valley, there is a significant Roma workforce. This meant that the collapse of the industry adversely affected the Roma population. Unemployment amongst Roma males reached 70 per cent. The Roma population faced both the loss of their main livelihood and significant labour market discrimination if they attempted to access other employment. The Odz Valley represents a case for environmental, social and labour market regeneration. In contrast to the examples from Scotland and Germany, there is a limited likelihood of 'top-down' regeneration or significant funds, though funding streams may become available when Hungary enters the European Union (a process that began early in 2003).

In place of 'top-down' regeneration, residents are developing 'bottom-up' solutions. However, they are starting from a very low base. In Odz, the establishment of a Civil College in 1997 began to offer residents the initial skills in community regeneration and development. The programmes of the College offer training in community development as well as offering retraining for employment (Grayson, 2000). There is a major focus on community appraisal and mapping of community needs. There is a particular strand of the programme for the Roma population. There is also a distinct cultural focus. The Civil College is working in the local Culture Houses spread across the neighbourhoods of Odz, re-designing them as Community Houses, offering residents opportunities for socializing, eating, drinking and discussion.

The nature of the regeneration challenge faced by Odz (and similar communities in Poland, former Yugoslavia and East Germany) is just beginning to be addressed. The work is building from a different base from the physical or environmental regeneration focus of the Scottish and German examples. Faced with uneconomic or despoiled resources, the residents are focusing on human resources and are building up the social and cultural capital of the locality.

There are questions as how community-led and -based organizations can supply, address and sustain the big visions needed to galvanize the politicians and planners to supply the resources for regeneration. There is also the practical question of how local organizations can obtain, manage and deliver complex funding programmes. The Hungarian example shows the value of civil society and the value of the sense of place that continues long after places have lost their economic rationale for being. Equally, Odz asks questions of how the top-down model can engage local residents and what it can offer them other than the promise of replacement employment, shops, new housing or challenging modern art.

What I have hoped to have shown in these three case studies is that areas are all recognisably Coketown clusters yet each has radically different histories and future trajectories. What is important to note is the positive role that education or learning can play in terms of uncovering these histories and planning trajectories. There cannot be what the Americans term a 'cookie-cutter approach', when the same approach is replicated regardless of situation. It also reveals 'the inadequacy of narrowly based professional specialisms' that cannot synthesize approaches from different disciplines (Bianchini and Parkinson, 1993: 210).

As such there appears to be an opportunity to begin to blend a cultural planning approach (with training focused on urban and regional economics, social and political science, cultural policy) with both physical regeneration *and* community development. What this approach might be like is explored in the next section by looking at some of the other identities of place in just one of the case studies of the European 'Coketown' clusters.

Coketown and its Alternative Futures – Linking Community Development and Cultural Planning Approaches in Craigmillar

This section of the chapter focuses on key areas that the Cragimillar master plan of 2000 did not address. These are the social and cultural history of the people of the area. The role of local people in consistently presenting their version of their experiences of Coketown and in formulating an alternative vision of regeneration that goes beyond the replacement of the built environment will be emphasized. This alternative vision of regeneration will, I believe, strike a chord in many other areas of the UK and Europe that are also undergoing regeneration. It also links the cultural planning approach with that of community development. I have taken a cultural planning approach and studied the original buildings, art works and cultural facilities of the area themselves as significant cultural texts that can be critically decoded and used for positive and socially progressive purposes by planners, academics, artists and community activists.

The majority of houses in the area were built after 1930 in a period of slum clearance and industrial re-location from central Edinburgh. Not only houses were built; there were also schools and workplaces. In Craigmillar primary school there is a wall mural painted by the Scottish artist John Maxwell in 1934 (see Figure 14.1). The wall mural focuses on and celebrates open space and sunshine. In doing so it welcomes the building of the estate as a release from the slums of central

Edinburgh for the residents, and particularly the children who were both the pupils of the school and the consumers of the fresh air and sunshine.

Figure 14.1 Mural by John Maxwell (Photo: P. Denning)

In both time period, subject, choice and use of imagery, the mural is an expression of much larger global social and artistic discourses that Ken Worpole identifies in *Here Comes the Sun* (2000), which focuses on the expression of these discourses in the built form via architecture in cities and housing estates around the UK and Europe in the inter-war period. The imagery of the mural also focuses on what we now would term 'quality of life'. This is expressed not only as access to fresh air and sun but also a sense of freedom and a desire to live an untroubled life. This would be particularly pertinent in the period following 'the war to end all wars' and in the boundaries of the Coketown clusters.

Whilst the Maxwell mural focuses on the celebratory features of the new estates, many other aspects were left out of the picture. Some provided a counterpoint to the ideologies of living on fresh air and sunshine alone. For example, one of the original residents, Helen Crummy (1992), draws attention to how it felt to actually live there as a child in the Great Depression of the 1930s, when unemployment in the coal industry was high, in an estate with no access to amenities and basic services such as a doctor. Like many 'new' working-class housing estates of the period (even when they offered greater standards of hygiene and comfort than the slums they replaced), Craigmillar was caught in the tension between the stated aspiration to build 'homes fit for heroes' and the reality of cost savings imposed by civic leaders that Swenarton (1981) has documented.

Other silenced aspects of the mural subverted the ideology itself. Interestingly, the mural presents the area as a 'new beginning', a clean slate. Maxwell, unlike other muralists of the time such as Diego Rivera, chose not to represent what else existed in the area as a contrast to inner-city slums besides fresh air, green open spaces and sunshine. The reality was somewhat different. Crummy (1992) makes no attempt to hide her watchmaker father's political views, particularly towards the ruling mine-owning aristocratic elite of the area. Furthermore, the estate was built on the land around and incorporating the mining and mill villages of Newcraighall, the Jewel and Niddrie. The majority of the men arriving in the area from across the UK and Europe in the agricultural depressions of the 1870-1910 and the post-World War I periods would find work in the newly-expanding mining industry. These 'new' residents were moving into spaces occupied by a number of differing communities. Each of these communities had its own collective actions, educational programmes and oral cultures. Far from being a 'new beginning', old struggles re-appeared from a new place. Both industrialization and innovation of the existing products of the area also took place, bringing the factory system to bear on the production of coal, beer, bricks, margarine, biscuits and dairy produce.

Standard writings on urban populations (particularly those who live on local authority housing estates) tend to stress the negative aspects of a limited social mix (see for example, Rogers and Power, 2000). This discounts the possibility that the working class is not homogenous in its composition. In Craigmillar, the mix of former inner-city dwellers (many of whom were immigrants from the Highlands, Ireland and central Europe with their own knowledges and skills) with industrial workers instead proved to be a potent brew in many ways.

Contemporaneously with the painting of the mural, Craigmillar is also notable in the siting and development of the People's College directly opposite the primary school. Founded by staff and students from the University of Edinburgh Settlement, the People's College focused on the human and educational development of non-school-age residents.

Once again this development is linked to wider social and educational movements and discourses. The People's College was drawing upon not only the rich ideas and examples of the University Settlement movement, but also the Village Colleges of Howard Morris, the 'People's Harvards' in the US (e.g. City University in New York) and the Labour Colleges of John MacLean that were all active in the first three decades of the twentieth century.

As Helen Crummy has documented in *Let the People Sing* (1992), in the midst of material deprivation, the residents of the new estate simultaneously engaged with a wide-ranging mix of political, cultural and artistic discourses, influences and inspirations that were probably not foreseen by the city fathers who built the estate. Examples of this ranged from the aesthetics and ideologies of the modern movement in their local built environment, the mass cultures of radio, publishing and film, the culturally-focused programmes of the People's College and the political-economy dominated curriculum of nearby Newbattle Abbey College which was part of the Scottish Labour College network.

Out of this mix over the period from 1940 to the early 1970s the area also produced a number of noteworthy cultural expressions and texts from residents of Coketown, such as the Bill Douglas film trilogy *My Childhood, My Ain Folk, My*

Way Home, that offer a radically different view of growing up in a coalfield community.

Over the last four decades of the twentieth century, residents developed the Craigmillar Festival Society which organized itself around the key issues for the local community such as unemployment, lack of educational opportunities, arts, youth, social welfare and the environment. These were explored using drama, carnival, festival, poetry, visual arts, sculpture and musical theatre, and achieved involvement and ownership by the local community in doing so. Consistent underlying themes were the need for investment in people via jobs, educational opportunities and amenities. Alongside these, there was a consistent moral challenge to preconceived notions as to the value and culture of local people in terms of their humanity. Again, Helen Crummy is quite explicit about this: 'Poverty is not only lack of an adequate income to live on, it is being classed as of little or no value to society, and as such, having one's capacity for self-fulfilment crippled at birth' (1992: 10).

Pierre Bourdieu (1984) sees such actions as signifiers of class conflict being contested within the cultural as well as the political fields and within specific historical and social settings. In terms of the critical attention paid by workers to the institutions and apparatuses of culture, it is notable that the formation of the Craigmillar Festival Society in the late 1950s is closely related to the development of the Edinburgh Festival in 1947 and in many ways is a critical response to this.

In terms of the development of a cultural politics that challenged dominant value systems, further research is required to place these distinct artistic forms of resistance and alignment within their wider social formation. The plays, musicals, sculptures, photographs, musicals, poems and songs within the archives of the Craigmillar Festival Society alone would reap a rich harvest in this respect (a personal retrospective of work by the artist Richard De Marco at Edinburgh's City Art Centre in 2001 was notable for the placing of the activities of the CFS within its artistic, cultural and social context of the last sixty years).

Conclusion

In terms of defining a sense and spirit of place as well as the multiple layers and identities of that place, the documents of the process and products of community development are of key importance to cultural planners. In spite of its stock of modern movement buildings and art forms from the 1930s, and the numerous public artworks that address the industrial heritage and the strength and pride of the local community that were commissioned by the Craigmillar Festival Society and which are spread over the community, there is little chance of Craigmillar ever being defined as a conservation area, industrial culture park or a sculpture or mural trail (as in Emscher Park or East Los Angeles). Instead, the Craigmillar master plan of 2000 ignores the industrial past of the area and envisages the destruction of these buildings and artefacts as part of a 'new beginning'. As Short (1999) has suggested, this process of silencing is a key part of a distinct discourse of urban representation whereby some issues, neighbourhoods or groups are either silenced or presented as dangerous and beyond the confines of reasonable debate.

The silencing of the community continues in other ways. A key problem facing any researcher is collating and analysing primary material. Although one of the founders of the CFS, Helen Crummy, has collected an archive of the posters, plays, music, songs, film, video, minutes and photography of the organization within her house and published a book on the organization, there has been no attempt to collect this material into the mainstream Scottish cultural research archives or libraries. Thus there is publicly accessible alternative memory of place.

The nature of culturally-focused community development work is based on people and short-lived events rather than physical art works or buildings. As a result there is the distinct possibility that work such as this will be lost to posterity and social memory, unless other means of storage are found. The richness of this archive is undoubted. Its potential value to a cultural planning approach lies as a tool that offers a more rounded and nuanced approach to neighbourhood regeneration that builds in community development techniques and resident involvement. Yet the fragility of this approach in the face of competing, larger and more powerful demands and interests should always be noted.

This fragility is all the more ironic given that the case for the economic regeneration of former industrial areas such as coalfield communities appears to be won in policy terms at both supranational and national levels. The UK government pledged £50 million of National Lottery Funds to the Coalfield Regeneration Trust in 1999 for three years. New funding for another three-year period has just been secured. The focus on community development and the acknowledgement of its importance is present in all three of the UK nations with coalfields.[2] These in turn are linked to the larger European programmes.

The social arguments for regenerating former coalfield communities would initially appear to reinforce the economic ones and vice versa. However, the UK government has been less effective at noting what the innovative actions to support social regeneration might be. I hope to have shown that there are also a wealth of traditions, memories, identities and experiences to draw upon. It is time to let these come in from the cold. Short (1999: 53-54) suggests a possible course of action in that 'There is need for an alternative representation, for urban imagineers who can represent the just, fair city'.

In many ways, from the wall murals of the 1930s to the present, coalfield communities like Craigmillar have continuously had representations, discourses, ideologies and solutions imposed from above. These have all sought to impose place upon people. As Short stresses, these representations are 'not politically neutral, neither are they devoid of social implications ... The dominant representations play down equality, social justice, and an inclusive definition of the good city' (54).

At present, the bulldozers and demolition squads are at work, erasing the past of the community. The builders are also at work, physically imposing an 'alternative sense of place' via another reconstruction of Craigmillar. If this is allowed to occur uncontested and unremarked, then Craigmillar will indeed become a 'ghost town', a 'non-place' devoid of historical context and stripped of the memories of collective action, like earlier parts of the European coalfields. On one hand we will have turned our backs upon a dirty, dangerous and polluting industry; on the other, we will have lost a key part of what made our cities the way they are today.

In this chapter, I have argued that a cultural planning approach, if linked to physical regeneration and community development approaches, can provide a counterpoint and a challenge to other more limited approaches based on economic development and physical regeneration alone. I would hope that fellow practitioners will recognize the links to their own work. I acknowledge that there are difficulties in accessing primary material and in making contact with what are often very resource-poor organizations (such as those in Odz). Yet in many ways the policy environment is such that these links are increasingly possible. I can only hope that we will see greater research on this area of practice in cultural planning seminars, conferences, journal articles and training programmes in the future.

Acknowledgements

I wish to thank the following for their consistent support, advice, feedback and critical encouragement in researching this area: Helen Crummy, Andrew Crummy and Dr Andrew MacDonald (in Craigmillar), Dr Franco Bianchini and Lia Ghilardi (at De Montfort University), Alison Seabrooke and Steve Brunt (at the Coalfields Learning Initiative Partnership), Dr Anja-Maaike Green, Martin Higgins, Mel Doyle, Dick Ellison, Frances Gillies and the late Dr Sheila Smith-Hobson.

Notes

1   My interests in this area are threefold: research interests, relationship to professional interests and personal history. For the last ten years, my research interests have broadly addressed the relationship between labour markets, educational providers (such as universities and colleges) and communities. A key element of this interest relates to the various ways and means by which local residents of such communities access (or not, as the case may be) wider urban labour markets and the higher levels of educational provision. I have studied this area via a number of study visits to projects in inner cities in Europe and the United States. The second reason for my interest relates to my professional interests. I am presently Chief Executive of the UK National Training Organization for the community-based learning and development sector. As a result of this, I am in daily contact with a huge range of community projects from across the UK, the majority of whom are engaged in community development and neighbourhood regeneration. A constant factor across the UK is on economic and environmental sustainability and quality of life as former ways of life based upon industries such as mining, textiles, manufacturing, agriculture and fishing are dying out. Therefore my interest in new approaches is both practical and timely. The third reason is personal. I come from a family of miners. I know from personal family history the reasons for economic migration as relatives live in Scotland, Kent, South Yorkshire and the Midlands. The major strikes of 1926 and 1984-85 as well as the nationalization of the mining industry after World War II deeply affected my family. It has been a source of personal pride drawn from family knowledge that the many families like mine in mining

communities across the UK made substantial contributions to the economic, social and political development of the UK. It has been a source of concern that these contributions are so rarely acknowledged. The collapse of former mining communities under pressure from high levels of unemployment, drug use and family breakdown that have been documented by researchers such as the Coalfields Task Force (DETR, 1998) and Turner (2000) only exacerbates my concerns.

2   Communities First programme in Wales, Neighbourhood Renewal in England, Community Regeneration in Scotland.

Chapter 15

The Culture of Neighbourhoods: A European Perspective

Franco Bianchini and Lia Ghilardi

Many cities have quarters or neighbourhoods that confer on them a sense of place and identity through the historic and cultural associations they provide. Such places are usually the product of the many, mostly organic, transformations undergone by their cities through time. Soho in London, New York's Lower East Side, or the Left Bank in Paris all grew out of what Roy Porter calls the 'response to the deep pulse of the city' (Porter, 1994: 153). Thus neighbourhoods are rarely autonomous functional zones and usually have a symbiotic relationship with the city, and tend to have a cultural substratum that identifies and distinguishes them, a cultural element which gives rise to what can be termed *neighbourhood culture*. For example, the neighbourhood culture of Soho today is a complex mixture of historical literary and bohemian associations with elements of a 'red-light district' reputation (with all its implications in terms of gangsterism and permissive tolerance) plus a much more recent and highly visible gay culture.

In terms of neighbourhood culture, over the past twenty years we have witnessed the emergence throughout the world of distinct social and spatial areas, cultural and ethnic quarters, where lifestyles, identities and forms of sociability are more than before packaged and promoted by policy-makers as attractions for visitors to consume. These new cultural quarters have often been used by policy-makers as a model for the regeneration of declining inner-urban areas with the result of putting neighbourhoods on the road to both gentrification and cultural banalization.

The concepts and policy issues related to neighbourhood cultures were discussed in our report, published in 1997 by the Council of Europe, containing the findings of a study conducted between 1993 and 1996 across neighbourhoods from eleven European cities.[1]

The 'Culture and Neighbourhoods' action research project was launched with the general aim of raising awareness among politicians, the media, policy-makers and the general public about the cultural needs, realities and potential of European urban neighbourhoods. From the point of view of policy, the objectives of the study were:

- To encourage local communities in European neighbourhoods to shape and evaluate their own cultural policies;
- To explore and maximize the potential contribution of neighbourhood culture to the cultural, economic and social dynamics and development of cities and regions;
- To examine the potential of neighbourhood cultures and cultural policies as resources for the implementation of new policies affecting the neighbourhood – for example, policies on social services, education, environmental improvement, economic and community development;
- To examine the role of the voluntary and non-profit making sector in neighbourhood cultural development.

In this chapter, we provide additional comments on the Council of Europe's study and discuss the specificity of neighbourhood cultures in relation to national and global cultural trends. The relevance of the neighbourhood as an entity in cultural policy-making, especially with regard to multicultural relations and cultural diversity, is also highlighted in the chapter, with reference to European cities. Finally, in the conclusion we propose different and more culturally integrated approaches to neighbourhood cultural policy-making and raise questions for further discussion and research.

The Concept of Neighbourhood Culture

In a new report published by the New York-based Center for an Urban Future, the arts and culture are cited as a 'primary component of growth' in New York City neighbourhoods over the past ten years (The Creative Engine, 2002). The report, which focuses on localized creative activity in seven different neighbourhoods, concludes that cultural development has exploded in NYC neighbourhoods outside of Central Manhattan over the past decade, and argues that the ingredients for successful cultural development at city level are mostly to be found in the neighbourhoods. However, gentrification and displacement are identified in the report as reasons for concern. In particular, the authors point out that the challenge in policy terms is that of finding ways to integrate artistic growth into neighbourhoods while at the same time respecting the integrity of their own local economies, longstanding residential communities, cultural organizations and artists.

These observations are similar in nature to the comments in the Council of Europe report. In particular, it was noted that European neighbourhoods are dynamic spaces of artistic and cultural experimentation where new institutional forms, based on proximity and projects, can be tried out. In this context, neighbourhoods are understood to be the result of collective work reflecting the processes of appropriation and production of social and cultural space by the groups of which they are made up.

The assumption here is that big cities' neighbourhoods are capable of developing their own distinctive cultural expression. This concept of 'neighbourhood culture', however, must not be understood as a yearning for a fixed identity made up of shared standards, values and mores; rather, it is much more like a fluid expression of the tension between the physical and functional elements of a place. In contrast to the determinism reflected in some interpretations of neighbourhoods – stressing their importance as instruments of acculturation and inevitable attachment – their relevance, instead, must be viewed more as the product of an elective process by the individuals that live there.

Thus, neighbourhood culture has its roots in both the meaning – the bricks and mortar of the place and in the historical memory of the activities that traditionally occurred in an area – as well as in the complexity of activity and networks required for its residents to pursue their personal aims successfully. As Giddens (1993) points out, the local is the area in the immediate vicinity where the individual obtains a certain degree of ontological security.

In discussing the potential for neighbourhood culture and in highlighting its opportunities, the Council of Europe study shows that participation in neighbourhood-based cultural activities tends to be mainly by people from the area. Hence, neighbourhoods often represent the first locus where certain individuals and groups within urban populations come into contact with cultural forms. The study also reveals that neighbourhoods tend to offer smaller-scale activities, involving direct participation by local people, and producing a greater beneficial impact on individual creativity, self-confidence and skills. Activities at neighbourhood level, moreover, tend to be less rigidly divided by cultural form than in the case of city centre-based professional arts activities; as a result, there is generally in the neighbourhood greater crossover between different forms of culture, with a positive impact on the potential for innovation and creativity.

However, contemporary society is formed and develops in widely varying spatio-temporal contexts, with social interaction being increasingly characterized by participation in a multiplicity of groups in which the various roles played by the individual become his/her identity, but only temporarily (Beck, 1994; Maffesoli, 1996). Thus neighbourhoods, like so many other elements of life in contemporary society, cannot be removed from the influence of ways of life and the resultant diverse lifestyles.

On this point the study throws up a number of challenges to the notion of a pre-eminence of neighbourhood culture over city-wide activity and to the concept of 'neighbourhood culture' itself. The concept of 'neighbourhood culture' was found to be useful by some of the cities involved in the Council of Europe's project, but even when accepted, it emerges as a controversial idea, provoking a variety of opinions on its applicability to policy-making. The authors of the Marseille case study, for instance, stressed that the notion of 'culture' underpinning cultural provision at neighbourhood level was not 'neighbourhood culture' but 'city culture'. The neighbourhood, in Marseille City Council's conception of cultural policy (as it was then), was the site where professionally-produced culture of high quality was made more widely available to citizens.

On the other hand, the Munich case studies include interviews with local residents which demonstrate that the concept of 'neighbourhood culture' is a living and important one for the everyday lives of neighbourhood residents. The Munich report provides a variety of opinions on the value of 'district culture', defined as neighbourhood-based cultural activities organized or supported by Munich City Council. According to the interviewees, district culture 'offers encouragement to take part, or to initiate something oneself ... [it] is also an opportunity to identify with one's own district ... [it] increases people's feeling of being part of their quarter ... it gets neighbourhoods to grow together, and people to meet and get to know one another'.

The study also shows that geographical location is an important factor. For example, in Southern European cities it is more important for people to be accepted at neighbourhood level, and, as a consequence, there are more multifunctional centres of community life with a mixing of different cultural activities than is usually the case in Northern European cities. Southern European cities tend to be characterized also by the presence of more unplanned, spontaneous street activities in the neighbourhood than is common in Northern Europe.

At the time of the study, larger geopolitical issues had an effect on comparisons between cities in different parts of Europe. For example, the effects of the changes in Eastern European countries were being felt at all levels of social and cultural life. In Prague, for instance, working life was taking up more time and energy than it used to and, as a consequence, the people interviewed in the case studies commented on the fact that there was now less time for local, participatory cultural activities. There was also a sense that indigenous culture had to compete with foreign products (books, film, music, TV, etc.) which were then swamping the market and which were becoming increasingly available in the domestic sphere, thus reducing the need to go out and participate in social life. Public cultural life in the two neighbourhoods studied was becoming more and more precarious: the steady march of privatization was having a deep impact on neighbourhood culture. In some cases, public policy has played a part in changing the social ecology of cultural life. In Bilbao, for example, the two neighbourhoods chosen for the study had recently undergone major regeneration transformations, and they both lacked an independent, vibrant neighbourhood culture but had a number of top-down cultural services provided by the City Council according to city-wide strategy and priorities.[2] Here too, independent neighbourhood cultural life was shrinking, with the urban and social changes brought by regeneration requiring a more top-down, place-marketing approach to cultural policy.

On the positive side, neighbourhood cultural activity appears from the results of the study to be a path of engagement to other forms of civic participation. The decline in political participation and the erosion of local citizens' trust in the traditional political process is a widely-felt problem in many European cities.[3] The study shows that while neighbourhood cultural policies are almost never directed to rekindling traditional forms of political engagement, they nevertheless are in some cases aimed at fostering 'non-political' forms of civic engagement. This way, cultural participation provides a basis for strengthening community bonds.

Links Between Neighbourhood Culture and Other Policies

Evidence from the study and from elsewhere shows that cultural participation at local level may be one of the key elements contributing to the strengthening of community bonds. Examples of attempts to combine social and cultural action were provided by the activities against drug abuse and AIDS undertaken by the Grava socio-cultural centre in Patissia (Athens), and by the Feierwerk Centre in Munich.[4] At the time of the study, this functioned as a home for refugees and other people in transit, as well as a meeting place for youth and an alternative arts centre. Another example of successful mix of social-cultural activities was provided by the Müsorfuzet cultural centre in Erzsébetváros, Budapest. The centre offered innovative programmes of activities targeted at the elderly as well as at Jewish and Gypsy minorities. Similar programmes are still offered today by the WUK in Vienna's Alsergrund district. From the beginning of its life in 1993, this centre has linked its activities with neighbourhood-based social services provision, especially for the young and the elderly.

Overall, although it is difficult to provide hard evidence of direct links between participation in cultural activity at neighbourhood level and the fostering of social cohesion, the case studies suggest that direct participation in cultural events and activities, rather than simple consumption of marketed goods, is an essential precondition for maximizing the contribution of culture to the development of human potential and to social cohesion in the neighbourhood.

Moreover, the impact that cultural participation at neighbourhood level can have in encouraging multiculturalism and in advancing intercultural understanding is also highlighted in the study. Multiculturalism and interculturalism are a relatively common experience at the level of individual consumption (food, music, crafts objects etc.), but it is generally much more difficult to encourage groups of people to participate in multicultural and intercultural projects. Neighbourhood-based cultural and social policies have traditionally aimed at multiculturalism, which generally means the strengthening of the distinctive cultural identities of different ethnic communities by enabling them to have their own cultural voices. This is a valuable objective, but it should be stressed that multiculturalism does not necessarily encourage communication between cultures. On the contrary, multicultural policies can sometimes contribute to entrenching particularisms and vested interests.

Two interesting examples of cultural activities aimed at building bridges between different communities and at producing innovative cultural hybrids have emerged from the Council of Europe study. They are the promotion by the Turin City Council of the production of the film *Piazza Saluzzo siamo noi* (We Are Piazza Saluzzo), and the creation of the *Werkstatt der Kulturen* (Workshop of Cultures) in Berlin. The film was made in 1996 with the double purpose of illustrating the richness of the physical, social and cultural environments and of counteracting the negative images that the San Salvario area of Turin had in the mainstream media at the time. The film was created entirely by local young people – including some belonging to ethnic minorities – under the guidance of a professional film director.

The development of the Berlin Workshop of Cultures is an example of how city government (in this case the Berlin Senate Commission for Foreign Affairs) can develop intercultural projects for civic spaces, while at the same time fostering an intercultural mentality in the city. The Workshop of Cultures is a building complex which includes a concert hall, auditorium, laboratories and studios, and is run jointly by representatives of German and migrant organizations. The aim is for young people to meet and engage in intercultural exchange and production projects. Since 1994, the Centre supports Radio Multikulti, a local public radio station run mainly by non-German DJs, and broadcasting world music and debates on social, cultural and political issues in sixteen languages (Vertovec, 1995; see also Soysal, 1996).

Using Culture to Aid the Physical Regeneration of Neighbourhoods

The use of cultural projects and policies to break cycles of physical decline in European cities is becoming more and more common. This is especially the case in city centres, where prestigious cultural facilities (such as museums, theatres and opera houses) have often acted as catalysts to counteract negative images of an area, attract private sector investment and start a cycle of renewal, usually linked with the development of tourism and wider city-marketing strategies aimed at pulling in footloose capital and mover firms. The case studies reveal that this process is much less common in neighbourhoods, probably due to their economic marginality in comparison with city centres, and despite the undoubted need for investment to improve and renew degraded buildings and the local public realm.

Nevertheless, some examples worth highlighting have emerged from the case studies. One of the most interesting is the Sidegaden project in Vesterbro, Copenhagen. The project's central aim was to offer homeless and unemployed young people cheap accommodation. Today, the young people living in the area have revitalized shop premises, with the opening of new crafts shops, a hairdresser, pubs and cafés. Similarly, another imaginative scheme is the reuse of the church of La Merced in La Vieja, a degraded neighbourhood of Bilbao. The church is now used by rock groups for rehearsals, recordings and concerts, as well as for dance and theatre activities.

There are other examples which are equally suggestive. A group of citizens living in the Augarten neighbourhood in Vienna – characterized by a very high concentration of immigrants (mainly from Turkey and the former Yugoslavia) – co-operated with Aktionradius, a locally-based group of community architects, to revitalize the long-neglected Augarten baroque gardens. They renovated the gardens' entrance gate, developed new play facilities for children, and co-operated with the local authority in designing a regeneration plan for the area. They also initiated concerts, conferences, festivals, music events and theatre performances with audiences of up to 5,000 (many of whom came from other parts of the city), and reminded the people of Vienna that the Augarten used to be one of the city's cultural foci under Emperor Joseph II. In the Gazi neighbourhood in Athens' Historic District, the City Council has restored the former gasworks to create an exhibition hall, artists' workshops, a theatre, plus other cultural facilities, cafés and restaurants. This is first and foremost a conservation and industrial archaeology project, and is the final stage of a tourist circuit linking all the city's archaeological sites.

The examples above are all the result of an 'organic' approach to regeneration, where the cultural resources of the neighbourhood are mobilized in response to local aspirations, thus engendering participation and a sense of ownership. By contrast, in districts where flagship venues were chosen as catalysts for development and increased consumption, these seem to have been largely unable to make their activities relevant to local people. The juxtaposition of commerce with culture, alongside or even taking the place of public (neighbourhood) culture in the form of cultural venues and facilities, appears to be a divisive issue for some of the neighbourhoods involved in the study.

Indeed, one of the key shifts in cultural policy-making in West European cities from the early 1980s and in East European cities from the early 1990s has been towards the use of prestigious, city centre-based facilities for 'high' cultural forms (concert halls, opera houses, museums etc.) as vehicles for improving the image of particular urban areas, and with the aim of attracting investment, tourists and skilled personnel. In other words there has been in European urban planning philosophy and practice a shift away from the idea of the city as a functioning whole, and towards the idea of the city as an image to be marketed nationally and internationally. As a consequence, local authority resources for neighbourhood and community-oriented projects have tended to shrink. This has often produced a defensive, inward-looking response from neighbourhood-based cultural groups. Energies which could have been channelled into creative innovation and communal celebration are increasingly giving rise to fragmentation, envy and even open conflict.

In some cases, as in Le Panier in Marseille, flagship cultural institutions are located in the neighbourhood itself. The case study of Le Panier shows that the resident population and people actively involved in cultural activities in the neighbourhood shared the view that flagship institutions embody an elitist cultural policy, which is 'unsuitable and alien' to the needs of local citizens. By contrast, local people interviewed during the study in the other Marseille neighbourhood (Saint Barthèlemy) largely supported the view that the local flagship, the Theatre du Merlan, had made a positive contribution to the locality's quality of life.

Moreover, a certain diffidence towards the cultural activities of the Lingotto complex still prevails among the residents of District IX in Turin, in part because of the relatively high ticket prices charged, for example for music performances. On the other hand, it is also true that local people are often proud of new flagship cultural projects. One example is the current positive attitude towards the Guggenheim Museum project among many residents of Bilbao La Vieja.

The dangers of developing mainly consumption-oriented urban cultural policies, such as those highlighted in some of the case studies above, have been discussed by Sharon Zukin over the past twenty years. Zukin's work shows that it is risky for cities to rely on consumption-oriented models, as they depend on factors over which local authorities have virtually no control, such as changes in the level of the residents' and visitors' disposable income (Zukin, 1995).

A related problem concerns the quality of the jobs generated by this type of cultural policy, which are often low-paid, part-time, and with a low skills content and satisfaction level. Moreover, creating new buildings – although popular among developers and city politicians anxious to be able to show tangible achievements to the electorate – can absorb most of the resources available to city authorities through maintenance costs and loan charges. Almost invariably, cultural buildings constructed as part of urban regeneration strategies are located in city centres. In times of financial stringency, municipal administrations are more likely to curtail funding for activities of experimental and participatory character in the neighbourhoods than to withdraw money invested in theatres, opera houses and other building-based flagship cultural institutions, mainly located in city centres.

Policy Implications

Implementation Issues

The case studies have identified a range of factors aiding the success of neighbourhood cultural initiatives, which include the leadership role of committed individuals and the adoption of consultative, open and transparent procedures for policy-making, involving also the use of artists as a creative resource. On the negative side, the main obstacles to successful implementation singled out by the case studies are the lack of co-operation between neighbourhood-based organizations, and the presence of excessively complicated bureaucratic procedures.

A good example of the central role played by committed and driven individuals is, according to one of the case studies, that of the extraordinary dedication to the success of the Pesthidegkut cultural centre (Budapest) by its charismatic director. In Marseille, the Saint-Barthélemy case study highlights the importance for the success of local cultural projects of the high levels of knowledge of the district and its people by professional cultural animateurs.

However, the role of individuals has to be balanced by and combined with mechanisms and actions to consult and involve local people. One example of good practice is provided by community architects Aktionradius, who have run an interesting consultation exercise on the subject of the future development of the Gaussplatz area of the Augartenviertel district in Vienna, with funding from Vienna City Council. Local residents attended information events focusing on the architecture and history of the area, and broadened their knowledge of urban design and planning. Representatives from local residents, together with experts, formed part of the jury which selected the winning project for the Gaussplatz.

The policy-makers in District IX in Turin encouraged public debate by raising awareness of the potential of local cultural resources through the organization of an open forum on 'culture as an opportunity for local development'. Similarly, the Munich case study highlights the importance of democratic procedures in the selection of the projects to be included in the 'District Weeks' organized by the City Council, in order to build a relationship of trust between the municipality and local citizens. The partnership between public authorities and local residents and associations in the Marseille neighbourhood of Saint Barthèlemy represents another example of good practice. On the other hand, the other Marseille case study, Le Panier, highlights the lack of consultation of cultural managers and policy-makers with the inhabitants of the neighbourhood, which has resulted in a series of missed opportunities.

The attempts detailed above to adopt open and transparent procedural methods for policy-making, involving local participation, are all indicative of a need for new and inclusive approaches aimed at urban neighbourhoods. The cultural policy-led urban regeneration strategies of the 1980s and 1990s in Europe adopted too narrow a concept of regeneration, which focused mainly on its economic and physical dimensions, and failed to integrate them with cultural, symbolic, social and political aspects. There is a feeling, among both cultural practitioners and policy-makers, that there needs to be a re-examination of policy delivery mechanisms, because national and supranational institutions often work through hierarchical departments which are too detached from local territorial dynamics.

From their experience of developing integrated cultural plans across Europe, we believe that the concept of 'cultural planning', which has been discussed since the early 1990s in North America, Australia and Europe (Bianchini, 1993, 1996; Ghilardi 2001; McNulty, 1991; Mercer, 1991), may provide a key to a more democratic and place-based process of cultural development for urban neighbourhoods.

The Cultural Planning Approach

Unlike traditional cultural policies – which are still mainly based on aesthetic definitions of 'culture' as 'art' – cultural planning adopts as its basis a broad definition of 'cultural resources', which consists of the following elements:

- Arts, the media and the heritage;
- The cultures of youth, ethnic minorities, communities of interest and 'neo-tribes';
- Local traditions, including archaeology, local dialects and rituals;
- Local and external perceptions of a place, as expressed in jokes, songs, literature, myths, tourist guides, media coverage and conventional wisdom;
- Topography, and the qualities of the natural and built environment, including public spaces;
- The diversity and quality of leisure, cultural, drinking, eating and entertainment facilities;
- The repertoire of local products and skills in the crafts, manufacturing and services.

While traditional cultural policies tend to take a sectoral focus – policies for the development of theatre, dance, literature, the crafts and other cultural forms – cultural planning adopts a territorial remit. Its purpose is to see how the pool of cultural resources identified above can contribute to the integrated development of a place (whether a neighbourhood, a city or a region).

By placing cultural resources at the centre of policy-making, two-way relationships can be established between these resources and any type of public policy – in fields ranging from economic development to housing, health, education, social services, tourism, urban planning, architecture, townscape design, and cultural policy itself.

Cultural planning cuts across the divides between the public, private and voluntary sectors, different institutional concerns, types of knowledge and professional disciplines. In addition, cultural planning encourages innovation in cultural production, for example through interculturalism, co-operation between artists and scientists, and crossovers between different cultural forms.

It is also important to clarify that cultural planning is not intended as the planning of culture – an impossible, undesirable and dangerous undertaking – but rather as a cultural approach to urban planning and policy. Advocates of cultural planning argue that policy-makers in all fields should not simply be making an instrumental use of cultural resources as tools for achieving non-cultural goals, but should let their own mindsets and assumptions be transformed by contact with local culture. This can happen if policy-makers learn from the five key sets of attributes of the types of thinking that characterize the processes of creative production. This thinking tends to be:

- Holistic, flexible, lateral, networking and interdisciplinary;
- Innovation-oriented, original and experimental;
- Critical, inquiring, challenging and questioning;
- People-centred, humanistic and non-deterministic;
- 'Cultured', and informed by critical knowledge of traditions of cultural expression.

In cultural planning, the cultural policy-maker, the artist and/or the cultural manager can become gatekeeper between the sphere of cultural production – the world of ideas and of the production of meaning – and any area of policy-making.

Issues for Discussion and Further Research

In order to adopt a cultural planning approach, neighbourhood cultural policy-makers need to be retrained, in order to expand their knowledge base from arts administration and cultural management to political economy, urban sociology, physical planning, urban history and other disciplines which are essential for an understanding of how neighbourhoods and cities develop. Their work could be organized more around cross-cutting issues and problems, and less shaped by the rigidities of departmental concerns. Innovative thinking in policy-making institutions could be encouraged through an extensive use of ideas competitions – not just for architectural, urban design and public art projects, but also for the design of cultural policies themselves. In other words, a culture of creativity and of the acceptance of risk could be encouraged in policy-making – a culture where policy-makers are not afraid of failure, or at least are able to distinguish between 'competent' and 'incompetent' failure, and see that the former may contain the seeds of future success.

The findings of the Council of Europe's project highlight two issues that are central to the development of urban cultural policies inspired by the principles of use value, local control and the search for local cultural identity. The first concerns the creation of a local public sphere and of spaces for social interaction, and the second the relationship between neighbourhood culture and city-wide culture.

Social cohesion may prove difficult to achieve in our cities, which are increasingly marked by economic and lifestyle differences. Precisely for this reason, it is important that policy-makers promote social interaction between different groups. Social interaction can be based on the simple but powerful fact that different social groups inhabit the same territory. The Council of Europe study has confirmed that cultural activities can play a key role in transforming this territory into a shared public space, and in counteracting trends towards conducting our public life within increasingly homogeneous social circles. However, to maximize the potential of cultural resources, it is important that they are co-ordinated with architecture and urban planning initiatives aimed at producing space which – in Michael Walzer's definition (1986) – is not designed with one particular type of usage in mind ('single minded space'), but is 'open minded': it is designed for 'a variety of uses, including unforeseen and unforseeable uses, and is used by citizens who do different things and are prepared to tolerate, even to take an interest in, things they do not do'.

Moreover, a notion of public space linked with strategies to recreate a local public sphere at neighbourhood level should make the most of the opportunities provided by the new information technologies, which are – according to Castells (2001) – the means by which places may continue to exist as such. Though sceptical about some of the claims made by the virtual community pioneers about the power of the internet to generate sociability without place, Castells argues that neighbourhood media strategies can contribute to counteracting the standardizing forces unleashed by the spaces of flows (of the increasingly globalized urban economies) and to asserting some local control over the external images of the neighbourhood itself.

Finally, one of the key issues to be discussed is: which strategies can be adopted at neighbourhood level to strengthen the identities and external images of these areas, in the context of the relationship between the neighbourhood and the rest of the city? In the words of Giandomenico Amendola – one of the advisers to the Council of Europe's project – how can we 'make sure that many different groups and cultures coexist and interact to produce reciprocal enrichment?' Such fruitful coexistence and interaction depends on the development of a civic identity alongside specific cultural identities, and of spaces and opportunities for intercultural exchange in the city. How should policy-makers relate to the innovative capacities of neighbourhoods, and especially to forms of creativity (such as those of French banlieue art, much British popular music, and many of the centri sociali in Italy, which are occupied buildings, self-managed by various groups mostly active in the environmentalist, anarchist and radical left fringes of Italian youth culture) emerging from deprived and/or marginalized areas, which have not yet been gentrified and regenerated? To this end, the Council of Europe (and other national, regional and local bodies for that matter) could take the lead in the process of re-orientation of urban cultural policies in Europe and, starting from neighbourhood experience: it could, for example, research best practice of new forms of neighbourhood cultural centres and of innovative approaches to providing spaces for cultural activities in the neighbourhood; community consultation and involvement at neighbourhood level in programmes aimed at tackling cultural diversity; and mechanisms, procedures and institutional arrangements to co-ordinate cultural policies at city-wide and neighbourhood level.

Notes

1   The research project focused on 24 neighbourhoods chosen from the following cities: Copenhagen, Liverpool, Munich, Vienna, Turin, Marseille, Bilbao, Prague, Budapest, Sofia and Athens.
2   The districts of La Vieja and San Pedro de Deusto.
3   On this topic see Burbidge (1998).
4   See the work of Matarasso (1997).

Chapter 16

Afterword: Thinking in Quarters

David Bell and Mark Jayne

The essays collected together in *City of Quarters* represent an intervention into the still-evolving discourses and practices of 'quartering' cities – of designating and branding particular spaces in an attempt to produce new forms of urban living and urban competitiveness, most commonly in a post-industrial context. As such, quartering is part of broader processes of entrepreneurial urban governance tied to the rise of the symbolic economy of cities (Scott, 2000). In this Afterword, we want to reflect on those processes and their outcomes, in an effort to think about urban quarters and what they do and mean for cities and their inhabitants, potential inhabitants and visitors. We want to begin by telling a particular quarter story – a story which, like so many in *City of Quarters*, visibilizes the forces at work in the production of these new urban spaces. From that starting point, we then want to move our focus out, in an attempt to site quarters and 'quarter-work' in the contested socio-spatial politics of the 'new urban order' – an order which, perhaps paradoxically, turns out to be not wholly new at all (Evans, this volume; Short, 1996).

Talking of Quarters

In February 2003, David was invited to join a small group of academics and university managers to discuss the designation of a University (or Learning) Quarter in Stoke-on-Trent, UK. The Quarter was to contain within its borders Staffordshire University (or, at least, its Stoke campuses), two Further Education colleges, two large urban parks and a proposed 'innovation village' (on land currently undergoing house clearance), together with substantial amounts of existing housing stock, some of it currently private-rented student accommodation. This inaugural meeting generated some interesting discussions about the idea of a University Quarter generally, about this University Quarter in Stoke-on-Trent specifically, and most tellingly about what (and who) such a quarter might actually be for.

It was clear that each participant at the meeting had their own ideas about the purpose of the quarter, and their own vision of what it might be like. For some, it was principally a branding exercise, a way of badging the University's role and presence in the city – and, to this end, there was much talk of 'flagship' buildings and gateways. For other participants, it offered a way of building 'ramps' to local communities, encouraging increased participation in education – especially by pulling together institutions of further and higher education already being corralled by the formation of Staffordshire University Regional Federation (SURF), as well as addressing what Habil Jan Hartman (2003: 87) calls the 'traditional extraterritoriality of the university against the city', that 'town and gown' mentality that separates the campus from its surroundings. The quarter was also seen as a statement of intent, as a landscape embodiment of the University's self-created role in local and regional regeneration (especially significant since the quarter was to look for finance from the regional development agency). It could also play a significant role in graduate retention, it was argued, since part of the vision was to include within the quarter business incubation units to house start-ups and spin-outs, notably in the high-technology and creative sectors. So, from widening participation to graduate retention, and from regeneration to place promotion, there was clearly a lot of work to be done by this quarter – it was, it seemed, an attempt to pull together and deliver on the many agendas and aspirations highlighted in the University's Corporate Plan, a move made all the more pressing by the recent UK government White Paper on the future of Higher Education. There was, at times, an almost utopian zeal to the meeting.

The idea of the University Quarter was also part of thinking and planning beyond the University itself. The city of Stoke-on-Trent already has at least one quarter – the Cultural Quarter within its city centre – and the (largely shelved) Cultural Strategy for the city prepared in 1990 by the Comedia consultancy had proposed quartering as a logical way to redevelop this strange, multi-centred place (see Jayne, 2000, 2003). Parallel to the discussion of the University Quarter, the sub-regional local regeneration partnership was also investigating the use of design as a motor for regeneration, potentially reheating previous unsuccessful attempts to produce a Design Quarter in the part of Stoke-on-Trent nominally historically associated with ceramic design (but now more associated with ceramic heritage given the decline in pottery manufacture in the city) (Bell and Jayne, 2003a, 2003b). The City Council's recently-produced Draft Local Plan, moreover, also mentioned the University Quarter as one possible development for the part of Stoke that the University inhabits – though the Plan was keen to also see the area develop its two other assets, the city's railway station and the Council's own Civic Centre.

So, the city was not new to the promise of being quartered, even though the publicity around the Cultural Quarter had been mixed to say the least (Jayne, 2000). Nevertheless, the Council and key local decision-makers were reportedly supportive of these new proposals, and the regional development agency had expressed its backing for the scheme, as part of a sizeable raft of initiatives aimed at reversing the city's deteriorating economic fortunes. The logic seemed initially unquestionable, and certainly the University seemed sure of the merit in undertaking this task and of the gains that would be realised. Plans had been drawn up, and an initial promotional prospectus mocked-up (using Photo-shopped images of other university quarters and campuses, and some aspirational PR copy). The Quarter was 'go'.

However, that first meeting brought to the surface numerous difficult issues and questions, many of which seemed to be symptomatic of the queries which quarters often provoke. There were concerns about boundaries, about exclusion and inclusion. Would the quarter be viewed negatively by locals, as the University's further colonization of an essentially mixed-use neighbourhood? Would this mean evicting or chasing out 'undesirable' land uses and populations? Was it essentially an elitist idea? Could the University itself sustain its territorial growth from a dispersed urban campus to a fully-fledged quarter? How would the quarter become legible in the landscape – how would people know they were in it? And would they *want* to be in it? PR and public consultation were offered as the obvious ways to make the quarter real and encourage local ownership. Getting the local press on-message was also seen as vital, given the rough ride they had given the Cultural Quarter (and the litany of other failed projects ghosting the city's regeneration agenda). Many of these queries were batted aside by the core team responsible for visioning the University Quarter, in the somewhat typical way in which University managers routinely refuse to hear voices of doubt or criticism. There was a seemingly unstoppable momentum to the project, and participants at the meeting were required to sign up to it, becoming themselves part of its promotional machinery, tasked with talking the 'quarter-talk' in their respective zones of influence. (Interestingly, at the time of writing this – in May 2003 – there has yet to be a follow-up meeting, and quarter-talk seems oddly absent from the University's organs, though it has appeared in the city's recent draft Community Strategy.)

Irrespective of whether or not the University Quarter becomes a reality on the streets of Stoke-on-Trent, this meeting and the surrounding paraphernalia of quarter-work seemed to draw out quite neatly some of the issues that academics, policy-makers, planners and city folk are currently grappling with, each in their own ways and for their own motives, in the broader context of urban quarterization. Setting aside the specificities of the University Quarter for a moment, we now want to attempt our own quarter-work and quarter-talk, and to ponder some of the things that happen when cities are subject to this process. We shall begin by considering quartering as an act of spatial and social ordering – a facet of quarters that looms large in the essays in this collection.

Topographic Tidying

One obvious – but nonetheless important – way of understanding quarters is to see them as the landscape embodiment of the process of ordering or purification – an act of tidying-up. Read like this, urban quarters are a response to the chaotic heterogeneity of the postmodern urban landscape. Cities have been misshaped and disordered by a whole set of social, spatial, political and economic processes, and the settled geography of the modern, industrial city has been profoundly *un*settled. The new emphasis on placelessness and disembedding brought about by globalization causes particularly pressing problems for urban geography, too (Bauman, 2001). Now, as Bruno Latour so eloquently describes in *We Have Never Been Modern* (1993), one of the core paradoxes of modernity has been the simultaneous desire for order (which he names purification) and the production of disorderly hybrids which refuse or refute that ordering (what he calls translation). The logic of modernity is shown here as one of tidying – of finding a place for everything, and everything in its place. Classificatory systems, cartographies and taxonomies – these are the rules by which modernity wants to know the world. In the context of cities, this is manifest in planning, zoning, Burgess's concentric ring models, and all the other ways in which attempts to impose and fix order are played out in the minds of planners and lives of city folk. The flipside to this fetish for order, as Latour says, is that modernity (and, in the urban context, perhaps even more so postmodernity) has actually produced things that cannot be classified in the simplistic ways modernity itself demands. Hybrid spaces, heterotopias, mixed-use zones, spaces-in-between – this kind of urban untidiness is anathema to the modern. Now, while the wilder excesses of postmodern theory (and at times even practice) have sought to accommodate – even celebrate – this category-busting heterodoxy, the day-to-day business of most city managers and planners remains firmly rooted in the modern, and centrally concerned with order. Quartering can thus be seen as the definitional act of urban ordering – reimposing tidiness on the heterogeneity of the postmodern cityscape. To borrow from Kevin Hetherington's (1997) discussion of the Potteries Museum & Art Gallery, also in Stoke-on-Trent, quartering is about the production of 'smooth space', about simplification, and about producing a particular kind of narrative, written into that space. So, *contra* Nigel Thrift's (2000) provocation, at least when they are quartered, cities *are* mirrors of modernity.

Whose Quarters?

The reference to museums is, in fact, quite helpful here; urban quarters, like museum displays, make most sense when seen as 'staged' or packaged – and, in that respect, they seek to speak to visitors, to provide a narrative of place that refuses resistant reading and confirms dominant narratives. Like museum displays, they provide a framework in which difference is contained and exhibited. In this sense, the inhabitants of quarters are like the 'cast members' acting out the past at heritage sites. This analogy is perhaps most apparent in 'ethnic quarters', where ethnic difference is packaged for the consumption of 'non-ethnic' visitors. This packaging is intimately tied to the city-marketing strategy that trades on discourses of cosmopolitanism or multiculturalism. Ethnic quarters are here made over as *tableaux vivants*, ever available for visitors to consume. Like Susan Willis's (1999) discussion of the experience of watching a polar bear swimming at the zoo, visiting an ethnic quarter brings up uncomfortable questions of colonization, appropriation, voyeurism and cultural fossilization – unless, like Iris Marion Young (1990), you are unable to see beyond the dazzling differences on display. Ethnic quarters offer cosmopolites the chance to engage in what Gassan Hage (1997) tellingly labels 'lazy cosmo-multiculturalism' – a safe engagement with the other that resides in surfaces. The 'staging' of quarters for visitors suggests that they can be understood primarily as a touristic topography – as providing a packaged itinerary for short-stay visitors keen to get their cultural fix. In this sense, the corralling of difference into distinct zones is part of the enclaving of the city, itself often part of the process of producing tourist geographies (Edensor, 1998). The enticements offered in quarters are safe, domesticated, zoned – there is no danger of wandering off the map, of encountering less desirable forms of difference; especially since, as is so often the case, these differences have been hounded out, erased, invisibilized.

Of course, quarters aim to attract more than passing trade; nevertheless, whether attempting to capture tourist dollars or footloose capital and transnational business types, quarters are facing outwards, trying to make sense to and attract actual or potential visitors, some of whom might become settlers. Reading the marketing materials promoting urban quarters, as shown in some of the chapters presented here, shows very clearly the kinds of quarter-talk and quarter-work being undertaken. As with the University Quarter, there is a firmly-encoded dominant discourse at the heart of quarter promotion, which denies alternative readings (often by figuring these as unprogressive, backward-looking, unfashionable, or reactionary). However, outside the sleek and shiny world of PR and place-marketing, the experience of quarters 'on the ground' at times threatens to disturb all the gloss and spin.

Borders, Edges and Dead Zones

The edges of quarters are perhaps their most interesting feature. Certainly, at the meeting to discuss Stoke's mooted University Quarter, the question of boundaries and boundary-marking occupied a lot of time. The spaces in between quarters represent a new 'zone in transition' for cities; like the dead zones present even in the most densely themed environments, such as leisure parks (Kelsall, 2003), these non-quarters are the left-overs, the cast-offs, the residue – non-spaces of the new urban quarter-order. What does it mean for part of a city to lie outside a quarter? What new gravitational forces and tensions are produced by quartering? Like the previous dread urban experience of off-centre and out-of-town developments, quarters can exert considerable pull, leading to the evacuation of surrounding areas. And, again echoing the new retail geography of megamalls matched by ghostly high streets, more-or-less monofunctional quarters can produce intense concentrations of activity within the quarter's walls, and a disappearance of that activity elsewhere. This effect heightens the theming imperative behind quarterization, producing a cityscape of peaks and troughs, and escalating the dereliction of marginal, non-quartered zones.

At the same time, designating every group of 'others' (apart from the utterly unassimilable) their own part of the city reveals quartering as quota-ing – as a manifestation of what David Goldberg (2000) calls the new segregation: a place for every*one*, and everyone in their place. Of course, the places allocated to different groups of urban residents reproduce (and even produce anew) distinct socio-economic and other inequalities. Even attempts to facilitate 'organic' or vernacular quarters – through community or neighbourhood empowerment – founder if they unquestioningly restate the purification logic of quartering. Moreover, this kind of 'bottom-up' approach can tend to the essentialistic in its attempts to produce place-identity through community participation. Such projects run the risk of replaying defensive or regressive territorial impulses, too – in trying to foster local pride and ownership, there is the ever-present risk of old territorialisms being reheated, and new exclusions being produced. In addition, as is highlighted in a number of chapters in this volume, such enterprises demand identification with particular narratives of place. As witnessed at the University Quarter meeting, there is here no space for dissent or disidentification, since opting out means being zoned out. In the push to quarter, what spaces (or non-spaces) remain for those who want to resist being themed or quartered? And what about the abject, the scapegoat, the un-quarterable other? Such questions raise the spectre of a disenfranchised and dismebedded urban underclass – a particularly vivid distillation of urban anxieties surrounding those who are 'out of place'.

One response to this anxiety, which produces particularly defensive forms of quartering, is the production of fortress communities, sealed off from the 'threatening' city beyond. In one sense, of course, all quarters are fortresses, but often their walling and gating is symbolic rather than material. In this mapping, as Zygmunt Bauman (2001) says, the flipside of the elective confinement of fortressing is the enforced confinement of the ghetto. Against the pseudo-progressive quarter-talk that seeks to produce an appropriate 'home' for all urban inhabitants, the ghetto-as-quarter works as a negative container of this residue, denied the possibility of participating in quarter-talk and quarter-work. As he puts it:

> Ghetto means the *impossibility of community*. This feature of the ghetto makes the policy of exclusion embodied in spatial segregation and immobilization a doubly safe, foolproof choice in a society which can no longer keep all its members playing 'the only game in town', but wishes to keep all the rest who can play it busy and happy, and first and foremost obedient (Bauman, 2001: 122-3).

It would appear, in the purifying agenda of urban quarterization, that the ghetto is the inevitable space to contain the uncontainable, since the alternative – to leave them roaming, equipped only with their footloose non-capital – threatens to unsettle the effort of tidying up urban space. This prompts some final questions, the first of which is: *how many quarters make a city?*

Quarters, Quarters, Everywhere...

Is the answer to the 'problem' of quarters merely to *carry on quartering*, until every part and person of the city is safely contained or corralled? Can a city *be a city* today without being quartered? It would appear that the logic of quartering demands such a spatial fix. For one thing, to be a city in this age of intense urban competitiveness means opting-in to the dominant models and discourses of city-shaping. This in itself places extreme strains on cities lower down the urban hierarchy, who cannot trade on their outsiderness ('City of No Quarters' would hardly work as a strapline), but can only adopt weak, 'me-too-ist' versions of what their bigger neighbours are doing far more successfully and resource-intensively (Jayne, 2000). So, to return to the question: how many quarters is it enough for a city to have? Having one quarter leads to conflict, since it focuses too much of the promotional machinery on one part of the city and its business: 'me-too-ism' exists within cities as much as between them. Moreover, having a solitary quarter replays the dreaded monofunctionalism seen as the kiss of death for modern cities, and made increasingly dangerous by the vagaries and faddishness of the market. Diversification and unique selling points are the (urban) order of the day. Of course, part of the irony of quartering is that many cities' USPs are in fact identical – cultural quarters, Chinatowns, high-tech corridors, gay villages. The limited lexicon of quartering ensures this, reproducing dominant ideal-types of quarter across the globe. But could there be another way? How else could quarters be imagined and produced? We shall finish this Afterword with a quote from mid-twentieth political art pranksters the Situationist International, who suggested a programme for planning the city based upon mood and effect rather than the imagined tastes of the new petit bourgeoisie. While as susceptible to criticism as any of the forms of quartering discussed in this book, there is something about its naïve utopianism that might enable us to think quarters differently; it even carries echoes of the ambition and boosterism of today's quarter-talkers:

> The districts of the city could correspond to the whole spectrum of diverse feelings that one encounters *by chance* in everyday life. Bizarre Quarter – Happy Quarter ... – Noble and Tragic Quarter ... – Historical Quarter ... – Useful Quarter ... – Sinister Quarter, etc. ... Perhaps also a Death Quarter, not for dying in but so as to have somewhere to *live in peace* ... Our first experimental city would largely live off tolerated and controlled tourism. Future avant-garde activities and productions would naturally gravitate there. In a few years it would become the intellectual capital of the world and would be universally recognised as such (Chtchelov, 1953/1981: 4).

Bibliography

Abercrombie, P. (1943), *Town and Country Planning* (2nd Edition), Oxford University Press, London.

ACME Housing Association Ltd (1990), *Studios for Artists*, London.

Adam, R. (1998), 'The Design of Housing', *MXD,* Issue 4.

Ajuntament de Barcelona (2001), *Barcelona: Urban Spaces 1981-2001*, Ajuntament de Barcelona, Barcelona.

Aldous, T. (ed.) (1995), *Economics of Urban Villages*, Urban Villages Forum, London.

Aldous, T. (1992), *Urban Villages: A Concept for Creating Mixed-Use Urban Developments on a Sustainable Scale*, Urban Villages Group, London.

Alvarez, M. (1997), 'Survival of a Superclub', *Sunday Telegraph Magazine,* 8th November.

Amin, A. and Graham, S. (1999), 'Cities of Connection and Disconnection', in J. Allen, D. Massey and M. Pryke (eds.), *Unsettling Cities,* Routledge, London, pp. 7-48.

Amin, A. and Thrift, N. (1994), 'Living in the Global', in A. Amin and N. Thrift (eds.), *Globalization, Institutions and Regional Development in Europe*, Oxford University Press, Oxford, pp. 1-22.

Anderson, K. (1995), 'Culture and Nature at the Adelaide Zoo: at the Frontiers of Human Geography', *Transaction of the Institute of British Geographers,* Vol. 20, pp. 275-94.

Aplin, G. J. (1982), 'Models of Urban Change: Sydney 1820-1870', *Australian Geographical Studies*, Vol. 20, pp. 144-57.

Arrigoni, P. (2000), 'The District of Leisure: Bars, Restaurants and Entrepreneurs of the "Milanesi Navigli"', *Journal of Urban Labour and Leisure*, Vol. 1(2), (www.lull.clara.net/vol1/2/00007.htm).

Ash, C. (2002), 'Cultural Quarters: Inner City Inspiration', *Arts Professional*, Vol. 27(42), pp. 5-6.

Ashton, P. (1993), *The Accidental City*, Hale and Iremonger, Sydney.

Ashworth, G. J. and Tunbridge, J. E. (eds.) (1990), *The Tourist-Historic City*, Belhaven Press, London.

Ashworth, G. J. and Voogd, H. (1990), *Selling the City: Marketing Approaches in Public Sector Urban Planning*, Belhaven Press, London.

Atkinson, R. and Kinestra, K. (2001), 'Disentangling Area Effects: Evidence from Deprived and Non-deprived Neighbourhoods', *Urban Studies,* Vol. 38(12), pp. 2277-2298.

Australian Bureau of Statistics (ABS) (1991), *Census of Population and Housing*, Australian Government Publishing Service, Canberra.

Australian Bureau of Statistics (ABS) (1976), *Census of Population and Housing*, Australian Government Publishing Service, Canberra.

Australian Financial Review (1997), 'Pyrmont – the Address for Business, Living and Leisure', City West Development Corporation Promotion, 26th September, p. 11.

Australian Property Monitor, http://www.apm.com.au [Accessed 2nd August 2002]

BAAA (1993), *The Artist in the Changing City*, British American Arts Association, London.

Backlund, A-K. and Sandberg, A. (2002), 'New Media Industry Development: Regions, Networks and Hierarchies – Some Policy Implications', *Regional Studies,* Vol. 36(1), pp. 87-91.

Badcock, B. (1997), 'Recently Observed Polarising Tendencies and Australian Cities', *Australian Geographical Studies*, Vol. 35(3), pp. 243-59.

Badgett, M. V. L. (2001), *Money, Myths and Change: The Economic Lives of Lesbians and Gay Men,* University of Chicago Press, Chicago.

Bailey, C. (2002), 'An Approach to Evaluating Large-scale Multi-agency Cultural Events: the Case of the Arts Council's Arts 2000 Series', paper given at the *Second International Conference on Cultural Policy Research,* Te Papa, Wellington, New Zealand, January.

Bailey, P. (1998), *Popular Culture and Performance in the Victorian City,* Cambridge University Press, Cambridge.

Bathelt, H. (2002), 'The Re-emergence of a Media Industry Cluster in Leipzig', *European Planning Studies,* Vol. 10(5), pp. 583-611.

Batt, R. *et al.* (2001), *Net Working: Patterns and Workforce Policies for the New Media Industry,* Economic Policy Institute, Washington DC.

Baum, S. (1997), 'Sydney, Australia: a Global City? Testing the Social Polarization Thesis', *Urban Studies,* Vol. 34(11), pp. 1881-1903.

Bauman, Z. (2001), *Community: Seeking Safety in an Insecure World,* Polity, Cambridge.

Beazley, M., Loftman, P. and Nevin, B. (1997), 'Downtown Redevelopment and Community Resistance: An International Perspective', in N. Jewson, and S. MacGregor (eds.), *Transforming Cities: Contested Governance and New Spatial Divisions,* Routledge, London, pp. 181-192.

Bech, H. (1997), *When Men Meet,* Polity Press, Cambridge.

Beck, U. (2002) 'The Cosmopolitan Society and its Enemies', *Theory, Culture and Society,* Vol. 19(1-2), pp. 17-44.

Beck, U. (1994), 'The Reinvention of Politics: Towards a Theory of Reflexive Modernization', in U. Beck, A. Giddens and S. Lash (1994), *Reflexive Modernization,* Polity Press, Cambridge.

Bell, D. (2001), 'Fragments for a Queer City', in D. Bell, J. Binnie, R. Holliday, R. Longhurst and R. Peace (eds.), *Pleasure Zones: Bodies, Cities, Spaces,* Syracuse University Press, Syracuse, NY, pp. 84-102.

Bell, D. and Binnie, J. (2003) 'Rethinking Sexual Citizenship in the City', paper presented at the annual meeting of the *Association of American Geographers,* New Orleans, LA, March.

Bell, D. and Binnie, J. (2000), *The Sexual Citizen: Queer Politics and Beyond,* Polity Press, Cambridge.

Bell, D. and Jayne, M. (2003a), 'Assessing the Role of Design in Urban and Regional Economies', *International Journal of Cultural Policy,* Vol. 9 (3). pp. 285-304.

Bell, D. and Jayne, M. (2003b), 'Design-led Urban Regeneration: a Critical Perspective', *Local Economy,* Vol. 18 (2). pp. 121-134.

Bell, D. and Valentine, G. (1997), *Consuming Geographies: We Are Where We Eat,* Routledge, London.

Bell, D. and Valentine, G. (1995*), Mapping Desire,* London, Routledge.

Benjamin, W. (2002), *The Arcades Project* (trans. H. Eiland and K. McLaughlin), Harvard, Cambridge, MA.

Benjamin, W. (1997), *Charles Baudelaire,* Verso, London.

Bennett, S. and Butler J. (eds.) (2000), *Locality, Regeneration and Divers[c]ities,* Intellect, Bristol.

Berelowitz, J-A. (1994), 'The Museum of Contemporary Art, Los Angeles: An Account of Collaboration Between Artists, Trustees and an Architect', in M. Pointon (ed.), *Art Apart: Art Institutions and Ideology Across Europe and North America,* Manchester University Press, Manchester, pp. 267-286.

Berger, K. (2002), 'What Just Happened Here? The Dot-Com Years', *San Francisco,* April, pp. 53-71.

Bianchini, F. (1999a), 'Cultural Planning for Urban Sustainability', in L. Nyström (ed.), *City and Culture – Cultural Processes and Urban Sustainability*, The Swedish Urban Environment Council, Stockholm, pp. 10-23.

Bianchini, F. (1999b), 'The Relationship Between Cultural Resources and Tourism Policies for Cities and Regions', in D. Dodd and A. van Hemel (eds.), *Planning Cultural Tourism in Europe: A Presentation of Theories and Cases*, Boekman Stichting, Amsterdam, pp.78-90.

Bianchini, F. (1996), 'Cultural Planning: an Innovative Approach to Urban Development', in J. Verwijnen and P. Lethovuori (eds.), *Creative Cities: Cultural Industries, Urban Development and the Information Society,* University of Art and Design Press, Helsinki, pp. 130-141.

Bianchini, F. (1993), 'Remaking European Cities: the Role of Cultural Policies', in F. Bianchini and M. Parkinson (eds.), *Cultural Policy and Urban Regeneration: The West European Experience*, Manchester University Press, Manchester, pp. 1-20.

Bianchini, F. Fisher, M., Montgomery, J. and Worpole, K. (1988) *City Centres, City Cultures*, Centre for Local Economic Strategies, Manchester.

Bianchini, F. and Ghilardi, L. (1997), *Culture and Neighbourhoods, Vol. 2, A Comparative Report*. Council of Europe Publishing, Strasbourg.

Bianchini, F. and Parkinson, M. (1993). *Cultural Policy and Urban Regeneration: The West European Experience*, Manchester University Press, Manchester.

Bianchini, F. and Schwengel, H. (1991), 'Re-imagining the City', in J. Corner *et al. Enterprise and Heritage*, London, Routledge, pp. 67-74.

Bianchini, F. and Torrigiani, M. (1995), 'Concepts and Projects around Culture and Neighbourhoods', in *Culture and Neighbourhoods, Vol. 1*, Council of Europe Publishing, pp. 13 - 40.

The Big Issue (2001), 'Peep Show', 12-18th March, London, pp.20-21.

Binnie, J. (2004), *Queer Globalization,* Sage, London (forthcoming).

Binnie, J. (1995), 'Trading Places: Consumption, Sexuality and the Production of Queer Space', in D. Bell and G. Valentine (eds), *Mapping Desire: Geographies of Sexualities,* Routledge, London, pp. 182-199.

Binnie, J. and Skeggs, B. (1999), 'Cosmopolitan Sexualities: Disrupting the Logic of Late Capitalism?', paper presented at the *Fourth International Metropolis Conference*, 8-11th December, Washington, DC.

Birmingham City Council Planning and Architecture Department (1996a), *Finding the Fifties*, Birmingham.

Birmingham City Council Planning and Architecture Department (1996b), *Chinese/Markets Quarter – Planning & Urban Design Framework, Consultation Draft*, Birmingham.

Birmingham City Council Planning and Architecture Department (1993), *The Birmingham Plan – Birmingham Unitary Development Plan 1993*, Birmingham.

Birmingham City Council (1992), *City Centre Strategy,* Birmingham.

Birmingham City Council Development Department (1989), *The Current State of the City Centre,* Birmingham.

Birmingham City Council (1988), *The Highbury Initiative: Proceedings of the Birmingham City Centre Challenge Symposium 25th – 27th March 1988.*

Birmingham City Council Leisure and Community Services (1984), *City Sound Archive C367 John Wong.*

Birmingham City Council and West Midlands County Council (1981), *Birmingham Central Area District Plan*, Birmingham.

Birmingham City Council and West Midlands County Council (1980a), *Birmingham Central Area District Plan – Draft Written Statement Discussion Document*, Birmingham.

Birmingham City Council and West Midlands County Council (1980b), *Birmingham Central Area District Plan Topic Papers – Employment*, Birmingham.

Birmingham Development Department (1989), *Developing Birmingham 1889-1989: 100 Years of Planning*, Birmingham.

Birmingham Enterprise Centre (1986), *Directory of Ethnic Minority Businesses,* Gibbons Barford, Wolverhampton.

Birmingham Evening Mail (1995), 'Brum Go-ahead Over Ethnic Street Names', 25th January.

Birmingham Post (2002), 'Top Officer Wants Prostitution Legalised' 4th October, p. 8.

Birmingham Post (2000) 'Why it's Time for Birmingham to go Full Bore', 1st November.

Birmingham Post (1991), 'City Warned of Refugee Chaos Threat', 19th June.

Birmingham Post (1988), '£1m Pagoda-style Complex on Way', 23rd November.

Birmingham Post (1983), 'Comments', 10th May.

BIS Schrapnel (1987), *Building in Australia/BIS Schrapnel*, Philip Shrapnel and Co., Sydney.

Boddy, T. (1999), 'Underground and Overhead: Building an Analogous City', in M. Sorkin (ed.), *Variations on a Theme Park*, Hill and Wang, New York.

Borja, J. and Castells, M. (1997), *Local and Global: Management of Cities in the Information Age*, Earthscan, London.

Bounds, M. and Morris, A. (2001), 'Economic Restructuring and Gentrification in the Inner City: A Case Study of Pyrmont Ultimo', *Australian Planner,* Vol. 38(3), pp. 128-132.

Bounds, M., Morris, A., McCormack, T., Moore, C. and Searle, G. (2000), *The Impact of the Sydney Casino on the Social Composition and Residential Amenity of the Residents of Pyrmont-Ultimo. Final Report of the Casino Community Benefit Fund, September 2000*, The Urban Studies Research Centre, University of Western Sydney Macarthur.

Bourdieu, P. (1984), *Distinction: A Social Critique of the Judgement of Taste* (trans. R. Nice), Harvard University Press, Cambridge.

Bovane, L. (1990) 'Cultural Intermediaries: a New Role for Intellectuals in the Post-Modern Age', *Innovation,* Vol. 3(1), pp. 104-115.

Boyle, M. (1997), 'Civic Boosterism in the Politics of Local Economic Development: 'Institutional Positions' and 'Strategic Outcomes' in the Consumption of Hallmark Events', *Environment and Planning A.,* Vol. 29(11), pp.1975-98.

Boyle, M. (1993), *Leisure, Place and Identity: Glasgow's Role as a European City of Culture,* unpublished PhD thesis, The University of Edinburgh, Edinburgh.

Braczyk, H-J., Fuchs, G. and Wolf, H-G. (eds.) (1999), *Multimedia and Regional Economic Restructuring*, Routledge, London.

Bray, C. (1980), *New Villages: Case Studies. No. 3. Christiania,*. Oxford Polytechnic, Oxford.

Brookfield, H. *et al.* (1991), *The City in the Village*, Oxford University Press, Oxford.

Brown, A., Cohen, S. and O'Connor, J. (2000) 'Local Music Policies Within a Global Music Industry: Cultural Quarters in Manchester and Sheffield', *Geoforum,* Vol. 31, pp. 94-105.

Bruggemeir, F. J. (1990), 'The Ruhr Basin 1850-1980: A Case of Large Scale Environmental Pollution', in P. Briddlecombe and C. Pfister (eds.), *The Silent Countdown: Essays in European Environmental History*, Springer Verlag, Berlin, pp. 101-120.

Buck, N., Gordon, I., Hall, P., Harloe, M. and Kleinman, M. (2003), *Working Capital: Life and Labour in Contemporary London,* Routledge, London.

Buck-Morss, S. (1991), *The Dialectics of Seeing: Walter Benjamin and the Arcades Project*, MIT, Cambridge, MA.

Burtenshaw, D., Bateman, M. and Ashworth, G. J. (1991), *The European City: A Western Perspective*, London, David Fulton.

Campbell, R., Coleman, S. and Torkington, P. (1996), *Street Prostitution in Inner City Liverpool*, Liverpool City Council, Liverpool.

Campbell, R. and O'Neill, M. (2002), *Prostitution Toolkit*, Home Office, London.

Castells, M. (2001) *The Internet Galaxy: Reflections on the Internet, Business, and Society*, Oxford, Oxford University Press.

Castells, M. (1996), *The Information Age: Economy Society and Culture, Vol. 1: The Rise of the Network Society*, Blackwell, Oxford.

Castells, M. (1989), *The Informational City: Information Technology, Economic Restructuring and the Urban-Regional Process*, Blackwell, Oxford.

Castells, M. (1977), *The Urban Question: a Marxist Approach*, Edward Arnold, London.

Caves, R. E. (2000), *Creative Industries: Contracts between Art and Commerce*, Harvard University Press, Cambridge, MA.

Chang, T. C. (2000), 'Renaissance Revisited: Singapore as a "Global City for the Arts"', *International Journal of Urban and Regional Research*, Vol. 24(4), pp. 818-831.

Cherry, G. E. (1994), *Birmingham: A Study in Geography, History and Planning*, John Wiley and Sons, Chichester.

Choay, F. (1997), *The Rule and the Model: On the Theory of Architecture and Urbanism*, MIT, Cambridge, MA.

Chtchelov, I. (1953/1981),'Formulary for a New Urbanism', in K. Knabb (ed.), *Situationist International Anthology*, Bureau of Public Secrets, Berkeley, pp. 1-4.

CIDA (1999), *Survey of Cultural Industries Firms in Spitalfields*, Tower Hamlets Cultural Industries Development Agency, London.

City of Edinburgh Council (2000), *Craigmillar Master Plan: A New Beginning*, City of Edinburgh Council, Edinburgh.

City West Development Corporation (n.d.), *Pyrmont. Perfect Sydney*, CityWest, Pyrmont.

City West Development Corporation and Park, M. (1997), *Doors Were Also Open: Recollections of Pyrmont and Ultimo*, City West Development Corporation, Pyrmont.

Civic Alliance to Rebuild Downtown New York (2002), *Listening to the City: Report of the Proceedings*, Civic Alliance to Rebuild Downtown New York, New York.

Clancy, L. (1997), 'Neon Words Upon the Walls', *The Irish Times*, 23rd July.

Cohen, S. (2002), 'Paying One's Dues: The Music Business, the City and Urban Regeneration', in M. Talbot (ed.), *The Business of Music*, University of Liverpool Press, Liverpool, pp. 167-180.

Cohen, S. (1999), 'Music Scenes', in B. Horner and T. Swiss (eds.), *Popular Music and Culture: New Essays on Key Terms*, Blackwell, Malden MA, pp. 202-118.

Cohen, S. (1998), 'Sounding Out the City: Music and the Sensuous Production of Place', in A. Leyshon, D. Matless and G. Revill (eds.), *The Place of Music: Music, Space and the Production of Place*, Guilford Press, New York, pp. 186-204.

Cohen, S. (1997), 'Popular Music, Tourism, and Urban Regeneration', in S. Abram, J. Waldren and D. McLeod (eds.), *Tourists and Tourism: Identifying with People and Places*, Berg, Oxford, pp. 71-90.

Cohen, S. (1994), 'Identity, Place and the "Liverpool Sound"', in M. Stokes (ed.) *Ethnicity, Identity and Music: the Musical Construction of Place*, Berg, Oxford, pp. 208-220.

Cohen, S. (1991a), 'Popular Music and Urban Regeneration: The Music Industries on Merseyside', *Cultural Studies*, Vol. 5(3), pp. 104-112.

Cohen, S. (1991b), *Rock Culture in Liverpool*, Oxford University Press, Oxford.

Cohen, S. and McManus, K. (1991), *Harmonious Relations*, National Museums and Galleries on Merseyside, Liverpool, pp. 1-59.

Comedia (1997), *A Cultural Industries Strategy for Tower Hamlets*, Comedia, London.

Comedia (1992), *The Importance of Culture for Urban Economic Development*, Comedia, Stroud.

Connell, J. (2000), *Sydney: The Emergence of a World City*, Oxford University Press, Melbourne.

Connell, J. and Gibson, C. (2002), *Sound Tracks: Popular Music, Identity and Place*, Routledge, London.

Cook, I. and Crang, P. (1996), 'The World on a Plate: Culinary Culture, Displacement and Geographical Knowledges', *Journal of Material Culture*, Vol. 1, pp. 131-153.

Cork, R. (1995), 'Message in a Bottle', *Modern Painters*, Spring, pp. 76-81.

Council for Cultural Cooperation (1995), *Council for Cultural Cooperation, Volume 1: Concepts and References*, Council of Europe Publishing, Netherlands.

Coupland, A. (1997), *Reclaiming the City*, E and FN Spon, London.

Cowles, B. R. and Piggott, S. G. (1975), 'Birmingham Inner Ring Road', *Proceedings of the Institution of Civil Engineers*, Vol. 58(1), pp. 453-456.

Cowles, B. R. and Piggott, S. G., (1974), 'Birmingham Inner Ring Road', *Proceedings of the Institution of Civil Engineers*, Vol. 56(1), pp. 513-535.

Crawford, M. (1992), 'The World in a Shopping Mall', in M. Sorkin (ed.), *Variations on a Theme Park*, Hill and Wang, New York.

Crewe, L. (1996), 'Material Culture: Embedded Firms, Organisational Networks and the Local Economic Development of a Fashion Quarter', *Regional Studies,* Vol. 30(3), pp. 257-72.

Crewe, L. and Beaverstock, J. (1998), 'Fashioning the City: Cultures of Consumption in Contemporary Urban Spaces', *Geoforum,* Vol. 29(3), pp. 287-308.

Crewe, L. and Davenport, E. (1992), 'The Puppet Show: Showcasing Buyer-supplier Relationships within Clothing Retailing', *Transactions of the Institute of British Geographers: New Series* 17, pp. 293-310.

Crewe, L. and Forster, Z. (1993), 'Markets, Design and Local Agglomeration: the Role of Small Independent Retailers in the Workings of the Fashion System', *Environment and Planning D: Society and Space,* Vol. 11, pp. 213-29.

Crewe, L. and Lowe, M. (1995), 'Gap on the Map? Towards a Geography of Consumption and Identity', *Environment and Planning A,* Vol. 27, pp. 1877-1898.

Crilley, D. (1993), 'Architecture and Advertising: Constructing the Image of Redevelopment', in G. Kearns and C. Philo (eds.), *Selling Places: The City as Cultural Capital, Past and Present*, Pergamon Press, Oxford, pp. 231-252.

Cronin, A. M. (2001), *Advertising and Consumer Citizenship: Gender, Images and Rights*, Routledge, London.

Crummy, H. (1992), *Let the People Sing*, Mainstream, Edinburgh.

Crump, J. (1986), 'Provincial Music Hall: Promoters and Public In Leicester, 1863-1929', in P. Bailey (ed.) *Music Hall: the Business of Pleasure*, Open University Press, Milton Keynes, pp. 86-104.

Cummins, C. (2001), 'High-tech Firms Plug in to Pyrmont', *Sydney Morning Herald*, February 24, p. 70.

Curran, J. and Blackburn, R. A. (1994), *Small Firms and Local Economic Networks: The Death of the Local Economy*, Routledge, London.

Cuthbert, A. (1995), 'Under the Volcano: Postmodern Space in Hong Kong', in S. Watson and K. Gibson (eds.), *Postmodern Cities and Spaces*, Blackwell, Oxford, pp. 223-249.

Daly, M. T. (1982), *Sydney Boom, Sydney Bust*, Allen and Unwin, Sydney.

Dane, C. and Feist, A. (1999), *A Sound Performance: The Economic Value of Music to the United Kingdom*, National Music Council, London.

Darley, G. (1978), *The Idea of the Village*, Arts Council of Britain, London.

Davies, L. (1996), 'Equality and Planning: Race', in C. Greed (ed.), *Implementing Town Planning: The Role of Town Planning in the Development Process,* Longman, London.

Davis, M. (1990), *City of Quartz: Excavating the Future of Los Angeles,* Vintage, London.

de Certeau, M. (1993), 'Walking in the City', in S. During (ed.), *The Cultural Studies Reader*, Routledge, London, pp. 207-224.

DeFilippis, J. (1997), 'From a Public Re-creation to Private Recreation: the Transformation of Public Space in South Street Seaport', *Journal of Urban Affairs*, Vol. 19(4), pp. 405-417.

Degen, M. (2002), 'Regenerating Public Life? A Sensory Analysis of Regenerated Public Places in El Raval, Barcelona', in J. Rugg and D. Hinchcliffe (eds.) *Advances in Art and Urban Futures Volume 2: Recoveries and Reclamations,* Intellect Books, Bristol, pp. 19-35.

Department of Culture, Media and Sport (2001), *Creative Industries Mapping Document*, Department for Culture, Media and Sport, London.

Department of Culture, Media and Sport (2000), *E-Business Strategy*, Department for Culture, Media and Sport, HMSO, London.

Department of Culture, Media and Sport (1999), *Draft Guidance for Local Cultural Strategies*, Department for Culture, Media and Sport, HMSO, London.

Department of Environment, Transport and the Regions (1998) *Coal Fields Task Force Report*, HMSO, London.

Department of the Environment (1987), *Managing Workspaces. Case Studies of Good Practice in Urban Regeneration*, Inner Cities Directorate, HMSO London.

Derrida, J. (1976), *Of Grammatology* (trans. G. C. Spivak), John Hopkins Press, London.

Desai, A. (2002), *We are the Poors*, Polity Press, Johannesburg.

Deutsche, R. (1988), 'Uneven Development: Public Art in New York City', *October*, Vol. 47, pp. 3-52.

Dodd, D. (1999), 'Barcelona, the Making of a Cultural City', in D. Dodd and A. van Hemel (eds.) *Planning Cultural Tourism in Europe: A Presentation of Theories and Cases*, Boekman Stichting, Amsterdam, pp. 53-64.

Dodd, D. and van Hemel, A. (eds.) (1999), *Planning Cultural Tourism in Europe: A Presentation of Theories and Cases*, Amsterdam, Boekman Stichting.

Dowling, R. and Mee, K. (2000), 'Tales of the City: Western Sydney at the End of the Millennium', in J. Connell (ed.) (2000), *Sydney: The Emergence of a World City*, Oxford University Press, Melbourne, pp. 273-291.

Downey, J. and McGuigan, J. (1999), *Technocities*, Routledge, London.

DPA (2000), *Creative Industries Strategy for London*, David Powell Associates for the London Development Partnership, London.

Drew, P. (1994), *The Coast Dwellers. A Radical Reappraisal of Australian Identity*, Penguin, Ringwood.

Du Noyer, R. (2002*), Liverpool: Wondrous Place: Music from the Cavern to Cream*, Virgin Books, Liverpool.

Dunn, K. (1993), 'The Vietnamese Concentration in Cabramatta: Site of Avoidance and Deprivation, or Island of Adjustment and Participation?' *Australian Geographical Studies*, Vol. 31(2), pp. 229-45.

Dunn, K. M., McGuirk, P. M. and Winchester, H. P. M. (1995), 'Place Making: the Social Construction of Newcastle', *Australian Geographical Studies*, Vol. 33(2), pp. 149-66.

The Economist (2001), 'Red Lights Ahead: Tightening up on the Sex Trade will Fail. Edinburgh shows a Better Way', 8th Sept, pp. 35-36.

The Economist (2000), *Clustering in Hackney*, 2nd March, p.9.

Edensor, T. (1998), *Tourists at the Taj*, Routledge, London.

Eisenschitz, A. (1997), 'The View from the Grassroots', in M. Pacione (ed.), *Britain's Cities: Geographies of Division in Urban Britain*, London, Routledge, pp.150-176.

Evans, G. L. (2003), 'Hard-Branding the Cultural City: from Prado to Prada', *International Journal of Urban and Regional Research*, Symposium Issue on 'Cities and the Global Entertainment Economy', June, (forthcoming).

Evans, G. L. (2002), 'Evaluating the UK Lottery and the Arts: the First Seven Years', *Circular,* No. 14, pp. 16-28.

Evans, G. (2001a), *Cultural Planning: an Urban Renaissance?* Routledge, London.

Evans, G. L. (2001b), 'Small is Beautiful?: ICT and SMTEs, a European Comparative', *Information Technology and Tourism,* Vol. 2 (3/4), pp. 1-15.

Evans, G. L. (2001c), *Islington Cultural Strategy: Survey and Mapping of Arts and Cultural Activity,* University of North London, London.

Evans, G. L. (2000a), 'Measuring the Arts and Cultural Industries - Does Size Matter?', in S. Roodhouse (ed.) *The New Cultural Map: A Research Agenda for the 21ˢᵗ Century,* Bretton Hall, Leeds University, Leeds, pp. 26-34.

Evans, G. L. (2000b), 'Contemporary Crafts as Artefacts and Functional Goods and their Role in Local Economic Diversification and Cultural Development', in M. Hitchcock and K. Teague (eds), *Souvenirs: The Material Culture of Tourism,* Aldershot, Ashgate, pp. 69-80.

Evans, G. L. (1996), *MultiMedia Sector: Employment and Labour Market Report,* City and Inner London Training & Enterprise Council (CILNTEC), London.

Evans, G. L. (1990), *Premises Needs and Problems of Crafts Firms in Clerkenwell,* London, Local Enterprise Research Unit, Polytechnic of North London, London.

Evans, G. L. (1989), *Survey of Employment in the Arts and Cultural Industries in Islington,* London Borough of Islington/Greater London Arts, London.

Evans, G. L. and Cleverdon, R. (2000), 'Fair Trade in Tourism: Community Development or Marketing Tool?' in G. Richards and D. Hall (eds.), *Tourism and Sustainable Community Development,* Routledge, London, pp. 137-153.

Evans, G. L. and Foord, J. (2003), 'Culture and Settlement in East London', in N. Kirkham and M. Miles (eds.) *Art and Urban Futures, Cultures & Settlement , Vol. 3* Intellect Books, Bristol, pp. 94-106.

Evans, G. L. and Foord, J. (2002), 'Shaping the Cultural Landscape: Local Regeneration Effects', in M. Miles and T. Hall (eds.), *Urban Futures: Critical Commentaries on Shaping the City,* Routledge, London, pp. 167-181.

Evans, G. and Foord, J (2000a), 'Landscapes of Cultural Production and Regeneration', in J. Benson and M. Rose (eds.), *Urban Lifestyles: Spaces, Places, People,* A.T. Balkema, Rotterdam, pp. 249-256.

Evans, G. L. and Foord, J. (2000b), 'European Funding of Culture: Promoting Common Culture or Regional Growth?' *Cultural Trends,* Vol. 36, pp. 53–87.

Express and Star (1995), 'Balti Boulevard, just off Dreadlock Drive!', 20ᵗʰ January , p. 8.

Featherstone, M. (1995), *Undoing Culture: Globalization, Postmodernism and Identity,* Sage, London.

Featherstone, M. (1991), *Consumer Culture and Postmodernism,* Sage, London.

Financial Times (1996), '£5m Pagoda is Testimony to Asian Success', 29ᵗʰ May, p.3.

Fincher, R. and Wulff, M. (1998), 'The Locations of Poverty and Disadvantage', in R. Fincher and J. Nieuwenhuysen (eds.), *Australian Poverty: Then and Now,* Melbourne University Press, Melbourne, pp. 144-164.

Fine, B. and Leopold, E. (1993), *The World of Consumption,* Routledge, London.

Fisher, M. and Owen, U. (eds.) (1991), *Whose Cities?,* Penguin, London.

Fitzgerald, S. and Golder, S. H. (1994), *Pyrmont and Ultimo Under Siege,* Hale and Iremonger, Sydney.

Fleming, T. (ed.) (1999), *The Role of Creative Industries in Local and Regional Development,* Government Office for Yorkshire and the Humber, Sheffield.

Flood, J. (2000), *Sydney Divided: Factorial Ecology Revisited,* Working Paper 2, Residential differentiation in Australian Cities, Urban Frontiers, University of Western Sydney, Sydney.

Florida, R. (2002), *The Rise of the Creative Class,* Basic Books, New York.

Foord, J. (1999) 'Creative Hackney: Reflections on Hidden Art', *Rising East,* Vol. 3(2), pp. 38-66.

Forest, R. and Kearns, A. (2001), 'Social Cohesion, Social Capital and the Neighbourhood', *Urban Studies,* Vol. 38(12), pp. 2125-2144.

Foucault, M. (1988), 'Space, Power and Knowledge' (an interview with P. Rainbow), in S. Dunning (ed.), *The Cultural Studies Reader,* Routledge, London, pp. 206-219.

Foucault, M. (1987), 'Space, Knowledge and Power', in P. Rabinow (ed.), *The Foucault Reader,* Penguin, Harmondsworth, pp.186-200.

Franck, D. (2002), *The Bohemians. The Birth of Modern Art: Paris 1900-1930,* Phoenix, London.

Fretter, A. D. (1993), 'Place Marketing: A Local Authority Perspective', in G. Kearns and C. Philo (eds.), *Selling Places: The City as Cultural Capital, Past and Present,* Pergamon Press, Oxford, pp. 102-118.

Gandy, M. (2002), *Concrete and Clay: Reworking Nature in New York City,* MIT, Cambridge, MA.

Gehl, J. (1999), 'Finding the Culture City', in L. Nyström and C. Fudge (eds.), *City and Culture: Cultural Processes and Urban Sustainability.* The Swedish Urban Environment Council, Stockholm, pp. 86-100.

Generalitat de Catalunya (2001), *Cerdà: The Barcelona Extension (Eixample),* Generalitat de Catalunya, Barcelona.

Ghilardi, L. (2001), 'Cultural Planning and Cultural Diversity', in T. Bennett (ed.), *Differing Diversities: Cultural Policy and Cultural Diversity,* Council of Europe Publishing, Stockholm, pp. 224-324.

Ghirardo, D. (1996), *Architecture after Modernism,* Thames and Hudson, London.

Gibbons, R. (1980), 'Improving Sydney 1908-1090', in J. Roe (ed.), *Twentieth Century Sydney: Studies in Urban and Social History,* Hale and Iremonger, Sydney, pp. 127-143.

Giddens, A. (1993), *Sociology,* Polity, Cambridge.

Giddens, A. (1990), *The Consequences of Modernity,* Polity/Blackwell, Cambridge.

Giddens, A. (1973), 'Review of Class Struggle of Advanced Societies', *British Journal of Sociology, Vol.* 29, pp. 10-15.

Gilloch, G. (2002), *Walter Benjamin: Critical Constellations,* Polity, Cambridge.

Gilloch, G. (1996), *Myth and Metropolis: Walter Benjamin and the City,* Polity, Cambridge.

Gimeno, E (2001), 'The Birth of the Barcelona Extension (*Eixample*)', in Generalitat de Catalunya, *Cerdà: The Barcelona Extension (Eixample),* Generalitat de Catalunya, Barcelona, pp. 20-23.

GLA (1990), *A Strategy for the Arts in London,* Greater London Arts, London.

GLC (1985), *State of the Arts or the Art of the State: Strategies for the Cultural Industries,* Greater London Council, London.

Goldberg, D. (2000), 'The New Segregation', in D. Bell and A. Haddour (eds.), *City Visions,* Prentice Hall, Harlow, pp. 179-204.

Gomez, M. V. (1998), 'Reflective Images: the Case of Urban Regeneration in Glasgow and Bilbao', *International Journal of Urban and Regional Research,* Vol. 22(1), pp. 106-21.

Gonzalez, J. M. (1993), 'Bilbao: Culture, Citizenship, and Quality of Life', in F. Bianchini and M. Parkinson (eds.), *Cultural Policy and Urban Regeneration: The West European Experience,* Manchester University Press, Manchester, pp. 73-89.

Good Jobs, New York (2002), *Breaking It Down: Business Assistance Programs for Lower Manhattan,* Good Jobs, New York, New York.

Goodwin, M. (1993), 'The City as Commodity: the Contest Spaces of Urban Development', in G. Kearns and C. Philo (eds.), *Selling Places: The City as Cultural Capital, Past and Present,* Pergamon Press, Oxford, pp. 145-162.

Gorz, A. (1999), *Reclaiming Work; Beyond the Waged Based Society*, Polity Press, Cambridge.

Gorz, A. (1989), *Critique of Economic Reason*, Verso, London.

Gorz, A. (1982), *Farewell to the Working Class*, Pluto, London.

Goss, J. (1997), 'Representing and Re-presenting the Contemporary City, Progress Report', *Urban Geography*, Vol. 18(2), pp. 180-188.

Gottdiener, M. (2000), 'Lefebvre and the Bias of Academic Urbanism. What can we Learn from the 'New' Urban Analysis?', *City*, Vol. 4(1), pp. 93-100.

Graham, S. and Guy, S. (2002), 'Digital Space Meets Urban Place: Sociotechnologies of Urban Restructuring in Downtown San Francisco', *City,* Vol. 6(3), pp. 369-382.

Gratz, R. B. (1989), *The Living City*, Simon and Schuster, New York.

Gratz, R. B. and Mintz, N. (1998), *Cities Back from the Edge: New Life for Downtown*, Wiley, New York.

Grayson, J (2002), 'Rebuilding Civil Society: Community Development in the Hungarian Coalfield' in D. Frances J. Grayson and P. Henderson, *Rich Seam: Community Development in Coalfield Communities,* Community Development Foundation Press, Norwich, pp. 25-34.

Green, N. (1999), 'Artists in the East End 1968-1980', *Rising East,* Vol. 3(2), pp 20-37.

Gregory, B. and Sheehan, P. (1998), 'Poverty and the Collapse of Full Employment', in R. Fincher and J. Nieuwenhuysen, J. (eds.), *Australian Poverty: Then and Now*, Melbourne University Press, Melbourne, pp. 103-126.

Gregory, R. G. and Hunter, B. (1997), *Technical Issues Related to Aggregation and Socio-economic Status* (appendix to Spatial Trends in Income and Employment in Australian Cities), report delivered to the New South Wales Department of Transport and Regional Development.

Gregory, R. G. and Hunter, B. (1995), *The Macro Economy and the Growth of Ghettos and Urban Poverty in Australia*, Discussion Paper No.325, Economics Program, Australian National University, Canberra.

Griffiths, R. (1998), 'Making Sameness: Place Marketing and the New Urban Entrepreneurialism', in N. Oakley (ed.), *Cities, Economic Competition and Urban Policy,* Paul Chapman Publishing, London, pp. 203-222.

Griffiths, S. (1996), *The Battle for Pyrmont: an Analysis of State/city Political Battles over the Redevelopment of Pyrmont and Ultimo*, unpublished undergraduate thesis, School of Architecture, University of New South Wales, Sydney.

Habermas, J. (1989), *The Structural Transformation of the Public Sphere* (trans. T. Burger), MIT Press, Cambridge, MA.

Hage, G. (1997), 'At Home in the Entrails of the West: Multiculturalism, Ethnic Food and Migrant Home-Building', in H. Grace, G. Hage, L. Johnson, J. Langsworth and M. Symonds, *Home/World: Space, Community and Marginality in Sydney's West*, Pluto, Annandale, New South Wales, pp. 99-153.

Hajer, M. A. (1993), 'Rotterdam: Re-designing the Public Domain', in F. Bianchini and M. Parkinson (eds.), *Cultural Policy and Urban Regeneration: The West European Experience*, Manchester University Press, Manchester, pp. 48-72.

Halfacre, H. and Kitchin, R. M. (1996), '"Madchester Rave On": Placing the Fragments of Popular Music', *Area,* Vol. 28 (1), pp47-55.

Hall, P. (1998), *Cities and Civilization: Culture, Innovation, and Urban Order*, Weidenfeld and Nicholson, London.

Hall, P. (1996), *Cities of Tomorrow: Updated Edition*, Blackwell, Oxford.

Hall, P. (1982), 'Enterprise Zones: a Justification', *International Journal of Urban and Regional Research*, Vol. 6, pp 416-421.

Hall, P. (1981), 'Retrospect and Prospect', in P. Hall (ed.), *The Inner City in Context: The Final Report of the Social Science Research Council Inner Cities Working Party,* Heinemann, London.

Hall, S. (1996), 'New Ethnicities', in D. Morley and K-H. Chen (eds.), *Stuart Hall: Critical Dialogues in Cultural Studies,* Routledge, London, pp. 68-80.

Hall, S. (1992), 'The Question of Cultural Identity', in S. Hall, D. Held and T. McGrew (eds.), *Modernity and its Futures,* Polity Press, Oxford, pp. 273-325.

Hall, T. and Hubbard, P. (eds.) (1998), *The Entrepreneurial City: Geographies of Politics, Regimes and Representation,* John Wiley and Sons, London.

Hannerz, U. (1996), *Transnational Connections: Culture, People, Places,* Routledge, London.

Hannerz, U. (1990), 'Cosmopolitans and Locals in World Cultures', in M. Featherstone (ed.), *Global Culture: Nationalism, Globalization and Modernity,* Sage, London, pp. 222-236.

Hannerz, U. (1987), 'The World in Creolization', *Afrika,* Vol. 57(4), pp. 546-59.

Hartman, J. H. (2003), 'The University Campus – a Ghost City', in M. Miles and N. Kirkham (eds.), *Cultures and Settlements,* Intellect, Bristol, pp. 87-90.

Harvey, D. (1993) 'From Space to Place and Back Again: Reflections on the Condition of Postmodernity', in J. Bird, T. Putnam and G. Robertson (eds.), *Mapping the Futures: Local Cultures, Global Change,* Routledge, London, pp. 3-29.

Harvey, D. (1989a), *The Urban Experience,* Johns Hopkins University Press, Baltimore.

Harvey, D. (1989b), 'From Managerialism to Entrepreneurialism: the Transformation of Urban Governance in Late Capitalism', *Geografiska Annaler (B),* Vol. 71, pp. 3-17.

Harvey, D. (1989c), *The Condition of Postmodernity: An Enquiry into the Origins of Cultural Change,* Blackwell, Oxford.

Harvey, D. (1985), *The Urbanization of Capital,* Blackwell, Oxford.

Haslam, D. (1999), *Manchester England: The Story of the Pop Cult City,* Fourth Estate, London.

Haylett, C. (2001), 'Illegitimate Subjects?: Abject Whites, Neoliberal Modernisation, and Middle-class Multiculturalism', *Environment and Planning D: Society and Space,* Vol. 19, pp. 351-370.

Healey, P., Graham, S. and Davoudi, S. (eds.) (1995), *Managing Cities, the New Urban Context,* John Wiley and Sons, London.

Held, D. and Pollitt, C. (eds.) (1986), *New Forms of Democracy,* Sage, London.

Henriques, E. B. and Thiel, J. (1998), 'The Cultural Economies of Cities: A Comparative Study of the Audio-Visual Sector in Hamburg and Lisbon', Paper to *Xth ACEI International Conference on Cultural Economics,* Barcelona.

Hesmondhalgh, D. (2002), *The Cultural Industries,* Sage, London.

Hetherington, K. (1997), 'Museum Topology and the Will to Connect', *Journal of Material Culture,* 2(2), pp. 199-218.

Hetter, K. (2002), 'Big Money to Stay Near WTC', *Newsday,* 3rd June.

Hewison, R. (1987), *The Heritage Industry: Britain in a Climate of Decline,* Methuen, London.

Hillier, J. and Searle, G. (1995), 'Rien Ne Va Plus: Fast Track Development and Public Participation in Pyrmont-Ultimo, Sydney', *Sydney Vision – UTS Papers in Planning,* Number 3, University of Technology Sydney, Sydney.

Hilton, T. (1991), 'Arts Schools and Urban Culture', in M. Fisher and U. Owen (eds.), *Whose Cities?,* Penguin, St. Ives, pp. 125-130.

Hirst, D. (1986), 'Associational Democracy', in D. Held and C. Pollitt (eds.), *New Forms of Democracy,* Sage, London, pp. 224-250.

HMSO (1977), *Policy for the Inner Cities,* HMSO, London.

Hobsbawm, E. J. (1977), *The Age of Capital 1848–1875*, Abacus, London.

Hodge, S. (1996), 'Disadvantage and "Otherness" in Western Sydney', *Australian Geographical Studies*, Vol. 34, pp. 32-44.

Hoher, D. (1986), 'The Composition of Music Hall Audiences, 1850-1900', in P. Bailey (ed.), *Music Hall: the Business of Pleasure*, Open University Press, Milton Keynes, pp. 236-250.

Home, R. K. (1982), *Inner City Regeneration*, E and FN Spon, London.

Hooper, B. (1998), 'The Poem of Male Desires: Female Bodies, Modernity, and "Paris, Capital of the Nineteenth Century"', in L. Sandercock (ed.), *Making the Invisible Visible: A Multicultural Planning History*, University of California Press, Berkeley, CA, pp. 227-254.

Horne, D. (1986), *The Public Culture: The Triumph of Industrialism*, Pluto Press, London.

Horvath, R. and Engels, B. (1985), 'The Residential Restructuring of Inner Sydney', in I. Burnley and J. Forrest (eds.), *Living in Cities*, Allen and Unwin, Sydney, pp. 143-159.

Hubbard, P. (1999), *Sex and the City: Geographies of Prostitution in the Urban West*, Ashgate, Aldershot.

Hutton, T. A. (2000), 'Reconstructed Production Landscapes in the Postmodern City: Applied Design and Creative Services in the Metropolitan Core', *Urban Geography*, Vol. 21, pp. 285-317.

Illich, I. (1973), *Tools for Conviviality*, Calder Boyars, London.

Jacobs, J. (1961), *The Death and Life of Great American Cities*, Random House, New York.

Jardine, L. (1996), *Worldly Goods: A New History of the Renaissance*, Macmillan, London.

Jayne, M. (2003), 'Too Many Voices, "Too Problematic to be Plausible"; Representing Multiple Responses to Local Economic Development Strategies', *Environment and Planning A.*, Vol. 35, pp. 959-981.

Jayne, M. (2000), 'Imag(in)ing a Post-Industrial Potteries', in D. Bell and A. Haddour (eds.), *City Visions*, Prentice Hall, Harlow, pp. 12-26.

Jencks, C. (1996), 'The City that Never Sleeps', *New Statesman*, 28th June, pp. 26–8.

Kasinitz, P. (ed.) (1995), *Metropolis. Centre and Symbol of Our Times*, Macmillan, Basingstoke.

Keilhacker, T. (1998), *Urban Densification in Today's Cities with reference to Pyrmont-Ultimo in Sydney and Dorotheen-Friedrichstadt in Berlin*, unpublished Master's thesis, Faculty of Architecture, University of Sydney, Sydney.

Keith, M. and Pile, S. (1996), 'Imaging the City', *Environment and Planning A*, Vol. 28(3), pp. 381-387.

Kelsall, G. (2003), *The Development, Production, Consumption of a Theme Park as a Multiple Landscape: A Case Study of Alton Towers, Staffordshire*, unpublished PhD thesis, Staffordshire University.

Kilian, T. (1998), 'Public and Private, Power and Space', in A. Light and J. M. Smith (eds.), *The Production of Public Space*, Rowman and Littlefield, Oxford, pp.67-89.

Kinnell, H. (2002), 'Tackling Violence Against Sex Workers', presented at *What Future Sex Workers!!: Reducing the Impact on the Community Through A Multi Agency Approach*, 28th May, Barbican Centre, London.

Knox, P. (1996), 'Globalization and Urban Change', *Urban Geography*, Vol. 17, pp. 115-117.

Knox, P. (1987), 'The Social Production of the Built Environment: Architects, Architecture and the Postmodern City', *Progress in Human Geography*, Vol. 21 (3), pp. 154-377.

Kockel, U. (2003), *Culture and Economy: Contemporary Perspectives*, Ashgate, Aldershot.

Krugman, P. (1991), *Geography and Trade*, MIT Press, Cambridge MA.

LAB (1992), *The Arts and Urban Policy*, National Arts & Media Strategy Seminar, London Arts Board, London.

Lacroix, J-G. and Tremblay, G. (1997), 'The Information Society and Cultural Industries Theory', *Current Sociology*, Vol. 45, pp. 106-124.

Landry, C. (2000), *The Creative City; a Toolkit for Urban Innovators*, Earthscan, London.

Lane, R. (1998), 'The Place of Industry', *Harvard Architecture Review* 10 [*Civitas/What City?*], pp. 151–61.

Lane, R. and Waitt, G. (2001), 'Authenticity in Tourism and Native Title: Space, Time and Spatial Politics in the East Kimberley', *Social and Cultural Geography,* Vol. 2(4), pp. 381-405.

Lash, S. and Urry, J. (1994), *Economies of Signs and Spaces,* Sage, London.

Latour, B. (1993), *We Have Never Been Modern*, Harvester Wheatsheaf, London.

Lazano, E. E. (1990), *Community Design and the Culture of Cities*, Cambridge University Press, Cambridge.

Leadbetter, C. and Oakley, K. (1995), *The Independents: Britain's New Cultural Entrepreneurs,* Demos, London.

Lefebvre, H. (1991), *The Production of Space*, Blackwell, Oxford.

LeGates, R. T. and Stout, F. (eds.) (1996), *The City Reader*, Routledge, London.

Leiss, W. (1978), *The Limits to Satisfaction*, Marion Boyars, London.

Lepani, B., Freed, G., Murphy, P., and McGillivray, A. (1995), *The Economic Role of Cities: Australia in the Global Economy*, Commonwealth Department of Housing and Regional Development, Australian Government Publishing Service (AGPS), Canberra.

Leslie, E. (2001), 'Tate Modern. A Year of Sweet Success', *Radical Philosophy*, Vol. 109, pp. 2-5.

Lin, J. (1998), *Reconstructing Chinatown: Ethnic Enclave, Global Change*, University of Minnesota Press, Minneapolis.

Lin, J. (1995), 'Ethnic Places, Postmodernism, and Urban Change in Houston', *The Sociological Quarterly*, Vol. 36(4), pp. 629-647.

Lincoln, C, (1993), 'City of Culture: Dublin and the Discovery of Urban Heritage', in B. O'Connor and M. Cronin, (eds.), *Tourism in Ireland: A Critical Analysis*, Cork University Press, Cork, pp. 226-240.

Lister, D. (1991) 'The Transformation of a City: Birmingham', in M. Fisher and U. Owen (eds.), *Whose Cities?* Penguin, St Ives, pp. 107-123.

LMDC (2001), *Governor and Mayor Name Lower Manhattan Redevelopment Corporation*, (press release), 29th November, LMDC, New York.

LMDC. (nd.), *Lower Manhattan Development Corporation and Port Authority of New York and New Jersey Preliminary Urban Design Study: For the Future of the World Trade Center Site and Adjacent Areas*, LMDC, New York.

Loftman, P. and Nevin, B. (1996a), 'Going for Growth: Prestige Projects in Three British Cities', *Urban Studies*, Vol. 33(6), pp. 991-1019.

Loftman, P. and Nevin, B. (1996b), 'Prestige Urban Regeneration Projects: Socio-Economic Impacts' in A. J. Gerrard and T. R. Slater (eds.), *Managing A Conurbation: Birmingham and its Region*, Brewin Books, Studley, pp. 121-141.

Logan, J. and Molotch, H. (1987), *Urban Fortunes: the Political Economy of Place*, University of California Press, Berkely, CA.

Loneragan, T. (2001), 'Pyrmont set to take on CBD Big Brother', *Sydney Morning Herald*, 4[th] August, p. 66.

Lorente, J. P. (2000), 'Art Neighbourhoods, Ports of Vitality', in S. Bennett and J. Butler (eds.), *Locality, Regeneration and Divers[c]ities*, Intellect, Bristol, pp. 79-97.

Louise, D. (2003), 'Encouraging Cultural Entrepreneurship', *Arts Professional,* Issue 42, p. 7.

Low, S. M. (2000), *On the Plaza: The Politics of Public Space and Culture*, University of Texas, Austin.

Lowe, D. M. (1982), *History of Bourgeois Perception*, University of Chicago Press, Chicago.

Luftig, V. (1996), 'Literary Tourism and Dublin's Joyce', in M. A. Wolleager, V. Luftig and R. Spoo (eds.), *Joyce and the Subject of History*, University of Michigan Press, Ann Arbor, pp. 24-40.

MacAvera, B. (1990), *Art, Politics and Ireland*, Open Air, Dublin.

Maffesoli, M. (1996), *The Time of the Tribes*, Sage, London.

Mahtani, M. and Salmon, S. (1988), 'Site Reading? Globalization, Identity and the Consumption of Place in Popular Music', in C. L. Harrington and D. Bielby (eds.), *Popular Culture: Production and Consumption,* Blackwell Publishing Ltd, Oxford, pp. 110-125.

Malouf, M. (1999), 'Forging the Nation: James Joyce and the Celtic Tiger', *Jouvert: A Journal of Postcolonial Studies*, Vol. 4(1), pp. 882-904.

Marcuse, P. (2003), 'The Ground Zero Architectural Competition: Designing Without a Plan, *Planners Network*, Vol. 154, pp. 10-13.

Marcuse, P. (2002), 'The Layered City', in G. Madsen and D. Plunz (eds.), *The City Under Attack,* Routledge, London. pp. 94-114.

Marcuse, P. (1995), 'Not Chaos, but Walls', in S. Watson and K. Gibson (eds.), *Postmodern Cities and Spaces*, Blackwell, Oxford, pp. 243-253.

Marcuse, P. (1989), '"Dual City": A Muddy Metaphor for a Quartered City', *International Journal of Urban and Regional Research*, Vol. 13(4), pp. 309-44.

Marshall, A. (1925), *Principles of Economics*, Macmillan, London.

Marx, K. (1973), *Grundrisse*, Penguin, London.

Massey, D. (1995), 'Power Geometry and a Progressive Sense of Place', in J. Bird, B. Curtis, T. Putnam and G. Robertson (eds.), *Mapping the Futures: Local Cultures, Global Change,* Routledge, London, pp.59-69.

Massey, D. (1994), *Space, Place and Gender,* Polity Press, Cambridge.

Massey, D. (1982), 'Enterprise Zones: a Political Issue', *International Journal of Urban and Regional Research*, Vol. 6, pp. 429-434.

Matless, D. (1993), 'Appropriate Geography: Patrick Abercrombie and the Energy of the World', *Journal of Design History*, Vol. 6(3), pp.167-178.

Matthews, M. (1982), *Pyrmont and Ultimo: A History*, Southwood Press, Sydney.

Mayer, M. (1995) 'Urban Governance in the Post-Fordist City', in P. Healey, S. Graham and S. Davoudi (eds.), *Managing Cities, the New Urban Context,* John Wiley and Sons, London, pp. 125-140.

McEwen, I. K. (1993), *Socrates' Ancestor: An Essay on Architectural Beginnings*, MIT, Cambridge, MA.

McGuigan, J. (1996) *Culture and the Public Sphere*, Routledge, London.

McGuirk, P. M., Winchester, H. P. M. and Dunn, K. M. (1996), 'Entrepreneurial Approaches to Urban Decline: the Honeysuckle Redevelopment in Inner Newcastle, New South Wales', *Environment and Planning: A*, Vol. 28, pp. 1815-1841.

McInnis, D. (2001), 'Inside the Outside: Politics and Gay and Lesbian Spaces in Sydney', in C. Johnston and P. van Reyk, (eds.) *Queer City: Gay and Lesbian Politics in Sydney*, Pluto Press, Annandale, NSW.

McKenna, J. (1986), *Birmingham Street Names*, Birmingham Public Libraries, Birmingham.

McManus, K. (1994a), *Nashville of the North: Country Music in Liverpool*, Institute of Popular Music, Liverpool.

McManus, K. (1994b), *Ceilis, Jigs and Ballads: Irish Music in Liverpool*, Institute of Popular Music, Liverpool.

McNeil, J. (2001), *Something New Under the Sun*, Penguin, London.

McNulty, R. (1999), *Partners for Liveable Places,* Partners for Liveable Places, Washington.

McNulty, R. (1991) 'Cultural Planning: a Movement for Civic Progress', *The Cultural Planning Conference*, Mornington, Victoria, Australia, EIT.

McNulty, R. and Page, C. (eds.) (1994), *The State of the American Community*, Partners for Liveable Communities, Washington DC.

Meaney, H. (1997), 'From the Heart of the Hibernian Metropolis', *The Irish Times*, Dublin, 16th June, p. 3.

Mee, K. (1994), 'Dressing-up the Suburbs: Representations of Western Sydney', in K. Gibson and S. Watson (eds.), *Metropolis Now: Planning and the Urban in Contemporary Australia*, Pluto Press, Sydney, pp. 60-77.

Meegan, R. and Mitchell, A. (2001), '"It's Not a Community Round Here, It's a Neighbourhood": Neighbourhood Change and Cohesion in Urban Regeneration Policies', *Urban Studies,* Vol. 38(12), pp. 2167-2194.

Mein, A. S. (1997), *Growing Pains: the Realities of Pyrmont-Ultimo*, unpublished undergraduate BSc thesis, School of Geography, University of New South Wales, Sydney.

Meller, H. (2001), *European Cities 1890-1930s: History, Culture and the Built Environment*, Wiley, Chichester.

Mellor, R. (2002), 'Hypocritical City: Cycles of Urban Exclusion', in J. Peck and K. Ward (eds.), *City of Revolution: Restructuring Manchester*, Manchester University Press, Manchester, pp. 214-235.

Mercer, C. (1996), 'By Accident or Design. Can Culture be Planned?', in F. Matarasso and S. Halls (eds.), *The Art of Regeneration*, Conference Papers, Nottingham and Bournes Green, Nottingham City Council, Nottingham.

Mercer, C. (1991), 'What is Cultural Planning?', paper presented to the *Community Arts Network National Conference*, Sydney, Australia, 10th October.

Miles, M. (2000), *The Uses of Decoration: Essays in the Architectural Everyday*, John Wiley, Chichester.

Milestone, K. (1996), 'Regional Variations: Northernness and New Urban Economies of Hedonism', in J. O'Connor and D. Wynne (eds.), *From the Margins to the Centre: Cultural Production and Consumption in the Post-industrial City,* Arena, Aldershot, pp. 106-123.

Miller, D. (1977), 'Idelfons Cerdà, an Introduction', *Architectural Association Quarterly*, Vol. 9, p. 1.

Mingione, E. (1995), 'Social and Employment Change in the Urban Area', in P. Healey, S. Graham and S. Davoudi (eds.), *Managing Cities, the New Urban Context,* John Wiley and Sons, London, pp. 67-80.

Mitchell, D. (1995), 'The End of Public Space/ People's Park, Definitions of the Public, and Democracy', *Annals of the Association of American Geographers*, Vol. 85, pp. 108-133.

Mitchell, K. (1998), 'Reworking Democracy: Contemporary Immigration and Community Politics in Vancouver's Chinatown', *Political Geography*, Vol. 17(6), pp. 729-750.

Mitchell, K. (1993), 'Multiculturalism, or the United Colors of Capitalism?', *Antipode*, Vol. 25(4), pp. 263-294.

Moles, A. (1995), *Council for Cultural Cooperation, Volume 1, Concepts and References*, Council of Europe Publishing, Netherlands.

Momass, H. (1997), *Globalisation and Cultural Policies; Implications for European Cities*, MA European Cultural Planning Seminar, DeMonfort University, Leicester.

Montgomery, J. (1995), 'Urban Vitality and the Culture of Cities', *Planning Practice and Research*, Vol. 10(2), pp. 236-250.

Moon, G. and Atkinson, R. (1997), 'Ethnicity', in M. Pacione (ed.), *Britain's Cities: Geographies of Division in Urban Britain* Routledge, London, pp. 286-302.

Morris, L. (2000), 'E-gulls Swoop on Dot Com Bay Bait', *Sydney Morning Herald*, 16th October, p. 37.

Mort, F. (1998), 'Consumption, Masculinities and the Mapping of London since 1950', *Urban Studies,* Vol. 35 (5-6), pp. 889-907.

Moss, L. (2002), 'Sheffield's Cultural Industries Quarter 20 Years On: What can be Learned from a Pioneering Example?', *International Journal of Cultural Policy,* Vol. 8(2), pp. 107-125.

Munt, I. (1994), 'Race, Urban Policy and Urban Problems: A Critique on Current UK Practice', in J. Thomas and V. Krishnarayan (eds.), *Race Equality and Planning: Policies and Procedures*, Avebury, Aldershot, pp. 224-260.

Murphy, P. and Watson, S. (1997), *Surface City. Sydney at the Millennium*, Pluto Press Australia, Annandale, NSW.

Murphy, P. and Watson, S. (1990), 'Restructuring of Sydney's Central Industrial Area: Process and Local Impacts', *Australian Geographical Studies*, Vol. 28, pp. 78-87.

Myerscough, J. (1988) *The Economic Importance of the Arts in Britain*, Policy Studies Institute, London.

National Housing Strategy (NHS) (1991), *Australian Housing: The Demographic, Economic and Social Environment*, Australian Government Publishing Service, Canberra.

Negrier, E. (1993), 'Montpellier: International Competition and Community Access', in F. Bianchini and M. Parkinson (eds.), *Cultural Policy and Urban Regeneration: The West European Experience*, Manchester University Press, Manchester, pp. 135-154.

New South Wales Department of Environment and Planning (1984), *Planning Issues in the Sydney Region: Urban Consolidation*, Department of Environment and Planning (NSW), Sydney.

New South Wales Department of Planning (1991), *City West Regional Environmental Study*, Department of Planning, Sydney.

New South Wales Department of Urban Affairs and Planning (DUAP) (1995a), *Urban Development Plan for Ultimo-Pyrmont Precinct. Draft 1995 Update*, Department of Planning, Sydney.

New South Wales Department of Urban Affairs and Planning (DUAP) (1995b), *City West Affordable Housing Program*, Department of Planning, Sydney.

Newby, H. (1979), *Green and Pleasant Land? Social Change in Rural England*, Billing and Sons, Worcester.

Newman, O. (1972), *Defensible Space: Crime Prevention Through Urban Design*, Macmillan, New York.

Newman, P. and Kenworthy, J. (1991), 'Sustainable Settlements: Restoring the Commons', *Habitat Australia,* Vol. 19, pp. 18-21.

Nittim Z. (1980), 'The Coalition of Resident Action Groups', in J. Roe (ed.) *Urban Problems and Planning in the Developed World*, Croom Helm, London, pp. 71-119.

Nixon, S. (1997), 'Circulating Culture', in P. Du Gay (ed.), *Production of Culture/Cultures of Production,* The Open University Press, Milton Keynes, pp. 177-234.

O'Brien, G. (1995), 'Plea on Heritage Sites', *Sydney Morning Herald,* 14th September, p.10.

O'Connor, J. (1998), 'Popular Culture, Cultural Intermediaries and Urban Regeneration', in T. Hall and P. Hubbard (eds.), *The Entrepreneurial City: Geographies of Politics, Regime and Representation,* John Wiley and Sons, Chichester, pp. 225-239.

O'Connor, K. and Stimson, R. (1995), *The Economic Role of Cities: Economic Change and City Development, Australia, 1971-1991*, Commonwealth Department of Housing and Regional Development, Urban Futures Research Programme, AGPS, Canberra.

O'Connor, J. and Wynne, D. (eds.) (1996), *From the Margins to the Centre: Cultural Production and Consumption in the Post-industrial City*, Ashgate, Aldershot.

O'Faolain, N. (1997), 'Men, the Presidency and Molly Bloom', *The Irish Times*, 13th October, pp. 2.

O'Kane, M. (2002), 'Mean Streets', *The Guardian*, 16th September, p. 16.

O'Neill, M. (2001), *Prostitution and Feminism: Towards a Politics of Feeling,* Polity, Cambridge.

O'Neill, M. and Campbell, R (2002), *Working Together To Create Change: Walsall Prostitution Consultation Research,* Walsall South Health Action Zone/Staffordshire University/Liverpool Hope University.

O'Neill, M., Campbell, R. and Webster, M. (2001), 'Prostitution, Ethno-mimesis and Participatory Arts: Processes and Practices of Inclusion', in J. Swift and T. Davies, (eds.), *Disciplines, Fields and Change in Art Education: Art Therapy, Psychology and Sociology*, University of Central England, Birmingham, pp. 224-249.

Olsen, D. J. (1982), *Town Planning in London: The Eighteenth and Nineteenth Centuries,* Yale University Press, New Haven and London.

Orchard, L. (1999), 'Shifting Visions in National Urban and Regional Policy 2', *Australian Planner,* Vol. 36(4), pp. 200-210.

Paba, G. and Paloscia, R. (1999), 'Living in the City', in L. Nyström and C. Fudge (eds.), *City and Culture*: *Cultural Processes and Urban Sustainability,* The Swedish Urban Environment Council, Stockholm, pp. 225-252.

Pacione, M. (ed.) (1997), *Britain's Cities: Geographies of Division in Urban Britain*, Routledge, London.

Parker, D. (1995), *Through Different Eyes: The Cultural Identities of Young Chinese People in Britain*, Avebury, Aldershot.

Parkinson, M and Bianchini, F, (1993), 'Liverpool: a Tale of Missed Opportunities?', in F. Bianchini and M. Parkinson (eds.), *Cultural Policy and Urban Regeneration: the Western European Experience,* Manchester University Press, Manchester, pp. 155-177.

Pearson, N. (1982), *The State and the Visual Arts*, Open University Press, Milton Keynes.

Peretti, J. (2002), 'Welcome to the Last Dance Saloon', *The Guardian*, 25th July, p. 35.

Phelan, S. (2001), *Sexual Strangers: Gays, Lesbians and Dilemmas of Citizenship*, Temple University Press, Philadelphia, PA.

Pick, J. (1988), *The Arts in a State: A Study of Government Arts Policies from Ancient Greece to the Present*, Bristol Classical Press, Bristol.

Pile, S., Brook, C. and Mooney, G. (1999), *Unruly Cities?*, Routledge, London.

Podmore, J. (1998), '(Re)-reading the "Loft-living" *Habitus* in Montreal's Inner City', *International Journal of Urban and Regional Research*, Vol. 22(2), pp. 283-302.

Pompidou (1994), *La Ville: Art et Architecture en Europe, 1870-1993*, Editions du Centre Pompidou, Paris.

Porter, M. (1990), *The Competitive Advantage of Nations*, Macmillan, London.

Portnov, B. A. and Erell, E. (2001), *Urban Clustering. The Benefits and Drawbacks of Location*, Ashgate, Aldershot.

Pratt, A. (2002), 'Hot Jobs in Cool Places. The Material Cultures of New Media Product Spaces: The Case of South of the Market, San Francisco', *Information, Communication and Society*, Vol. 5(1), pp. 27-50.

Pratt, A. (2000), 'New Media, the New Economy and New Spaces', *Geoforum*, Vol. 31(4), pp. 425-436.

Pritchard, W. N. (2000), 'Beyond the Modern Supermarket: Geographical Approaches to the Analysis of Contemporary Australian Retail Restructuring', *Australian Geographical Studies,* Vol. 38(2), pp. 204-218.

Probyn, E. (2000), 'Sporting Bodies: Dynamics of Shame and Pride', *Body & Society*, Vol. 6(1), pp. 13-28.

Prud'homme, R. (1995), 'On the Economic Role of Cities', *Cities and the New Global Economy*, OECD/Australian Government, Canberra, Vol. 3, pp. 732.

Purvis, S. (1996), 'The Interchangeable Roles of the Producer, Consumer and Cultural Intermediary: the New "Pop" Fashion Designer', in J. O'Connor and D. Wynne (eds.), *From the Margins to the Centre: Cultural Production and Consumption in the Post-industrial City*, Ashgate, Aldershot, pp. 68-75.

Pusey, M. (1991), *Economic Rationalism in Canberra: A Nation-building State Changes Its Mind*, Cambridge University Press, Melbourne.

Putnam, R. (2000): *Bowling Alone: the Collapse and Revival of American Community*, Simon and Schuster, London.

Raban, J. (1974), *Soft City*, Hamish Hamilton, London.

Raffo, C., O'Connor, J., Lovatt, A. and Banks, M. (1999), 'Risk and Trust in the Cultural Industries', *Geoforum*, Vol. 24, pp. 224-254.

Rahnema, M. (1997), 'Afterword: Towards Post-Development: Searching for Signposts, A New Language and New Paradigm', in M. Rahnema and V. Bawtree (eds), *The Post-Development Reader*, Zed Books, London, pp. 104-124.

Rains, S. (1999), 'Touring Temple Bar: Cultural Tourism in Dublin's "Cultural Quarter"', *International Journal of Cultural Policy*, Vol. 6(1), pp. 225-267.

Rantisi, N. M. (2002), 'The Local Innovation System as a Source of "Variety": Openness and Adaptability in New York City's Garment District', *Regional Studies*, Vol. 36(6), pp. 587-602.

Reid, P. (1992), 'City West Reviewed at Tusculum', *Architecture Bulletin*, July, pp. 3-7.

Relf, J. (1993), 'Utopia the Good Breast: Coming Home to Mother', in K. Kunnar and S. Bann (ed.), *Utopias and the Millennium*, Reaktion Books, London, pp. 224-253.

Remesar, A. and Pol, E. (2000) 'Civic Participation Workshops in Sant Adrià de Besòs: a Creative Methodology', in S. Bennett and J. Butler (eds.) (2000), *Locality, Regeneration and Divers[c]ities*, Intellect, Bristol, pp. 153-8.

Renton, A. (2002), 'Is Hoxton Still Hot?', *Evening Standard*, 27th August, p. 53.

Report of the Chief Executive to the City Centre Steering Group (1989), *Birmingham City Centre: Towards the Year 2000*, Birmingham City Council, Birmingham.

Richards, L. (1994), 'Suburbia: Domestic Dreaming', in L. C. Johnston (ed.), *Suburban Dreaming*, Deakin University Press, Geelong, pp. 114-129.

Roberts, M., Salter, M., and Marsh, C. (1993), *Public Art in Private Places*, University of Westminster, London.

Robertson, R. (1995), 'Glocalisation: Time-Space and Homogeneity-Heterogeneity', in M. Featherstone, S. Lash and R. Robertson (eds.), *Global Modernities*, Sage, London, pp. 68-82.

Robins, K. (1995), 'Collective Emotion and Urban Culture', in P. Healey, S. Graham and S. Davoudi (eds.), *Managing Cities, the New Urban Context*, John Wiley and Sons, London, pp. 160-175.

Robson, B. (2002), 'Mancunian Ways: the Politics of Regeneration', in J. Peck and K. Ward (eds.), *City of Revolution: Restructuring Manchester*, Manchester University Press, Manchester, pp. 34-49.

Roche, M. (1994), 'Mega-events and Urban Policy', *Annals of Tourism Research*, Vol. 21, pp. 1-19.

Rogers, R. (1997), *Cities for a Small Planet*, Faber and Faber, London.

Rogers, R. and Power, A. (2000), *Cities for a Small Country*, Faber and Faber, London.

Rojek, C. (2000), *Leisure and Culture*, Macmillan, London.

Rose, N. (2000), 'Governing Cities, Governing Citizens', in E. Isin (ed.), *Democracy, Citizenship and the Global City,* Routledge, London, pp. 95-109.

Rosler, M. (1991), 'Fragments of a Metropolitan Viewpoint', in B. Wallis (ed.), *If You Lived Here,* Seattle, Bay Press, pp. 15-44.

Ross, A. (2002), 'The Odour of Publicity', in M. Sorkin and S. Zukin (eds.), *After the World Trade Center: Rethinking New York City,* Routledge, New York.

RTPI/CRE (1983), *Planning for a Multi-racial Britain,* Commission for Racial Equality, London.

Rugg, J. and Hinchcliffe, D,. (eds.) (2002), *Recoveries and Reclamations,* Intellect, Bristol.

Rushbrook, D. (2002), 'Cities, Queer Space, and the Cosmopolitan Tourist', *GLQ,* Vol. 8(1-2), pp. 183-206.

Russell, M. (1996), 'Pyrmont Braced for Dramatic Transformation', *Sydney Morning Herald,* 5th October, p 4.

Ryan, B. (1992), *Making Capital from Culture,* Walter de Gruyter, New York and Berlin.

Ryan, J. and Fitzpatrick, H. (1996), 'The Space that Difference Makes: Negotiation and Urban Identities Through Consumption Practices', in J. O'Connor and D. Wynne (eds), *From the Margins to the Centre: Cultural Production and Consumption in the Post-industrial City,* Ashgate, Aldershot, pp. 169-202.

Sandercock, L. (ed.) (1998), *Making the Invisible Visible: A Multicultural Planning History,* University of California Press, Berkeley, CA.

Sant, M. and Jackson, S. (1991), 'Strategic Planning and Urban Restructuring: the Case of Pyrmont-Ultimo', *Australian Geographer,* Vol. 22(2), pp. 136-146.

Sassen,·S. (1994), *Cities in a World Economy,* Pine Forge Press, Thousand Oaks, CA.

Sassen, S. (1991), *The Global City: New York, London, Tokyo,* Princeton University Press, Princeton.

Sassen, S. and Roost, F. (1999), 'The City: Strategic Site for the Global Entertainment Industry', in D. R. Judd and S. S. Fainstein (eds.), *The Tourist City,* Yale University Press, New Haven and London, pp. 143–154.

Savage, M. and Warde, A. (1993), *Urban Sociology, Capitalism and Modernity,* Macmillan, Basingstoke.

Schumacher, E. F. (1974), *Small is Beautiful: A Study of Economics as if People Really Mattered,* Abacus, London.

Schwarz, W. and Schwarz, D. (1999), *Living Lightly: Travels in Post-Consumer Society,* John Carpenter, London.

Scott, A. (2002), 'A New Map of Hollywood: The Production and Distribution of American Motion Pictures', *Regional Studies,* Vol. 36(9), pp. 957-976.

Scott, A. (2001), 'Capitalism, Cities, and the Production of Symbolic Forms', *Transactions of the Institute of British Geographers,* Vol. 26, pp. 11-23.

Scott, A. (2000), *The Cultural Economy of Cities,* Sage, London.

Scott, A. (1997), 'The Cultural Economy of Cities', *International Journal of Urban and Regional Research,* Vol. 21.2, pp. 323-39.

Seed, P. and Lloyd, G. (1997), *Quality of Life,* Jessica Kingsley, London.

Selwood, S. (1995), *The Benefits of Public Art,* Policy Studies Institute, London.

Sen, A. (1999), *Development as Freedom,* Oxford University Press, Oxford.

Sennett, R. (1995), *Flesh and Stone,* Faber and Faber, London.

Sennett, R. (1986), *The Fall of Public Man,* Faber and Faber, London.

Serratosa, A. (2001a), 'Cerdà's Magic: Housing Begets a City', in Generalitat de Catalunya, *Cerdà: The Barcelona Extension (Eixample),* Generalitat de Catalunya, Barcelona, pp. 10-12.

Serratosa A (2001b) 'The Value of Cerdà's *Eixample* Today', in Generalitat de Catalunya, *Cerdà: The Barcelona Extension (Eixample),* Generalitat de Catalunya, Barcelona, pp. 37-9.

Seve, L. (1978), *Man in Marxist Theory and the Psychology of Personality*, Harvester Press, Brighton.

Shank, B. (1994), *Dissonant Identities: The Rock'n'Roll Scene in Austin, Texas*, Wesleyan University Press, Austin.

Shaw, P. (1999), *The Arts and Neighbourhood Renewal: A Research Report*, Policy Action Team 10, Department for Culture, Media and Sport, London.

Shaw, W. S. (forthcoming), 'Sydney's SoHo Syndrome', *Urban Studies*.

Shaw, W. S. (2000), 'Ways of Whitness: Harlemising Sydney's Aborignal Redfern', *Australian Geographical Studies,* Vol. 38(3), pp. 291-305.

Sherlock, H. (1991), *Cities are Good for Us*, Paladin, London.

Short, J. (1999), 'Urban Imagineers: Boosterism and the Representation of Cities', in A. Jonas and D. Wilson (eds.), *The Urban Growth Machine: Critical Perspectives and Reflections*, SUNY Press, New York, pp. 37-54.

Short, J. R. (1996), *The Urban Order: An Introduction to Cities, Culture and Power*, Blackwell, Oxford.

Short, J. R., Benton, L. M., Luce, W. B. and Walton, J. (1993), 'Reconstructing the Image of an Industrial City', *Annals of the Association of American Geographers*, Vol. 83(2), pp. 207-224.

Simmie, J. (ed.) (2001), *Innovative Cities*, E and F.N. Spon, London.

Skelton, T. (1995), "Boom, Bye, Bye': Jamaican Ragga and Gay Resistance', in D. Bell and G. Valentine (eds.), *Mapping Desire: Geographies of Sexualities*, Routledge, London, pp. 264-283.

Smart, A. and Smart, J. (1996), 'Monster Homes: Hong Kong Immigration to Canada, Urban Conflicts, and Contested Representations of Space', in J. Caulfield and L. Peake, (eds.), *City Lives and City Forms: Critical Research and Canadian Urbanism*, University of Toronto Press, Toronto.

Smith, A. (1776), *The Wealth of Nations,* Bantam Books, London.

Smith, N. (1996), *The New Urban Frontier: Gentrification and the Revanchist City*, New York, Routledge.

Smith, N. and Williams, P. (1986), *Gentrification of the City*, Allen and Unwin, Boston.

Smyth, H. (1994), *Marketing the City: the Role of Flagship Developments in Urban Regeneration,* E and FN Spon, London.

Söderlind, J. (1999), 'Culture and Sustainability', in L. Nyström, and C. Fudge (eds.) (1999) *City and Culture: Cultural Processes and Urban Sustainability,* The Swedish Urban Environment Council, Stockholm, pp. 257-280.

Soja, E. (1996), *Thirdspace: Journey to Los Angeles and Other Real and Imagined Places,* Blackwell, London.

Soja, E. (1989), *Postmodern Geographies: the Reassertion of Space in Critical Social Theory,* Verso, London.

Solomos, J. (1993), *Race and Racism in Britain,* Macmillan Press, London.

Soria y Puig, A. (ed.) (1999), *Cerdà: The Five Bases of the General Theory of Urbanization*, Electa, Madrid.

Sorkin, M. (ed.) (1992), *Variations on a Theme Park*, Hill and Wang, New York.

Soysal, Y. (1996), 'Boundaries and Identity: Immigrants in Europe', *Florence, European Forum, European University Institute, EUI Working Paper* EUF, Florence, pp. 96/3.

Spencer, K., Taylor, A., Smith, B., Mawsin, J., Flynn, N. and Battey, R. (1986), *Crisis in the Industrial Heartland: a Study of the West Midlands,* Clarendon Press, Oxford.

Spivak, G. C. (1999), *A Critique of Postcolonial Reason: Toward a History of the Vanishing Present,* Harvard University Press, London.

Stanworth, J., Purdy, D. and Kirby, D. (1992), *The Management of Success in 'Growth Corridors'*, Small Business Research Trust, Open University, Milton Keynes.

Stimson, R. (2001), 'Dividing Societies: the Socio-political Spatial Implications of Restructuring in Australia', *Australian Geographical Studies,* Vol. 39(2), pp. 198-216.

Storper, M. (1995), 'The Resurgence of Regional Economies, Ten Years Later: the Region as a Nexus of Untraded Interdependencies', *European Urban and Regional Studies,* Vol. 2(3), pp. 191-221.

Sutcliffe, A. and Smith, R. (1974), *History of Birmingham Volume 3,* Oxford University Press, London.

Swenarnton, M. (1981), *Homes Fit for Heroes: the Politics and Architecture of Early State Housing in Britain,* Heinemann: London.

Sydney City Council (1980), *1980 City of Sydney Strategic Plan,* Sydney City Council, Sydney.

Sydney Harbour Foreshore Authority (2000), *Utimo-Pyrmont Post Occupancy Survey,* Report Reference TRC-737/738/741-CJ, Sydney Harbour Foreshore Authority, Sydney, September.

Sydney Morning Herald (2002) 'Reflecting the Best of Harbourside Living ...', Lend Lease Development Promotion, 8th June , p. 17.

Sydney Morning Herald (1997), 'City-linked Living ... a Style Apart', Walker Corporation promotion, 24th April, p. 20.

Tarragó, S. (2001), 'Three Holistic Proposals for a Complete, New, Integrated City', in Generalitat de Catalunya (2001), *Cerdà: The Barcelona Extension (Eixample),* Generalitat de Catalunya, Barcelona, pp. 5-9.

Tausz, K (1990), 'The Case of Eastern Europe: Why Community Development Still has to Find a Role in Hungary', *Community Development Journal,* 25(4), pp. 68-76.

Taylor, N. (1998), *Urban Planning Theory Since 1945,* Sage, London.

Taylor, N. (1973), *The Village in the City,* Temple Smith, London.

Teedon P. (2002), 'New Urban Spaces: Regenerating a Design Ethos', in J. Rugg and D. Hinchcliffe (2002), *Advances in Art and Urban Futures Volume 2: Recoveries and Reclamations,* Intellect Books, Bristol, pp. 49-59.

Thake, S. and Stauback, R. (1993), *Investing in People: Rescuing Communities from the Margin,* Joseph Rowntree Foundation, York.

Tiesdell, S., Oc, T. and Heath, T. (1996), *Revitalizing Historic Urban Quarters,* Architectural Press, Oxford.

Thomas, H. (1994), 'The New Right: 'Race' and Planning in Britain in the 1980s and 1990s', *Planning Practice and Research,* Vol. 9(4), pp. 353-366.

Thomas, H. and Krishnarayan, V. (1994), 'Introduction: Securing a Fair Planning System for Britain's Ethnic Minorities', in H. Thomas and V. Krishnarayan (eds.), *Race Equality and Planning: Policies and Procedures,* Avebury, Aldershot.

Thrift, N. (2000), "Not a Straight Line but a Curve", or, Cities are Not Mirrors of Modernity', in D. Bell and A. Haddour (eds.), *City Visions,* Prentice Hall, Harlow, pp. 233-263.

Totaro, P. (1997), '$800 Million to Turn Pyrmont high-tech', *Sydney Morning Herald,* 4th April, p. 2.

Towse, R. (1993), *Singers in the Market Place. The Economics of the Singing Profession,* Clarendon Press, Oxford.

Tranick, R. (1986), *Finding Lost Spaces: Theories of Urban Design,* Van Norstrand Rheinhold, New York.

Tuan, Y-F. (1977), *Space and Place: The Perspective of Experience,* Minnesota University Press, Minneapolis.

Turner, R. (2000), *Coal was Our Life,* Sheffield Hallam University Press, Sheffield.

Ulldemolins, J. R. (2000), 'From "Chino" to Raval. Art Merchants and the Creation of a Cultural Quarter in Barcelona', paper given at the *Cultural Change and Urban Contexts* Conference, Manchester, September.

URBED (1988), *Developing the Cultural Industries Quarter in Sheffield*, Sheffield City Council, Sheffield.

Urry, J. (1995), *Consuming Places*, London and New York, Routledge.

Urry, J. (1990), *The Tourist Gaze: Leisure and Travel in Contemporary Societies*, Sage Publications, London.

Van Doorninck, M. (1999), 'Business Like Any Other: Managing the Sex Industry in the Netherlands', paper presented at *Prostitution in a Global Context: Intertwined Histories, Present Realities*, University of Aalborg, Denmark, 16-18th November.

Vervaeke, M. and Lefebvre, B. (2002), 'Design Trades and Inter-firm Relationships in the Nord-Pas de Calais Textile Industry', *Regional Studies*, Vol. 36(6), pp. 661-673.

Verwijen, J. (1999), 'The Creative City as a Field Condition: Can Urban Innovation and Creativity Overcome Bureaucracy and Technocracy?', *Built Environment*, Vol. 24(2/3), pp. 142-54.

Verwijen, J. and Lehtovuori, P. (1999), *Creative Cities: Cultural Industries, Urban Development and the Information Society*, University of Art and Design Press, Helsinki.

Viapong, J., Castle, K. and Cardew, R. (1998), 'Revival in Inner-city Areas', *Australian Planner*, Vol. (35), pp. 215-222.

Visser, J. H. (1998), 'Selling Private Sex in Public Places: Managing Street Prostitution in the Netherlands', paper presented at *Changing Perspectives on Female Prostitution: A Regional Day Conference*, University of Liverpool Greenbank Conference Centre, Liverpool, 7th February.

Waitt, G. (1999), 'Playing Games with Sydney: Marketing Sydney for the 2000 Olympics', *Urban Studies*, Vol. 36(7), pp. 1055-1077.

Walder, S. (2002), 'Case Study of the "Quarter21" Cluster in the Museums Quarter, Vienna', Sheffield (2002) *Creative Clusters Conference Handbook* , 'First International Summit Conference on Creative Industries Regeneration', Cultural Industries Quarter, Sheffield, 20th-23rd November, pp. 260.

Walker, S. (1996), 'Dublin Masque', in P. Quinn (ed.), *Temple Bar: The Power of an Idea*, Temple Bar Properties, Dublin.

Wallis, B. (ed.) (1991), *If You Lived Here*, Bay Press, Seattle.

Walmsely, D. J. and Weinand, H. C. (1997), 'Well-being and Settlement Type', *Urban Policy and Research*, Vol. 15, pp. 43-50.

Walzer, M. (1986), 'Pleasures and Costs of Urbanity', *Dissent*, Summer, pp. 224-256.

Walzer, M. (1983), *Spheres of Justice,* Blackwell, Oxford.

Ward, K. (2000), 'From Rentiers to Rantiers: "Active Entrepreneurs", "Structural Speculators" and the Politics of Marketing the City', *Urban Studies*, Vol. 37, pp. 1093-1108.

Watson, S. (1990), 'Gilding the Smokestacks: the New Symbolic Representations of De-industrialised Regions', *Environment and Planning D: Society and Space*, Vol. 9, pp. 59-70.

Watson, S. (1988), *Accommodating Inequality: Gender and Housing*, Allen and Unwin, Sydney.

Webber, G. P. (1973), *The Design of Sydney: Three Decades of Change in the City Centre*, Law Book Co., Sydney.

Weber, M. (1978), *Economy and Society: An Outline of Interpretative Sociology*, University of California Press, Berkeley.

Webster, M. (1997), *Finding Voices, Making Choices,* Educational Heretics Press, Nottingham.

Wedd, K., Peltz, L. and Ross, C. (2001), *Creative Quarters: the Art World in London 1700-2000*, Merrell/Museum of London, London.

Wells, R. (1990), 'The Development of the English Rural Proletariat and Social Protest, 1700 – 1850', in, M. Reed and R. Wells (eds.), *Class, Conflict and Protest in the English Countryside*, Frank Cass and Co, London.

Wheelan, K. (2002), 'The Memories of "The Dead"', *The Yale Journal of Criticism*, Vol.15(1), pp. 86-100.

Whitehead, M. (2003), 'Love Thy Neighbour: Rethinking the Politics of Scale and Walsall's Struggle for Neighbourhood Democracy', *Environment and Planning A*, Vol. 35, pp. 277-300.

Wiggins, P. and Lang, T. (1985), *The West Midlands Food Industries 1985: A Report to the West Midlands County Council Economic Development Committee*, The London Food Commission, London.

Williams, P. (1997), 'Inclusionary Zoning and Strategic Planning: Affordable Housing Case Study', *Australian Planner*, Vol. 34(1), pp. 16-21.

Williams, R. (1989), *The Politics of Modernism*, Verso, London.

Willis, S. (1999) 'Looking at the Zoo', *The South Atlantic Quarterly*, 98(4), pp. 669-687.

Wilson, E. (2003), *Bohemians: The Glamorous Outcasts*, Tauris Parke, London.

Withers, G., Clarke, R. and Johnstone, K. (1995), *Income Distribution in Australia: Recent Trends and Research*, Australian Government Publishing Service, Canberra.

Worpole, K. (2000), *Here Comes the Sun*, Faber and Faber, London.

Worpole, K. (1991), 'Trading Places: the City Workshop', in M. Fisher and U. Owen (eds.) *Whose Cities?* Penguin, St Ives, pp. 142-152.

Wynne, D. (1992), *The Culture Industry: The Arts in Urban Regeneration*, Avebury, Aldershot.

Wynne, D. and O'Connor, J. (1998), 'Consumption and the Postmodern City', *Urban Studies*, Vol. 35, pp. 841-861.

Young, I. M. (1990), *Justice and the Politics of Difference*, Princeton University Press, Princeton.

Young, K., Gosschalk, B. and Hatter, W. (1996), *In Search of Community Identity*, Joseph Rowntree Foundation, York.

Zeidler, E. H. (1983), *Multi-use Architecture in the Urban Context*, van Nostrand Reinhold, New York.

Zukin, S. (2001), 'How to Create a Culture Capital: Reflections on Urban Markets and Places', in I. Blazwick (ed.), *Century City: Art and Culture in the Modern Metropolis*, Tate Publishing, London, pp. 259-264.

Zukin, S. (1998), 'Urban Lifestyles: Diversity and Standardisation in Spaces of Consumption', *Urban Studies*, Vol. 35 (8), pp. 825-839.

Zukin, S. (1995), *The Cultures of Cities*, Blackwell, Cambridge.

Zukin, S. (1992), 'Postmodern Urban Landscapes: Mapping Culture and Power', in S. Lash and J. Friedman (eds.), *Modernity and Identity*, Blackwell, Oxford, pp. 221-247.

Zukin, S. (1991), *Landscapes of Power: from Detroit to Disney World*, University of California Press, Oxford.

Zukin, S. (1990), 'Socio-spatial Prototypes of a New Organisation of Consumption: the Role of Real Cultural Capital', *Sociology*, Vol. 24, pp. 37-56.

Zukin, S. (1982), *Loft-living: Culture and Capital in Urban Change*, The John Hopkins Press Ltd, London.

Index